Practical Probabilistic Programming

Practical Probabilistic Programming

AVI PFEFFER

MANNING

SHELTER ISLAND

For online information and ordering of this and other Manning books, please visit
www.manning.com. The publisher offers discounts on this book when ordered in quantity.
For more information, please contact

    Special Sales Department
    Manning Publications Co.
    20 Baldwin Road
    PO Box 761
    Shelter Island, NY 11964
    Email: orders@manning.com

Manning Publications Co.
20 Baldwin Road
PO Box 761
Shelter Island, NY 11964

Development editor:	Dan Maharry
Technical development editors:	Ravishankar Rajagopalan, Shabeesh Balan
Copyeditor:	Sharon Wilkey
Proofreader:	Katie Tennant
Technical proofreader:	Alex Ihler
Typesetter:	Dennis Dalinnik
Cover designer:	Marija Tudor

ISBN: 9781617292330
Printed in the United States of America
1 2 3 4 5 6 7 8 9 10 – EBM – 21 20 19 18 17 16

In loving memory of my mother, Claire Pfeffer

z"l
(May her memory be blessed)

brief contents

contents

foreword

In 1814, Pierre-Simon Laplace wrote, "Life's most important questions are, for the most part, nothing but probability problems." For well over a hundred years after that, the only way to answer such questions (while remaining true to the dictum) was to analyze each problem with pen and paper, obtain a formula for the result, and evaluate the formula by plugging in the numbers by hand. The advent of computers did not change this very much. It simply meant that more-complicated formulas could be evaluated, with more numbers, and the pen-and-paper analyses became more ambitious, often stretching to hundreds of pages.

The analysis of a probability problem requires the formulation of a *probability model* that lays out the space of possibilities and, in some fashion, assigns a numerical probability to each of them. In the past, probability models were written down using a combination of natural language text and semi-formal mathematical notation. From the model, a formula or algorithm for calculating answers was derived by further mathematical manipulation. Each of these stages was laborious, error-prone, and problem-specific, placing severe practical limits on the applicability of probability theory. Despite Laplace, life's most important questions remained unanswered.

The first major step forward was the development of *formal languages*, such as Bayesian networks and Markov networks, for defining probability models. A formal language has a precise syntax, defining what counts as a correct expression, and a precise semantics, defining what each correct expression means (i.e., exactly which probability model is represented by each expression). It thus became possible to describe probability models in machine-readable form and to develop a single algorithm for computing the consequences of *any* expressible probability model.

In the foregoing narrative, there is a fly in the ointment: the lack of *expressible* probability models. The formal languages of Bayesian and Markov networks are, in fact, quite limited in their expressive power. They are, in a sense, probabilistic analogs of Boolean circuits. To get a sense of what this limitation means, consider the problem of writing payroll software for a large company. In a high-level programming language such as Java, this might involve tens of thousands of lines of code. Now, imagine trying to implement exactly the same functionality by wiring together Boolean gates. Such a task seems utterly impossible. The circuit would be unimaginably large, complicated, and opaque, because circuits lack the expressive power to capture the structure of the problem.

In 1997, Avi Pfeffer, the author of this book and then still a student, along with his advisor Daphne Koller and collaborator David McAllester, published the seminal paper on probabilistic programming languages (PPLs), providing the key idea linking probability theory with the expressive power of high-level programming languages. The idea was to let programs be probability models by introducing stochastic elements and defining the meaning of a program to be the probability of each possible execution trace. This idea tied together in a productive way two of the most important branches of mathematics, and we are just beginning to explore the new possibilities that have emerged from it.

This book takes the reader gently through these ideas using the Figaro language to illustrate the concepts and their applications. It avoids unnecessary mathematics and concentrates on real-world examples, which are laid out in detail and carefully explained. It is suitable for someone with a typical programming background. As a by-product of working through the book, the reader will, with less effort than usual, acquire a strong grasp of the principles and techniques of Bayesian inference and statistical learning. Perhaps most importantly, the reader will learn the skill of modeling, which is among the most critical skills any scientist or engineer can have. Figaro and other PPLs allow one to express that skill directly, rapidly, and precisely.

The book is an important step in moving probabilistic programming from the research laboratories where it has been developed, out into the real world. Undoubtedly the capabilities of PPL systems will, in some ways, fail to meet this challenge, and those research laboratories will have their work cut out. On the other hand, readers of this book will undoubtedly find creative ways to apply Figaro and its relatives to a wide range of new problems never imagined by the author.

STUART RUSSELL
PROFESSOR OF COMPUTER SCIENCE
UNIVERSITY OF CALIFORNIA, BERKELEY

preface

Probabilistic programming is an exciting new field that is quickly gathering interest, moving out of the academic arena and into the world of programmers. In essence, probabilistic programming is a new way of creating models for probabilistic reasoning, which lets you predict or infer things you don't know from observations. Probabilistic reasoning has long been one of the core approaches to machine learning, where you use a probabilistic model to describe what you know and learn from experience. Before probabilistic programming, probabilistic reasoning systems were limited to models with simple and fixed structures like Bayesian networks. Probabilistic programming sets probabilistic reasoning systems free from these shackles by providing the full power of programming languages to represent models. It's analogous to moving from circuits to high-level programming languages.

Although I didn't realize it at the time, I've been working on probabilistic programming since my teens, when I developed a soccer simulation in BASIC. The simulation used instructions like "GOTO 1730 + RANDOM * 5" to express random sequencing of events. After careful tuning, the simulation was realistic enough to keep me entertained for hours. Of course, in the intervening years, probabilistic programming has matured a long way from GOTO statements with random targets.

In 1997, I coauthored, with Daphne Koller and David McAllester, one of the first papers on probabilistic programming. The paper introduced a probabilistic Lisp-like language, but the main innovation of the paper was an algorithm for inferring likely aspects of the program based on evidence about its output. This innovation took probabilistic programming beyond typical probabilistic simulation languages by providing a means not only to run the program forward to obtain possible executions, but also to reason backward and infer why an observed result was produced.

In the early 2000s, I developed IBAL (pronounced "eyeball"), which was the first general-purpose probabilistic programming system based on functional programming. IBAL was highly expressive and contained novel inference algorithms, but over the years I gradually became dissatisfied with its limitations, chief among which was the difficulty of interacting with data and integrating with applications. These limitations motivated me, in 2009, to begin developing a new probabilistic programming system, which I named Figaro. Figaro was designed with practicality as the foremost goal, without sacrificing the power of probabilistic programming. This led to the design decision of implementing Figaro as a Scala library, which makes it easy to integrate probabilistic programming models into a Java Virtual Machine application. At the same time, Figaro has possibly the widest range of representational features and inference algorithms of any probabilistic programming system I know of. Figaro is now an open source GitHub project and is up to version 3.3.

Probabilistic programming can be a challenging technique to master because it requires multiple skills, principally the ability to write probabilistic models and the ability to write programs. For many programmers, writing programs comes naturally, but probabilistic modeling is a bit mysterious. This book is designed to take the mystery out of probabilistic modeling, to show you how to program effectively when creating probabilistic models, and to help you use probabilistic programming systems effectively. The book assumes no background in machine learning or probabilistic reasoning. Some experience with functional programming and Scala will be helpful, but you don't have to be a Scala wizard to use the book, and your Scala expertise will probably grow as a result of reading it.

After reading this book, you should be able to design probabilistic models for many applications to get meaningful information from your data, without needing a PhD in machine learning. If you're an expert in some domain, the book will help you express the models you have in your head or on paper and make them operational, enabling you to evaluate and analyze different possibilities. If you are a data scientist, the book can help you develop richer, more detailed, and potentially more accurate models than are feasible with other tools. If you are a software engineer or architect looking to incorporate into your systems the ability to reason under uncertainty, this book will help you not only build models for handling uncertainty but also integrate these models into your application. Whatever reason you have for picking up this book, I hope you enjoy it and find it useful.

acknowledgements

This book has been many years in the making: from the first ideas about probabilistic programming through creating the IBAL and Figaro systems to conceiving, writing, and polishing the book with Manning. Countless people have contributed their efforts over the years to help make this book possible.

This book owes its existence largely to the efforts of my team at Charles River Analytics: Joe Gorman, Scott Harrison, Michael Howard, Lee Kellogg, Alison O'Connor, Mike Reposa, Brian Ruttenberg, and Glenn Takata. Thanks also to Scott Neal Reilly who supported Figaro from the start.

I learned most of what I know in artificial intelligence and machine learning from Daphne Koller, my mentor and collaborator. Stuart Russell gave me the first opportunity to study artificial intelligence and has provided me with encouragement throughout my career, as well as being a recent collaborator and the author of the foreword to this book. Mike Stonebraker gave me my first research opportunity on his Postgres project, and I learned a lot about building systems from working in his group. Alon Halevy invited me to spend the summer with him at AT&T Labs, where I first started talking about probabilistic programming with David McAllester; this resulted in the probabilistic Lisp paper with Daphne. Lise Getoor, office mate and collaborator, was someone I could talk to about these ideas when they were first germinating.

My deep appreciation goes to Alex Ihler, who graciously lent his expertise to carefully read the book for technical accuracy. Alex has also been a tremendously useful sounding board for all things relating to inference in the past couple of years.

Many others offered comments at various stages of development, including Ravishankar Rajagopalan and Shabeesh Balan, Chris Heneghan, Clemens Baader, Cristofer Weber, Earl Bingham, Giuseppe de Marco, Jaume Valls, Javier Guerra Giraldez, Kostas Passadis, Luca Campobasso, Lucas Gallindo, Mark Elston, Mark Miller, Nitin Gode, Odisseyas Pentakolos, Peter Rabinovitch, Phillip Bradford, Stephen Wakely, Taposh Dutta Roy, and Unnikrishnan Kumar.

Thank you to the many great people at Manning Publications who have helped in making this book a reality. Thanks especially to my editor, Dan Maharry, who made this a far better book than I could have myself, and to Frank Pohlmann, who gave me the initial encouragement to write the book and helped prepare me for the process.

Thank you to the Air Force Research Laboratory (AFRL) and to the Defense Advanced Research Projects Agency (DARPA) for funding some of the work described in this book under the Probabilistic Programming for Advancing Machine Learning (PPAML) program. Thanks in particular to several DARPA program managers, Bob Kohout, Tony Falcone, Kathleen Fisher, and Suresh Jagannathan, who believed in probabilistic programming and worked to help make it a practical reality. This material is based on work supported by the United States Air Force under Contract No. FA8750-14-C-0011. Any opinions, findings and conclusions or recommendations expressed in this material are those of the author and do not necessarily reflect the views of the United States Air Force.

Lastly, this book would not have been possible without the love and support of my family. Thank you to my wife Debby Gelber and my children Dina, Nomi, and Ruti for being the wonderful people you are. And to my mother Claire Pfeffer, who raised me with love, my eternal gratitude. This book is dedicated to your memory.

about this book

Lots of decisions, whether in business, science, the military, or everyday life, involve judgment calls under uncertainty. When different factors sway you in different directions, how do you know what to pay attention to the most? Probabilistic models enable you to express all the relevant information about your situation. Probabilistic reasoning lets you use these models to determine the probability of the variables that make the most difference to your decision. You can use probabilistic reasoning to *predict* the things that are most likely to happen: will your product be a success at your target price; will the patient respond well to a particular treatment; will your candidate win the election if she takes a certain position? You can also use probabilistic reasoning to *infer* the likely reasons behind what happened: if the product failed, is it because the price was too high?

Probabilistic reasoning is also one of the main approaches to machine learning. You encode your initial beliefs about your domain in a probabilistic model, such as the general behavior of users in response to products in your market. Then, given training data, perhaps about the response of users to specific products, you update your beliefs to get a new model. Now you can use your new model to predict future outcomes, like the success of a planned product, or infer likely causes of observed outcomes, like the reasons behind the failure of a new product.

In the past, probabilistic reasoning used dedicated languages to represent probabilistic models. In recent years, we have come to realize that you can use ordinary programming languages, which has resulted in probabilistic programming. This has three major benefits. First, you get to benefit from all the features of the programming language, like rich data structures and control flow, when building your models. Second, your probabilistic model can easily be integrated with other applications. And third, you benefit from general-purpose inference algorithms for reasoning with your models.

This book aims to provide you with the knowledge to use probabilistic programming in your everyday activities. In particular, it tells you

- How to build probabilistic models and express them as probabilistic programs
- How probabilistic reasoning works and is implemented in a variety of inference algorithms
- How to use the Figaro probabilistic programming system to build practical probabilistic programs

Figaro is implemented as a Scala library. Like Scala, it combines functional and object-oriented programming styles. It will be useful to you to know a little bit about functional programming. The book doesn't make use of advanced functional programming concepts, so you should be able to understand it with just a little knowledge. Likewise, it will be helpful to you to know some Scala. Although Scala constructs are often explained in the book, this book in not an introduction to Scala. Again, the book generally does not use the more esoteric features of Scala, so a little exposure should be enough.

Roadmap

Part 1 of the book is an introduction to probabilistic programming and Figaro. Chapter 1 begins by explaining what probabilistic programming is and why it is useful and then provides a brief introduction to Figaro. Chapter 2 is a tutorial on using Figaro, which will quickly get you up to speed on writing probabilistic programs. Chapter 3 provides a complete probabilistic programming application in the form of a spam filter, including a component that reasons about whether a given email is normal or spam and a component that learns the probabilistic model from training data. The goal of chapter 3 is to provide you with the big picture of how everything fits together before you get into the detail of modeling techniques.

Part 2 is all about building probabilistic programs. It begins in chapter 4 with basic material on probabilistic models and probabilistic programs that is important to understand so you really know what you're doing when you create probabilistic programs. Chapter 5 presents the two modeling frameworks that lie at the heart of probabilistic programming, Bayesian networks and Markov networks. Chapters 6 through 8 describe a set of useful programming techniques for building more advanced programs. Chapter 6 talks about using Scala and Figaro collections to organize programs involving many variables of the same type. Chapter 7 talks about object-oriented programming, which is as beneficial for probabilistic programming as it is for ordinary programs. Chapter 8 is about modeling dynamic systems. A dynamic system is a system whose state changes over time, and it's an extremely common and important application of probabilistic reasoning that is discussed in depth in this chapter.

Part 3 teaches you about probabilistic inference algorithms. It's important to understand inference to use probabilistic programming effectively, so you can use the right algorithm for a task, configure it in the right way, and express your model in a way that supports effective reasoning. Part 3 strikes a balance between teaching you the theory behind the algorithms and giving you practical tips on how to use them. Chapter 9 is a foundational chapter that presents the three rules that capture the main ideas used in probabilistic inference. Chapters 10 and 11 describe the two main families of inference algorithms. Chapter 10 describes factored algorithms, including an introduction to factors and how they work, and the variable elimination and belief propagation algorithms. Chapter 11 covers sampling algorithms, with a particular focus on importance sampling and Markov chain Monte Carlo algorithms. While chapters 10 and 11 focus on the basic query of computing the probability of variables of interest, chapter 12 shows you how factored and sampling algorithms can be used to compute other queries, such as the joint probability of multiple variables, the most likely values of variables, and the probability of the observed evidence. Finally, chapter 13 discusses two advanced but important inference tasks: monitoring a dynamic system as it changes over time, and learning the numerical parameters of a probabilistic model from data.

Each of the chapters has a set of exercises. These exercises range from simple calculations through programming tasks to open-ended thought exercises.

The book also contains two appendixes. Appendix A contains installation instructions to get started with Figaro. Appendix B is a brief survey of other probabilistic programming systems.

About the code and exercises

The code in the book is presented in a `fixed-width font like this` to separate it from ordinary text. Code annotations accompany many of the listings, highlighting important concepts. In some cases, numbered bullets link to explanations that follow the listing.

The book contains many code examples, most of which are available in the online code base, which can be found at the book's website, www.manning.com/books/practical-probabilistic-programming. The website also includes answers to selected exercises.

about the author

Avi Pfeffer is a probabilistic programming pioneer, having been active in the field since its earliest days. Avi is the lead designer and developer of Figaro. At Charles River Analytics, Avi is engaged in applying Figaro to diverse problems including malware analysis, vehicle health monitoring, climate modeling, and evaluating engineered systems.

In his spare time, Avi is a singer, composer, and music producer. Avi lives in Cambridge, Massachusetts with his wife and three kids.

Author Online

Purchase of *Practical Probabilistic Programming* includes free access to a private web forum run by Manning Publications where you can make comments about the book, ask technical questions, discuss exercises, and receive help from the author and from the community. To access the forum and subscribe to it, go to www.manning.com/ books/practical-probabilistic-programming. This page provides information on how to get on the forum once you're registered, what kind of help is available, and the rules of conduct on the forum.

Manning's commitment to our readers is to provide a venue where a meaningful dialog between individual readers and between readers and the author can take place. It's not a commitment to any specific amount of participation on the part of the author, whose contribution to the forum remains voluntary (and unpaid). We suggest you try asking the author some challenging questions lest his interest stray!

The Author Online forum and the archives of previous discussions will be accessible from the publisher's website as long as the book is in print.

about the cover illustration

The figure on the cover of *Practical Probabilistic Programming* is captioned "The Venetian." The illustration is taken from a French travel book, *Encyclopédie des Voyages* by J. G. St. Saveur, published in 1796. Travel for pleasure was a relatively new phenomenon at the time and travel guides such as this one were popular, introducing both the tourist and the armchair traveler to the inhabitants of other regions of France and abroad.

The diversity of the drawings in the *Encyclopédie des Voyages* speaks vividly of the uniqueness and individuality of the world's towns and provinces just 200 years ago. This was a time when the dress codes of two regions separated by a few dozen miles identified people uniquely as belonging to one or the other. The travel guide brings to life a sense of isolation and distance of that period and of every other historic period except our own hyperkinetic present.

Dress codes have changed since then and the diversity by region, so rich at the time, has faded away. It is now often hard to tell the inhabitant of one continent from another. Perhaps, trying to view it optimistically, we have traded a cultural and visual diversity for a more varied personal life—or a more varied and interesting intellectual and technical life.

We at Manning celebrate the inventiveness, the initiative, and the fun of the computer business with book covers based on the rich diversity of regional life two centuries ago brought back to life by the pictures from this travel guide.

Part 1

Introducing probabilistic programming and Figaro

What is probabilistic programming? Why is it useful? How do you use it? These questions are the main subject of part 1. Chapter 1 introduces you to the basic ideas of probabilistic programming. It begins with the concept of a probabilistic reasoning system and shows you how probabilistic programming marries the traditional concept of probabilistic reasoning systems with programming language technology.

In this book, you'll use a probabilistic programming system called Figaro. Chapter 1 briefly introduces Figaro, while chapter 2 presents a quick tutorial of all the main Figaro concepts, so you can quickly start writing probabilistic programs. Chapter 3 presents a complete probabilistic programming application to give you a big-picture overview of how a practical application is put together. Though this chapter is placed near the beginning of the book so you start with the big picture, it's worth revisiting as you read more of the book and have learned some of the deeper concepts.

Probabilistic programming in a nutshell

This chapter covers

- What is probabilistic programming?
- Why should I care about it? Why should my boss care?
- How does it work?
- Figaro—a system for probabilistic programming
- A comparison between writing a probabilistic application with and without probabilistic programming

In this chapter, you'll learn how to make everyday decisions by using a probabilistic model and an inference algorithm—the two main components of a probabilistic reasoning system. You'll also see how modern probabilistic programming languages make creating such reasoning systems far easier than a general-purpose language such as Java or Python would. This chapter also introduces *Figaro*, the probabilistic programming language based on Scala that's used throughout the book.

1.1   *What is probabilistic programming?*

Probabilistic programming is a way to create systems that help us make decisions in the face of uncertainty. Lots of everyday decisions involve judgment in determining relevant factors that we don't directly observe. Historically, one way to help make decisions under uncertainty has been to use a probabilistic reasoning system. *Probabilistic reasoning* combines our knowledge of a situation with the laws of probability to determine those unobserved factors that are critical to the decision. Until recently, probabilistic reasoning systems have been limited in scope, and have been hard to apply to many real-world situations. Probabilistic programming is a new approach that makes probabilistic reasoning systems easier to build and more widely applicable.

To understand probabilistic programming, you'll start by looking at decision making under uncertainty and the judgment calls involved. Then you'll see how probabilistic reasoning can help you make these decisions. You'll look at three specific kinds of reasoning that probabilistic reasoning systems can do. Then you'll be able to understand probabilistic programming and how it can be used to build probabilistic reasoning systems through the power of programming languages.

1.1.1   *How do we make judgment calls?*

In the real world, the questions we care about rarely have clear yes-or-no answers. If you're launching a new product, for example, you want to know whether it will sell well. You might think it will be successful, because you believe it's well designed and your market research indicates a need for it, but you can't be sure. Maybe your competitor will come out with an even better product, or maybe it has a fatal flaw that will turn off the market, or maybe the economy will take a sudden turn for the worse. If you require being 100% sure, you won't be able to make the decision of whether to launch the product (see figure 1.1).

The language of probability can help make decisions like these. When launching a product, you can use prior experience with similar products to estimate the probability that the product will be successful. You can then use this probability to help decide whether to go ahead and launch the product. You might care not only about whether the product will be successful, but also about how much revenue it will bring, or alternatively, how much you'll lose if it fails. You can use the probabilities of different outcomes to make better-informed decisions.

Okay, so probabilistic thinking can help you make hard decisions and judgment calls. But how do you do that? The general principal is expressed in the Fact note.

> **FACT**   A judgment call is based on *knowledge + logic*.

You have some knowledge of the problem you're interested in. For example, you know a lot about your product, and you might have done some market research to find out what customers want. You also might have some intelligence about your competitors and access to economic predictions. Meanwhile, logic helps you get answers to your questions by using your knowledge.

Figure 1.1 Last year everyone loved my product, but what will happen next year?

You need a way of specifying the knowledge, and you need logic for getting answers to your questions by using the knowledge. Probabilistic programming is all about providing ways to specify the knowledge and logic to answer questions. Before I describe what a probabilistic programming system is, I'll describe the more general concept of a probabilistic reasoning system, which provides the basic means to specify knowledge and provide logic.

1.1.2 Probabilistic reasoning systems help make decisions

Probabilistic reasoning is an approach that uses a model of your domain to make decisions under uncertainty. Let's take an example from the world of soccer. Suppose the statistics show that 9% of corner kicks result in a goal. You're tasked with predicting the outcome of a particular corner kick. The attacking team's center forward is 6' 4" and known for her heading ability. The defending team's regular goalkeeper was just carted off on a stretcher and has been replaced by a substitute playing her first game.

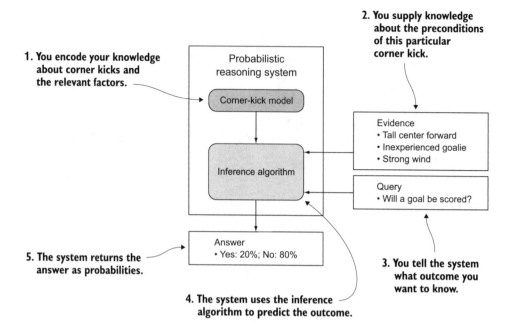

1. You encode your knowledge about corner kicks and the relevant factors.

2. You supply knowledge about the preconditions of this particular corner kick.

Probabilistic reasoning system

Corner-kick model

Inference algorithm

Evidence
• Tall center forward
• Inexperienced goalie
• Strong wind

Query
• Will a goal be scored?

Answer
• Yes: 20%; No: 80%

5. The system returns the answer as probabilities.

3. You tell the system what outcome you want to know.

4. The system uses the inference algorithm to predict the outcome.

Figure 1.2 How a probabilistic reasoning system predicts the outcome of a corner kick

Besides that, there's a howling wind that makes it difficult to control long kicks. So how do you figure out the probability?

Figure 1.2 shows how to use a probabilistic reasoning system to find the answer. You encode your knowledge about corner kicks and all the relevant factors in a corner-kick model. You then supply evidence about this particular corner kick, namely, that the center forward is tall, the goalie is inexperienced, and the wind is strong. You tell the system that you want to know whether a goal will be scored. The inference algorithm returns the answer that a goal will be scored with 20% probability.

KEY DEFINITIONS

General knowledge—What you know to hold true of your domain in general terms, without considering the details of a particular situation

Probabilistic model—An encoding of general knowledge about a domain in quantitative, probabilistic terms

Evidence—Specific information you have about a particular situation

Query—A property of the situation you want to know

Inference—The process of using a probabilistic model to answer a query, given evidence

In probabilistic reasoning, you create a *model* that captures all the relevant general knowledge of your domain in quantitative, probabilistic terms. In our example, the model might be a description of a corner-kick situation and all the relevant aspects of players and conditions that affect the outcome. Then, for a particular situation, you apply the model to any specific information you have to draw conclusions. This specific information is called the *evidence*. In this example, the evidence is that the center forward is tall, the goalie is inexperienced, and the wind is strong. The conclusions you draw can help you make decisions—for example, whether you should get a different goalie for the next game. The conclusions themselves are framed probabilistically, like the probability of different skill levels of the goalie.

The relationship between the model, the information you provide, and the answers to queries is well defined mathematically by the laws of probability. The process of using the model to answer queries based on the evidence is called *probabilistic inference*, or simply *inference*. Fortunately, computer algorithms have been developed that do the math for you and make all the necessary calculations automatically. These algorithms are called *inference algorithms*.

Figure 1.3 summarizes what you've learned.

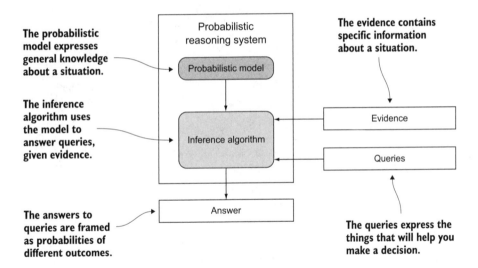

Figure 1.3   The basic components of a probabilistic reasoning system

In a nutshell, what we've just discussed are the constituents of a probabilistic reasoning system and how you interact with one. But what can you do with such a system? How does it help you make decisions? The next section describes three kinds of reasoning that can be performed by a probabilistic reasoning system.

1.1.3 *Probabilistic reasoning systems can reason in three ways*

Probabilistic reasoning systems are flexible. They can answer queries about any aspect of your situation, given evidence about any other aspect. In practice, probabilistic reasoning systems perform three kinds of reasoning:

- *Predict future events.* You've already seen this in figure 1.2, where you predict whether a goal will be scored based on the current situation. Your evidence will typically consist of information about the current situation, such as the height of the center forward, the experience of the goalie, and the strength of the wind.

- *Infer the cause of events.* Fast-forward 10 seconds. The tall center forward just scored a goal with a header, squirting under the body of the goalie. What do you think of this rookie goalkeeper, given this evidence? Can you conclude that she's poorly skilled? Figure 1.4 shows how to use a probabilistic reasoning system to answer this question. The model is the same corner-kick model you used before to predict whether a goal would be scored. (This is a useful property of probabilistic reasoning: the same model that can be used to predict a future result can be used after the fact to infer what caused that result.) The evidence here is the same as before, together with the fact that a goal was scored. The query is the skill level of the goalie, and the answer provides the probability of various skill levels.

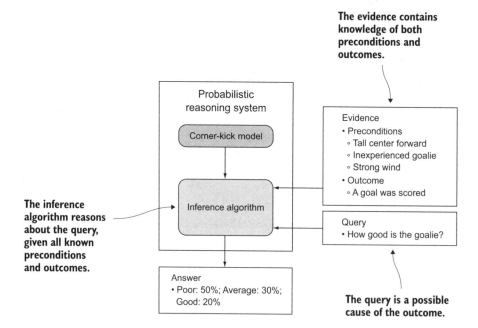

Figure 1.4 By altering the query and evidence, the system can now infer why a goal was scored.

If you think about it, the first reasoning pattern describes reasoning forward in time, predicting future events based on what you know about the current situation, whereas the second reasoning pattern describes reasoning backward in time, inferring past conditions based on current outcomes. When you build probabilistic models, typically the models themselves follow a natural temporal sequence. A player takes the corner kick, then the wind operates on the ball as it's coming in, then the center forward leaps up to try to head the ball, and then the goalie tries to make a save. But the reasoning can go both forward and backward. This is a key feature of probabilistic reasoning, which I'll repeat throughout the book: the direction of reasoning doesn't necessarily follow the direction of the model.

- *Learn from past events to better predict future events.* Now fast-forward another 10 minutes. The same team has won another corner kick. Everything is similar to before in this new situation—tall center forward, inexperienced goalie—but now the wind has died down. Using probabilistic reasoning, you can use what happened in the previous kick to help you predict what will happen on the next kick. Figure 1.5 shows how to do this. The evidence includes all evidence from last time (making a note that it was from last time), as well as the new information about the current situation. In answering the query about whether a goal

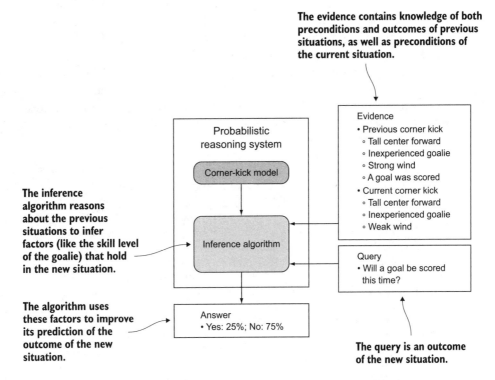

Figure 1.5 By taking into account evidence from the outcome of the last corner kick, the probabilistic reasoning system can produce a better prediction of the next corner kick.

will be scored this time, the inference algorithm first infers properties of the situation that led to a goal being scored the first time, such as the skill levels of the center forward and goalie. It then uses these updated properties to make a prediction about the new situation.

All of these types of queries can help you make decisions, on many levels:

- You can decide whether to substitute a defender for an attacker based on the probability that a goal will be scored with or without the extra defender.
- You can decide how much to offer the goalie in her next contract negotiation based on your assessment of her skill.
- You can decide whether to use the same goalie in the next game by using what you've learned about the goalie to help predict the outcome of the next game.

LEARNING A BETTER MODEL

The preceding three reasoning patterns provide ways to reason about specific situations, given evidence. Another thing you can do with a probabilistic reasoning system is learn from the past to improve your general knowledge. In the third reasoning pattern, you saw how to learn from a particular past experience to better predict a specific future situation. Another way to learn from the past is to improve the model itself. Especially if you have a lot of past experiences to draw on, such as a lot of corner kicks, you might want to learn a new model representing your general knowledge of what typically happens in a corner kick. As figure 1.6 shows, this is achieved by a learning algorithm. Somewhat different from an inference algorithm, the goal of a learning algorithm is to produce a new model, not to answer queries. The learning algorithm begins with the original model and updates it based on the experience to produce the new model. The new model can then be used to answer queries in the future. Presumably, the answers produced when using the new model will be better informed than when using the original model.

Probabilistic reasoning systems and accurate predictions

Like any machine learning system, a probabilistic reasoning system will be more accurate the more data you give it. The quality of the predictions depends on two things: the degree to which the original model accurately reflects real-world situations, and the amount of data you provide. In general, the more data you provide, the less important the original model is. The reason for this is that the new model is a balance between the original model and the information contained in the data. If you have very little data, the original model dominates, so it had better be accurate. If you have lots of data, the data will dominate and the new model will tend to forget the original model, which doesn't matter as much. For example, if you're learning from an entire soccer season, you should be able to learn the factors that contribute to a corner kick quite accurately. If you have only one game, you'll need to start out with a good idea of the factors to be able to make accurate predictions about that game. Probabilistic reasoning systems will make good use of the given model and available data to make as accurate a prediction as possible.

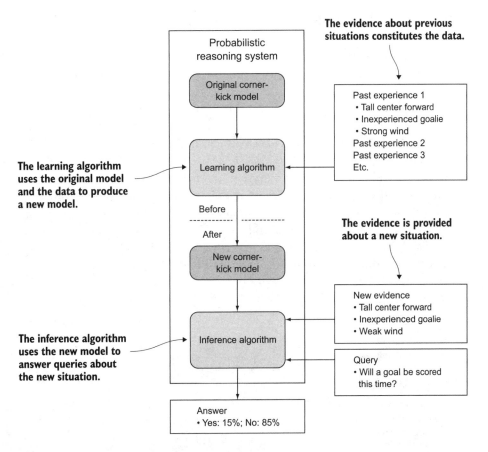

The evidence about previous situations constitutes the data.

The evidence is provided about a new situation.

The learning algorithm uses the original model and the data to produce a new model.

The inference algorithm uses the new model to answer queries about the new situation.

Figure 1.6 You can use a learning algorithm to learn a new model based on a set of experiences. This new model can then be used for future inferences.

Now you know what probabilistic reasoning is. What then, is probabilistic programming?

1.1.4 *Probabilistic programming systems: probabilistic reasoning systems expressed in a programming language*

Every probabilistic reasoning system uses a *representation language* to express its probabilistic models. There are a lot of representation languages out there. You may have heard of some of them, such as Bayesian networks (also known as belief networks) and hidden Markov models. The representation language controls what models can be handled by the system and what they look like. The set of models that can be represented by a language is called the *expressive power* of the language. For practical applications, you'd like to have as large an expressive power as possible.

A *probabilistic programming* system is, very simply, a probabilistic reasoning system in which the representation language is a programming language. When I say *programming language*, I mean that it has all the features you typically expect in a programming language, such as variables, a rich variety of data types, control flow, functions, and so on. As you'll come to see, probabilistic programming languages can express an extremely wide variety of probabilistic models and go far beyond most traditional probabilistic reasoning frameworks. Probabilistic programming languages have tremendous expressive power.

Figure 1.7 illustrates the relationship between probabilistic programming systems and probabilistic reasoning systems in general. The figure can be compared with figure 1.3 to highlight the differences between the two systems. The main change is that models are expressed as programs in a programming language rather than as a mathematical construct like a Bayesian network. As a result of this change, evidence, queries, and answers all apply to variables in the program. Evidence might specify particular values for program variables, queries ask for the values of program variables, and answers are probabilities of different values of the query variables. In addition, a probabilistic programming system typically comes with a suite of inference algorithms. These algorithms apply to programs written in the language.

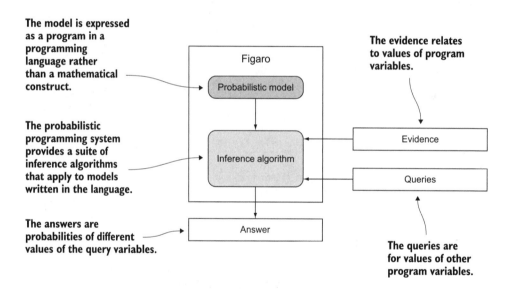

Figure 1.7 A probabilistic programming system is a probabilistic reasoning system that uses a programming language to represent probabilistic models.

Although many kinds of probabilistic programming systems exist (see appendix B for a survey), this book focuses on functional, Turing-complete systems. *Functional* means that they're based on functional programming, but don't let that scare you—you don't need to know concepts such as lambda functions to use functional probabilistic programming systems. All this means is that functional programming provides the theoretical foundation behind these languages that lets them represent probabilistic models. Meanwhile, *Turing-complete* is jargon for a programming language that can encode any computation that can be done on a digital computer. If something can be done on a digital computer, it can be done with any Turing-complete language. Most of the programming languages you're familiar with, such as C, Java, and Python, are Turing-complete. Because probabilistic programming languages are built on Turing-complete programming languages, they're extremely flexible in the types of models that can be built.

KEY DEFINITIONS

Representation language—A language for encoding your knowledge about a domain in a model

Expressive power—The ability of a representation language to encode various kinds of knowledge in its models

Turing-complete—A language that can express any computation that can be performed on a digital computer

Probabilistic programming language—A probabilistic representation language that uses a Turing-complete programming language to represent knowledge

Appendix B surveys some probabilistic programming systems besides Figaro, the system used in this book. Most of these systems use Turing-complete languages. Some, including BUGS and Dimple, don't, but they're nevertheless useful for their intended applications. This book focuses on the capabilities of Turing-complete probabilistic programming languages.

REPRESENTING PROBABILISTIC MODELS AS PROGRAMS

But how can a programming language be a probabilistic modeling language? How can you represent probabilistic models as programs? I'll hint at the answer to this question here but save a deeper discussion for later in the book, when you have a better idea of what a probabilistic program looks like.

A core idea in programming languages is *execution*. You execute a program to generate output. A probabilistic program is similar, except that instead of a single execution path, it can have many execution paths, each generating a different output. The determination of which execution path is followed is specified by random choices throughout the program. Each random choice has a number of possible outcomes, and the program encodes the probability of each outcome. Therefore, a probabilistic program can be thought of as a program you randomly execute to generate an output.

Figure 1.8 illustrates this concept. In the figure, a probabilistic programming system contains a corner-kick program. This program describes the random process of generating the outcome of a corner kick. The program takes some inputs; in our example, these are the height of the center forward, the experience of the goalie, and the strength of the wind. Given the inputs, the program is randomly executed to generate outputs. Each random execution results in a particular output being generated.

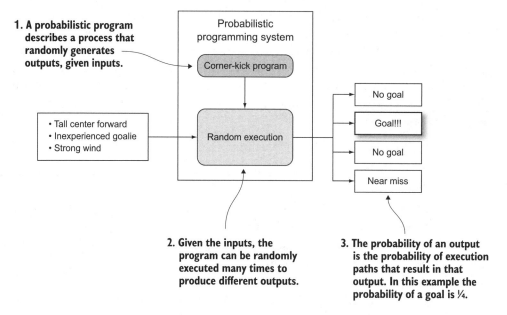

Figure 1.8   A probabilistic program defines a process of randomly generating outputs, given inputs.

Because every random choice has multiple possible outcomes, many possible execution paths exist, resulting in different outputs. Any given output, such as a goal, can be generated by multiple execution paths.

Let's see how this program defines a probabilistic model. Any particular execution path results from a sequence of random choices having specific outcomes. Each random choice has a probability of occurring. If you multiply all these probabilities together, you get the probability of the execution path. So the program defines the probability of every execution path. If you imagine running the program many times, the fraction of times any given execution path will be generated is equal to its probability. The probability of an output is the fraction of times the program is run that result in that output. In figure 1.8, a goal is generated by 1/4 of the runs, so the probability of a goal is 1/4.

> **NOTE** You might be wondering why the block in figure 1.8 is labeled Random Execution rather than Inference Algorithm, as it has been in other figures. Figure 1.8 shows what a probabilistic program means, as defining a random execution process, rather than how you use a probabilistic programming system, which is by using an inference algorithm to answer queries, given evidence. So although the structure of the figures is similar, they convey different concepts. As a matter of fact, random execution forms the basis for some inference algorithms as well, but many algorithms aren't based on simple random execution.

MAKING DECISIONS WITH PROBABILISTIC PROGRAMMING

It's easy to see how you can use a probabilistic program to predict the future. Just execute the program randomly many times, using what you know about the present as inputs, and observe how many times each output is produced. In the corner-kick example of figure 1.8, you executed the program many times, given the inputs of tall center forward, inexperienced goalie, and strong wind. Because 1/4 of those runs resulted in a goal, you can say that the probability of a goal, given these inputs, is 25%.

The magic of probabilistic programming, however, is that it can also be used for all the kinds of probabilistic reasoning described in section 1.3.1. It can be used not only to predict the future, but also to infer facts that led to particular outcomes; you can "unwind" the program to discover the root causes of the outcomes. You can also apply a program in one situation, learn from the outcome, and then use what you've learned to make better predictions in the future. You can use probabilistic programming to help make all the decisions that can be informed by probabilistic thinking.

How does this work? Probabilistic programming became practical when people realized that inference algorithms that work on simpler representation languages like Bayesian networks can be extended to work on programs. Part 3 of this book presents a variety of inference algorithms that make this possible. Fortunately, probabilistic programming systems come with a range of built-in inference algorithms that apply automatically to your programs. All you have to do is provide your knowledge of your domain in the form of a probabilistic program and specify the evidence, and the system takes care of the inference and learning.

In this book, you'll learn probabilistic reasoning through probabilistic programming. You'll learn, first of all, what a probabilistic model is and how it can be used to draw conclusions. You'll also learn some basic manipulations that are performed to draw those conclusions from a model made up of simple components. You'll learn a variety of modeling techniques and how to implement them by using probabilistic programming. You'll also gain an understanding of how the probabilistic inference algorithms work, so you can design and use your models effectively. By the end of this book, you'll be able to use probabilistic programming confidently to draw useful conclusions that inform your decisions in the face of uncertainty.

1.2 *Why probabilistic programming?*

Probabilistic reasoning is one of the foundational technologies of machine learning. It's used by companies such as Google, Amazon, and Microsoft to make sense of the data available to them. Probabilistic reasoning has been used for applications as diverse as predicting stock prices, recommending movies, diagnosing computers, and detecting cyber intrusions. Many of these applications use techniques you'll learn in this book.

From the previous section, two points stand out:

- Probabilistic reasoning can be used to predict the future, infer the past, and learn from the past to better predict the future.
- Probabilistic programming is probabilistic reasoning using a Turing-complete programming language for representation.

Put these two together and you have a slogan expressed in the Fact note.

FACT   Probabilistic reasoning + Turing-complete = probabilistic programming

The motivation for probabilistic programming is that it takes two concepts that are powerful in their own right and puts them together. The result is an easier and more flexible way to use computers to help make decisions under uncertainty.

1.2.1   *Better probabilistic reasoning*

Most existing probabilistic representation languages are limited in the richness of the systems they can represent. Some relatively simple languages such as Bayesian networks assume a fixed set of variables and aren't flexible enough to model domains in which the variables themselves can change. More-advanced languages with more flexibility have been developed in recent years. Some (for example, BUGS) also provide programming-language features including iteration and arrays, without being Turing-complete. The success of languages such as BUGS shows a need for richer, more structured representations. But moving to full-fledged, Turing-complete languages opens a world of possibilities for probabilistic reasoning. It's now possible to model long-running processes with many interacting entities and events.

Let's consider the soccer example again, but now imagine that you're in the business of sports analytics and want to recommend personnel decisions for a team. You could use accumulated statistics to make your decisions, but statistics don't capture the context in which they were accumulated. You can achieve a more fine-grained, context-aware analysis by modeling the soccer season in detail. This requires modeling many dependent events and interacting players and teams. It would be hard to imagine building this model without the data structures and control flow provided by a full programming language.

Now let's think about the product launch example again, and look at making decisions for your business in an integrated way. The product launch isn't an isolated incident, but follows phases of market analysis, research, and development, all of which have uncertainty in their outcome. The results of the product launch depend on all these phases, as well as an analysis of what else is available in the market. A full analysis will also look at how your competitors will respond to your product, as well as any new products they might bring. This problem is hard, because you have to conjecture about competing products. You may even have competitors you don't know about yet. In this example, products are data structures produced by complex processes. Again, having a full programming language available to create the model would be helpful.

One of the nice things about probabilistic programming, however, is that if you want to use a simpler probabilistic reasoning framework, you can. Probabilistic programming systems can represent a wide range of existing frameworks, as well as systems that can't be represented in other frameworks. This book teaches many of these frameworks using probabilistic programming. So in learning probabilistic programming, you'll also master many of the probabilistic reasoning frameworks commonly used today.

1.2.2　*Better simulation languages*

Turing-complete probabilistic modeling languages already exist. They're commonly called *simulation languages*. We know that it's possible to build simulations of complex processes such as soccer seasons by using programming languages. In this context, I use the term *simulation language* to describe a language that can represent the execution of complex processes with randomness. Just like probabilistic programs, these simulations are randomly executed to produce different outputs. Simulations are as widely used as probabilistic reasoning, in applications from military planning to component design to public health to sports predictions. Indeed, the widespread use of sophisticated simulations demonstrates the need for rich probabilistic modeling languages.

But a probabilistic program is much more than a simulation. With a simulation, you can do only one of the things you can do with a probabilistic program: predict the future. You can't use it to infer the root causes of the outcomes that are observed. And, although you can update a simulation with known current information as you go along, it's hard to include unknown information that must be inferred. As a result, the ability to learn from past experience to improve future predictions and analyses is limited. You can't use simulations for machine learning.

A probabilistic program is like a simulation that you can analyze, not just run. The key insight in developing probabilistic programming is that many of the inference algorithms that can be used for simpler modeling frameworks can also be used on simulations. Hence, you have the ability to create a probabilistic model by writing a simulation and performing inferences on it.

One final word. Probabilistic reasoning systems have been around for a while, with software such as Hugin, Netica, and BayesiaLab providing Bayesian network systems. But the more expressive representation languages of probabilistic programming are so new that we're just beginning to discover their powerful applications. I can't honestly tell you that probabilistic programming has already been used in a large number of fielded applications. But some significant applications exist. Microsoft has been able to determine the true skill level of players of online games by using probabilistic programming. Stuart Russell at the University of California at Berkeley has written a program to help enforce the United Nations Comprehensive Nuclear-Test-Ban Treaty by identifying seismic events that could indicate a nuclear explosion. Josh Tenenbaum at the Massachusetts Institute of Technology (MIT) and Noah Goodman at Stanford University have created probabilistic programs to model human cognition with considerable explanatory success. At Charles River Analytics, we've used probabilistic programming to infer components of malware instances and determine their evolution. But I believe these applications are only scratching the surface. Probabilistic programming systems are reaching the point where they can be used by larger numbers of people to make decisions in their own domains. By reading this book, you have a chance to get in on this new technology on the ground floor.

1.3   *Introducing Figaro: a probabilistic programming language*

In this book, you'll use a probabilistic programming system called Figaro. (I named Figaro after the character from Mozart's opera "The Marriage of Figaro." I love Mozart and played Dr. Bartolo in a Boston production of the opera.) The main goal of the book is to teach the principles of probabilistic programming, and the techniques you learn in this book should carry over to other probabilistic programming systems. Some of the available systems are listed with a brief description in appendix B. A secondary goal, however, is to give you hands-on experience with creating practical probabilistic programs, and provide you with tools you can use right away. For that reason, a lot of the examples are made concrete in Figaro code.

Figaro, which is open source and maintained on GitHub, has been under development since 2009. It's implemented as a Scala library. Figure 1.9 shows how Figaro uses

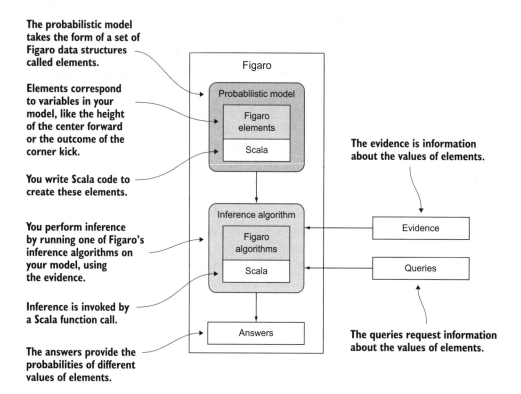

Figure 1.9   How Figaro uses Scala to provide a probabilistic programming system

Scala to implement a probabilistic programming system. The figure elaborates on figure 1.7, which describes the main components of a probabilistic programming system. Let's start with the probabilistic model. In Figaro, the model consists of any number of data structures known as *elements*. Each element represents a variable that can take on any number of values in your situation. These data structures are implemented in Scala, and you write a Scala program to create a model using these data structures. You can supply evidence by providing information about the values of elements, and you can specify which elements you want to know about in your query. For the inference algorithm, you choose one of Figaro's built-in inference algorithms and apply it to your model, to answer your query, given the evidence. The inference algorithms are implemented in Scala, and invoking an inference algorithm is simply a Scala function call. The results of inference are probabilities of various values of your query elements.

Figaro's embedding in Scala provides some major advantages. Some of these come from embedding in a general-purpose host language, compared to a standalone probabilistic language. Others come specifically because of the favorable properties of Scala. Here's why it's good to embed a probabilistic programming language in a general-purpose host language:

- The evidence can be derived using a program in the host language. For example, you might have a program that reads a data file, processes the values in some way, and provides that as evidence for the Figaro model. It's much harder to do this in a standalone language.
- Similarly, you can use the answers provided by Figaro in a program. For example, if you have a program used by a soccer manager, the program can take the probability of a goal being scored to recommend to the manager what to do.
- You can embed general-purpose code inside the probabilistic program. For example, suppose you have a physics model that simulates the trajectory of a headed ball through the air. You can incorporate this model inside a Figaro element.
- You can use general programming techniques to build your Figaro model. For example, you might have a map containing Figaro elements corresponding to all the players in your squad and choose the appropriate elements for a situation based on the players involved in that situation.

Here are some reasons that Scala is a particularly good choice of language for embedding a probabilistic programming system in:

- Because Scala is a functional programming language, Figaro gets to benefit from functional programming too. Functional programming has been instrumental in probabilistic programming, and many models can be written naturally in a functional manner, as I'll show in part 2.
- Scala is object-oriented; one of the beauties of Scala is that it is both functional and object-oriented. Figaro is also object-oriented. As I'll describe in part 2, object-orientation is a useful way to express several design patterns in probabilistic programming.

Finally, some of Figaro's advantages go beyond its embedding in Scala. These include the following:

- Figaro can represent an extremely wide range of probabilistic models. The values of Figaro elements can be any type, including Booleans, integers, doubles, arrays, trees, graphs, and so on. The relationships between these elements can be defined by any function.
- Figaro provides a rich framework for specifying evidence by using its conditions and constraints.
- Figaro features a good variety of inference algorithms.
- Figaro can represent and reason about dynamic models of situations that vary over time.
- Figaro can include explicit decisions in its models and supports inferring optimal decisions.

Using Scala

Because Figaro is a Scala library, you'll need a working knowledge of Scala to use Figaro. This is a book on probabilistic programming, so I don't teach Scala in this book. Many great resources for learning Scala are available, such as Twitter's Scala School (http://twitter.github.io/scala_school). But in case you aren't yet confident with Scala, I explain the Scala features used in the code as I go along. You'll be able to follow the book even if you don't know Scala yet.

You don't need to be a Scala wizard to benefit from probabilistic programming and Figaro, and I avoid using some of the more advanced and obscure features of Scala in this book. On the other hand, improving your Scala skills can help you become a better Figaro programmer. You might even find that your Scala skills improve as a result of reading this book.

For several reasons, Figaro is a favorable language for learning probabilistic programming:

- Being implemented as a Scala library, Figaro can be used in Java and Scala programs, making it easy to integrate into applications.
- Also related to being implemented as a library, rather than its own separate language, Figaro provides the full functionality of the host programming language to build your models. Scala is an advanced, modern programming language with many useful features for organizing programs, and you automatically benefit from those features when using Figaro.
- Figaro is fully featured in terms of the range of algorithms it provides.

This book emphasizes practical techniques and practical examples. Wherever possible, I explain the general modeling principle, as well as describe how to implement it in Figaro. This will stand you in good stead no matter what probabilistic programming system you end up using. Not all systems will be capable of easily implementing all the techniques in this book. For example, few object-oriented probabilistic programming systems currently exist. But with the right foundation, you can find a way to express what you need in your chosen language.

1.3.1 *Figaro vs. Java: building a simple probabilistic programming system*

To illustrate the benefits of probabilistic programming and Figaro, I'll show a simple probabilistic application written two ways. First, I'll show you how to write it in Java, with which you might be familiar. Then, I'll show you what it looks like in Scala using Figaro. Although Scala has some advantages over Java, that's not the main difference I'll point out here. The key idea is that *Figaro provides capabilities for representing probabilistic models and performing inference with them that aren't available without probabilistic programming.*

Our little application will also serve as a Hello World example for Figaro. Imagine someone who gets up in the morning, checks if the weather is sunny, and utters a greeting that depends on the weather. This happens two days in a row. Also, the weather on the second day is dependent on the first day: the second day is more likely to be sunny if the first day is sunny. These English language statements can be quantified numerically by the numbers in table 1.1.

Table 1.1   Quantifying the probabilities in the Hello World example

Today's weather		
Sunny	0.2	
Not sunny	0.8	
Today's greeting		
If today's weather is sunny	"Hello, world!"	0.6
	"Howdy, universe!"	0.4
If today's weather isn't sunny	"Hello, world!"	0.2
	"Oh no, not again"	0.8
Tomorrow's weather		
If today's weather is sunny	Sunny	0.8
	Not sunny	0.2
If today's weather isn't sunny	Sunny	0.05
	Not sunny	0.95
Tomorrow's greeting		
If tomorrow's weather is sunny	"Hello, world!"	0.6
	"Howdy, universe!"	0.4
If tomorrow's weather isn't sunny	"Hello, world!"	0.2
	"Oh no, not again"	0.8

The forthcoming chapters explain exactly how to interpret these numbers. For now, it's enough to have an intuitive idea that today's weather will be sunny with probability 0.2, meaning that it's 20% likely that the weather will be sunny today. Likewise, if tomorrow's weather is sunny, tomorrow's greeting will be "Hello, world!" with probability 0.6, meaning that it's 60% likely that the greeting will be "Hello, world!" and it's 40% likely that the greeting will be "Howdy, universe!"

Let's set for ourselves three reasoning tasks to perform with this model. You saw in section 1.1.3 that the three types of reasoning you can do with a probabilistic model are to *predict* the future, *infer* past events that led to your observations, and *learn* from past events to better predict the future. You'll do all of these with our simple model. The specific tasks are as follows:

1 Predict the greeting today.

2 Given an observation that today's greeting is "Hello, world!" infer whether today is sunny.

3 Learn from an observation that today's greeting is "Hello, world!" to predict tomorrow's greeting.

Here's how to do these tasks in Java.

Listing 1.1 Hello World in Java

```java
class HelloWorldJava {
  static String greeting1 = "Hello, world!";              Define the
  static String greeting2 = "Howdy, universe!";           greetings
  static String greeting3 = "Oh no, not again";

  static Double pSunnyToday = 0.2;
  static Double pNotSunnyToday = 0.8;
  static Double pSunnyTomorrowIfSunnyToday = 0.8;
  static Double pNotSunnyTomorrowIfSunnyToday = 0.2;
  static Double pSunnyTomorrowIfNotSunnyToday = 0.05;
  static Double pNotSunnyTomorrowIfNotSunnyToday = 0.95;   Specify the
  static Double pGreeting1TodayIfSunnyToday = 0.6;         numerical
  static Double pGreeting2TodayIfSunnyToday = 0.4;         parameters
  static Double pGreeting1TodayIfNotSunnyToday = 0.2;      of the model
  static Double pGreeting3IfNotSunnyToday = 0.8;
  static Double pGreeting1TomorrowIfSunnyTomorrow = 0.5;
  static Double pGreeting2TomorrowIfSunnyTomorrow = 0.5;
  static Double pGreeting1TomorrowIfNotSunnyTomorrow = 0.1;
  static Double pGreeting3TomorrowIfNotSunnyTomorrow = 0.95;

  static void predict() {                                  Predict
    Double pGreeting1Today =                               today's
         pSunnyToday * pGreeting1TodayIfSunnyToday +        greeting
         pNotSunnyToday * pGreeting1TodayIfNotSunnyToday;   using the
    System.out.println("Today's greeting is " + greeting1 + rules of
      "with probability " + pGreeting1Today + ".");         probabilistic
  }                                                         inference
```

```
static void infer() {
    Double pSunnyTodayAndGreeting1Today =
        pSunnyToday * pGreeting1TodayIfSunnyToday;
    Double pNotSunnyTodayAndGreeting1Today =
        pNotSunnyToday * pGreeting1TodayIfNotSunnyToday;
    Double pSunnyTodayGivenGreeting1Today =
        pSunnyTodayAndGreeting1Today /
        (pSunnyTodayAndGreeting1Today +
         pNotSunnyTodayAndGreeting1Today);
    System.out.println("If today's greeting is " + greeting1 +
        ", today's weather is sunny with probability " +
        pSunnyTodayGivenGreeting1Today + ".");
}
```

Infer today's weather given the observation that today's greeting is "Hello, world!" using the rules of probabilistic inference

```
static void learnAndPredict() {
    Double pSunnyTodayAndGreeting1Today =
        pSunnyToday * pGreeting1TodayIfSunnyToday;
    Double pNotSunnyTodayAndGreeting1Today =
        pNotSunnyToday * pGreeting1TodayIfNotSunnyToday;
    Double pSunnyTodayGivenGreeting1Today =
        pSunnyTodayAndGreeting1Today /
        (pSunnyTodayAndGreeting1Today +
            pNotSunnyTodayAndGreeting1Today);
    Double pNotSunnyTodayGivenGreeting1Today =
        1 - pSunnyTodayGivenGreeting1Today;
    Double pSunnyTomorrowGivenGreeting1Today =
        pSunnyTodayGivenGreeting1Today *
            pSunnyTomorrowIfSunnyToday +
        pNotSunnyTodayGivenGreeting1Today *
            pSunnyTomorrowIfNotSunnyToday;
    Double pNotSunnyTomorrowGivenGreeting1Today =
        1 - pSunnyTomorrowGivenGreeting1Today;
    Double pGreeting1TomorrowGivenGreeting1Today =
        pSunnyTomorrowGivenGreeting1Today *
            pGreeting1TomorrowIfSunnyTomorrow +
        pNotSunnyTomorrowGivenGreeting1Today *
            pGreeting1TomorrowIfNotSunnyTomorrow;
    System.out.println("If today's greeting is " + greeting1 +
        ", tomorrow's greeting will be " + greeting1 +
        " with probability " +
        pGreeting1TomorrowGivenGreeting1Today);
}
```

Learn from observing that today's greeting is "Hello, world!" to predict tomorrow's greeting using the rules of probabilistic inference

```
public static void main(String[] args) {
    predict();
    infer();
    learnAndPredict();
}
}
```

Main method that performs all the tasks

I won't describe how the calculations are performed using the rules of inference here. The code uses three rules of inference: the chain rule, the total probability rule, and

Bayes' rule. All these rules are explained in detail in chapter 9. For now, let's point out two major problems with this code:

- *There's no way to define a structure to the model.*

  The definition of the model is contained in a list of variable names with double values. When I described the model at the beginning of the section and showed the numbers in table 1.1, the model had a lot of structure and was relatively understandable, if only at an intuitive level. This list of variable definitions has no structure. The meaning of the variables is buried inside the variable names, which is always a bad idea. As a result, it's hard to write down the model in this way, and it's quite an error-prone process. It's also hard to read and understand the code afterward and maintain it. If you need to modify the model (for example, the greeting also depends on whether you slept well), you'll probably need to rewrite large portions of the model.

- *Encoding the rules of inference yourself is difficult and error-prone.*

  The second major problem is with the code that uses the rules of probabilistic inference to answer the queries. You have to have intimate knowledge of the rules of inference to write this code. Even if you have this knowledge, writing this code correctly is difficult. Testing whether you have the right answer is also difficult. And this is an extremely simple example. For a complex application, it would be impractical to create reasoning code in this way.

Now let's look at the Scala/Figaro code.

Listing 1.2   Hello World in Figaro

```
import com.cra.figaro.language.{Flip, Select}                          Import Figaro
import com.cra.figaro.library.compound.If                              constructs
import com.cra.figaro.algorithm.factored.VariableElimination

object HelloWorld {
  val sunnyToday = Flip(0.2)
  val greetingToday = If(sunnyToday,
      Select(0.6 -> "Hello, world!", 0.4 -> "Howdy, universe!"),
      Select(0.2 -> "Hello, world!", 0.8 -> "Oh no, not again"))     Define the
  val sunnyTomorrow = If(sunnyToday, Flip(0.8), Flip(0.05))          model
  val greetingTomorrow = If(sunnyTomorrow,
      Select(0.6 -> "Hello, world!", 0.4 -> "Howdy, universe!"),
      Select(0.2 -> "Hello, world!", 0.8 -> "Oh no, not again"))

  def predict() {                                                     Predict
    val result = VariableElimination.probability(greetingToday,       today's
                "Hello, world!")                                      greeting using
    println("Today's greeting is \"Hello, world!\" " +               an inference
          "with probability " + result + ".")                        algorithm
  }
```

```
def infer() {
  greetingToday.observe("Hello, world!")
  val result = VariableElimination.probability(sunnyToday, true)
  println("If today's greeting is \"Hello, world!\", today's " +
      "weather is sunny with probability " + result + ".")
}
```

> **Use an inference algorithm to infer today's weather, given the observation that today's greeting is "Hello, world!"**

```
def learnAndPredict() {
  greetingToday.observe("Hello, world!")
  val result = VariableElimination.probability(greetingTomorrow,
          "Hello, world!")
  println("If today's greeting is \"Hello, world!\", " +
      "tomorrow's greeting will be \"Hello, world!\" " +
      "with probability " + result + ".")
}
```

> **Learn from observing that today's greeting is "Hello, world!" to predict tomorrow's greeting using an inference algorithm**

```
def main(args: Array[String]) {
  predict()
  infer()
  learnAndPredict()
}
}
```

> **Main method that performs all the tasks**

I'll wait until the next chapter to explain this code in detail. For now, I want to point out that it solves the two problems with the Java code. First, the model definition describes exactly the structure of the model, in correspondence with table 1.1. You define four variables: sunnyToday, greetingToday, sunnyTomorrow, and greeting-Tomorrow. Each has a definition that corresponds to table 1.1. For example, here's the definition of greetingToday:

```
val greetingToday = If(sunnyToday,
        Select(0.6 -> "Hello, world!", 0.4 -> "Howdy, universe!"),
        Select(0.2 -> "Hello, world!", 0.8 -> "Oh no, not again"))
```

This says that if today is sunny, today's greeting is "Hello, world!" with probability 0.6 and "Howdy, universe!" with probability 0.4. If today isn't sunny, today's greeting is "Hello, world!" with probability 0.2 and "Oh no, not again" with probability 0.8. This is exactly what table 1.1 says for today's greeting. Because the code explicitly describes the model, the codes is much easier to construct, read, and maintain. And if you need to change the model (for example, by adding a sleepQuality variable), this can be done in a modular way.

Now let's look at the code to perform the reasoning tasks. It doesn't contain any calculations. Instead, it instantiates an algorithm (in this case, the variable elimination algorithm, one of several algorithms available in Figaro) and queries the algorithm to get the probability you want. Now, as described in part 3, this algorithm is based on the same rules of probabilistic inference that the Java program uses. All the hard work of organizing and applying the rules of inference is taken care of by the algorithm. Even for a large and complex model, you can run the algorithm, and all the inference is taken care of.

1.4   Summary

- Making judgment calls requires knowledge + logic.
- In probabilistic reasoning, a probabilistic model expresses the knowledge, and an inference algorithm encodes the logic.
- Probabilistic reasoning can be used to predict future events, infer causes of past events, and learn from past events to improve predictions.
- Probabilistic programming is probabilistic reasoning, where the probabilistic model is expressed using a programming language.
- A probabilistic programming system uses a Turing-complete programming language to represent models and provides inference algorithms to use the models.
- Figaro is a probabilistic programming system implemented in Scala that provides functional and object-oriented programming styles.

1.5   Exercises

Solutions to selected exercises are available online at www.manning.com/books/practical-probabilistic-programming.

1   Imagine that you want to use a probabilistic reasoning system to reason about the outcome of poker hands.

 a   What kind of general knowledge could you encode in your model?

 b   Describe how you might use the system to predict the future. What's the evidence? What's the query?

 c   Describe how you might use the system to infer past causes of current observations. What's the evidence? What's the query?

 d   Describe how the inferred past causes can help you with your future predictions.

2   In the Hello World example, change the probability that today's weather is sunny according to the following table. How do the outputs of the program change? Why do you think they change this way?

Today's weather	
Sunny	0.9
Not sunny	0.1

3   Modify the Hello World example to add a new greeting: "Hi, galaxy!" Give this greeting some probability when the weather is sunny, making sure to reduce the probability of the other greetings so the total probability is 1. Also, modify the program so that all the queries print the probability of "Hi, galaxy!" instead of "Hello, world!" Try to do this for both the Java and Figaro versions of the Hello World program. Compare the process for the two languages.

A quick Figaro tutorial

Now that you've seen what probabilistic programming is all about, you're ready to get up to speed in Figaro so that you can write your own simple programs and answer queries with them. My goal in this chapter is to introduce you to the most important concepts in Figaro as quickly as possible. Future chapters provide detailed explanations of what the models mean and how they should be understood. So let's go.

2.1 Introducing Figaro

To start, let's take a high-level look at Figaro. *Figaro*, introduced in chapter 1, is a probabilistic reasoning system. Before you look at its components, let's review the components of a probabilistic reasoning system in general so you can see how Figaro compares. Figure 2.1 reproduces the gist of the probabilistic reasoning system

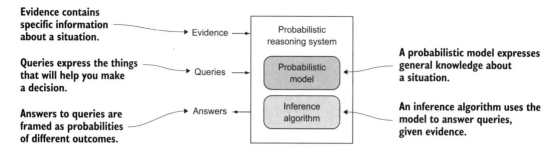

Figure 2.1   Review of probabilistic reasoning essentials

in chapter 1. As a reminder, general knowledge about a situation is encoded in the probabilistic model, while evidence provides specific information about a particular situation. An inference algorithm uses the model and the evidence to answer queries about your situation.

Now let's look at Figaro. Figure 2.2 shows the key concepts of Figaro. As you can see, the figure has the same components as figure 2.1. You express your general knowledge in the *Figaro model*. You provide specific knowledge about a situation in the form of *evidence*. *Queries* tell the system what you're interested in finding out. A *Figaro inference algorithm* takes the evidence and uses the model to provide *answers* to the queries.

Now let's look at each of these pieces in turn. The majority of Figaro's interface provides ways to specify Figaro models. A Figaro model consists of a set of data structures called *elements*. Each element represents a variable in your situation that can take on one of a set of values. The element encodes information that defines the probabilities of different values. You'll see the basic definition of elements in the context of the Hello World example in section 2.2.1.

There are two main kinds of element: atomic and compound. You can think of Figaro as providing a construction kit for building models. *Atomic elements* are the basic building blocks. Atomic elements represent basic probabilistic variables that don't depend on any other elements. Section 2.3 discusses atomic elements and presents a variety of examples. *Compound elements* are the connectors. They depend on one or more elements to build up more-complex elements. You'll learn about compound elements in section 2.4. Although Figaro provides a variety of compound elements, two are particularly important. These are called *Apply* and *Chain*, and you'll learn how to use them in section 2.5.

Next, you come to the evidence. Figaro provides a rich mechanism for specifying evidence. Most of the time, you'll use the simplest form of evidence, which is an *observation*. An observation specifies that an element is known to have a specific value. You'll learn how to specify observations in section 2.2.3. Sometimes you need a more general

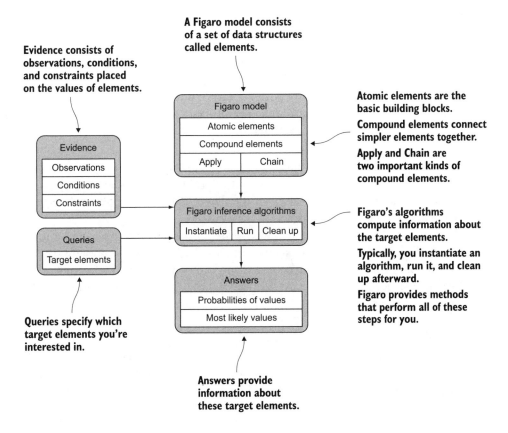

Figure 2.2 The key concepts of Figaro and how they fit together

way to specify evidence. Figaro provides *conditions* and *constraints* for this purpose. Conditions and constraints and their uses are described in section 2.6.

Queries in Figaro are specified by saying which *target elements* you're interested in and what you want to know about them. You use an inference algorithm to find out information about your target elements, given the evidence. Typically, you need to *instantiate* an algorithm, *run* it, and *clean up* afterward. I've provided simple methods that perform all these steps for you by using default settings. After you run the algorithm, you can get answers to your queries. Most often, these answers take the form of *probabilities of values* of the target elements. Sometimes, instead of probabilities, they tell you the *most likely values* of each target element. For each target element, the answer tells you which value has the highest probability. You'll see how to specify queries, run algorithms, and get answers in section 2.2.2.

2.2 Creating models and running inference: Hello World revisited

Now that you've seen an overview of Figaro concepts, let's see how they all fit together. You'll take another look at the Hello World example from chapter 1, and specifically at how all the concepts from figure 2.2 show up in this example. You'll look at how to build a model out of atomic and compound elements, observe evidence, ask queries, run an inference algorithm, and get answers.

You can run the code in this chapter in two ways. One is to use the Scala console, entering statements line by line and getting immediate responses. To do this, navigate to the book's project root directory PracticalProbProg/examples and type `sbt console`. You'll be greeted with a Scala prompt. Then you can enter each line of code as it appears and see the response.

The second way is the usual way: write a program with a `main` method that contains the code you want to execute. In this chapter, I don't provide the boilerplate for turning your code into a program you can run. I provide only the code that's relevant to Figaro. I'll make sure to indicate what you need to import and where to import it from.

2.2.1 Building your first model

To start, you'll build the simplest possible Figaro model. This model consists of a single atomic element. Before you can build a model, you have to import the necessary Figaro constructs:

```
import com.cra.figaro.language._
```

This imports all the classes in the `com.cra.figaro.language` package, which contains the most basic Figaro constructs. One of the classes is called `Flip`. You can build a simple model using `Flip`:

```
val sunnyToday = Flip(0.2)
```

Figure 2.3 explains this line of code. It's important to be clear about which parts are Scala and which parts are Figaro. In this line of code, you've created a Scala variable named sunnyToday and assigned it the value `Flip(0.2)`. The Scala value `Flip(0.2)` is a Figaro element that represents a random process that results in a value of `true` with probability 0.2 and `false` with probability 0.8. An *element* is a data structure

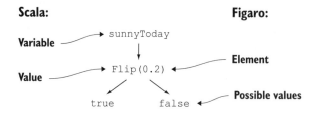

Figure 2.3 The relationship between Scala variables and values, and Figaro elements and possible values

representing a process that randomly produces a value. A random process can result in any number of outcomes. Each possible outcome is known as a *value* of the process. So `Flip(0.2)` is an element whose possible values are the Booleans `true` and `false`. To summarize, you have a Scala variable with a Scala value. That Scala value is a Figaro element, and it has any number of possible values representing different outcomes of the process.

In Scala, a type can be parameterized by another type that describes its contents. You might be familiar with this concept from Java generics, where you can have, for example, a list of integers or a list of strings. All Figaro elements are instances of the `Element` class. The `Element` class is parameterized by the type of values an element can take. This type is known as the *value type* of the element. Because `Flip(0.2)` can take Boolean values, the value type of `Flip(0.2)` is `Boolean`. The notation for this is that `Flip(0.2)` is an instance of `Element[Boolean]`.

KEY DEFINITIONS

Element—A Figaro data structure representing a random process

Value—A possible outcome of the random process

Value type—The Scala type representing the possible values of the element

There was a lot to say about this simple model. Fortunately, what you've learned applies to all Figaro models. Figaro models are created by taking simple Figaro elements—the building blocks—and combining them to create more-complex elements and sets of related elements. The definitions you've just learned of elements, values, and value types are the most important definitions in Figaro.

Before going on to build more-complex models, let's look at how to reason with this model.

2.2.2 *Running inference and answering a query*

You've built a simple model. Let's run inference so you can query the probability that `sunnyToday` is `true`. First, you need to import the inference algorithm you'll use:

```
import com.cra.figaro.algorithm.factored.VariableElimination
```

This imports the algorithm known as *variable elimination*, which is an exact inference algorithm, meaning it computes exactly the probabilities implied by your model and the evidence. Probabilistic inference is complex, so exact algorithms sometimes take too long or run out of memory. Figaro provides approximate algorithms that usually compute answers in the ballpark of the exact answers. This chapter uses simple models, so variable elimination will for the most part work.

Now, Figaro provides a single command to specify a query, run an algorithm, and get an answer. You can write the following code:

```
println(VariableElimination.probability(sunnyToday, true))
```

This command prints 0.2. Your model consists only of the element Flip(0.2), which comes out true with probability 0.2. Variable elimination correctly computes that the probability sunnyToday is true is 0.2.

To elaborate, the command you've just seen accomplishes several things. It first creates an instance of the variable elimination algorithm. It tells this instance that the query target is sunnyToday. It then runs the algorithm and returns the probability that the value of sunnyToday is true. The command also takes care of cleaning up after itself, releasing any resources used by the algorithm.

2.2.3 *Building up models and making observations*

Now let's start building up a more interesting model. You need a Figaro construct called If, so let's import it. You also need a construct named Select, but you already imported that along with the rest of com.cra.figaro.language:

```
import com.cra.figaro.library.compound.If
```

Let's use If and Select to build a more complex element:

```
val greetingToday = If(sunnyToday,
    Select(0.6 -> "Hello, world!", 0.4 -> "Howdy, universe!"),
    Select(0.2 -> "Hello, world!", 0.8 -> "Oh no, not again"))
```

The way to think about this is that an element represents a random process. In this case, the element named greetingToday represents the process that first checks the value of sunnyToday. If this value is true, it selects "Hello, world!" with probability 0.6 and "Howdy, universe!" with probability 0.4. If the value of sunnyToday is false, it selects "Hello, world!" with probability 0.2 and "Oh no, not again" with probability 0.8. greetingToday is a compound element, because it's built out of three elements. Because the possible values of greetingToday are strings, greetingToday is an Element[String].

Now, let's say that you've seen the greeting today and it's "Hello, world!" You can specify this evidence by using an observation as follows:

```
greetingToday.observe("Hello, world!")
```

Next, you can find out the probability that today is sunny, given that the greeting is "Hello, world!"

```
println(VariableElimination.probability(sunnyToday, true))
```

This prints 0.4285714285714285. Note that this is significantly higher than the previous answer (0.2). This is because "Hello, world!" is more likely if today is sunny than otherwise, so the evidence provides support for today being sunny. This inference is a simple example of Bayes' rule in action, which you'll learn about in chapter 9.

You're going to be extending this model and running more queries with different evidence, so you'll want to remove the observation on the variable greetingToday. You can do this with the following command:

```
greetingToday.unobserve()
```

Now, if you ask your query

```
println(VariableElimination.probability(sunnyToday, true))
```

you get the same answer, 0.2, as before you specified the evidence.

To finish this section, let's elaborate the model further:

```
val sunnyTomorrow = If(sunnyToday, Flip(0.8), Flip(0.05))
val greetingTomorrow = If(sunnyTomorrow,
    Select(0.6 -> "Hello, world!", 0.4 -> "Howdy, universe!"),
    Select(0.2 -> "Hello, world!", 0.8 -> "Oh no, not again"))
```

You compute the probability that tomorrow's greeting is "Hello, world!" both without and with evidence about today's greeting:

```
println(VariableElimination.probability(greetingTomorrow, "Hello, world!"))
// prints 0.27999999999999997

greetingToday.observe("Hello, world!")
println(VariableElimination.probability(greetingTomorrow, "Hello, world!"))
// prints 0.3485714285714286
```

You can see that after observing that today's greeting is "Hello, world!" the probability increases that tomorrow's greeting is "Hello, world!" Why? Because today's greeting being "Hello, world!" makes it more likely that today is sunny, which in turn makes it more likely that tomorrow is sunny, which finally makes it more likely that tomorrow's greeting will be "Hello, world!" As you saw in chapter 1, this is an example of inferring the past to better predict the future, and Figaro takes care of all of these calculations.

2.2.4 *Understanding how the model is built*

Now that you've seen all of the steps in creating a model, specifying evidence and queries, and running evidence and getting answers, let's take a closer look at the Hello World model to understand how it's built up from the building blocks (atomic elements) and connectors (compound elements).

Figure 2.4 is a graphical depiction of this model. The figure first reproduces the model definition, with each Scala variable in a separate box. In the second half of the figure, each node represents a corresponding element in the model, again in separate boxes. Some elements are values of Scala variables themselves. For example, the value of the sunnyToday Scala variable is the Flip(0.2) element. If an element is the value of a Scala variable, the graph shows both the name of the variable and the element. The model also contains some elements that aren't the values of specific

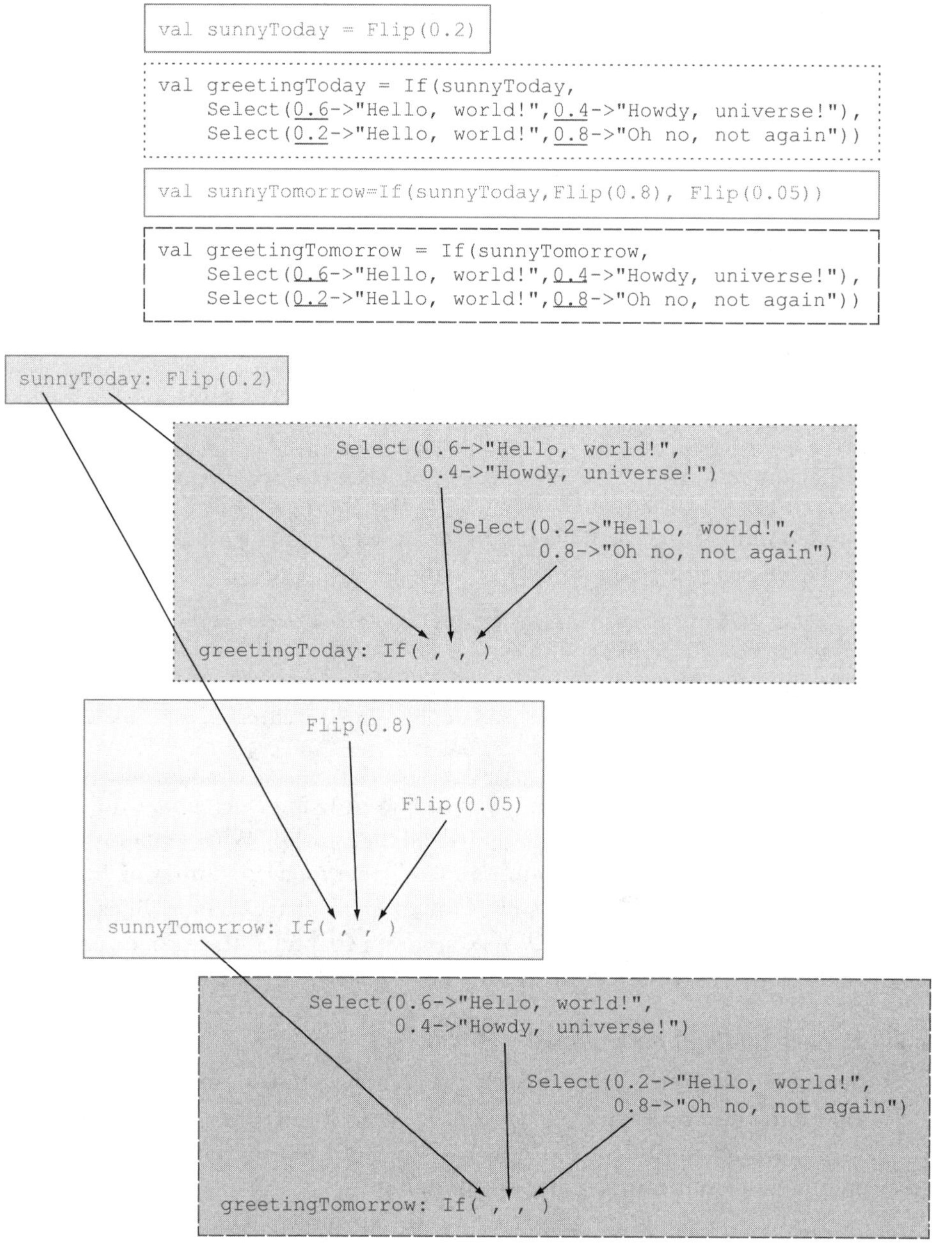
val sunnyToday = Flip(0.2)
val greetingToday = If(sunnyToday,
Select(0.6->"Hello, world!",0.4->"Howdy, universe!"),
Select(0.2->"Hello, world!",0.8->"Oh no, not again"))
val sunnyTomorrow=If(sunnyToday,Flip(0.8), Flip(0.05))
val greetingTomorrow = If(sunnyTomorrow,
Select(0.6->"Hello, world!",0.4->"Howdy, universe!"),
Select(0.2->"Hello, world!",0.8->"Oh no, not again"))
sunnyToday: Flip(0.2)
Select(0.6->"Hello, world!",
0.4->"Howdy, universe!")
Select(0.2->"Hello, world!",
0.8->"Oh no, not again")
greetingToday: If(, ,)
Flip(0.8)
Flip(0.05)
sunnyTomorrow: If(, ,)
Select(0.6->"Hello, world!",
0.4->"Howdy, universe!")
Select(0.2->"Hello, world!",
0.8->"Oh no, not again")
greetingTomorrow: If(, ,)

Figure 2.4 Structure of the Hello World model as a graph. Each node in the graph is an element. Edges in the graph show when one element is used by another element.

Scala variables, but still appear in the model. For example, because the definition of `sunnyTomorrow` is `If(sunnyToday, Flip(0.8), Flip(0.05))`, the elements `Flip(0.8)` and `Flip(0.05)` are also part of the model, so they're shown as nodes in the graph.

The graph contains edges between elements. For example, there's an edge from `Flip(0.8)` to the `If` element that's the value of `sunnyTomorrow`. The element `Flip(0.8)` is used by `If`. In general, there's an edge from one element to another if the second element uses the first element in its definition. Because only compound elements are built out of other elements, only compound elements can be the destination of an edge.

2.2.5 *Understanding repeated elements: when are they the same and when are they different?*

One point to notice is that `Select(0.6 -> "Hello, world!", 0.4 -> "Howdy, universe!")` appears twice in the graph, and the same for `Select(0.2 -> "Hello, world!", 0.8 -> "Oh no, not again")`. This is because the definition itself appears twice in the code, once for `greetingToday` and once for `greetingTomorrow`. These are two distinct elements, even though their definitions are the same. They can take different values in the same execution of the random process defined by this Figaro model. For example, the first instance of the element could have the value `"Hello, world!"` whereas the second could have the value `"Howdy, universe!"` This makes sense, because one is used to define `greetingToday`, and the other is used to define `greetingTomorrow`. It's quite possible that today's greeting and tomorrow's greeting will be different.

This is similar to ordinary programming. Imagine that you have a `Greeting` class and this code:

```
class Greeting {
  var string = "Hello, world!"
}
val greetingToday = new Greeting
val greetingTomorrow = new Greeting
greetingTomorrow.string = "Howdy, universe!"
```

Even though their definitions are exactly the same, `greetingToday` and `greetingTomorrow` are two distinct instances of the `Greeting` class. Therefore, it's possible for `greetingTomorrow.string` to have a different value from `greetingToday.string`, which will still be equal to "Hello, world!" In a similar way, the Figaro constructors, such as `Select`, create new instances of the corresponding class of elements. So `greetingToday` and `greetingTomorrow` are two different instances of the `Select` element, and therefore can take different values in the same run.

On the other hand, notice that the Scala variable `sunnyToday` also appears twice in the code, once in the definition of `greetingToday` and once for `sunnyTomorrow`. But the element that's the value of `sunnyToday` appears only once in the graph. Why? Because `sunnyToday` is a Scala variable, not the definition of a Figaro element. When a Scala variable appears more than once in a piece of code, it's the same variable, and so the same value is used. In our model, this makes sense; it's the same day's weather that's being used in the definitions of greetingToday and sunnyTomorrow, so it'll have the same value in any random execution of the model.

The same thing would happen in ordinary code. If you write

```
val greetingToday = new Greeting
val anotherGreetingToday = greetingToday
anotherGreetingToday.string = "Howdy, universe!"
```

anotherGreetingToday is exactly the same Scala variable as greetingToday, so after running this code, the value of greetingToday is also "Howdy, universe!" In the same way, if the same Scala variable representing an element appears multiple times in a program, it'll have the same value in every run.

It's essential to understand this point in order to know how to build Figaro models, so I suggest rereading this subsection to make sure you grok it. At this point, you should have a general idea of all the main concepts of Figaro and how they fit together. In the next few sections, you'll look at some of these concepts in more detail. You'll start in the next section with atomic elements.

2.3   *Working with basic building blocks: atomic elements*

Now it's time to build up your knowledge of Figaro elements. I'll start with the basic building blocks of models, the atomic elements. The name *atomic* means that they don't depend on any other elements but are completely self-contained. I won't provide you with an exhaustive list of atomic elements here, just some of the most common examples.

Atomic elements are divided into discrete elements and continuous elements, depending on their value type. *Discrete* atomic elements have value types like Boolean and Integer, while *continuous* atomic elements typically have the value type Double. Technically, discrete means that the values are well separated. For example, the integers 1 and 2 are well separated in that there are no integers between them. Continuous, meanwhile, means that the values lie in a continuum with no separation, such as the real numbers. Between any two real numbers, there are more real numbers. The distinction between discrete and continuous elements makes a difference in how probabilities are defined, as you'll see in chapter 4.

> **WARNING** Some people think *discrete* means *finite*. This isn't the case. For example, there are infinitely many integers, but the integers are well separated, so they're discrete.

KEY DEFINITIONS

Atomic element—Self-contained element that doesn't depend on any other elements

Compound element—Element built out of other elements

Discrete element—Element whose value type is well separated

Continuous element—Element whose value type has no separations

2.3.1   *Discrete atomic elements*

Let's look at some examples of discrete atomic elements: Flip, Select, and Binomial.

FLIP

You've already seen the discrete atomic element Flip. Flip is contained in the com.cra.figaro.language package, which includes many of the most commonly used elements. I suggest always importing everything in this package at the start of your programs. In general, Flip takes a single argument p, which represents the probability that the value of the element is true. p should be a number between 0 and 1 inclusive. The probability that the value of the element is false is $1 - p$. For example:

```
import com.cra.figaro.language._
val sunnyToday = Flip(0.2)
println(VariableElimination.probability(sunnyToday, true))
// prints 0.2

println(VariableElimination.probability(sunnyToday, false))
// prints 0.8
```

The official type of Flip(0.2) is AtomicFlip, which is a subclass of Element[Boolean]. This is to distinguish it from CompoundFlip, which you'll see later.

SELECT

You've also seen the Select element in the Hello World program. Here's an example of Select: Select(0.6 -> "Hello, world!", 0.3 -> "Howdy, universe!", 0.1 -> "Oh no, not again"). Figure 2.5 shows how this element is built up. Inside the parentheses are a number of clauses. Each clause consists of a probability, a right arrow, and a possible outcome. The number of clauses is variable; you can have as many as you like. The figure has three clauses. Because all of the outcomes are of type String, this is an Element[String]. Again, the official type is AtomicSelect[String], which is a subclass of Element[String].

Naturally, a Select element corresponds to a process in which each possible outcome is selected with the corresponding probability. Here's how it works for this example:

```
val greeting = Select(0.6 -> "Hello, world!", 0.3 -> "Howdy, universe!", 0.1
    -> "Oh no, not again")
println(VariableElimination.probability(greeting, "Howdy, universe!"))
// prints 0.30000000000000004
```

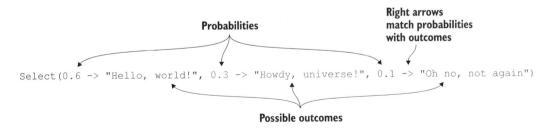

Figure 2.5   Structure of a Select element

Note that in a `Select`, the probabilities don't have to add up to 1. If they don't add up to 1, the probabilities are *normalized*. They're made to add up to 1 while the ratios between the probabilities are maintained. In the following example, each probability is twice what it was in the previous example, so they add up to 2. Normalizing restores the probabilities in the previous example so the outcome is the same.

```
val greeting = Select(1.2 -> "Hello, world!", 0.6 -> "Howdy, universe!", 0.2
    -> "Oh no, not again")
println(VariableElimination.probability(greeting, "Howdy, universe!"))
//prints 0.30000000000000004
```

BINOMIAL

One useful discrete element is `Binomial`. Imagine that you have the seven days of a week, and every day has a sunny element, which is `Flip(0.2)`. Now you want an element whose value is the number of sunny days in the week. This can be achieved by using the element `Binomial(7, 0.2)`. The value of this element is the number of trials that come out `true`, when there are seven total trials and each trial has probability 0.2 of coming out `true`. You can use it as follows:

```
import com.cra.figaro.library.atomic.discrete.Binomial
val numSunnyDaysInWeek = Binomial(7, 0.2)
    println(VariableElimination.probability(numSunnyDaysInWeek, 3))
//prints 0.114688
```

In general, `Binomial` takes two arguments: the number of trials and the probability that each trial comes out `true`. The definition of `Binomial` assumes that the trials are independent; the first trial coming out true doesn't change the probability that the second trial will come out `true`.

2.3.2 *Continuous atomic elements*

This section presents a couple of common examples of continuous atomic elements, `Normal` and `Uniform`. Chapter 4 explains continuous elements in detail. Continuous probability distributions are a little different from discrete distributions, in that instead of specifying the probability of each value, you specify the *probability density* of each value, which describes the probability of each interval around the value. You can still think of a probability density as similar to an ordinary probability, indicating how likely a value is compared to others. Because this chapter is a tutorial on Figaro, and chapter 4 explains probabilistic models, I'll defer further discussion until then. Rest assured that this will be made clear later.

NORMAL

One continuous probability distribution you're probably familiar with is the normal distribution. The *normal distribution* goes by other names, including the *bell curve* and the *Gaussian distribution*. Figure 2.6 shows the probability density function of a normal distribution. (If we're being picky, it's properly called a *univariate normal distribution*

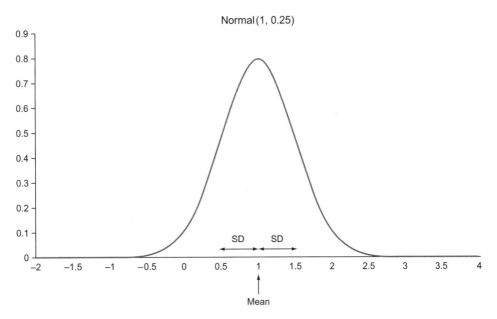

Figure 2.6   **Probability density function of a normal distribution**

because it defines a distribution over one single real-valued variable, and you can also have multivariate normal distributions that define a distribution over multiple variables, but we're not being picky, so a normal distribution it is.) The function has a *mean*, which is its center point (1 in the figure), and a *standard deviation*, which is a measure of the degree to which the function is spread around the center point (0.5 in the figure). About 68% of the time, generating a value from a normal distribution will result in a value within one standard deviation of the mean. In statistics and probabilistic reasoning, a normal distribution is typically specified using the mean and the *variance*, which is the square of the standard deviation. Because the standard deviation in the figure is 0.5, the variance is 0.25. So the standard specification for this particular normal is Normal(1, 0.25).

Figaro follows exactly this convention. It provides a Normal element, which takes the mean and variance as arguments. You can define a Normal element like this:

```
import com.cra.figaro.library.atomic.continuous.Normal
val temperature = Normal(40, 100)
```

The mean is 40, and the variance is 100, meaning the standard deviation is 10. Now, suppose you want to run inference using this element. It turns out that Figaro's variable elimination works only for elements that can take on a finite number of values. In particular, it doesn't work for continuous elements. So you need to use a different algorithm. You'll use an algorithm called *importance sampling*, which is an approximation algorithm that works well with continuous elements. You can run the algorithm as follows:

```
import com.cra.figaro.algorithm.sampling.Importance
def greaterThan50(d: Double) = d > 50
println(Importance.probability(temperature, greaterThan50 _))
```

The importance sampling algorithm is a randomized algorithm that produces a different answer every time, which should generally be in the ballpark of the true value. The answer you get will be close to 0.1567, but yours will most likely be slightly different.

Notice that the query here is a little different from before. With a continuous element, the probability that it'll take on a single particular value, such as 50, is usually 0. The reason is that there are infinitely many values with no separation. The chance that the process will come out exactly 50 rather than 50.000000000000001 or something in between is infinitesimally small. So you don't usually query continuous elements for the probability of an exact value.

Instead, you query the probability that the value falls in a range. The query is the predicate `greaterThan50`, which is a predicate that takes a `Double` as an argument and returns `true` if the argument is greater than 50. A predicate is a Boolean function of the value of an element. When you query whether an element satisfies a predicate, you ask for the probability that applying the predicate to a value of the element will return `true`. In this example, your query computes the probability that the temperature is greater than 50.

> **SCALA NOTE** The underscore after `greaterThan50` tells Scala to treat `greater-Than50` as a functional value being passed to the `Importance.probability` method. Without the underscore, Scala might think that you're trying to apply the function to zero arguments, which would be an error. Sometimes Scala can figure this out automatically without you having to provide the explicit underscore. But sometimes it fails to do so and tells you to provide it.

UNIFORM

Let's have one more example of a continuous element, again a familiar one. A *uniform element* is one that takes values in a given range, with every value in the range being equally likely. You can create and use a uniform element as follows:

```
import com.cra.figaro.library.atomic.continuous.Uniform
val temperature = Uniform(10, 70)
Importance.probability(temperature, greaterThan50 _)
// prints something like 0.3334
```

Specifically, a uniform element takes two arguments: the minimum and maximum values. The probability density of all values from the minimum to the maximum is the same. In the preceding example, the minimum is 10 and the maximum is 70, so the size of the range is 60. Your query predicate is whether the value is between 50 and 70; the size of this range is 20. So the probability of the predicate is 20/60 or 1/3, and you can see that importance sampling gets close to this answer.

Last, a comment: the official name of this element is the *continuous uniform*. There's also a discrete uniform, which can be found in the com.cra.figaro.library .atomic.discrete package. As you might expect, the discrete uniform makes each of an explicitly listed set of values equally likely.

Okay, now that you've seen the building blocks, let's see how to combine them to create bigger models.

2.4 *Combining atomic elements by using compound elements*

In this section, you'll look at some compound elements. Recall that a compound element is an element that builds on other elements to make more-complex elements. There are many examples of compound elements. You'll first look at two specific examples, If and Dist, and then see how you can use compound versions of most atomic elements.

2.4.1 *If*

You've already seen one example of a compound element in If. It's made up of three elements: a test, a then clause, and an else clause. If represents the random process that first checks the test. If the value of the test is true, it produces the value of the then clause; otherwise, it produces the value of the else clause. Figure 2.7 shows an example of an If element. If takes three arguments. The first argument is an Element[Boolean], in this case the element sunnyToday. This argument represents the test. The second argument is the then clause; when the value of the test element is true, this element is chosen. If the value of the test element is false, the third argument, the else clause, is chosen. The then and else clauses must have the same value type, which becomes the value type of the If element.

```
                                   ── Test
If(sunnyToday, ◄─────
                                                              ── Then clause
    Select(0.6 -> "Hello, world!", 0.4 -> "Howdy, universe!"), ◄──
                                                              ── Else clause
    Select(0.2 -> "Hello, world!", 0.8 -> "Oh no, not again")) ◄──
```

Figure 2.7 Structure of an If element

Here's this If element in action:

```
val sunnyToday = Flip(0.2)
val greetingToday = If(sunnyToday,
     Select(0.6 -> "Hello, world!", 0.4 -> "Howdy, universe!"),
     Select(0.2 -> "Hello, world!", 0.8 -> "Oh no, not again"))
println(VariableElimination.probability(greetingToday, "Hello world!"))
// prints 0.27999999999999997
```

The reason this prints 0.28 (within rounding error) is that the then clause is chosen with probability 0.2 (when sunnyToday is true), and "Hello, world!" results in this case with probability 0.6. Meanwhile, the else clause is chosen with probability 0.8, and in this case "Hello, world!" results with probability 0.2. So the total probability of "Hello, world!" is (0.2 × 0.6) + (0.8 × 0.2) = 0.28. You can see this by explicitly evaluating the two cases:

```
sunnyToday.observe(true)
println(VariableElimination.probability(greetingToday, "Hello, world!"))
// prints 0.6 because the then clause is always taken

sunnyToday.observe(false)
println(VariableElimination.probability(greetingToday, "Hello, world!"))
// prints 0.2 because the else clause is always taken
```

2.4.2 *Dist*

A useful compound element is Dist. Dist is similar to Select, except that instead of choosing among one of a set of values, Dist chooses one of a set of elements. Each of the choices is itself an element, which is why Dist is a compound element. Dist is useful when you want to select between complex options that are themselves random processes. For example, a corner kick in soccer might begin with a short pass or an aerial cross. This could be represented by a Dist choosing between two processes, one beginning with a short pass and one an aerial cross.

Dist is in the com.cra.figaro.language package. Here's an example of a Dist element:

```
val goodMood = Dist(0.2 -> Flip(0.6), 0.8 -> Flip(0.2))
```

Its structure, shown in figure 2.8, is similar to that of figure 2.5 for Select. The difference is that instead of having outcome values, you have outcome elements. You can think of it like this: Select selects one of a set of possible values directly, without any intervening process. Dist is indirect; it selects one of a set of processes to run, which generates a value when you run it. In this case, with probability 0.2, the process represented by the element Flip(0.6) is selected, while with probability 0.8, it's the process represented by Flip(0.2).

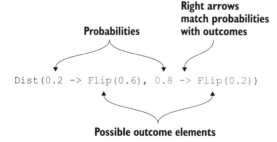

Figure 2.8 Structure of a Dist element

Here's what you get when you query this element:

```
println (VariableElimination.probability(goodMood, true))
// prints 0.28 = 0.2 * 0.6 + 0.8 * 0.2
```

2.4.3 *Compound versions of atomic elements*

You've seen examples of atomic elements that take numeric arguments. For example, Flip takes a probability, whereas Normal takes a mean and a variance. What if you're uncertain about the values of these numeric arguments? In Figaro, the answer is simple: you make them elements themselves.

When you make the numeric arguments elements, you get compound versions of the original atomic elements. For example, the following code defines and reasons with a compound Flip:

```
val sunnyTodayProbability = Uniform(0, 0.5)
val sunnyToday = Flip(sunnyTodayProbability)
println(Importance.probability(sunnyToday, true))
// prints something like 0.2548
```

Here, the element sunnyTodayProbability represents your uncertainty about the probability that today is sunny; you believe that any value from 0 to 0.5 is equally likely. Then sunnyToday is true with probability equal to the value of the sunnyToday-Probability element. In general, a compound Flip takes a single argument, which is an Element[Double] representing the probability that the Flip comes out true.

Normal offers more possibilities. It's common in probabilistic reasoning to assume that the normal has a particular known variance, while representing uncertainty over the mean. For example, you might assume that the temperature has a variance of 100, and the mean is somewhere around 40, but you're not quite sure what it is. You can capture this with the following:

```
val tempMean = Normal(40, 9)
val temperature = Normal(tempMean, 100)
println(Importance.probability(temperature, (d: Double) => d > 50))
// prints something like 0.164
```

Alternatively, you might also be uncertain about the variance, and think that it's either 80 or 105. You can use the following code:

```
val tempMean = Normal(40, 9)
val tempVariance = Select(0.5 -> 80.0, 0.5 -> 105.0)
val temperature = Normal(tempMean, tempVariance)
println(Importance.probability(temperature, (d: Double) => d > 50)
// prints something like 0.1549
```

FOR MORE INFORMATION This chapter shows a small fraction of the atomic and compound elements provided by Figaro. You can see more useful examples by looking at Figaro's Scaladoc. The Scaladoc (www.cra.com/Figaro) is an automatically generated HTML documentation of the Figaro library, similar to Javadoc. Alternatively, it's contained in the Figaro binary download, also available from the Figaro web page. This download includes a file that looks like figaro_2.11-2.2.2.0-javadoc.jar. The contents of this archive can be extracted by using a program such as 7-Zip or WinZip.

2.5   *Building more-complex models with Apply and Chain*

Figaro provides two useful tools for building models, called `Apply` and `Chain`. Both are important kinds of elements. `Apply` lets you utilize the whole power of Scala in Figaro models by bringing Scala into Figaro. `Chain` lets you create dependencies between elements in limitless ways. The compound elements you've seen so far, such as `If` and compound `Flip`, let you create dependencies in specific predefined ways. `Chain` lets you go beyond these predefined dependencies to create any dependencies you want.

2.5.1   *Apply*

Let's start with `Apply`, which is in the `com.cra.figaro.language` package. `Apply` takes an element and a Scala function as arguments. It represents the process of applying the Scala function to the value of the element to get a new value. For example:

```
val sunnyDaysInMonth = Binomial(30, 0.2)
def getQuality(i: Int): String =
  if (i > 10) "good"; else if (i > 5) "average"; else "poor"
val monthQuality = Apply(sunnyDaysInMonth, getQuality)
println(VariableElimination.probability(monthQuality, "good"))
// prints 0.025616255335326698
```

The second and third lines define a function named `getQuality`. This function takes an `Integer` argument; the local name of the argument in the `getQuality` function is i. The function returns a String according to the code in line 3.

The fourth line defines `monthQuality` to be an `Apply` element. The structure of an `Apply` element is shown in figure 2.9. `Apply` takes two arguments. The first is an element; in this example, it's `sunnyDaysInMonth`, an `Element[Int]`. The second argument is a function, where the type of the argument is the same as the value type of the element. In our example, the function `getQuality` takes an `Integer` argument, so it matches up. The function can return a value of any type; in our example, it returns a String.

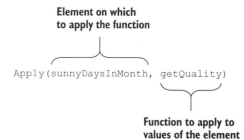

**Element on which
to apply the function**

`Apply(sunnyDaysInMonth, getQuality)`

**Function to apply to
values of the element**

**Figure 2.9   Structure of an
`Apply` element**

Here's how the Apply element defines a random process. It first generates a value for the first, element argument. In our example, it generates a particular number of sunny days in the month. Let's say it generates 7. Then the process takes the second, function argument and applies it to the value that was generated. In our case, the process applies the function getQuality to 7 to obtain the result average. This becomes the value of the Apply element. You can see from this that the possible values of Apply have the same type as the return type of the function argument. In our case, the Apply element is an Element[String].

If you're new to Scala, let me introduce you to *anonymous functions*. Having to define a separate function for each Apply element can be annoying when you're going to use it in only one place, especially when it's short like this one. Scala provides anonymous functions that can be defined directly in the place they're used. Figure 2.10 shows the structure of an anonymous function that defines the same function as getQuality. The components of this structure are similar to the named function. There's a function argument named i. It has the type Integer. The symbol => indicates that you're defining an anonymous function. Finally, there's the function body, which is the same as for getQuality.

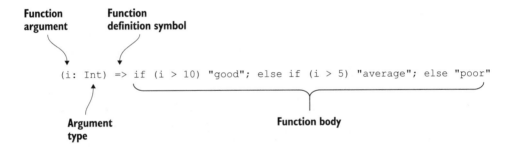

Figure 2.10 Structure of an anonymous function

You can define an Apply element equivalent to the previous element by using an anonymous function:

```
val monthQuality = Apply(sunnyDaysInMonth,
  (i: Int) => if (i > 10) "good"; else if (i > 5) "average"; else "poor")
```

Now you can query monthQuality. You get the same answer, whichever version of monthQuality you use:

```
println(VariableElimination.probability(monthQuality, "good"))
// prints 0.025616255335326698
```

Although this example of `Apply` is contrived, there are many practical reasons you might want to use it. Here are a few examples:

- You have a `Double` element whose value you want to round to the nearest integer.
- You have an element whose value type is a data structure, and you want to summarize a property of the data structure. Perhaps you have an element over lists and you want to know the probability that the number of items in the list is greater than 10.
- The relationship between two elements is best encoded by a physics model. In this case, you would use a Scala function to represent the physical relationship and embed the physical model into Figaro by using `Apply`.

MULTI-ARGUMENT APPLY

With `Apply`, you're not restricted to Scala functions of only one argument. `Apply` in Figaro is defined for up to five arguments. Using `Apply` with more than one argument is a good way of bringing multiple elements together to bear on another element. For example, here's an `Apply` of two arguments:

```
val teamWinsInMonth = Binomial(5, 0.4)
val monthQuality = Apply(sunnyDaysInMonth, teamWinsInMonth,
    (days: Int, wins: Int) => {
    val x = days * wins
    if (x > 20) "good"; else if (x > 10) "average"; else "poor"
    })
```

Here, the two element arguments to `Apply` are `sunnyDaysInMonth` and `teamWinsInMonth`, which are both `Element[Int]`s. The `Apply`'s function argument takes two `Integer` arguments named `days` and `wins`. This function creates a local variable named x whose value is equal to `days * wins`. Note that because `days` and `wins` are ordinary Scala `Integer`s, x is also an ordinary Scala variable, not a Figaro element. In fact, everything inside the `Apply`'s function argument is ordinary Scala. `Apply` takes this ordinary Scala function that operates on ordinary Scala values and "lifts" it to a function that operates on Figaro elements.

Now let's query this version of `monthQuality`:

```
println(VariableElimination.probability(monthQuality, "good"))
// prints 0.15100056576418375
```

The probability has gone up quite a bit. It looks like my softball team has a chance to cheer me up. More significantly, despite being a simple example, this probability would have been difficult to compute without Figaro.

2.5.2 *Chain*

As its name indicates, `Chain` is used to chain elements together into a model in which one element depends on another element, which in turn depends on other elements, and so forth. It relates to the chain rule of probability, which you'll see in chapter 5. But you don't need to know the chain rule to understand `Chain`.

Chain is also in the `com.cra.figaro.language` package. The easiest way to explain Chain is through a picture. Figure 2.11 shows two elements; the element goodMood depends on the element monthQuality. If you think about this as a random process, the process first generates a value for monthQuality and then, using that value, generates a value for goodMood. This is a simple example of a Bayesian network, which you'll learn about in chapter 4. The figure borrows terminology from Bayesian networks: monthQuality is called the *parent*, and goodMood is called the *child*.

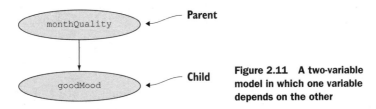

Figure 2.11 A two-variable model in which one variable depends on the other

Because goodMood depends on monthQuality, goodMood is defined by using Chain. The element monthQuality has already been defined in the previous subsection. Here's the definition of goodMood:

```
val goodMood = Chain(monthQuality, (s: String) =>
    if (s == "good") Flip(0.9)
    else if (s == "average") Flip(0.6)
    else Flip(0.1))
```

Figure 2.12 shows the structure of this element. Like Apply, this Chain takes two arguments: an element and a function. In this case, the element is the parent, and the function is known as the *chain function*. The difference between Chain and Apply is that whereas the function in Apply returns ordinary Scala values, the function in Chain returns an element. In this example, the function returns a Flip, with the exact choice of which Flip depending on the value of monthQuality. So, this function takes an argument of type String and returns an Element[Boolean].

The random process defined by this Chain is illustrated in figure 2.13. This process has three steps. First, a value is generated for the parent. In this example, the value

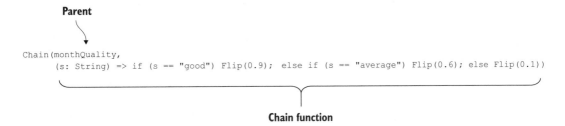

Figure 2.12 Structure of a Chain element

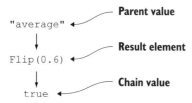

"average" ← —— **Parent value**

Flip(0.6) ← —— **Result element**

true ← —— **Chain value**

Figure 2.13   Random process defined by a `Chain` **element. First, a value is generated for the parent. Next, the result element is chosen according to the chain function. Finally, a value is generated from the result element.**

average is generated for monthQuality. Second, you apply the chain function to this value to get an element, which is called the *result element*. In this example, you can check the definition of the chain function to see that the result element is Flip(0.6). Third, you generate a value from the result element; in this example, you generate true. This value becomes the value of the child.

Let's summarize by checking the type of everything that's involved in a Chain. A Chain is parameterized by two types, the parent's value type (which you'll call T) and the child's value type (which you'll call U):

- The *parent* has type Element[T].
- A *parent value* has type T.
- The *chain function* has type T => Element[U]. This means that it's a function from type T to an Element[U].
- A *result element* has type Element[U].
- A *chain value* has type U.
- The *child* has type Element[U]. This is the type of the Chain as a whole.

In our example, goodMood is an Element[Boolean], so you can query the probability that it's true:

```
println(VariableElimination.probability(goodMood, true))
// prints 0.3939286578054374
```

MULTI-ARGUMENT CHAIN

Let's consider a slightly more complex model, where goodMood depends on both monthQuality and sunnyToday, as shown in figure 2.14.

You can capture this by using a two-argument Chain. In this example, the function inside the chain takes two arguments, a String named quality and a Boolean named

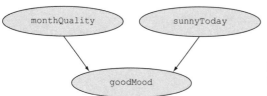

Figure 2.14   A three-variable model in which goodMood **depends on the other two variables**

sunny, and returns an `Element[Boolean]`. goodMood is again an `Element[Boolean]`.
Here's the code:

```
val sunnyToday = Flip(0.2)
val goodMood = Chain(monthQuality, sunnyToday,
  (quality: String, sunny: Boolean) =>
    if (sunny) {
      if (quality == "good") Flip(0.9)
      else if (quality == "average") Flip(0.7)
      else Flip(0.4)
    } else {
      if (quality == "good") Flip(0.6)
      else if (quality == "average") Flip(0.3)
      else Flip(0.05)
    })
println(VariableElimination.probability(goodMood, true))
// prints 0.2896316752495942
```

NOTE Unlike `Apply`, the `Chain` construct is defined for only one or two arguments. If you need more arguments, you can combine `Chain` with `Apply`. First you use `Apply` to package the argument elements into a single element whose value is a tuple of values of the arguments. This single element is passed to `Chain`. The chain then has all the information it needs in the value of this element.

map and flatMap using Apply and Chain

A note to the Scala knowledgeable among you. Figaro elements are, in a way, like Scala collections such as `List`. Whereas a list contains a list of values, an element contains a random value. And just as you can apply a function to every value in a list to get a new list, you can apply a function to the random value contained in an element to get a new element. But this is exactly what `Apply` does! For lists, applying a function to every value in the list is performed by using the `map` method. You've similarly defined `map` for elements by using `Apply`. So you can write `Flip(0.2).map(!_)` for `Apply(Flip(0.2), (b: Boolean) => !b)`.

Likewise, for lists, you can apply a function to each value that returns a list, and then flatten all the resulting lists into a single list, using `flatMap`. In the same way, `Chain` applies a function to the random value contained in an element to get another element, and then gets the value out of that element. So `flatMap` for elements is defined using `Chain`. Therefore, you can write `Uniform(0, 0.5).flatMap(Flip(_))` for `Chain(Uniform(0, 0.5), (d: Double) => Flip(d))`. (As an aside, note how you've defined a compound `Flip` by using `Chain`. Many of Figaro's compound elements can be defined using `Chain`.)

One of the really cool things about Scala is that any type that has `map` and `flatMap` defined can be used in a `for` comprehension. You can use `for` notation for elements. You can write this:

```
for { winProb <- Uniform(0, 0.5); win <- Flip(winProb) } yield !win
```

That's our tour of how to build complex models out of simpler elements. Before ending this chapter, I want to describe some ways of applying evidence and constraining models.

2.6   Specifying evidence by using conditions and constraints

By now, I've gone into a fair amount of detail about how to build models. Much of your energy when using Figaro will be spent on creating models. But let's not ignore specifying evidence. Figaro provides three mechanisms for specifying evidence: observations, conditions, and constraints.

2.6.1   Observations

You've already seen one way to specify evidence, by using observations. You saw an example in the Hello World program, where you used this:

```
greetingToday.observe("Hello, world!")
```

In general, observe is a method defined on an element that takes as an argument a possible value of the element. Its effect is to say that the element has to take on that value. Any random execution in which the element takes on a different value is ruled out. This observation has an effect on the probabilities of related elements. For example, in the Hello World program, you saw that asserting this observation makes sunny-Today more likely to be true, because according to the model, a sunny day today is more likely to result in a "Hello, world!" greeting than a non-sunny day.

You also saw another method related to observations:

```
greetingToday.unobserve()
```

This removes the observation on greetingToday (if it had one), so that no random executions are ruled out. As a result, there will be no effect from evidence about greetingToday on the probabilities of other elements.

2.6.2   Conditions

observe specifies a particular value of the element. What happens if you know something about the value of the element but don't know exactly what it is? Figaro allows you to specify any predicate as evidence. This is called a *condition*. A condition specifies a Boolean function that needs to be true for a value to be possible. For example:

```
val sunnyDaysInMonth = Binomial(30, 0.2)
println(VariableElimination.probability(sunnyDaysInMonth, 5)
sunnyDaysInMonth.setCondition((i: Int) => i > 8)
println(VariableElimination.probability(sunnyDaysInMonth, 5)
```

Prints
0.172279182850003

Evidence that more than 8 days are sunny

Prints 0, because 5 sunny days contradicts the evidence

Observing evidence and using it to infer the probabilities of other variables is central to probabilistic reasoning. For example, by observing the number of sunny days in the month, you could infer whether someone is likely to have a good mood. Using the example from section 2.5:

```
val sunnyDaysInMonth = Binomial(30, 0.2)
val monthQuality = Apply(sunnyDaysInMonth,
  (i: Int) => if (i > 10) "good"; else if (i > 5) "average"; else "poor")
val goodMood = Chain(monthQuality, (s: String) =>
    if (s == "good") Flip(0.9)
    else if (s == "average") Flip(0.6)
    else Flip(0.1))
println(VariableElimination.probability(goodMood, true))
// prints 0.3939286578054374 with no evidence
```

You set the condition that specifies that the value of sunnyDaysInMonth must be more than 8. You can then see its effect on goodMood:

```
sunnyDaysInMonth.setCondition((i: Int) => i > 8)
println(VariableElimination.probability(goodMood, true))
// prints 0.6597344078195809
```

The probability of a good mood has gone up significantly because you've ruled out the bad months with 8 or fewer sunny days.

Figaro allows you to specify multiple conditions that are satisfied by an element. This is achieved using the addCondition method, which adds a condition to any existing conditions on the element. The result of adding a condition is that both the new and existing conditions must hold the value of the element.

```
sunnyDaysInMonth.addCondition((i: Int) => i % 3 == 2)
```

This says that in addition to being greater than 8, the value of sunnyDaysInMonth must be two more than a multiple of 3. This rules out 9 and 10 as possible values, so the smallest possible value is 11. Naturally, when you query the probability of a good mood, you see that it has gone up again:

```
println(VariableElimination.probability(goodMood, true))
// prints 0.9
```

You can remove all the conditions on an element by using removeConditions:

```
sunnyDaysInMonth.removeConditions()
println(VariableElimination.probability(goodMood, true))
// prints 0.3939286578054374 again
```

By the way, an observation is just a special case of a condition in which you require that an element take on a single particular value. To summarize the methods associated with conditions:

- setCondition is a method on an element that takes a predicate as an argument. The predicate must be a function from the element's value type to a Boolean.

The setCondition method makes this predicate the only condition on the element, removing existing conditions and observations.

- addCondition is also a method on an element that takes a predicate as an argument that must be a function from the element's value type to a Boolean. The addCondition method adds this predicate to any existing conditions and observations.

- removeConditions is a method on an element that removes all conditions and observations from the element.

2.6.3   *Constraints*

Constraints provide a more general means to say things about elements. Constraints generally serve two purposes: (1) as a means of specifying "soft" evidence; (2) as a way of providing additional connections between elements in a model.

CONSTRAINTS FOR SOFT EVIDENCE

Suppose you have some evidence about an element, but you're not quite sure about it. For example, you think I look grumpy, but you can't tell my mood from the outside. So rather than specifying hard evidence that goodMood is false, you specify soft evidence that goodMood is more likely to be false than true.

This is achieved using a constraint. A *constraint* is a function from the value of an element to a Double. Although this isn't enforced by Figaro, constraints work best when the value of this function is always between 0 and 1 (inclusive). For example, to express evidence that my mood appears to be grumpy but you're not sure, you could add a constraint to goodMood that produces a value of 0.5 when goodMood is true and 1.0 when goodMood is false:

```
goodMood.addConstraint((b: Boolean) => if (b) 0.5; else 1.0)
```

This soft constraint is interpreted as saying that all else being equal, goodMood being true is half as likely as goodMood being false, because 0.5 is half of 1.0. The precise mathematics of this is discussed in chapter 4, but the short version is that the probability of a value of an element is multiplied by the constraint results for that value. So in this example, the probability of true is multiplied by 0.5, and the probability of false is multiplied by 1.0. When you do this, the probabilities don't necessarily add up to 1, so they're scaled so they add up to 1. Suppose that without this evidence, I think that goodMood being true and false are equally likely, so they both have probability 0.5. After seeing the evidence, I would first multiply both probabilities by the constraint result, so true has probability 0.25 and false has probability 0.5. These don't add up to 1, so I scale them to get the final answer that the probability of goodMood being true is 1/3, while the probability goodMood is false is 2/3.

The difference between a condition and a constraint is that in a condition, some of the states are declared to be impossible (have a probability of zero). In contrast, constraints change the probability of different states but don't make a state impossible unless the constraint result is zero. Conditions are sometimes called *hard conditions*, because they set a hard-and-fast rule about the possible states, while constraints are called *soft constraints*.

Getting back to the example program, when you query goodMood after adding this constraint, you see that the probability has gone down because of the soft evidence, but is not zero, which it would have been had we set hard evidence that I was grumpy:

```
println(VariableElimination.probability(goodMood, true))
// prints 0.24527469450215497
```

Constraints offer a parallel set of methods to conditions. Specifically:

- setConstraint is a method on an element that takes a predicate as argument. The predicate must be a function from the element's value type to a Double. The setConstraint method makes this predicate the only constraint on the element.
- addConstraint is also a method on an element that takes a predicate as an argument that must be a function from the element's value type to a Double. The addConstraint method adds this predicate to any existing constraints.
- removeConstraints is a method on an element that removes all constraints from the element.

The conditions and constraints are separate, so setting a condition or removing all conditions doesn't remove any existing constraints, and vice versa.

CONSTRAINTS FOR CONNECTING ELEMENTS

Here's a powerful usage of constraints. Suppose you believe that two elements have values that are related, but this isn't captured in their definitions as elements. For example, suppose your softball team wins 40% of its games, so each game is defined by Flip(0.4). Suppose you also believe that your team is streaky, so adjacent games are likely to have the same result. You can capture this belief by adding a constraint to pairs of adjacent games, with the constraint saying they're more likely to have the same values than different values. You can achieve this with the following code. I'm presenting it for three games, but it can be generalized to any number of games with arrays and for comprehensions.

First, you'll define the results of the three games:

```
val result1 = Flip(0.4)
val result2 = Flip(0.4)
val result3 = Flip(0.4)
```

Now, to demonstrate what's happening, you'll create an allWins element whose value is true whenever all the results are true:

```
val allWins = Apply(result1, result2, result3,
  (w1: Boolean, w2: Boolean, w3: Boolean) => w1 && w2 && w3)
```

Let's see the probability that all the games result in a win before adding any constraints:

```
println(VariableElimination.probability(allWins, true))
// prints 0.064000000000000002
```

Now let's add the constraints. You'll define a `makeStreaky` function that takes two results and adds a streakiness constraint to them:

```
def makeStreaky(r1: Element[Boolean], r2: Element[Boolean]) {
  val pair = Apply(r1, r2, (b1: Boolean, b2: Boolean) => (b1, b2))
    pair.setConstraint((bb: (Boolean, Boolean)) =>
    if (bb._1 == bb._2) 1.0; else 0.5
  )}
```

This function takes two `Boolean` elements as arguments, representing the results of two games. Because a constraint can be applied to only a single element, and you want to use a constraint to create a relationship between both elements, you first package the two elements into a single element whose value is a pair. This is achieved by `Apply(r1, r2, (b1: Boolean, b2: Boolean) => (b1, b2))`. Now you have a single element whose value is a pair of the results of the two games. You then set the constraint of the pair to the function that takes a pair bb of `Boolean`s and returns 1.0 if `bb._1 ==` `bb._2` (the first and second components of the pair are equal), and returns 0.5 otherwise. This constraint says that, all else being equal, the two results are twice as likely to be the same as different.

Now, you can make each pair of adjacent results streaky and query the probability that all games resulted in a win:

```
makeStreaky(result1, result2)
makeStreaky(result2, result3)
println(VariableElimination.probability(allWins, true))
// prints 0.11034482758620691
```

You see that the probability has gone up significantly because of the streakiness of the team.

NOTE For those in the know about probabilistic graphical models, you'll notice that the use of constraints demonstrated in this subsection enables Figaro to represent undirected models such as Markov networks.

You've reached the end of our whirlwind tour of Figaro. In the next chapter, you'll see a complete end-to-end example that uses Figaro in an application.

2.7 *Summary*

- Figaro uses the same overall structure as other probabilistic reasoning systems, with models, evidence, queries, and inference algorithms that provide answers.
- A Figaro model is made up of a set of elements.
- Figaro elements are Scala data structures representing random processes that generate a value of their value type.

- Figaro models are put together by starting with atomic elements and building them up using compound elements.
- Using `Apply`, you can lift any Scala function into your Figaro model.
- Using `Chain`, you can create many interesting and complex dependencies between elements.
- Conditions and constraints provide a rich framework for specifying evidence and additional relationships between elements.

2.8   Exercises

Solutions to selected exercises are available online at www.manning.com/books/ practical-probabilistic-programming.

1 Extend the Hello World program to add a variable representing the side of bed you got out of (right or wrong). If you got out of the wrong side of the bed, the greeting is always "Oh no, not again!" If you got out of the right side of the bed, the greeting logic is the same as before.

2 In the original Hello World program, observe that today's greeting is "Oh no, not again!" and query today's weather. Now observe the same evidence and ask the same query on your modified program from exercise 1. What happened to the answer to the query? Can you explain the result intuitively?

3 In Figaro, you can use the code x === z as shorthand for

```
Apply(x, z, (b1: Boolean, b2: Boolean) => b1 === b2
```

In other words, it produces an element whose value is true if the values of its two arguments are equal. Without running Figaro, try to guess what the following two programs will produce:

a
```
val x = Flip(0.4)
val y = Flip(0.4)
val z = x
val w = x === z
println(VariableElimination.probability(w, true))
```

b
```
val x = Flip(0.4)
val y = Flip(0.4)
val z = y
val w = x === z
println(VariableElimination.probability(w, true))
```

Now check your answers by running the Figaro program.

4 In the following exercises, you'll find the `FromRange` element useful. `FromRange` takes two integers *m* and *n* and produces a random integer from *m* to *n* − 1. For example, `FromRange(0, 3)` produces 0, 1, or 2 with equal probability. Write a Figaro program to compute the probability of rolling a total of 11 when you roll two fair six-sided dice.

5 Write a Figaro program to compute the probability that the first die is a 6 when you roll two fair six-sided dice and the total is greater than 8.

6 In Monopoly, doubles happen when you roll two fair six-sided dice and both dice show the same number. If you roll three doubles in a row, you go to jail. Write a Figaro program to compute the probability that this will happen to you on any given turn.

7 Imagine a game where you have a spinner and five dice with different numbers of sides. The spinner has five possible outcomes with equal probability: 4, 6, 8, 12, and 20. In the game, you first spin the spinner. Then you roll a fair die whose number of sides is the result of the spinner. Write a Figaro program to represent this game.

   a Compute the probability that you rolled a 12-sided die.
   b Compute the probability that you rolled a 7.
   c Compute the probability that you rolled a 12-sided die given that you rolled a 7.
   d Compute the probability that you rolled a 7 given that you rolled a 12-sided die.

8 Now modify the game from exercise 7 so that the spinner has a tendency to get stuck and land on the same outcome two turns in a row. Using similar logic to makeStreaky, encode a constraint that two adjacent spins are more likely to have the same value than different values. You play the game twice in a row.

   a Compute the probability that you rolled a 7 on the second roll.
   b Compute the probability that you rolled a 7 on the second roll given that you rolled a 7 on the first roll.

Creating a probabilistic programming application

This chapter covers

- Using a common architecture for probabilistic programming applications
- Designing a realistic model using only simple language features
- Learning models from data and using the results to reason about future instances

You've now had a whirlwind introduction to many of the features of Figaro. What can you do with it? How do you build useful software with it? This chapter gives you a glimpse of how to use Figaro to build a realistic application.

In this chapter, you'll see a complete design of a spam filter based on probabilistic programming, including the design of a model, a component to reason about incoming emails and classify them as normal or spam, and a component to learn the spam-filtering model from a training set of emails. In the process, you'll learn about an architecture that's often used in probabilistic programming applications.

3.1 Understanding the big picture

You're going to build a spam filter. How does it fit into a larger email application? Figure 3.1 illustrates how it works. Imagine that you have an email server. One of its

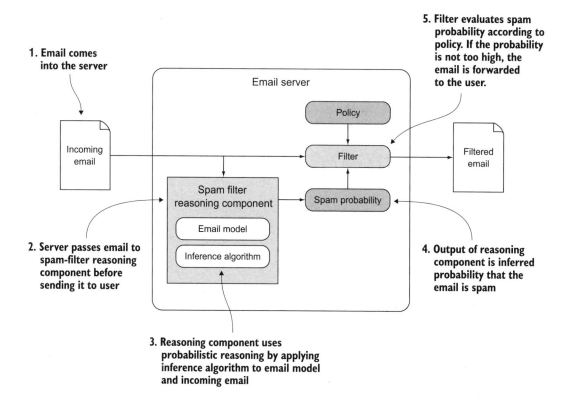

Figure 3.1   How a spam filter fits in an email server. This is an online process that happens every time a new email arrives.

jobs is to take incoming emails and direct them to users. When an incoming email arrives, the server passes it to the spam filter reasoning component. This component uses probabilistic reasoning to determine the probability that the email is spam. This probability is then passed to a filter, which uses the spam probability to decide whether to allow the email to pass, based on a certain policy.

As you may recall from chapter 1, a probabilistic reasoning system uses an inference algorithm operating on a model to answer a query, given evidence. In this case, the system uses a model of normal and spam emails, contained in the email model. The query is whether the email is spam, and the answer is the spam probability. In order to work, the reasoning component needs to get the email model from somewhere. Where does it come from? It's learned from training data by a learning component.

In probabilistic reasoning, *learning* is the process of taking training data and producing a model. Chapter 1 briefly introduced learning as something a probabilistic reasoning system can do. For example, a soccer reasoner can use a season's worth of corner kicks to learn a corner-kick model that it can then use to predict the next

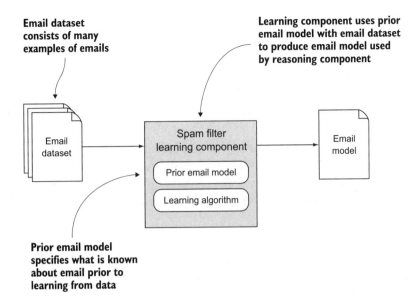

Email dataset consists of many examples of emails

Learning component uses prior email model with email dataset to produce email model used by reasoning component

Prior email model specifies what is known about email prior to learning from data

Figure 3.2 How a learning component produces the email model. This learning process can take a long time and happens offline.

corner kick. Learning is used in practical applications as a method to create the model used for probabilistic reasoning. The other method is to hand-engineer the model by using knowledge of the system being modeled.

Figure 3.2 shows the process by which the learning component produces the email model. This is an offline component; the process doesn't happen with every email and is allowed to take a long time to produce the best model it possibly can. The learning component has to finish its job and produce the email model before the reasoning component can run. After it's finished, the learning component isn't needed anymore, unless you want to update the email model at some future date.

The learning component uses training data consisting of a set of emails. This dataset includes both normal and spam emails, but they don't necessarily have to be all labeled as normal or spam. The learning component doesn't start without any knowledge; rather, it uses a learning algorithm operating on the dataset to take a prior email model and turn it into the email model used by the reasoning component. At this point, you might be thinking that I've just punted the issue of creating the model. If the goal of the learning component is to create the email model, where does the prior email model come from?

In this case, the prior email model contains the minimal structural assumptions needed to build a spam filter. In particular, this model states that whether an email is spam depends on the presence or absence of certain words, but it doesn't state which words indicate spam, or with what probability. Those are learned from the data. The prior model also states that the number of unusual words in an email has something to do with an email being spam, but it doesn't stipulate what the relationship is. Again, this relationship is learned from the data.

I'll go into detail a little later on what exactly the learning component learns, but in a nutshell, it consists of the following information:

- Which words are useful in classifying emails as normal or spam. These are called the *feature words*.
- A set of parameters that represent things like the probability that any given email is spam before you observe the email; the probability that a particular word appears in the email, given that it's either normal or spam; and the probability that an email contains many unusual words, again given that it's either normal or spam.

The first item, the set of feature words, is read immediately from the dataset when it's first read. The guts of the learning component are in learning the parameters. These same parameters are then used by the reasoning component.

A lot of research has been done on how to build an effective spam filter. This chapter provides a relatively simple solution that's enough to show you the principles, but you can do a lot more to put together an effective application.

3.2   *Running the code*

In the body of the chapter, you'll see all the code for this application that's relevant to probabilistic programming. The application contains a fair amount of code dedicated to file I/O, particularly for reading emails from a file and for writing a learned model to a file and reading it back from the file. I won't show you that code, because it's not particularly germane to the topic of probabilistic programming and would make the chapter overly long. The code you'll see in this chapter is in fragments. To run it, you'll need the full code, which can be found at http://manning.com/pfeffer/ PPP_SourceCode.zip.

The learning component needs data. You also need data for testing and evaluating your system while it's under development. Although several real spam datasets exist, their presence on the internet is unreliable, so to ensure that you have a concrete dataset to work with, I've generated my own. This isn't a dataset of real emails; each "email" is represented as a list of words found in the emails with no attempt to make them into sentences or to include headers. But the distribution of words in the normal and spam "emails" was derived from real normal and spam emails, so it's realistic from that point of view. For the purpose of explaining the concepts in this chapter, this dataset will suffice. For a real application, you'd want to work with proper emails.

Inside the directory named Chapter3Data, the dataset contains two subdirectories: Training contains 100 example emails used for training, of which 60 are normal and 40 are spam; and Test contains a total of 100 emails used for testing the results of the learning. In addition, a Labels.txt file contains labels (1 for spam or 0 for normal) for all the emails. The learning component uses these labels to help learn the model. The reasoning model doesn't use the labels; that would be cheating. But when you want to evaluate the model, you'll use the labels to check whether the reasoning component got the right answer. In principle, labels might not be supplied for all the training emails. Learning can work even if only a subset of emails is labeled, and the code in this chapter works with only a subset labeled. But to keep things simple, all emails in this dataset have labels.

When you're building a learning application, you need a way to evaluate the application during development. The code in the repository contains an evaluator whose job it is to evaluate the quality of the learned model. Because this isn't part of the deployed application, I don't describe it in the body of the text. Its operation is straightforward, and you should be able to understand the code in Evaluator.scala, given the explanations in the text.

The easiest way to run the code in this chapter is to use the Scala build tool, sbt. First, you'll run the learning component on some training data. The learning component takes three arguments: the path of the directory containing the training emails, the path of the file containing the labels, and the path of the file to store the results of learning. For example, you can call

```
sbt "runMain chap03.LearningComponent Chapter3Data/Training Chapter3Data/
Labels.txt Chapter3Data/LearnedModel.txt"
```

This produces output like the following. (This shows only the most relevant lines, not the full verbose output.)

```
Number of elements: 31005
Training time: 4876.629
```

This shows that 31,005 Figaro elements were created, and learning took 4,876 seconds.

The most important outcome of running the learning component is that now you have a file named LearnedModel.txt in your project directory. LearnedModel.txt is a text file that contains the information needed from learning to support reasoning. In particular, it contains a list of all the relevant words that are used for classification and the values of all the parameters of the model. The format of this file is specific to the spam-filtering application, and the reasoning component knows how to read it.

NOTE The learning component uses a lot of memory. You may find that you need to explicitly set the heap space used by the Java virtual machine. You can do this by including an option like -Xmx8096m in your Java initialization. In Eclipse, you would put this option in the eclipse.ini file in the directory in which Eclipse is installed. In this case, the option is telling Java to allocate 8096 MB (8 GB) to the heap.

Now that you have this model, you can use the reasoning model to classify whether a particular email is spam. To do this, you run the reasoning component, which takes as arguments the path to the email you want to classify and the path to the learned model. For example, you might call

```
sbt "runMain chap03.ReasoningComponent Chapter3Data/Test/TestEmail_3.txt
Chapter3Data/LearnedModel.txt"
```

This produces output of the probability that test email 3 is spam.

Finally, you can evaluate the learning results on a test set. To do this, you call the evaluator. This takes four arguments. The first three arguments are the path to the directory containing test emails, the path to the file containing labels, and the path to the file containing the learned model. The final argument corresponds to the policy shown in figure 3.1. This argument provides a threshold probability for classifying an email as spam. If the reasoning component thinks the probability that an email is spam is above this threshold, it classifies it as spam; otherwise, it classifies it as normal. This threshold controls how sensitive the spam filter is. If you set the threshold to 99%, the filter will block only emails that it's pretty sure are spam, but many spam emails will probably get through. If the threshold is 50%, a large number of nonspam emails might be blocked. For example, running

```
sbt "runMain chap03.Evaluator Chapter3Data/Test Chapter3Data/Labels.txt
Chapter3Data/LearnedModel.txt 0.5"
```

produces output that ends with lines like these:

```
True positives: 44
False negatives: 2
False positives: 0
True negatives: 54
Threshold: 0.5
Accuracy: 0.98
Precision: 1.0
Recall: 0.9565217391304348
```

These lines summarize the performance of the spam filter. *True positives* means cases that are spam that are classified as spam by the filter. *False positives* means cases that aren't spam but are mistakenly classified as spam. *False negatives* are the opposite: emails that are spam but are classified as normal. Finally, *true negatives* are the emails correctly classified as normal. The next line shows the threshold used for classification. The last three lines show various metrics of performance. The topic of measuring the performance of classifiers is an interesting one but not particularly salient to probabilistic programming in general, so I've provided details in the sidebar "Measuring performance of classifiers."

The code in this chapter works reasonably quickly on training sets of up to 200 emails. You can use Figaro to learn from much larger datasets by using advanced methods discussed in chapter 12.

Measuring performance of classifiers

Quantifying the performance of classifiers can be tricky. The most obvious measure to use is accuracy, meaning the fraction of classifications that are correct. But this can be misleading if most of the cases you're interested in are negative and you're interested in finding the positives. For example, suppose 99% of the cases are negative. You could get 99% accuracy just by classifying everything as negative, but in reality, you would have a poor classifier because it would never find the cases you're interested in. Therefore, people often use metrics like precision and recall. *Precision* is a measure of how well the classifier avoids false positives. *Recall* measures how well it recognizes the positive cases (how well it avoids false negatives).

The precise definitions are as follows. *TP* stands for the number of true positives, *FP* is the number of false positives, *FN* is the number of false negatives, and *TN* is the number of true negatives.

$$\text{Accuracy} = \frac{TP + TN}{TP + FP + FN + TN}$$

$$\text{Precision} = \frac{TP}{TP + FP}$$

$$\text{Recall} = \frac{TP}{TP + FN}$$

Now that you understand how to train and run the spam filter, let's look at how it works. You'll start with the general architecture of the application before learning details of the model and the code.

3.3 Exploring the architecture of a spam filter application

Going back to section 3.1, our spam filter consists of two components. An online component performs probabilistic reasoning to classify an email as normal or spam, and filter it or pass it on to the user appropriately. An offline component learns the email model from a training set of emails. The following sections describe the architecture of the reasoning component and then of the learning component. As you'll see, they have a lot of parts in common.

3.3.1 Reasoning component architecture

When deciding on the architecture for a component, the first things you need to determine are the inputs, the outputs, and the relationships between them. For our spam filter application, your goal is to take an email as input and determine whether it's a normal email or spam. Because this is a probabilistic programming application, the application won't produce a Boolean spam/normal classification as output. Instead, it will produce the probability with which it thinks the email is spam. Also, to keep things simple, you'll assume that the email input is a text file.

To summarize your spam-filtering reasoning component:

- *Input*—A text file representing an email
- *Output*—A `Double` representing the probability that the email is spam

Now you'll build up the architecture of your spam filter, step by step.

STEP 1: DEFINE THE HIGH-LEVEL ARCHITECTURE AS A PROBABILISTIC REASONING SYSTEM

To start, you can go back to the basic architecture of a probabilistic reasoning system, first found in chapter 1, and get your first cut at the architecture of your spam-filtering application, shown in figure 3.3. Your *spam filter reasoning component* is used to determine whether an email is normal or spam. It takes as evidence the text of the email. The query is whether the email is spam. The answer it produces is the probability that the email is spam.

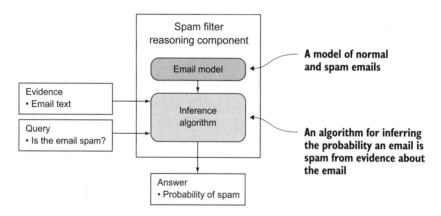

Figure 3.3   First cut at spam filter reasoning architecture. The spam filter uses an inference algorithm operating on an email model to determine the probability that an email is spam, given the email text.

To get this answer, the reasoning component uses an *email model* and an *inference algorithm*. The email model is a probabilistic model that captures your general knowledge about emails, including both the properties of an email itself and whether the email is spam. The inference algorithm uses the model to answer the query of whether the email is spam, given evidence.

STEP 2: REFINE THE ARCHITECTURE FOR THE SPAM-FILTERING APPLICATION

You want to represent your probabilistic model by using a probabilistic program. In Figaro, a probabilistic program has elements in it. Remember from chapter 2 that in Figaro, evidence is applied to individual elements as conditions or constraints. So you need a way to turn your email text into evidence that can be applied to individual elements in the model. In machine learning, the component that turns raw data into evidence about model elements is typically called a *feature extractor*. Those aspects of the data that are applied as evidence to the model are called *features*. As figure 3.4 shows,

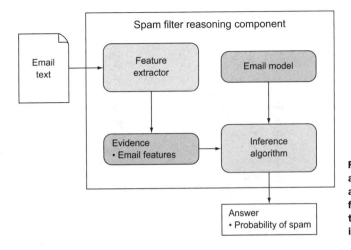

Figure 3.4 Second cut at spam filter reasoning architecture. You've added a feature extractor and removed the query, because the query is always the same.

the feature extractor takes the email text as input and turns it into a set of email features, which becomes the evidence for the inference algorithm.

Also, this particular probabilistic reasoning application always answers the same query: is the email spam? You don't need to make a query an input to the application; therefore, you drop the query from the architecture.

STEP 3: SPECIFY THE ARCHITECTURE IN DETAIL

It's time to take a closer look at the model. Figure 3.5 shows a refinement of the reasoning architecture that breaks the model into three parts: the process, which contains structural knowledge programmed in by the model designer; the parameters, which are learned from the data; and auxiliary knowledge that's not directly related to elements but is used for reasoning.

Creating a model takes skill, and this book includes many examples, but in general, a probabilistic model has the same kinds of constituents in it. I'll go into all these constituents in detail in section 3.4 for the spam filter application, but I want to introduce them here. The model contains five separate constituents:

- *Templates defining which elements are in the model.* For example, an element represents whether the email is spam, and other elements represent the presence of particular words in the email. The exact words aren't specified; that's part of the knowledge, which is explained at the end of this list. Choosing the elements of the spam filter model is discussed in section 3.4.1.
- *The dependencies between the elements.* For example, an element indicating the presence of a particular word depends on the element representing whether the email is spam. Remember that in a probabilistic model, the direction of the dependencies isn't necessarily the direction of reasoning. You use the words to determine whether the email is spam, but in the model, you can think of the email sender as first deciding what kind of email to send ("I'm going to send

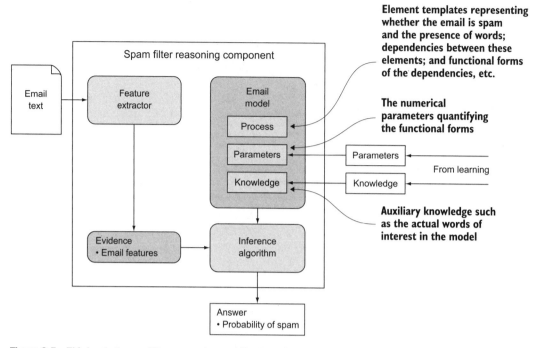

Figure 3.5 Third cut at spam filter reasoning architecture. The model is broken into process, parameters, and knowledge. The parameters and knowledge come from learning.

you a spam email") and then deciding what words go in it. You typically model dependencies in the causal direction. Because the kind of email causes the words, the dependency goes from the element representing whether the email is spam to each of the words. Determining the dependencies in the spam filter model is discussed in more detail in section 3.4.2.

- The *functional forms of these dependencies*. The functional form of an element indicates what type of element it is, such as an If, an atomic Binomial, or a compound Normal. The functional form doesn't specify the parameters of the element. For example, the preceding dependency takes the form of an If with two Flips: if the email is spam, then the word *rich* is present with one probability; otherwise, it's present with some other probability. The functional forms for the spam filter model are defined in section 3.4.3.

These first three constituents, which make up the process in figure 3.5, are what's assumed by the spam filter application to be known before learning. They're defined by the designer of the application. Together, they constitute the structure of the email model.

- The *numerical parameters of the model*, shown as Parameters in figure 3.5. For example, the probability that an email is spam is one parameter. The probability that the word *rich* is present if the email is spam is another parameter, and the probability that *rich* is present if the email isn't spam is a third parameter. The parameters are separated out from the process because the parameters will be learned from training data. The parameters of the email model are discussed in section 3.4.4.

- *The knowledge.* Figure 3.5 shows the auxiliary knowledge used in constructing the model and applying evidence to it in a particular situation. I use the term "knowledge" for anything learned from the training data that isn't specifically related to the elements, their dependencies, functional forms, or numerical parameters. In our spam filter application, this knowledge will consist of a dictionary of the words that appear in the training emails along with the number of times each word appears. For example, you need the knowledge to tell you that the word *rich* is one you're interested in. As a result, the knowledge helps define the parameters of the model; the probability that *rich* appears if the email is spam is a parameter only if *rich* is a word you're interested in. The auxiliary knowledge is discussed further in section 3.4.5.

At this point, the architecture of the reasoning component is fairly complete. It's time to look at the learning component.

3.3.2 Learning component architecture

Harking back to section 3.1, you know that the job of the learning component is to produce the email model used by the reasoning component, given a dataset of emails. Just as you did for reasoning, the first thing to do is determine the inputs and outputs of the learning component. Looking at figure 3.5, you know that the output needs to be the parameters and knowledge of the email model. But what about the input? You can assume that you're given a training set of emails from which to learn, so that makes up part of the input. But learning is much easier if someone has also labeled some of those emails as normal or spam. You'll assume that you're given a training set of emails, as well as labels for some of those emails. But not all the emails have to be labeled; you can use a large dataset of unlabeled emails in addition to a smaller dataset of emails with labels.

To summarize your spam-filtering learning component:

- *Inputs*
  - A set of text files representing emails
  - A file with normal/spam labels for a subset of the emails
- *Outputs*
  - Numerical parameters characterizing the generative process
  - Auxiliary knowledge to use in the model

Figure 3.6 shows the architecture of the spam filter learning component. It uses many elements similar to the reasoning component, but with some important differences:

- The learning component centers on a *prior email model*. This model contains the same parts as the email model in the reasoning component, except that you use

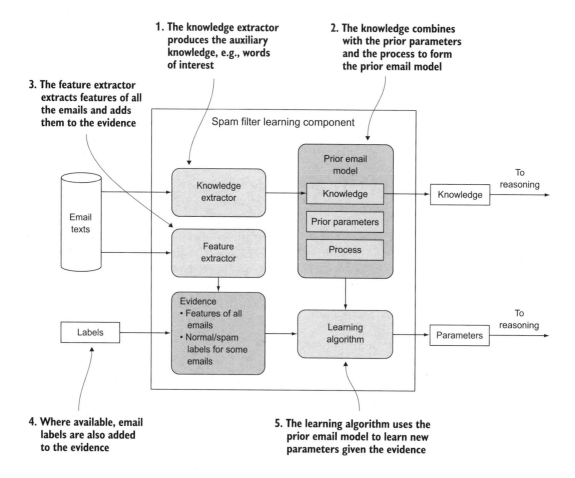

1. The knowledge extractor produces the auxiliary knowledge, e.g., words of interest

2. The knowledge combines with the prior parameters and the process to form the prior email model

3. The feature extractor extracts features of all the emails and adds them to the evidence

Spam filter learning component

Email texts

Knowledge extractor

Feature extractor

Prior email model

Knowledge

Prior parameters

Process

Knowledge — To reasoning

Labels

Evidence
• Features of all emails
• Normal/spam labels for some emails

Learning algorithm

Parameters — To reasoning

4. Where available, email labels are also added to the evidence

5. The learning algorithm uses the prior email model to learn new parameters given the evidence

Figure 3.6   Learning component architecture

prior parameters for the parameters instead of parameters produced by the learning component. As you'll see in chapter 5, prior parameters are the parameters of your model before you've seen any data. Because the learning component hasn't seen any data before it operates, it uses prior parameter values. The other two parts of the model, the *process* and the *knowledge*, are exactly the same as for the reasoning component.

■ The knowledge itself is extracted directly from the training emails by a *knowledge extractor*. For example, the knowledge might consist of the most common words appearing in the emails. This knowledge is also output from the learning component and sent to the reasoning component.

■ Just as in the reasoning component, the *feature extractor* extracts features of all the emails and turns them into evidence. The normal/spam labels are turned into evidence for the emails for which you have labels.

- Instead of an inference algorithm, you have a *learning algorithm*. This algorithm takes all the evidence about all the emails, and uses the model to learn parameter values. Like reasoning algorithms, Figaro provides learning algorithms, which you'll learn about later in the book.

Those are all the pieces of the learning component. One of the nice things about this architecture, with its division into reasoning and learning components, is that the learning component can be run once and the results can be used many times by the reasoning component. Learning from training data can be a time-consuming operation, and you wouldn't want to do it every time you want to reason about a new email. Your design allows you to do the learning once and export the learned parameters and knowledge, and use them to reason rapidly about incoming emails.

Now that you've seen the architecture, it's time to look at how it works in practice. The next section presents the design of the model and shows the code that builds the model for each email. Then, you'll see the implementation of the reasoning component, and finally, the implementation of the learning component.

3.4 Designing an email model

This section shows how to design the probabilistic model that models normal and spam emails. Because both the reasoning and learning components use the same process and knowledge and differ only in the parameters, the design here applies to both.

When you build a probabilistic model in Figaro, you put together four main ingredients:

- The elements in the model.
- The way the elements are connected to each other (the dependencies between the elements).
- The functional forms of the dependencies. These are the element class constructors used to implement the dependencies. For example, atomic `Flip` is an element class constructor for `Boolean` elements that don't depend on any other element, whereas compound `Flip` is a constructor for a `Double` element that depends on another element for its mean.
- The numerical parameters of those functional forms.

Let's look at each of these in turn. At the end, I'll also describe the auxiliary knowledge that goes into the model.

3.4.1 Choosing the elements

When you're designing a spam filter, you need to consider what things about an email might tell you whether it's spam or normal. Some of these items include the following:

- Particular words in the header or body of the email. For example, the word *rich* might be more likely in a spam email than a normal email.
- Misspellings and other unusual words. Spam email often has misspelled words or words that don't appear in other emails.

- The appearance of particular words near other words.
- Natural language features such as parts of speech.
- Features of the header, such as the From and To addresses, servers used, and the like.

To keep the application relatively simple, you'll make these simplifying design decisions:

- You'll use only the first two of these items: the words in the email, as well as the presence of unusual words.
- Although it might be beneficial to reason separately about the header and body of the email, you'll lump both together.
- When it comes to creating an element about a word in an email, you have two options. One is to use an integer element whose value is the number of times the word appears in an email. The second is to use a `Boolean` element whose value indicates the presence or absence of the word, regardless of the number of times it appears. You'll use the second option.
- For unusual words, you could look up each word in a language dictionary to see whether it's a well-defined word or an unusual word. To avoid relying on an external application, you'll use a different approach. For this example, an unusual word is one that doesn't appear in any other email.

Given these assumptions, your next task is to choose the elements of the model. You'll have three sets of elements. The first set indicates whether the email is spam. This is achieved through a single `Boolean` element. The second consists of the presence or absence of particular words in the email. The third set relates to the number of unusual words in the email.

REPRESENTING PRESENCE OR ABSENCE OF WORDS

When it comes to creating elements to represent the presence or absence of words, thought needs to be put into which words to include in the model. You could have an element for every single word that appears in any of the training emails. But that would result in a huge number of elements. For example, a typical training set of 1,000 emails contains over 40,000 distinct words.

Having too many elements is bad for two reasons. First, it leads to *overfitting*, meaning that you learn a model that fits the training data well but doesn't generalize well. When you have a huge number of elements, it's likely that some of them will spuriously explain the training data, even when they're not predictive of whether something is spam. To see this, imagine that you take a word and randomly put it in five emails. Suppose 1/3 of your set of training emails are spam. The probability that all five emails in which the word appears are spam is about 1/250. That means that if you have 40,000 words that appear five times, about 160 of them will appear only in spam emails. These 160 words might explain all of the spam emails. But by the assumption of the experiment, these words were put randomly in the training emails, so they have no predictive power.

Another reason having too many elements is bad is that it makes both the reasoning and learning slow. You want reasoning to be as fast as possible, because you want to apply it to every email that comes into your server. Meanwhile, learning a probabilistic model can be a slow process, especially when you have thousands of training instances or more. Using a large number of elements can make it impracticably slow.

Based on these considerations, you'll create elements for 100 words in the model. The next question is, which 100 words? A machine learning technique called *feature selection* can be used to decide which features or elements to include in a model. In a spam filter, the goal of feature selection is to identify the words that are most likely to be indicative of an email being normal or spam. Feature selection techniques can be sophisticated. If you were building a production spam filter, you'd probably use one of these sophisticated techniques. But for this chapter, you'll use a simple technique.

This technique is based on two considerations. First, using words that occur too infrequently leads to overfitting, as they're more likely to appear too randomly to be predictive. Second, frequent words such as *the* and *and* are also unlikely to be predictive, because they appear in lots of normal and spam emails. These kinds of words are called *stop words*. So to create your list of words in the model, you'll remove all words that are too frequent, and then use the next 100 most frequent words.

REPRESENTING THE NUMBER OF UNUSUAL WORDS

The motivation for including the number of unusual words in the model is that spam tends to contain more unusual words than ordinary email. In fact, in a 1,000-email training set, 28% of words in spam emails are unusual, whereas only 18% of words in ordinary emails are unusual. But a closer look at the data reveals a more nuanced picture. Some spam emails have a lot of unusual words, and others appear to be like normal emails in terms of their unusual word count. To capture this detail, you add a `hasUnusualWords` element into the model to represent whether this is an email that has a lot of unusual words. This is a *hidden element*. It's not directly present in the data, but including it in the model can make the model more accurate.

To summarize, the elements in your email model are as follows:

- `isSpam`—A `Boolean` element whose value is `true` if the email is spam.
- `hasWord1`, ..., `hasWord100`—A `Boolean` element for each word whose value is `true` if the word is present in the email.
- `hasManyUnusualWords`—A `Boolean` element whose value is `true` if the email tends to have a lot of unusual words.
- `numUnusualWords`—An `Integer` element whose value is the number of words in the email that don't appear in any other email.

You can summarize the elements in the model with the following `Model` class. This abstract `Model` class declares the elements in the model without providing a definition for them. The purpose of creating an abstract `Model` class is to extend it with both a `ReasoningModel` and a `LearningModel`. As you'll see later, subtle differences exist between the reasoning model and the learning model that necessitate creating two classes. Using an abstract base class means that you can write methods, such as for applying evidence, that apply to either kind of model. In chapter 12, you'll learn a pattern for creating reasoning and learning components by using a single model class so that you don't have to go to the trouble of creating two classes, but that pattern uses Figaro features you haven't learned yet.

Listing 3.1 Abstract `Model` class

> The model class takes a dictionary as an argument. As you'll see in section 3.4.5, the dictionary contains auxiliary knowledge about the words in the training set.

```
abstract class Model(val dictionary: Dictionary) {                ◁──────┘
  val isSpam: Element[Boolean]
  val hasManyUnusualWords: Element[Boolean]
  val numUnusualWords: Element[Int]

  val hasWordElements: List[(String, Element[Boolean])]           ◁──────┐
}
```

> Declarations of the elements in the model, as described in the previous paragraphs

> hasWordElements is a list of (word, element) pairs, where each element represents whether the corresponding word is in the email.

3.4.2 Defining the dependencies

To start, let's define the dependency model for the `isSpam` element and all of the word elements. When defining the dependencies of a probabilistic model, a common rule of thumb is that the class of an object determines the properties of the object, meaning that the properties depend on the class in the dependency model. In our example, whether an email is spam determines the presence or absence of all the words.

I made this point earlier in the chapter, but it bears repeating, because it's important and people often get confused by it. You're using the words to determine whether the email is spam. So why am I saying that the class of the email determines the words, and not vice versa? The key point to remember is that in probabilistic reasoning, the direction of inference isn't necessarily the direction of dependencies in the model. As often as not, the direction of inference is the opposite of the direction of the dependencies, as you try to determine the factors that caused an observed outcome. Here, you're modeling the intrinsic nature of the email (whether it's spam or normal) as the unobserved factor that causes the observed words. So the dependency in the model goes from the class of the email to the words.

That being given, one thing you need to decide is whether you're going to model dependencies between the words. In English or any language, the choice of the first word of a sentence is closely related to the second word. The words aren't, in reality, independent. But to keep this chapter relatively simple, I'll make the assumption that the words are independent, after the class (normal or spam) of the email is given.

You can draw a diagram called a *Bayesian network* that shows the dependencies in the model. Bayesian networks are explained in detail in chapter 5. For now, the main

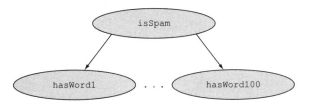

Figure 3.7 Naïve Bayes' dependency model for `isSpam` and `word` elements

point is that an edge exists in the network from one node to another if the second node depends on the first. For our spam filter so far, you get the Bayesian network shown in figure 3.7. This kind of network is called a *Naïve Bayes' model*—naïve because it makes the assumption that the words are independent.

Now let's introduce the elements for unusual words. Remember that you have two elements: `hasManyUnusualWords` and `numUnusualWords`. `hasManyUnusualWords` characterizes whether the words in this email tend to be unusual, whereas `numUnusual-Words` is the number. Because an email with unusual words tends to have more unusual words than an email that doesn't, it's natural that `numUnusualWords` should depend on `hasManyUnusualWords`. In turn, `hasManyUnusualWords`, which is a property of the email, depends on `isSpam`, which represents the class of the email. Finally, continuing with the Naïve Bayes' assumption, you assume that the presence of unusual words is independent from the presence of any given particular word, after the class is known. You end up with the Bayesian network in figure 3.8. This is the final dependency model for your spam filter application.

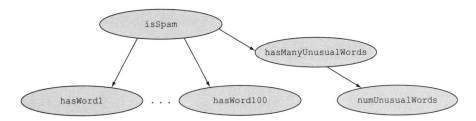

Figure 3.8 Full dependency model including unusual words

3.4.3 *Defining the functional forms*

You need to define functional forms for your four sets of elements. Again, the functional forms are the element class constructors used to build the model. They're everything you need to express the model except that the numbers aren't specified. I'll go through each in turn. First, let's define these functional forms for the reasoning component, where you assume that parameter values have been produced by the learning component. Here's the code for the reasoning model. I'll explain the definition of each of the elements in detail after the code.

Listing 3.2   Reasoning model

The arguments to the reasoning model are the dictionary and parameters produced by learning.

```
class ReasoningModel(
    dictionary: Dictionary,
    parameters: LearnedParameters
) extends Model(dictionary) {
    val isSpam = Flip(parameters.spamProbability)
```

ReasoningModel implements the abstract Model class

Element indicating whether the email is spam

```
    val hasWordElements = {
        for { word <- dictionary.featureWords } yield {
            val givenSpamProbability =
                parameters.wordGivenSpamProbabilities(word)
            val givenNormalProbability =
                parameters.wordGivenNormalProbabilities(word)
            val hasWordIfSpam = Flip(givenSpamProbability)
            val hasWordIfNormal = Flip(givenNormalProbability)
            val hasWord = If(isSpam, hasWordIfSpam, hasWordIfNormal)
            (word, hasWord)
        }
    }
```

Elements indicating whether a word is present in the email. This code creates a list of (word, element) pairs, one for each feature word.

```
    val hasManyUnusualIfSpam =
        Flip(parameters.hasManyUnusualWordsGivenSpamProbability)
    val hasManyUnusualIfNormal =
        Flip(parameters.hasManyUnusualWordsGivenNormalProbability)
    val hasManyUnusualWords =
        If(isSpam, hasManyUnusualIfSpam, hasManyUnusualIfNormal)
```

Element indicating whether the email has many unusual words

```
    val numUnusualIfHasMany =
        Binomial(Model.binomialNumTrials,
                parameters.unusualWordGivenManyProbability),
    val numUnusualIfHasFew =
        Binomial(Model.binomialNumTrials,
                parameters.unusualWordGivenFewProbability),
    val numUnusualWords =
        If(hasManyUnusualWords, numUnusualIfHasMany, numUnusualIfHasFew)
}
```

Element representing the number of unusual words

Now let's look at each of the elements in the model in detail:

- `isSpam`—This `Boolean` element is `true` with a certain probability, which is the probability that a given email is spam. So you define it by using a `Flip` element. In Figaro, this is defined by `val isSpam = Flip(parameter.spamProbability)`. This reflects your belief that the email is spam before seeing any of the words. Because the words depend on whether it's spam, and you get to observe the words, you infer from the words whether the email is spam. This is why the direction of the dependency can be different from the direction of inference. In probabilistic reasoning, you can infer backward from the effects of a cause to determine the cause.

■ word1, …, word100—Each word is present with a certain probability. This probability depends on whether the email is normal or spam. The If construct is perfect for this. The basic form is

```
val hasWordIfSpam = Flip(givenSpamProbability)
val hasWordIfNormal = Flip(givenNormalProbability)
val hasWord = If(isSpam, hasWordIfSpam, hasWordIfNormal)
```

WARNING If you look at the definition of hasWord, you might think you could simplify it by eliminating hasWordIfSpam and hasWordIfNormal and writing this:

```
val hasWord = If(isSpam, Flip(givenSpamProbability),
Flip(givenNormalProbability))
```

Unfortunately, Figaro has the restriction that an element that depends on a parameter to be learned (such as Flip(givenSpamProbability), which depends on the learned parameter givenSpamProbability) can't be defined inside a Chain. Because If is a kind of Chain, an element that depends on a parameter to be learned also can't be defined inside an If. We hope to lift this restriction in a future release of Figaro.

■ givenSpamProbability *and* givenNormalProbability—These are derived from the learning results, and they're different for every word. You'll create one of these If forms for every word that's used as a feature. In Scala, you create a list in which each word is paired with its hasWord element. Here's the code for this:

dictionary.featureWords produces a list of the 100 words used as features. This loop cycles through all of these words.

```
val hasWordElements = {
  for { word <- dictionary.featureWords } yield {
    val givenSpamProbability =
      parameters.wordGivenSpamProbabilities(word)
    val givenNormalProbability =
      parameters.wordGivenNormalProbabilities(word)
    val hasWordIfSpam = Flip(givenSpamProbability)
    val hasWordIfNormal = Flip(givenNormalProbability)
    val hasWord = If(isSpam, hasWordIfSpam, hasWordIfNormal)
    (word, hasWord)            ◁
  }
}
```

The probability of a word appearing, depending on whether the email is spam or normal

Creates the Figaro element representing whether this word is present

A pair of the word and its element. All of these pairs are strung together in a list by the for comprehension.

- hasManyUnusualWords—This element is `true` with a given probability, depending on whether the email is spam or normal. Again, the appropriate form is `If`:

```
val hasManyUnusualIfSpam =
  Flip(parameters.hasManyUnusualWordsGivenSpamProbability)
val hasManyUnusualIfNormal =
  Flip(parameters.hasManyUnusualWordsGivenNormalProbability)
val hasManyUnusualWords =
  If(isSpam, hasManyUnusualIfSpam, hasManyUnusualIfNormal)
```

- numUnusualWords—This `Integer` element represents the number of unusual words in an email. The more words in an email, the more unusual words it's likely to have. You model each individual word as having some probability of being unusual. The natural way to represent this is with a binomial distribution in which the number of trials is equal to the total number of words in the email. But the number of words in an email could be more than 1,000, and when the number of trials is that large, many values of `numUnusualWords` will have extremely low probability. So the probability of an email can be extremely small. This can lead to underflow errors when you have lots of emails: probabilities get rounded to 0 because they're too small to represent on a computer.

  To get around this problem, you set the number of trials to a fixed number, such as 20. This number is represented in the code as the constant `Model .binomialNumTrials`. Then, the number of unusual words in an email is scaled down so that it represents a fraction out of 20. You'll take care of this when you apply evidence later. Using this method, the definition of `numUnusualWords` is given by the following:

```
val numUnusualIfHasMany =
  Binomial(Model.binomialNumTrials,
           parameters.unusualWordGivenManyProbability),
val numUnusualIfHasFew =
  Binomial(Model.binomialNumTrials,
           parameters.unusualWordGivenFewProbability),
val numUnusualWords =
  If(hasManyUnusualWords, numUnusualIfHasMany, numUnusualIfHasFew)
```

That's it for the reasoning model. The learning model is exactly the same, except that instead of a particular probability from the learning results being used, an element representing the prior probability is used. For example:

```
val isSpam = Flip(parameters.spamProbability)
```

Compare this to what you saw previously for the reasoning component:

```
val isSpam = Flip(parameters.spamProbability)
```

These look exactly the same. But a significant difference exists. In the reasoning model, `parameters.spamProbability` is a fixed number. On the other hand, in the learning model, `parameters.spamProbability` is an element; it represents a random element that can take on one of many possible values. When you're learning, you don't know the probability that a particular email is spam, so you represent this probability with a random element. The result of learning is a particular value for this probability, which is then used for reasoning. The code for the learning model is as follows:

```
class LearningModel(
    dictionary: Dictionary,
    parameters: PriorParameters
) extends Model(dictionary) {
    // body is exactly the same as for the reasoning model
}
```

The elements representing the priors for the parameters

LearningModel also extends the abstract Model class

3.4.4 Using numerical parameters

This leads us right into the discussion of numerical parameters. In the reasoning component, these parameters are provided by the learning results. The `LearnedParameters` class defines all the parameters used by the model, as shown in the following listing.

Listing 3.3 `LearnedParameters` class

```
class LearnedParameters(
    val spamProbability: Double,
    val hasManyUnusualWordsGivenSpamProbability: Double,
    val hasManyUnusualWordsGivenNormalProbability: Double,
    val unusualWordGivenManyProbability: Double,
    val unusualWordGivenFewProbability: Double,
    val wordGivenSpamProbabilities: Map[String, Double],
    val wordGivenNormalProbabilities: Map[String, Double]
)
```

For the learning component, you need to specify prior parameter values. Our model uses compound `Flip` and `Binomial` elements. Recall from chapter 2 that they both take an `Element[Double]` as an argument. This `Element[Double]` is the parameter of the compound `Flip` and `Binomial`. You typically want a continuous atomic element for this parameter. There's a kind of continuous atomic element, called a `Beta` element, that works well as the parameter of a compound `Flip` or `Binomial`, so that's what you'll use. You'll learn more about `Beta` elements in chapters 4 and 5.

The atomic `Beta` element takes as arguments two `Double` values. In the following code, the values of these arguments have been chosen carefully, but you'll have to wait for upcoming chapters to understand why these particular values were used. Here's the `PriorParameters` class.

Listing 3.4   `PriorParameters` class

```
class PriorParameters(dictionary: Dictionary) {
  val spamProbability = Beta(2,3)
```
Prior for the spam probability

Probability a word is present in a spam or normal email

```
  val wordGivenSpamProbabilities =
    dictionary.featureWords.map(word => (word, Beta(2,2)))
  val wordGivenNormalProbabilities =
    dictionary.featureWords.map(word => (word, Beta(2,2)))

  val hasManyUnusualWordsGivenSpamProbability = Beta(2,2)
  val hasManyUnusualWordsGivenNormalProbability = Beta(2, 21)
  val unusualWordGivenManyProbability = Beta(2,2)
  val unusualWordGivenFewProbability = Beta(2,7)
```
Prior for whether the email has many unusual words, given whether it's spam or normal

Prior for the probability that an individual word is unusual, given whether the email has many unusual words

Tells the learning algorithm which parameters to learn. See sidebar.

```
  val fullParameterList =
    spamProbability ::
    hasManyUnusualWordsGivenSpamProbability ::
    hasManyUnusualWordsGivenNormalProbability ::
    unusualWordGivenManyProbability ::
    unusualWordGivenFewProbability ::
    wordGivenSpamProbabilities.map(pair => pair._2) :::
    wordGivenNormalProbabilities.map(pair => pair._2)
}
```

Let's look at the following lines more closely:

```
val wordGivenSpamProbabilities =
  dictionary.featureWords.map(word => (word, Beta(2,2)))
val wordGivenNormalProbabilities =
  dictionary.featureWords.map(word => (word, Beta(2,2)))
```

For each word, there's a probability that the word appears in a spam email, and likewise for a normal email. The prior for each word is a `Beta(2,2)`. This code creates a list of (word, element) pairs, one for each feature word. For each feature word, the element is the `Beta(2,2)` prior. One important detail: this is a different `Beta` element for every word. Every word has its own individual probability of being present in a normal or spam email.

Scala notation

Let's take a close look at the code defining `fullParameters`. This code creates a list consisting of all the parameters in the model. There are two things to note in this code.

First, look at the line `wordGivenNormalProbabilities.map(pair => pair._2)`. This goes through each (word, element) pair in `wordGivenNormalProbabilitiies`. For each (word, element) pair, it applies the function that takes a pair and returns its second argument. In other words, it returns the element. So this entire line returns all the elements associated with the probability of any feature word, given normal emails. The line `wordGivenSpamProbabilities.map(pair => pair._2)` is similar except for spam emails.

The second thing to note is the way all the elements are put together to form a list. If you look carefully at the definition, you'll see that the first five lines consist of a single element each, while the last two lines consist of lists of elements. In Scala, the `::` operator takes an element `x` and a list `xs` and appends `x` at the front of `xs`. Meanwhile, the `:::` operator concatenates two lists together. So this code creates a single list consisting of all elements that are parameters of the model.

3.4.5 *Working with auxiliary knowledge*

To construct a model for a particular email, you need to know which words are feature words. You also need to be able to tell whether a particular word is unusual. These services are provided by a data structure called the `Dictionary`. Here's the code for the `Dictionary` class. The full explanation of this class is found in the annotations.

Listing 3.5 Dictionary class

The Dictionary class maintains the number of emails from which it was built. initNumEmails is the initial count.

A map from words to the number of emails in which they appear

```scala
class Dictionary(initNumEmails: Int) {

  val counts: Map[String, Int] = Map()

  var numEmails = initNumEmails

  def addWord(word: String) {
    counts += word -> (getCount(word) + 1)
  }

  def addEmail(email: Email) {
    numEmails += 1
    for { word <- email.allWords } {
      addWord(word)
    }
  }

  object OrderByCount extends Ordering[String] {
    def compare(a: String, b: String) = getCount(b) - getCount(a)
  }
  def words = counts.keySet.toList.sorted(OrderByCount)

  def nonStopWords =
    words.dropWhile(counts(_) >=
                    numEmails * Dictionary.stopWordFraction)
  def featureWords = nonStopWords.take(Dictionary.numFeatures)

  def getCount(word: String) =
    counts.getOrElse(word, 0)

  def isUnusual(word: String, learning: Boolean) =
    if (learning) getCount(word) <= 1
    else getCount(word) <= 0
}
```

The number of emails from which this Dictionary is built

Add a word to the Dictionary by incrementing its count by 1

Add an email to the Dictionary by incrementing numEmails and adding each word in the email

The words in the Dictionary, ordered by count

Take the numFeatures most frequent of the remaining words

Get the words that don't appear too frequently

Get the number of emails in which the given word appears

Determine if the word is unusual

Some comments on this code:

- The argument to the `Dictionary` class, `initNumEmails`, is the initial number of emails in the dictionary. In the reasoning component, the total number of emails is already known from the learning component, so `initNumEmails` is set to the number of emails. In the learning component, emails are added one at a time, so `initNumEmails` is set to 0.

- `numEmails` is the number of emails in the dictionary. It begins with `initNumEmails` and is incremented each time an email is added. Emails are added to the dictionary only by the learning component.

- `words` is a list of all the words in the dictionary, ordered by count, from most frequent to least frequent. The sorted method takes an `Ordering` argument that provides a `compare` method to order two elements in the list. The ordering is implemented by the `OrderByCount` object.

- The feature words form the full set of words in two steps. In the first step, you go through the sorted list of words and drop all words that are too frequent (stop words). A word is considered a stop word if it appears in at least `Dictionary.stopWordFraction` of the emails. For example, if `Dictionary.stopWordFraction` is 0.2, and there are 50 emails, a stop word is one that appears in at least 10 emails. In the second step, you take the first `Dictionary.numFeatures` words out of the `nonStopWords`.

- `getCount` uses the `getOrElse` method from the Scala library. `getOrElse` looks for the word in the counts map and, if it's not found, returns 0.

- Here's the logic behind `isUnusual`. A word is considered unusual if it doesn't appear in any other emails. During learning, because the word appears in the email in question, its count is <= 1. During reasoning, the dictionary consists only of emails seen during training, so for the word to be unusual, it can't appear in the dictionary at all.

3.5   *Building the reasoning component*

Let's take another look at the reasoning component architecture, reproduced again in figure 3.9. You've already seen the parts of the email model, the generative process, parameters coming from learning, and the knowledge in the form of a dictionary produced during learning. You'll still need to learn about the feature extractor, how evidence is asserted, and running the inference algorithm.

For extracting features and observing evidence, you use an `Email` class. Here's the code for that class, explained in the annotations. With all the work you've done on the model, extracting features from an email and observing evidence is simple.

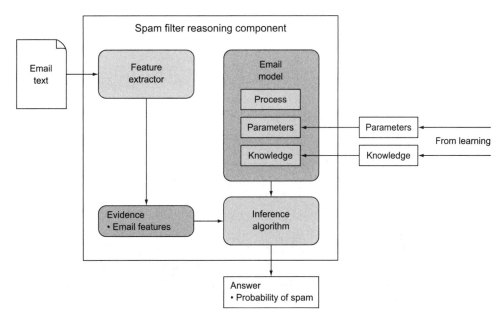

Figure 3.9 Reasoning component architecture reproduced

Listing 3.6 `Email` class

```
class Email(file: File) {
  def getAllWords() = …
```
Get all the words in the email using I/O operations (not shown)

```
  val allWords: Set[String] = getAllWords()
```

The model on which to observe the evidence
```
  def observeEvidence(
    model: Model,
    label: Option[Boolean],
    learning: Boolean
  ) {
```
A method to observe evidence on a model, based on the email's features

A label option that may or may not be present

A flag indicating whether you're currently learning or reasoning
```
    label match {
      case Some(b) => model.isSpam.observe(b)
      case None => ()
    }
```
If the label is present, apply it to the model's isSpam element

```
    for {
      (word, element) <- model.hasWordElements
    } {
      element.observe(allWords.contains(word))
    }
```
For each word and its corresponding element in the model, observe whether the email's allWords contains that word

```
    val obsNumUnusualWords =
      allWords.filter((word: String) =>
        model.dictionary.isUnusual(word, learning)).size
```
Count the number of unusual words in the document

```
    val unusualWordFraction =
      obsNumUnusualWords * Model.binomialNumTrials / allWords.size
    model.numUnusualWords.observe(unusualWordFraction)
  }
}
```
Apply an observation to the model's numUnusualWords element

Again, some comments on this code are in order:

- When an `Email` object is created, it performs some I/O on its file argument to get all the words out of the email. These are stored in the `allWords` field. Note that `allWords` is a set, consistent with your model in which you care only if a word is present or absent in the email, not the number of times it appears.
- The type of the `label` argument to `observeEvidence` is `Option[Boolean]`, indicating that the `label` is optionally present. Scala's `Option` data structure can either have the value `Some(c)` or `None`. In this case, if the email has a known class, `c` will be that class. If the class of the email is unknown, the label is `None`. If the label is present (the value of the label option is `Some(c)`), it will be applied as evidence to `model.isSpam`.
- Counting the number of unusual words in the document uses the standard Scala `filter` method. Here, the `filter` method takes `allWords`, which is a set of strings, and removes all strings that don't satisfy its argument. The argument to `filter` is a function that returns `true` if the word is unusual. So the `filter` method removes all strings that aren't unusual. You then take the size of the resulting set to get the number of unusual words. Note that the `isUnusual` method takes the learning flag as its second argument.
- The last three lines assert an observation about the number of unusual words. Remember that `numUnusualWords` is defined by a binomial distribution in which the number of trials is given by `Model.binomialNumTrials`. So you scale down the full `obsNumUnusualWords` to the appropriate fraction of `Model.binomialNumTrials`.

Now that you know how to extract features and apply evidence, and you have a model including the learned parameters, you can classify emails as normal or spam. You could use any inference algorithm for this. You're going to use variable elimination (VE), which is an exact algorithm. On a single email, this algorithm is fast enough for our purposes, and because it's exact, it produces the best possible answer. Here's the code.

Listing 3.7   The `classify` method

```
def classify(
  dictionary: Dictionary,
  parameters: LearnedParameters,
  fileName: String
) = {
```
The classify method takes the learning results, in the form of a dictionary and parameters, and the name of the file containing the email to classify, and returns the probability that the email is spam.

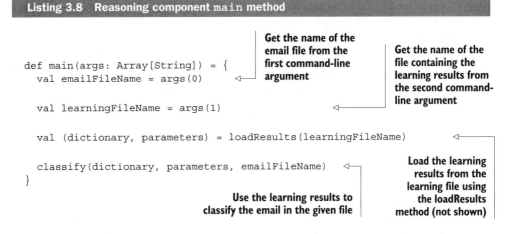

```
val file = new File(fileName)          Create the Email object from
val email = new Email(file)            the file pointed to by fileName
```

Observe evidence about this particular email on the model. Because you're not learning, the optional label is None and the learning flag is false.

Create the reasoning model using the learning results

```
val model = new ReasoningModel(dictionary, parameters)

email.observeEvidence(model, None, false)
```

Create and run a VE algorithm with the model's isSpam element as the query target

```
val algorithm = VariableElimination(model.isSpam)
algorithm.start()
```

```
val isSpamProbability = algorithm.probability(model.isSpam, true)
println("Spam probability: " + isSpamProbability)
```

```
algorithm.kill()
```
Clean up by killing the algorithm. You make sure not to kill the algorithm until after you've gotten the answer to the query you need.

Get the probability that the email is spam and print an appropriate message

```
isSpamProbability
}
```
Return the probability the email is spam

Finally, the reasoning application has a main method. This method is called when the reasoning application is invoked from the command line.

Listing 3.8 Reasoning component `main` method

```
def main(args: Array[String]) = {
  val emailFileName = args(0)

  val learningFileName = args(1)

  val (dictionary, parameters) = loadResults(learningFileName)

  classify(dictionary, parameters, emailFileName)
}
```

Get the name of the email file from the first command-line argument

Get the name of the file containing the learning results from the second command-line argument

Load the learning results from the learning file using the loadResults method (not shown)

Use the learning results to classify the email in the given file

---

I don't show the code of the loadResults method, because it's ordinary I/O and verbose. If you're interested in seeing it, please look at the code in the repository. All this code does is the following:

1 Read in the general parameters of the model, such as the probability of spam and the probability that an email has a lot of unusual words
2 Read in all of the words, along with the number of times they appear
3 Read in the feature words and the probabilities that each is present, given that the email is spam or normal

The format of this file was designed for this particular application; Figaro has no general format for the results of learning.

3.6   *Creating the learning component*

After you've defined the model and built the reasoning component, you already have most of the pieces in place for the learning component. Let's take another look at the architecture of the learning component, reproduced in figure 3.10. You've already seen the email model. As mentioned, a difference between the learning email model and the one used for reasoning is that the learning model uses prior parameters consisting of Beta elements for each parameter of the model.

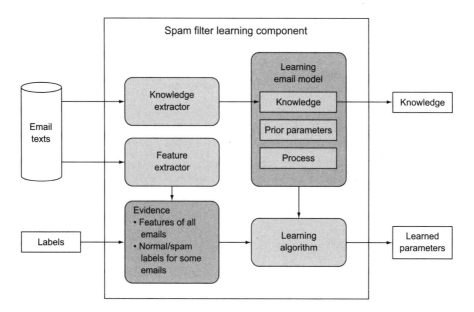

Figure 3.10   Learning component architecture reproduced

You've also seen the feature extractor in the reasoning component and how the evidence is applied, given an email and an optional normal/spam label. In the reasoning component, you reasoned about a single email. In contrast, in the learning component, you have an entire training set of emails. Your feature extractor will extract the features of all the emails and compile the evidence for each one. It will also read a Labels file that contains labels for some of the emails in the training set, and apply the appropriate evidence if there's a label.

Looking at the architecture in figure 3.10, you can see that there's now a knowledge extractor whose job is to get the auxiliary knowledge out of the email texts. You've already seen that the knowledge consists of a dictionary, and you've already seen that the Dictionary class has an addEmail method, so the knowledge extractor in your spam filter is simple. You define a Scala object named `Dictionary`. In Scala, an object is like a class that has only a single instance. It can be used to define the analogue of Java static methods. You'll define a `fromEmails` method that constructs a `Dictionary` from a `Traversable` of `Emails` (`Traversable` is a Scala base class for many kinds of collections such as lists or sets). You can call this method by using `Dictionary.fromEmails(emails)`. Note that you already have a `Dictionary` class; the same name can be used for both a class and an object.

Listing 3.9   Dictionary object

```
object Dictionary {
  def fromEmails(emails: Traversable[Email]) = {
    val result = new Dictionary(0)
    for { email <- emails } { result.addEmail(email) }
    result
  }
}
```

> Create an instance of the Dictionary class where the initial number of emails is 0. Add each of the emails to the dictionary and return it.

Now you finally come to the meat of the learning component, which is the code that applies the learning algorithm to learn the parameters of the model. The learning algorithm you'll use is called *expectation maximization* (EM). EM is a "meta-algorithm," because it employs a regular inference algorithm in its inner loop. You'll learn all about EM in chapter 12. On a high level, EM begins with a guess about the parameter values, computes probabilities of elements in the model using this guess, and then uses these probabilities to improve its guess. This process is repeated as many times as desired. The inference algorithm is used in the step of computing the probabilities of elements.

Figaro provides implementations of EM by using inference algorithms. In this application, you'll use *belief propagation* (BP). BP is a similar algorithm to VE but works faster on large models. BP works by propagating messages between the elements and goes through some number of iterations of propagating messages. When running EM with BP, you need to choose the number of iterations of both EM and BP. For this application, you'll use the default values of 10 for both, which work well here.

The code for applying the learning algorithm is shown next in the `learnMAP` method, which takes the prior parameters as its argument and returns the learned parameters. *MAP* stands for *maximum a posteriori*, which is the learning approach we're using: you return the values of the parameters that maximize the posterior probability of the parameters, given the data. These MAP values are produced by the EM algorithm.

Listing 3.10   The `learnMAP` method

```
def learnMAP(params: PriorParameters): LearnedParameters = {
  val algorithm =
    EMWithBP(params.fullParameterList:_*)
  algorithm.start()
```

> Instantiate and run an EM algorithm that uses BP to compute probabilities. The default numbers of EM and BP iterations are used.

For each feature word, compute the most likely Double value of the parameter representing the probability that the word is present in a spam email, and likewise for a normal email. Put all these values together in a list of (word, value) pairs.

Compute the most likely Double value of each parameter element

```
val spamProbability = params.spamProbability.MAPValue
val hasUnusualWordsGivenSpamProbability =
  params.hasManyUnusualWordsGivenSpamProbability.MAPValue
val hasUnusualWordsGivenNormalProbability =
  params.hasManyUnusualWordsGivenNormalProbability.MAPValue
val unusualWordGivenHasUnusualProbability =
  params.unusualWordGivenManyProbability.MAPValue
val unusualWordGivenNotHasUnusualProbability =
  params.unusualWordGivenFewProbability.MAPValue

val wordGivenSpamProbabilities =
  for { (word, param) <- params.wordGivenSpamProbabilities }
  yield (word, param.MAPValue)
val wordGivenNormalProbabilities =
  for { (word, param) <- params.wordGivenNormalProbabilities }
  yield (word, param.MAPValue)

algorithm.kill()

new LearnedParameters(
  spamProbability,
  hasUnusualWordsGivenSpamProbability,
  hasUnusualWordsGivenNormalProbability,
  unusualWordGivenHasUnusualProbability,
  unusualWordGivenNotHasUnusualProbability,
  wordGivenSpamProbabilities.toMap,
  wordGivenNormalProbabilities.toMap
)
}
```

Clean up by killing the algorithm. Note that you don't kill the algorithm until after you have the MAP values, as they would be invalid after the algorithm has been killed.

Return an instance of Learned-Parameters with the learned values of all the parameters

Finally, the learning component has a `main` method that's called when learning is invoked from the command line. This method takes three arguments: the name of the directory containing all the emails in the training set, the name of the file containing labels for some of the training samples, and the name of the file in which to store learning results. First, it reads the information from its input files and extracts the dictionary. Next, it creates models for each of the emails. Finally, it runs the learning algorithm and exports the results. These results can then be used by the reasoning component as many times as it wants.

An important thing to note is that all the emails share the same parameters. This makes it possible to learn the same parameters from all the emails. But each of the emails has a different set of elements in the model. For example, the `isSpam` element for each email is different. If they weren't all different, all the emails would have the same value for the element, so they would either be all spam or all normal. On the other hand, the models for each of the different emails are all identical in structure and parameters.

Here's the code for the `main` method.

Listing 3.11 Learning component `main` method

Build the models and observe evidence. Note that all the models share the same prior parameters but have different instances of the LearningModel. Also, notice how for the optional label argument of observeEvidence, you use labels.get (filename). This will be None if there's no label, or Some(class) if the label is a particular class.

```
def main(args: Array[String]) {
    val trainingDirectoryName = args(0)
    val labelFileName = args(1)
    val learningFileName = args(2)

    val emails = readEmails(trainingDirectoryName)

    val labels = readLabels(labelFileName)

    val dictionary = Dictionary.fromEmails(emails.values)

    val params = new PriorParameters(dictionary)
    val models =
      for { (fileName, email) <- emails }
      yield {
        val model = new LearningModel(dictionary, params)
        email.observeEvidence(model, labels.get(fileName), true)
        model
      }
    val learnedParameters = learnMAP(params)

    saveResults(learningFileName, dictionary, learnedParameters)
  }
}
```

Read all the emails from the training directory. readEmails (not shown) returns a map from filenames to Email instances.

Read the labels from a label file. readLabels (not shown) returns a map from filenames to labels. Any file that doesn't have a label won't be in this map.

Construct the dictionary from the values of the emails map (the actual emails)

Run the learning algorithm

Save the learning results to a file using I/O for use by the reasoning component (not shown)

So there you have it. You've seen a complete application, starting with the architecture and then going through the design of the model, the implementation of the reasoning component, and the implementation of the learning component. At this point, you should have a basic handle on Figaro's features. You've seen how to build an application, so you already have a fair bit of power at your disposal.

The next part of the book presents a deeper view of modeling. First, you'll step back for a deeper understanding of probabilistic models and inference. Then you'll look at a variety of creative ways to use Figaro to create rich, practical probabilistic models.

3.7   Summary

- Probabilistic programs are often used in applications that learn a model from training data and then apply the model as many times as desired to specific instances.
- Many probabilistic programming applications have a similar architecture, with a reasoning component and a learning component.

- The reasoning and learning components both use a model, which includes a specification of the generative process, the parameters of that process, and auxiliary knowledge.
- The learning component uses prior parameters and learns values for those parameters, which are used by the reasoning component.

3.8   Exercises

Solutions to selected exercises are available online at www.manning.com/books/practical-probabilistic-programming.

The exercises in this chapter are high-level thought exercises, asking you to think about how you would design a probabilistic reasoning and learning application for a real-world problem, along the lines of the example in this chapter. When you work on these exercises, think about the overall architecture and design, without worrying about details of the model.

1   You're building an intelligent search engine for images that lets you search for images containing objects you're interested in, even if the images aren't explicitly labeled with those objects. Your search engine will contain an object recognizer that can tag an image with the objects it contains. You've decided to develop the object recognizer as a probabilistic reasoning and learning application.

   a   Sketch an architecture of the search engine and the role the object recognizer plays.
   b   Sketch an architecture for the reasoning component. What are the inputs and outputs of the recognizer? Rather than working with raw pixels, you might want your recognizer to first extract high-level image features such as color histograms and edge detections. How would this fit in the architecture?
   c   Sketch an architecture of the learning component. What are its inputs and outputs? How are the results of learning communicated to the reasoning component?

2   You're designing a component of a security guard application, whose task is to detect anomalous activity in a department store. In your approach, anomalous activity is defined to be activity that has low probability. You'll learn a probabilistic model of network activity. Anytime you see activity from the network, you compute the probability of the activity. If the probability is low, you signal an anomaly.

   a   What are the inputs and outputs of the anomaly detector and how does it fit in with the whole security guard application?
   b   In this design, you don't have a variable representing the class of the activity. Instead, you create a probabilistic model over the variables describing an activity. What might some of those variables be? What kinds of relationships and dependencies exist between the variables?

c What will the training data for your anomaly detector consist of? What kind of knowledge can you learn from this data?

3 You're designing an intelligent poker player. You have two goals: to play well against an opponent the first time you play against them and to become even better when you play against an opponent over time.

a In poker, there are two main sources of randomness: the deal of the cards and the actions of the players. Describe some of the variables that will be relevant to your poker player and label each one with its source of randomness. From the point of view of a learning application, why do you think it makes a difference whether a variable is the result of the deal of the cards or the actions of players?

b In your poker player, you want two kinds of learning. First, you want to learn how people play in general. This will help you play well the first time you meet an opponent. Second, when you play repeatedly against a particular player, you want to learn the tendencies of that player. Describe an architecture for a learning system that can perform both kinds of learning. What information gets communicated between the different components?

Part 2

Writing probabilistic programs

P art 2 is all about writing probabilistic programs to represent whatever situation you're interested in. The goal of this part of the book is not only to give you the tools to write programs but also to make sure you understand what these programs mean and why you might choose to use a certain programming technique. Chapter 4 provides an introduction to probabilistic modeling and the basic concepts of probabilistic programming; although there's little programming in this chapter, it will help you approach the task of writing a probabilistic program in a well-grounded, principled way. Chapter 5 presents the two main modeling paradigms that are at the center of probabilistic programming: Bayesian networks and Markov networks. Chapters 6 through 8 build on the material of chapters 4 and 5 with more-advanced modeling techniques, including using collections, object-oriented programming, and modeling dynamic systems.

Probabilistic models and probabilistic programs

This chapter covers

- The definition of a probabilistic model
- How probabilistic models are used to answer queries
- The ingredients of a probabilistic model, including variables, dependencies, functional forms, and numbers
- How a probabilistic program represents the ingredients of a probabilistic model

Part 1 of this book introduced probabilistic programming. You learned that a probabilistic reasoning system uses a probabilistic model to answer queries, given evidence, and that probabilistic programming uses a program to represent the probabilistic model. This part of the book goes deeper into representing probabilistic models. You'll learn a variety of programming techniques for writing probabilistic programs.

But first you need to develop a basic understanding of probabilistic models and how they're constructed and used to answer queries. This chapter provides that understanding. You've already used some of the ideas intuitively in part 1, but now it's time to get into the fundamentals.

This chapter elaborates on the themes of chapter 1 in much greater depth, so it'll be useful if you've read that chapter. This chapter also describes how probabilistic programs, and Figaro programs in particular, define probabilistic models, so the basic knowledge of Figaro presented in chapter 2 will be helpful.

4.1 Probabilistic models defined

A *probabilistic model* is a way of encoding the general knowledge you have of an uncertain situation. Imagine, for example, that you're an art expert who's trying to decide whether a painting is a genuine Rembrandt or a forgery. You have the following pieces of information:

1 Rembrandt liked to use dark colors in his paintings.
2 He often painted people.
3 Genuine newly discovered paintings by masters are rare, but forgeries are a dime a dozen.
4 This painting has a big splash of bright yellow.
5 The painting is a picture of a sailor.
6 The painting was sold at an auction in 2003.

Items 1–3 are *in-general* knowledge. Items 4–6 are *here-and-now* knowledge. Notice how the in-general knowledge is stated in terms of tendencies: "liked to use," "often," "rare," "a dime a dozen." The here-and-now knowledge is specific: "This painting has," "The painting is a picture of," "The painting was sold." In probabilistic modeling, you encode your in-general knowledge in a *probabilistic model*, and apply it to your here-and-now knowledge to reason about the specific situation you're dealing with. The here-and-now knowledge is also called *evidence*, and the thing you're trying to find out, which is whether the painting is a genuine Rembrandt, is the *query*. So here, you're trying to apply your general knowledge about painting and Rembrandt contained in assertions 1–3 to the evidence encoded in assertions 4–6 to answer the query of whether this painting is genuine.

4.1.1 Expressing general knowledge as a probability distribution over possible worlds

Figure 4.1 shows examples of general domain knowledge. The in-general knowledge says two things: (1) what's possible, and (2) what's likely. First, let's talk about what's possible: when you create a probabilistic model, you envision many possible states of affairs—and each one is called a *possible world*. For example, one possible world is that the painting is a forgery; another is that it's a genuine Rembrandt landscape. Each possible world describes a situation that you consider possible before seeing any evidence. For example, a Rembrandt landscape is one possible world before you see any

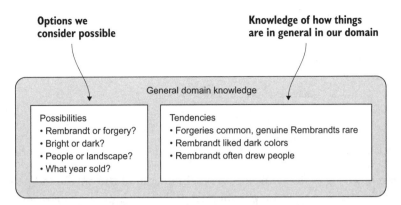

Figure 4.1   General domain knowledge includes what's possible and what's likely.

evidence. Later, if you see evidence that the painting is of people, you'd use that evidence to rule out this possible world. This fits into our distinction between in-general knowledge and here-and-now knowledge. A possible world is something that could happen in general: having a landscape by Rembrandt is possible. Evidence characterizes what you know in the here-and-now: this is a people painting.

For example, in this situation, you may envision the following possible worlds:

- w_1—The painting is a forgery.
- w_2—The painting is a genuine Rembrandt about people with dark colors.
- w_3—The painting is a genuine Rembrandt about people with bright colors.
- w_4—The painting is a genuine Rembrandt landscape.

Note that the possible worlds are what you consider possible before you see any evidence. It's important to understand that evidence isn't part of a probabilistic model. The model itself describes general knowledge. Probabilistic reasoning uses a model that encodes general knowledge and applies it to evidence about a specific situation, in order to answer queries about that situation. Because evidence isn't part of the model, and the model is made up of possible worlds, you can't use the evidence to decide what the possible worlds should be. So you get worlds like w_2 and w_4, which contradict the evidence in statements 4 and 5.

Now let's talk about the second thing included in the general knowledge: what's likely. This is encoded by assigning a number to each possible world, called its *probability*. Table 4.1 shows an assignment of probabilities to the four possible worlds w_1 to w_4. The probabilities of all possible worlds must add up to 1. The assignment of probabilities to possible worlds is called a *probability distribution*. This term is used to mean any assignment of probabilities to possible worlds, whatever knowledge that assignment is based on.

Table 4.1   A probability distribution, defined by assigning probabilities to possible worlds that sum to 1

Possible world	Description	Probability
w_1	Forgery	0.9
w_2	Rembrandt, people, dark	0.09
w_3	Rembrandt, people, bright	0.009
w_4	Rembrandt, landscape	0.001

The process of taking general knowledge, including all of the envisioned possibilities and the tendencies among those possibilities, and representing it as a probability distribution over possible worlds, is summarized in figure 4.2. The possibilities determine the definition of the possible worlds. Then the tendencies—what's likely—determine the probability of each possible world.

Now that you understand possible worlds and probability distributions, it's time to define a probabilistic model. A *probabilistic model* is a formal representation of a probability distribution over possible worlds.

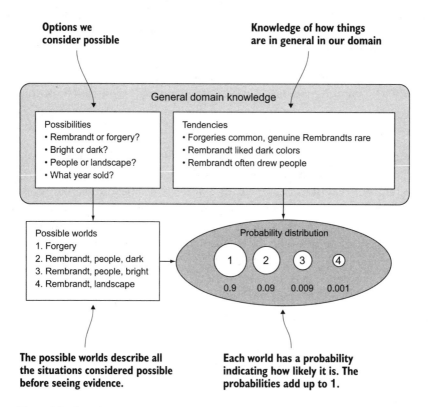

Figure 4.2   Domain knowledge is represented as a probability distribution over possible worlds. In this figure, the probabilities are represented by the sizes of the worlds.

That's all there is to it. The definition doesn't say that a probabilistic model *is* a probability distribution. Rather, it's a *representation* of such a distribution. The distribution itself is a mathematical concept that explicitly assigns a number to every possible world. The number of possible worlds might be enormous, and the distribution has to assign a probability to every single one. The representation is something you can write down and work with. Although the simplest kind of probabilistic model is a table explicitly listing the probabilities of possible worlds, as you'll see throughout this book, the model can be quite compact even when the number of possible worlds is enormous. The definition does say that the representation has to be formal. Clear rules specify how the probability of every possible world is defined, even though you might not explicitly create that probability.

Although I've defined a probabilistic model, I haven't described how you create one—how you specify the possible worlds and the probabilities. The art and science of probabilistic modeling is all about representing probability distributions in a precise and compact way. You'll learn all about how to do that in this book.

Now that you've seen the central importance of probability distributions to probabilistic modeling, let's look at the concept more closely.

4.1.2 Exploring probability distributions further

In addition to telling you the probability of individual possible worlds, a probability distribution also tells you the probabilities of various facts. Any given fact will hold in some possible worlds and not others. To get the probability of the fact, you add up the probabilities of the worlds in which the fact holds.

For example, consider the fact that the painting is a genuine Rembrandt. This fact holds in worlds w_2, w_3, and w_4 but not in w_1. The probability of this fact is the sum of the probabilities of the possible worlds in which the fact holds. The probability that the painting is a Rembrandt is the sum of the probabilities assigned to w_2, w_3, and w_4, which is $0.09 + 0.009 + 0.001 = 0.1$. So you say that the probability that the painting is a Rembrandt is 0.1, or, colloquially speaking, 10%. Standard notation for this conclusion is $P(\text{Rembrandt}) = 0.1$. This concept is illustrated in figure 4.3.

This probability distribution, before you see any evidence, is commonly called the *prior probability distribution*. The name, naturally, means that it's prior to any

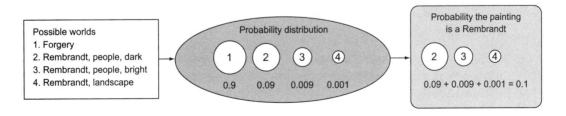

Figure 4.3 The probability of a fact is the sum of the probabilities of possible worlds consistent with the fact.

considerations about the here-and-now (prior to seeing the evidence). It's contrasted with the *posterior probability distribution*, which is the distribution you get after considering the evidence. Likewise, the P(Rembrandt) computed in the previous paragraph is called the *prior probability of this fact*, as opposed to the posterior probability you'll get after looking at the evidence. You'll see how to take the evidence into account to get the posterior probability in the next section.

There are many ways to enumerate the possible worlds and to assign probabilities. The probability distribution appearing in table 4.1, shown again in table 4.2, happens to match the general knowledge described in items 1, 2, and 3 at the beginning of this section. Item 3 says that forgeries are more common than genuine Rembrandts, and indeed, forgery is true in world w_1, whose probability is 0.9, whereas Rembrandt is true in the other three worlds, whose total probability is 0.1. Item 1 says that Rembrandt liked to use dark colors. If you look at the table, you see that w_2 (Rembrandt, people, dark) is 10 times as likely as w_3 (Rembrandt, people, bright). Although the remaining world w_4 doesn't say anything about colors, it's extremely unlikely in the prior distribution, because it has only probability 0.001. Finally, item 2 says that Rembrandt often painted people. Both w_2 and w_3 are consistent with the fact that the painting is about people, so according to our model, the probability that the painting is by Rembrandt and about people is equal to the total probability of w_2 and w_3, which is 0.099. Meanwhile, the probability of a landscape by Rembrandt is only 0.001, 99 times less likely than people.

In this example, you can put together a plausible-looking model without any real method, but this gets difficult with more-complex situations. In section 4.3 you'll start looking at more-structured ways to represent probability distributions.

Table 4.2 Our probabilistic model revisited. Forgery is much more likely than Rembrandt, so the probability of w_1 is more than the other three put together. Similarly, if the painter is Rembrandt, it's more likely to be a painting of people than a landscape, and a dark painting of people is more likely than a bright one.

Possible world	Description	Probability
w_1	Forgery	0.9
w_2	Rembrandt, people, dark	0.09
w_3	Rembrandt, people, bright	0.009
w_4	Rembrandt, landscape	0.001

Before you get into the specifics of representing models, however, you need to first understand in the most basic terms how models are used to reason about a particular situation.

4.2 Using a probabilistic model to answer queries

You've encoded your general knowledge as a probability distribution over possible worlds. How do you apply this model to evidence (here-and-now knowledge) to answer a query? For example, you know that this painting has a big splash of bright yellow, is a picture of a sailor, and was sold at auction in 2003. This is your evidence. You want to know if the painting is a Rembrandt—that's your query. How do you use the model to infer an answer to your query, given the evidence? Your state of knowledge is summarized in table 4.3.

Table 4.3 The model and evidence comprising your knowledge in this situation. Each piece of evidence is annotated with its relevance to the model.

Model		Evidence
Forgery	0.9	Big splash of bright yellow ==> Bright
Rembrandt, people, dark	0.09	Picture of a sailor ==> People
Rembrandt, people, bright	0.009	Sold in 2003 (irrelevant)
Landscape	0.001	

4.2.1 Conditioning on the evidence to produce the posterior probability distribution

The process of using the probability distribution to take into account the evidence is called *conditioning on the evidence*. The result of conditioning is also a probability distribution and is known as the *posterior probability distribution*.

The conditioning process is simple, and consists of two steps:

1 *Eliminate all possible worlds that are inconsistent with the evidence.*
   Looking at your possible worlds, you see that two are inconsistent with the evidence: w_2, which has dark colors, and w_4, which is a landscape. So you "cross out" those worlds, assigning them probability 0. The fact that the painting was sold at auction in 2003 doesn't rule out any possible worlds; that piece of evidence is irrelevant to the model.

2 *Adjust the probabilities of the remaining worlds upward so that they sum to 1 again.*
   This is called *normalizing* the probabilities. When normalizing, the remaining worlds have to absorb the probability of the crossed-out worlds. The amount of probability that each world absorbs is proportional to its prior probability. For example, because the prior probability of w_1 was 100 times as large as the prior probability of w_3, the amount of probability of crossed-out worlds absorbed into w_1 is 100 times the amount absorbed into w_3. This ensures that after absorbing, the probability of w_1 will still be 100 times the probability of w_3.

   There's an easy mathematical way to normalize the probabilities correctly. First, you add up the probabilities of the worlds that are consistent with the evidence and aren't crossed out. The total is called the *normalizing factor*. In our case, the normalizing factor is 0.9 + 0.009 = 0.909. You then divide the probabilities of each of the consistent worlds by the normalizing factor. This guarantees that the probabilities will sum to 1 and the proportions will be maintained. As a result of this process, you get the probability distribution in table 4.4.

Table 4.4 Posterior probability distribution after conditioning on the evidence. First, you reduce the probability of inconsistent worlds to 0. Then, you normalize by dividing each of the remaining probabilities by the sum of the probabilities of consistent worlds. This ensures that the probabilities sum to 1.

World	Description	Probability
w_1	Forgery	0.9 / 0.909 = 0.9901
w_2	Rembrandt, people, dark	0
w_3	Rembrandt, people, bright	0.009 / 0.909 = 0.0099
w_4	Rembrandt, landscape	0

Conditioning on the evidence consists of crossing out possible worlds inconsistent with that evidence and normalizing the remaining probabilities. The probability distribution you get after conditioning on the evidence is called the posterior probability distribution because it comes after seeing the evidence. The process of starting with a prior probability distribution, conditioning on the evidence, and obtaining a posterior probability distribution, is illustrated in figure 4.4.

4.2.2 *Answering queries*

Now that you have the posterior probability distribution, how do you answer queries? In our example, the query is whether the painter is Rembrandt. In the previous section, I said that a probability distribution specifies the probability not only of individual possible worlds but also of any fact that holds in some worlds and not others. For example, w_3 is the only possible world consistent with Rembrandt whose posterior probability is greater than 0. So the posterior probability that the painter is Rembrandt is 0.0099.

You use notation for the answer to a query, given evidence. You write P(Rembrandt | bright yellow, picture of sailor, sold in 2003) = 0.0099. In this notation, the pipe symbol (|) separates the query from the evidence. To the left of the pipe symbol go the things you want to know the probability of. To the right go the things you're given as evidence. This notation is also called a *conditional probability*, because it represents the probability of a query conditioned on some evidence. Figure 4.5 shows how a conditional probability statement is built this way.

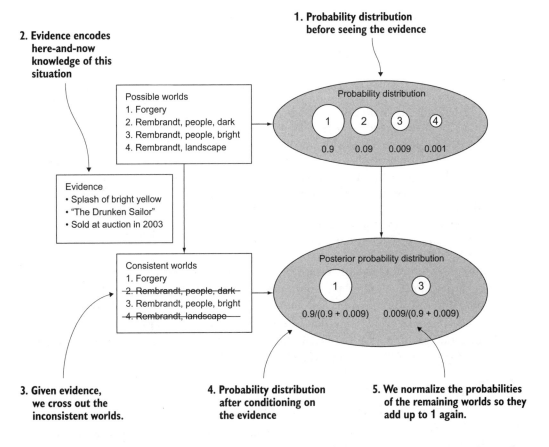

Figure 4.4   Conditioning on the evidence. Given evidence, you cross out your inconsistent worlds and normalize the probabilities of the remaining worlds so they sum to 1.

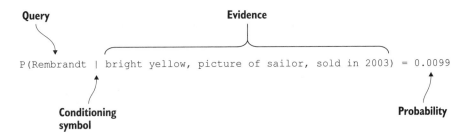

Figure 4.5   Structure of a conditional probability statement

WARNING If you look only at the notation, it seems to be possible to condition on evidence that you believe to be impossible (evidence that has probability 0). For example, what would happen if you try to observe evidence that the painting is a still life by Rembrandt? Let's say you want to query the brightness of the painting. Using our conditional probability notation, you could try to compute P(bright | still life, Rembrandt). But the evidence that the painting is a still life by Rembrandt has probability zero, because it's inconsistent with all of the possible worlds. When you condition on this evidence, you'll cross out all possible worlds and be left with no worlds. Consequently, you won't be able to produce a posterior probability distribution, and you won't be able to say with what probability the painting is bright. A lot of ink has been spilled trying to make sense of conditioning on impossible evidence, but the bottom line is, you should avoid it. If you do condition on impossible evidence, the results will be unpredictable, and will vary from one probabilistic programming system to another.

Figure 4.6 pulls all of the ideas of the previous two sections together into the big picture of probabilistic modeling. You use your general domain knowledge to encode a probability distribution over possible worlds. Then, your here-and-now knowledge takes the form of evidence, which is used to produce a posterior probability distribution. Finally, your posterior distribution is used to answer queries about particular facts of interest, in light of the evidence.

KEY DEFINITIONS

Possible worlds—All states you consider possible

Probability distribution—An assignment of a probability between 0 and 1 to each possible world, such that all of the probabilities add up to 1

Probabilistic model—A formal representation of a probability distribution over possible worlds

Evidence—Knowledge that you have about a specific situation

Prior probability distribution—The probability distribution before seeing any evidence

Conditioning on the evidence—The process of applying evidence to a probability distribution

Posterior probability distribution—The probability distribution after seeing the evidence; the result of conditioning

Normalizing—The process of proportionally adjusting a set of numbers so they add up to 1

Now you know what a probabilistic model is and the basic principles behind answering queries. But how do you put this into practice? The number of possible worlds could be enormous; it's not practical to go about checking each one to see if it's

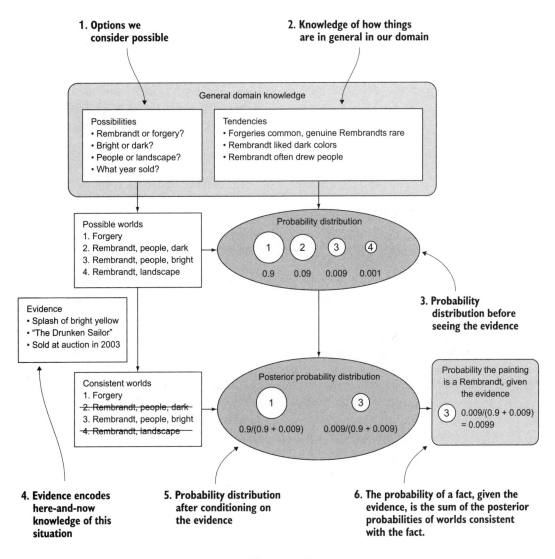

Figure 4.6 The big picture of how to use a probabilistic model.

consistent with the evidence. The goal of probabilistic inference algorithms is to answer queries efficiently.

4.2.3   *Using probabilistic inference*

The main goal of probabilistic inference is to compute the posterior probability distribution over variables of interest, given evidence. In our example, it was simple to cross out the worlds that disagree with the evidence and normalize the probabilities of the remaining worlds. In practice, for real problems, the number of possible worlds can be huge; you can have an exponential number of variables in the model. So you can't even write down all possible worlds, let alone compute their probabilities. You need a probabilistic inference algorithm that can compute posterior probabilities efficiently. Probabilistic programming systems such as Figaro provide these kinds of algorithms.

Such algorithms are based on three rules of probabilistic inference: the chain rule, the total probability rule, and Bayes' rule. You'll learn the details of these rules in part 3. For now, you need to know only that probabilistic programming inference algorithms are mechanical ways of implementing these rules and other rules derived from them. These algorithms are designed to work with the constructs of the probabilistic programming language for which they're defined, so they can be used even with complex programs written in the language. This is one of the benefits of probabilistic programming: if you can write a program in the language, you can apply an inference algorithm to it.

In practice, even though the algorithm will work in principle, probabilistic inference can be difficult. With ordinary programs, it's easy to write programs that have exponential complexity and take a long time on the problems you care about. In a similar way, it's easy to write probabilistic programs in which the inference algorithm takes a long time to produce accurate answers. For many typical uses, you can write your program, and inference will work the way you need it to. On large and complex problems, however, even the best and most efficient algorithm might take a long time to produce an answer.

Probabilistic inference algorithms can be exact or approximate. *Exact* means that the posterior probabilities they compute follow mathematically from the three rules of inference. Exact inference can be expensive, so approximate algorithms are needed. *Approximate* algorithms usually come close to the right answer but don't always provide guarantees.

Probabilistic programming systems often provide a choice of algorithms for a given problem, including both exact and approximate algorithms. Some of these algorithms might also be configurable in various ways. In addition, the way you express a model can have significant impact on the difficulty of inference. So if you're going to be using a probabilistic programming language to build large, complex models, it's worth taking the time to learn how inference works and gain techniques that will help you choose the best algorithm and make inference on your problem more efficient. You'll gain this knowledge in part 3 of this book.

4.3 *The ingredients of probabilistic models*

A probabilistic model is a formal representation of a probability distribution, and many representations are possible. One representation is a table of explicit probabilities, but that's not practical for all but the simplest problems. This section introduces a general and practical approach to building probabilistic models using four ingredients. This isn't the only way to build models, but it's widely used. It's also the foundation for probabilistic programming.

You've seen the four ingredients in the spam filter model of chapter 3, but here you'll go into them in detail. A model has four ingredients:

- The *variables* involved, such as whether a painting is a Rembrandt or a forgery.
- *Dependencies* between the variables; for example, the brightness of a painting depends on whether it's a Rembrandt.
- *Functional forms* these dependencies take; for example, whether the painting is a Rembrandt can be modeled as the result of a coin toss with a certain weight.
- *Numerical parameters* for these forms, such as the weight of the coin used to determine whether the painting is a Rembrandt.

In the following subsections, you'll see how to specify each of these ingredients.

4.3.1 Variables

The first step is to decide what variables you want to include in the model. Just as in a programming language, a *variable* is something that can take on various values. A possible world specifies a specific value for every variable. In any given possible world, the variable will have one particular value, but it might have a different value in other worlds. Even though specifying variables is just the first step in building a probabilistic model, there's a lot of creativity here, just as in programming. The decisions you make will be crucial to the effectiveness of the model.

In the example in section 4.1, implicit in our specification of possible worlds were the following variables:

- Rembrandt: Is the painting a genuine Rembrandt or a forgery?
- Brightness: Does it have bright or dark colors?
- Subject: Is it a painting of people or a landscape?

Notice that we didn't include a variable indicating whether it had been sold at an auction. Even though that variable was part of our here-and-now knowledge, we considered it irrelevant.

Every variable has a *type*, which defines the kinds of values it can take. *Continuous* variables take on real numbered values (like `Double` variables)—for example, height could be measured in centimeters. You could also have enumerations, or integers, or structured variables like lists. Variables that aren't continuous are called *discrete*. All of the variables you've seen so far have been discrete, and more specifically, enumerations. Variables whose type is an enumeration are often called *categorical*. A variable also has a *range*, which is the set of values you consider possible for the variable. For example, a variable might be an integer variable, but you consider only values between 1 and 10 possible, so its range is the integers 1 to 10. Examples of variables you might use in the Rembrandt example, their types, and some of their possible values, are shown in table 4.5.

Table 4.5 Examples of variables, their types, and possible values

Variable	Type	Example values
Rembrandt	Boolean	true, false
Size	Enumeration	small, medium, large
Height (in cm)	Real	25.3, 14.9, 68.24
Last year sold	Integer	1937, 2003
All years sold	List[Integer]	List(1937), List(1969, 2003)

An obvious relationship exists between the variables in a probabilistic model and those in a probabilistic program. In Figaro, the elements in your program will correspond to the variables in the model, and their value types will be a computational representation of the corresponding types in the model. For example, you might have the following:

```
val rembrandt: Element[Boolean] = // definition goes here
val size: Element[Symbol] = // definition goes here
val height: Element[Double] = // definition goes here
val lastYearSold: Element[Int] = // definition goes here
val allYearsSold: Element[List[Integer]] = // definition goes here
```

Given a set of variables, the simplest way to construct the possible worlds is to create a table, with a column for each variable, and a row for every possible set of values of the variables. For example, table 4.6 shows the eight possible worlds if the variables are Rembrandt, Brightness, and Subject.

Table 4.6 Possible worlds for the variables Rembrandt, Brightness, and Subject. There's a possible world for each combination of values of these variables.

	Rembrandt	Brightness	Subject
w_1	False	Dark	People
w_2	False	Dark	Landscape
w_3	False	Bright	People
w_4	False	Bright	Landscape
w_5	True	Dark	People
w_6	True	Dark	Landscape
w_7	True	Bright	People
w_8	True	Bright	Landscape

4.3.2   *Dependencies*

I've claimed that dependencies can be used to provide structure to a probability distribution. *Dependencies* characterize the way variables are related to each other. Intuitively, the enormous probability distribution over all possible worlds is divided into local model components that characterize these relationships.

Going back to our example, you now have three variables: Rembrandt, Brightness, and Subject. How are these variables related? In probabilistic modeling, relationships between variables are characterized by dependencies, which describe the ways a value of a variable depends on the values of other variables. Just as important as dependencies are *independence relationships*, which describe situations where the value of one variable doesn't depend on the value of another variable at all.

UNDERSTANDING INDEPENDENCE RELATIONSHIPS

Two variables are independent if knowing about one doesn't tell you anything about the other. For example, imagine you have another variable called Size (with possible values Small, Medium, and Large), indicating the size of the painting. What would it mean to say that Size is independent of Brightness? This has a precise meaning.

Consider any particular value for Brightness—say, Dark. You have its prior probability P(Brightness = Dark). Now consider any particular value for Size—say, Large. You're asking the question of whether knowing that Size = Large provides any new information about whether Brightness = Dark. For this question, the evidence is Size = Large, while the query is Brightness = Dark, because that's the fact whose probability you want to know. If you condition the model on the evidence Size = Large, you get a posterior probability for Dark, P(Brightness = Dark | Size = Large). Now, if Brightness and Size are independent, this posterior probability must be the same as the prior probability. Telling you that the size is large didn't change your belief that the painting is dark one bit. For Brightness and Size to be independent, this has to hold no matter what values for Brightness and Size you choose. You need the following equations to be true. See figure 4.7 for a description of how to read these equations.

P(Brightness = Dark | Size = Large) = P(Brightness = Dark)

P(Brightness = Dark | Size = Medium) = P(Brightness = Dark)

P(Brightness = Dark | Size = Small) = P(Brightness = Dark)

P(Brightness = Bright | Size = Large) = P(Brightness = Bright)

P(Brightness = Bright | Size = Medium) = P(Brightness = Bright)

P(Brightness = Bright | Size = Small) = P(Brightness = Bright)

Independence is a symmetric property. If you know that telling you about the size of the painting doesn't provide any new information about its brightness, the same is

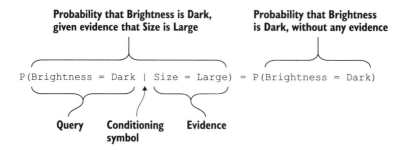

Figure 4.7   Breakdown of an equation describing an independence relationship

true in the opposite direction: telling you about its brightness provides no new information about the painting's size. In mathematical notation,

$$P(\text{Brightness} = \text{Dark} \mid \text{Size} = \text{Large}) = P(\text{Brightness} = \text{Dark})$$

implies

$$P(\text{Size} = \text{Large} \mid \text{Brightness} = \text{Dark}) = P(\text{Size} = \text{Large})$$

The independence equation is illustrated in figure 4.8. You begin with a prior probability distribution over Size and Brightness. The probability that Brightness is Dark is the sum of the probabilities of the possible worlds in which Brightness = Dark, which is 0.8. You then observe evidence that Size = Small and cross out the inconsistent

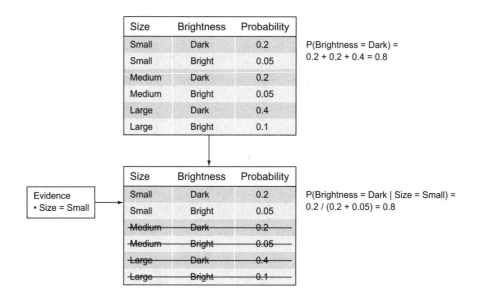

Figure 4.8   Independence: the probability that Brightness is Dark doesn't change after observing that Size is Small.

worlds. You obtain the posterior probability of Brightness = Dark by normalizing the probabilities of the worlds consistent with the evidence. The posterior probability comes out to 0.8, which is the same as it was before you observed the evidence. If you look at the prior distribution, you can see that for any value of Size, the ratio of the probability of the possible world in which Brightness is Dark to the probability of the possible world in which Brightness is Bright is the same, 4:1. Because the ratio is the same, observing a particular value for Size doesn't change the ratio of Dark to Bright from what it was prior to observing the evidence.

UNDERSTANDING CONDITIONAL INDEPENDENCE

The next step is to consider that the relationship between two variables depends on what you already know. In some cases, two variables may not be independent, given no additional information, but may become independent with added information. For example, say that landscapes are more likely to be large and more likely to be bright. Then Size and Brightness aren't independent, because telling you that the painting is large increases your belief that the painting is a landscape, which in turn makes it more likely to be bright. On the other hand, if you already know that the painting is a landscape, telling you it's large doesn't provide any new information about what type of painting it is, so it doesn't change your belief that it's bright. In this case, you say that Brightness and Size are *conditionally independent* given that Subject = Landscape. You can write equations like this:

P(Brightness = Dark | Size = Small, Subject = Landscape) =
P(Brightness = Dark | Subject = Landscape)

You can have an equation like this for every possible value of Brightness, Size, and Subject.

To understand this equation, imagine a two-step process, illustrated in figure 4.9. You start out knowing nothing about the painting and having a prior probability distribution over Subject, Size, and Brightness. According to this prior distribution, P(Brightness = Dark) = 0.7. You then observe the evidence that Subject = Landscape, and get the posterior probability distribution P(Brightness = Dark | Subject = Landscape) = 0.3. According to our prior distribution, landscapes are less likely to be dark than people paintings, so the evidence that Subject = Landscape has lowered your belief that Brightness = Dark. Now here's the trick: this posterior distribution becomes the prior distribution for the next piece of evidence, where you now observe that Size = Small. You get a new posterior distribution. According to this new distribution, P(Brightness = Dark | Size = Small, Subject = Landscape) = 0.3, so the extra evidence that Size = Small hasn't provided any new information about Brightness, after you already know that Subject = Landscape. If you look closely at the prior distribution, you can see that in the bottom half of the table, where Subject = Landscape, the ratio for Brightness between Dark and Bright is always 3:7, whereas in the top half, where Subject = People, the ratio is always 4:1. The two ratios are different, but after you fix

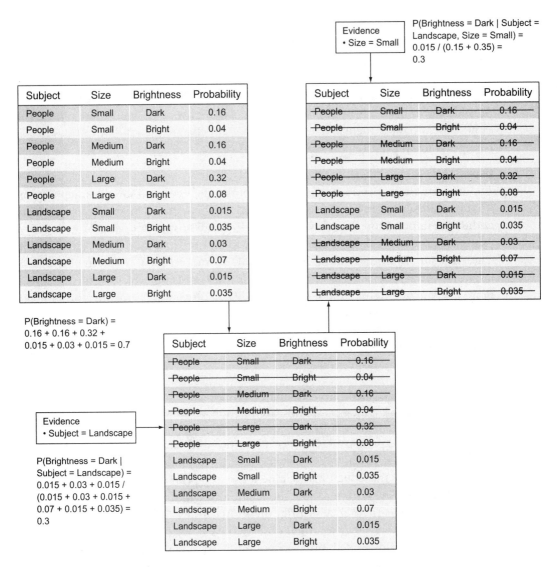

Figure 4.9   Conditional independence: evidence that Subject = Landscape changes your belief that Brightness = Dark, but subsequent evidence that Size = Small doesn't provide any new information.

Subject, the ratio becomes fixed, so Size and Brightness are conditionally independent, given Subject.

ENCODING DEPENDENCIES IN A PROBABILISTIC PROGRAM

Chapter 5 details the subject of dependencies. The main representation used in that chapter is Bayesian networks. I'll give you a preview of them here.

One of the main themes of this book is that dependencies between variables can be encoded as a network, in which there's an arrow from a parent variable to a child variable if the value of the parent influences the value of the child. In our example, you imagine the painter first choosing the Subject, which then influences Size and Brightness, but Size and Brightness don't influence each other. These relationships can be captured by the network structure depicted in figure 4.10. In brief, an edge in a Bayesian network goes in a single direction from parent to child, and usually the edge indicates that the parent causes the child in some way. Chapter 5 provides details of these causal relationships and how to draw the Bayesian network structure.

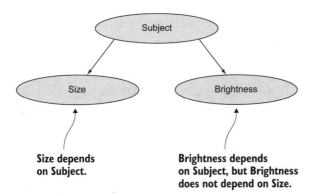

Size depends
on Subject.

Brightness depends
on Subject, but Brightness
does not depend on Size.

**Figure 4.10   A simple Bayesian
network structure encoding the
conditional independence between
Size and Brightness, given Subject**

A network that shows the dependencies between variables in this manner is known as a *Bayesian network*. The nodes in the network correspond to variables in the model, and there's an edge between two nodes if the first one influences the second one. As you'll see in chapter 5, an awful lot of information about dependencies in the model is encoded in the Bayesian network.

A Bayesian network structure naturally translates into the structure of a probabilistic program. If one variable is the parent of another variable in the network, the first variable influences the second. If you think about ordinary programs, one variable influences another one if the second variable uses it in its definition. It's the same way in probabilistic programming: if there's an edge from one variable to another in a Bayesian network, the second variable will use the first one in its definition. This is one of the fundamental connections between probabilistic modeling and programming that makes probabilistic programming possible.

With this understood, representing dependencies in probabilistic programs becomes simple. In Figaro, you have the following program skeleton:

```
val subject = // definition
val size = // definition uses subject
val brightness = // definition uses subject
```

Crucially, the definition of brightness doesn't use size. In chapter 5, you'll learn that this captures the fact that brightness is conditionally independent of size, given subject.

At this point, you have your variables, and you know their dependencies, described in the form of a network. Although we've talked about a variable depending on other variables, you haven't yet seen what these dependencies look like and what forms they take. That's accomplished with the next two ingredients: functional forms and numerical parameters.

4.3.3 *Functional forms*

Okay, so you've chosen your variables, and you've specified your dependencies in the form of a network. I've said that dependencies are key to defining probability distributions over many variables using simple components. These components must characterize variables only in terms of the variables they're related to. The next step is to define the precise forms that the components characterizing these relationships take. In the example of figure 4.10, this involves specifying how the value of Subject is chosen, and how that value is used to choose the value of Size and the value of Brightness.

BASIC FUNCTIONAL FORMS

Let's start with the first problem: specifying how the value of Subject is chosen. Because Subject doesn't depend on any other variable, all you have to do is specify a probability distribution over the values of Subject. In our example, Subject has an enumeration type with values People and Landscape, so you need to specify the probability of People and Landscape. Specifying the probabilities explicitly is the simplest way to express a probability distribution. But when you have a lot of values, or when the explicit probabilities are hard to come up with directly, this explicit specification can be infeasible.

Instead, you often specify that the probability distribution takes on one of a standard set of functional forms. In general, the available forms depend on the type of the variable. Each form has particular properties and is used for particular use cases. It's good to understand how different functional forms are used so you can pick an appropriate one for your application.

For example, a common form for a continuous variable is a normal distribution. Another is an exponential distribution. For integer variables, binomial and geometric are two common forms. For the most part, this book doesn't go into a lot of details about individual functional forms. A huge amount of material is available, with good articles on Wikipedia on most of these forms.

Figaro has representations of many common functional forms, as you saw in chapter 2. When representing the form of a single variable, you'll typically use an atomic element. For example, `Select` represents an explicit assignment of probabilities, `Normal` represents the continuous normal distribution with a given mean and variance, and `Binomial` represents the binomial distribution with a particular number of trials and probability of success in each trial.

CONDITIONAL PROBABILITY DISTRIBUTIONS

Now, what about the other two variables, Size and Brightness, that depend on Subject? You can't just specify a basic functional form for them; you also have to specify how their probability distribution changes for different values of Subject. For this, you define a *conditional probability distribution* (CPD). You'll specify, for each value of Subject, a probability distribution over Size. For example, you'll specify the probability that Size = Large given Subject = Landscape, or, in our notation, P(Size = Large | Subject = Landscape). The easiest way to do this is by specifying, for every possible value of Subject, a corresponding functional form for Size.

In our example, Size is an enumeration, so this functional form is naturally an explicit specification of probabilities. You can present the CPD of Size given Subject by using a table, as shown in table 4.7. I use a standard form for CPD tables that shows which variable the CPD belongs to and which are the conditioning variables. The conditioning variables go down the left. In this example, there's just one conditioning variable, Subject, and it's in the left column. You might imagine a dependency model in which a variable depends on more than one other variable. In this case, all these conditioning variables will go on the left. On the right goes the variable whose CPD is being defined, with a column for each possible value of that variable. So here you have Size, with a column for each possible value Small, Medium, and Large. Then there's a row in the CPD for each possible value of the conditioning variables. In our case, there are two values, People and Landscape, so there's a row for each. If you have more than one conditioning variable, there will be a row for every combination of values of those variables. Finally, in the cell in the table corresponding to row i and column j, there's an entry for the probability that the variable whose CPD is being defined has the value in column j, given that the conditioning variables have the values specified by row i. So, for example, in the cell whose row is People and column is Small, you have P(Size = Small | Subject = People). I've given each of these probabilities a label from p1 through p6. These labels are used in the following code snippet; you can use them to cross-reference between the table and the code.

Table 4.7 The form of a CPD of Size given Subject

Subject	Size		
	Small	**Medium**	**Large**
People	p1 = P(Size = Small | Subject = People)	p2 = P(Size = Medium | Subject = People)	p3 = P(Size = Large | Subject = People)
Landscape	p4 = P(Size = Small | Subject = Landscape)	p5 = P(Size = Medium | Subject = Landscape)	p6 = P(Size = Large | Subject = Landscape)

In Figaro, a CPD can be implemented by using a compound element. The compound element specifies precisely how the variable depends on other variables. In chapter 2, you saw that `Chain` is a general kind of compound element that defines a function from a value of the conditioning variable to an element over the conditioned variable. This function can be anything you like, so `Chain` is the most general Figaro concept for representing CPDs. But many more specific forms are also available.

One useful form is called, naturally enough, CPD. The Figaro CPD form can be used in our example as follows:

```
val size = CPD(subject,
  'people -> Select(p1 -> 'small, p2 -> 'medium, p3 -> 'large),
  'landscape -> Select(p4 -> 'small, p5 -> 'medium, p6 -> 'large)
)
```

The Scala variables p1 to p6 represent the numerical probabilities, which you'll learn about in the next section.

> **NOTE** The quote notation ' indicates that I'm using the Scala Symbol type. A symbol is a unique name for something. For example, 'small is a symbol that's equal to every other occurrence of 'small and different from every other symbol. You can't do much with a symbol other than compare it for equality. A symbol is useful when you want to create a specific set of values for a variable.

If you have more than two variables, you can also use CPD. For example, imagine there's a Price variable that depends on whether the painting is a Rembrandt and what its subject is. You can write its form as follows:

```
val price = CPD(rembrandt, subject,
  (false, 'people)    -> Flip(p1),
  (false, 'landscape) -> Flip(p2),
  (true, 'people)     -> Flip(p3),
  (true, 'landscape)  -> Flip(p4)
)
```

The CPD constructor takes two sets of arguments:

1 *The parents of the variable being defined*—You can have up to five parents.
2 *A number of clauses*—This number varies depending on the possible values of the parents. Each clause consists of a *case* of the parents and an *outcome element*. For example, in the first clause for the CPD of size, the case is 'people and the outcome element is Select(p1 -> 'small, p2 -> 'medium, p3 -> 'large). This clause means that if the value of subject is 'people, then the value of size is chosen according to this Select element. If there's only one parent, the case will simply be a value of the parent. If there's more than one parent, the case will be a tuple of parent values. For example, in the first clause of the CPD of price, the case is (false, 'people), meaning that this clause applies if rembrandt has value false and subject has value 'people.

OTHER WAYS OF SPECIFYING DEPENDENCIES IN FIGARO

Figaro provides another constructor called RichCPD that enables you to represent CPDs much more compactly than providing the complete table. RichCPD is just like CPD, except that the case in each clause specifies a set of possible values for each parent, rather than a single value. You can specify these sets in one of three ways: (1)

OneOf(values) specifies that the value of the parent must be one of the given values for the clause to apply; (2) NoneOf(values) specifies that the value of the parent can't be any of the given values; and (3) * means that the parent can take any value and the clause will apply, assuming the other parents have appropriate values. Given a particular set of values for the parents, the first matching clause is chosen and defines the distribution for the element.

RichCPD is a more advanced construct that can be useful when you have CPDs involving multiple parents. Ordinarily, the number of rows in a CPD is equal to the product of the number of values of each of the parents. When you have one parent with two values, one with three, and one with four, the number of rows in the CPD is $2 \times 3 \times 4 = 24$. You can see that becomes tedious to specify when you have more parents, or the parents have more values. RichCPD is designed to help in these situations. Here's an example:

```
val x1 = Select(0.1 -> 1, 0.2 -> 2, 0.3 -> 3, 0.4 -> 4)
val x2 = Flip(0.6)
val y = RichCPD(x1, x2,
  (OneOf(1, 2), *) -> Flip(0.1),
  (NoneOf(4), OneOf(false)) -> Flip(0.7),
  (*, *) -> Flip(0.9))
```

A RichCPD with two parents

Matches cases where x1 is 1 or 2, and x2 is anything

Matches cases where x1 is anything but 4, and x2 is false

Default case that matches everything

WARNING It's important that the cases of CPD and RichCPD cover all possible values of the parents that have positive probability. Otherwise, Figaro won't know what to do when it encounters values that don't match any clause. For CPD, this implies that you have to provide the complete table. For RichCPD, you can use a "default" clause at the end that uses * for each parent, as in the RichCPD example.

CPD and RichCPD are two explicit ways of writing dependencies that are useful when you have discrete variables. I don't want you to get the impression that these are the only ways to write dependencies in Figaro; they're just two simple and explicit ways. In Figaro, the two general ways of specifying dependencies are to use Apply and Chain. Recall from chapter 2 the following:

- Apply takes a number of argument elements and a function. The result of Apply is an element whose value is the given function applied to the values of the arguments. Therefore, Apply defines a dependency from the arguments to the result.
- Chain takes an argument element and a function that takes a value of the argument and returns a new element. The result of the Chain is an element whose value is generated by taking the value of the argument, applying the function to get a new element, and generating a value from that element. Therefore, Chain also defines a dependency from the argument to the result.

- Many elements, such as If and compound Normal, are defined using Chain. Therefore, they also define dependencies.

Up to this point, you've seen what functional forms are, and you know that Figaro provides a variety of them. But without numbers to fill in their parameters, they're just empty shells. Next, you'll look at providing these numbers.

4.3.4   *Numerical parameters*

The final ingredient in a probabilistic model is the numerical parameters. Conceptually, this is the simplest part. Any functional form you choose will have particular parameters, and you fill in numbers for those parameters. The one constraint is that you have to make sure those values are legal for the functional form. For example, when specifying explicit probabilities for a set of values, the probabilities must add up to 1. Table 4.8 shows the filled-in CPD of Size, given Subject. Note how each row adds up to 1. This is necessary because each row is a probability distribution over Size.

Table 4.8   **The filled-in CPD of Size, given Subject**

Subject	Size		
	Small	**Medium**	**Large**
People	0.5	0.4	0.1
Landscape	0.1	0.6	0.3

Despite its conceptual simplicity, filling in the numbers can be the hardest step in practice. Estimating probabilities based on expertise can be challenging. If you go back to the beginning of the chapter, you had some general statements about tendencies among paintings: Rembrandt "liked" to use dark colors in his paintings; he "often" painted people; genuine newly discovered paintings by masters are "rare," but forgeries are "a dime a dozen." It's relatively easy, if you're an expert in a subject, to come up with general tendencies like this, but putting numbers on them is different. Rembrandt "liked" to use dark colors in his paintings—does that mean that P(Brightness = Dark | Rembrandt = True) = 0.73? It's hard to say.

There are two pieces of good news. First, it turns out that in many cases, getting the exact numbers right isn't critical. Answers to queries will usually be about the same even if the numerical probabilities are somewhat different. For example, if the model says that P(Brightness = Dark | Rembrandt = True) = 0.77, you'll get roughly the same prediction as to whether the painting is a forgery as if the probability were 0.73. This isn't true, however, about extremely small probabilities that are close to 0. Changing a probability from 0.001 to 0.0001 can cause drastic changes in the conclusions. It's the orders of magnitude that are important at the extremes. On the other hand, these orders of magnitude are sometimes easier for experts to provide.

The other piece of good news is that these numbers can usually be learned from data. You've already seen an example of this in chapter 3. A caveat, as you saw in that chapter, is that even when you learn parameters from data, you need to specify some prior parameters. But these prior parameters can make minimal assumptions, and, given a reasonable amount of data, these prior parameter values have little impact on the final numbers. Furthermore, the ability to specify prior parameter values is a good thing, because it provides an opportunity to use your expert knowledge to influence the learning. If you don't have expert knowledge, you can specify neutral prior parameter values that tend not to influence the learning in any direction.

In chapters 9 and 12, you'll learn the basic principles behind parameter learning. Chapter 9 describes two general approaches to parameter learning. In one approach, known as the Bayesian learning approach, a probability distribution over the parameter values themselves is included in the model. Learning the parameter values is then accomplished using ordinary probabilistic inference, which produces a posterior probability distribution over these parameter values. The second approach doesn't learn a posterior probability distribution over parameter values, and instead generates a single estimate of the parameter values after seeing the training data. Chapter 12 then shows you how to implement these approaches in Figaro.

So there you have all of the ingredients of a practical approach to representing probabilistic models. But I've left an important question unanswered. Suppose you build a probabilistic model using these ingredients. How does it represent a probability distribution over possible worlds? The next section presents generative models, an essential concept to understanding probabilistic programming and how programs represent probabilistic models.

4.4 *Generative processes*

This chapter began with a definition of a probabilistic model as a formal representation of a probability distribution over possible worlds. Section 4.3 showed how to build probabilistic models by specifying variables, dependencies, functional forms, and numerical parameters, and, furthermore, that this representational approach is essential to probabilistic programming. To clearly understand what probabilistic programs mean, it's essential to close the loop and see how a probabilistic model defined in this way specifies a probability distribution over possible worlds. This understanding centers on the concept of a *generative process.*

Probabilistic programming relies on an analogy between probabilistic models and programs in a programming language. The essence of this analogy is as follows:

- Probabilistic models like Bayesian networks can be viewed as defining a process for generating values of variables. This generative process defines a probability distribution over possible worlds.
- In a similar way, ordinary, nonprobabilistic programs define a process for generating values of variables.

- Combining these two, a probabilistic program uses a programming language to describe a process for generating values of variables involving random choices. This generative process defines a probability distribution over possible worlds.

That last sentence needs justification. I'll explain how Bayesian networks define a probability distribution over possible worlds by using a generative process. Then, I'll make the analogy to probabilistic programs.

Let's see how a Bayesian network defines a process for generating values of variables. Figure 4.11 reproduces the Bayesian network of figure 4.10, along with the CPD for each variable, given the variables it depends on.

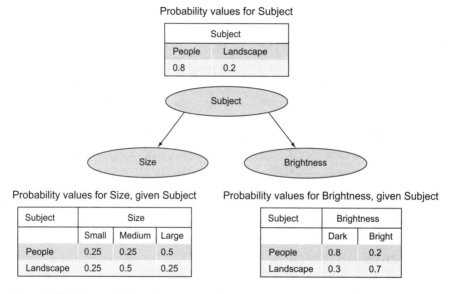

Figure 4.11 **Three-node Bayesian network with CPDs**

You can imagine a process for generating values of all of the variables in this network. You make sure not to generate a value for a variable until you already have values for the variables it depends on. This process is illustrated in figure 4.12. You start with Subject, because it doesn't depend on any other variables. According to Subject's CPD, People has probability 0.8 and Landscape has probability 0.2. So you randomly choose People or Landscape, each with the appropriate probability. Let's say you choose Landscape.

You then go on to choose Size. You can do this because you've already chosen a value for Subject, which is the only variable Size depends on. Because you've chosen Subject = Landscape, you use the appropriate row in Size's CPD. In this row, Small has probability 0.25, Medium is 0.5, and Large is 0.25. So you randomly choose a value for Size with these probabilities. Let's say you choose Medium.

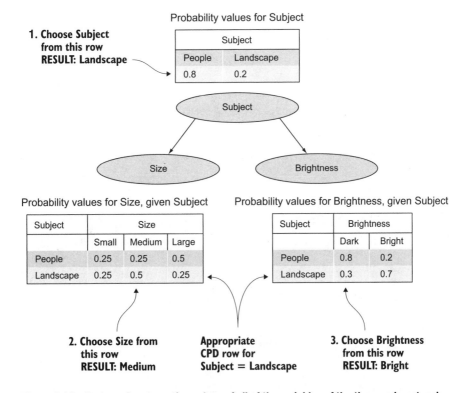

Figure 4.12 Process for generating values of all of the variables of the three-node network. The value of a variable is generated by choosing a value using the probabilities in the appropriate CPD row, depending on the values of its parents.

Finally, you choose a value for Brightness. This is similar to choosing a value for Size, because Brightness depends only on Subject, whose value is Landscape. Let's say you choose the value Bright for Brightness. You've now generated values for all of the variables: Subject = Landscape, Size = Medium, Brightness = Bright.

When you go through this process of generating values for all of the variables, multiple possibilities exist for each variable. You can draw a tree that captures all possibilities. For our example, figure 4.13 shows the tree. The root of the tree is the first variable, Subject. Subject has a branch for each of its possible values, People and Landscape. Each branch is annotated with the probability of that choice. For example, according to the CPD of Subject, Landscape has probability 0.2. You then get to the next variable, Size, which appears in two nodes in the tree, corresponding to the possible choices for Subject. At each Size node, the tree has three branches corresponding to each of its values. Note that the numbers associated with these branches are different for the two Size nodes. This is because these numbers are derived from the appropriate row of Size's CPD. This row is different depending on whether Subject is People or Landscape. After each branch of the Size node, there's a Brightness node

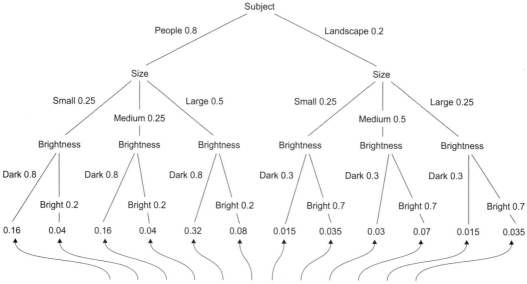

Probabilities of possible worlds are computed by multiplying probabilities
of choices on path. These probabilities add up to 1.

Figure 4.13   Tree of generation possibilities for three-node Bayesian network

with two branches for Dark and Bright. Again, the probabilities are drawn from the
appropriate row of Brightness's CPD. Notice that the three Brightness nodes on the
left all have the same probabilities, and similarly for the three Brightness nodes on the
right. This is because Brightness depends only on Subject and not on Size. The three
Brightness nodes on the left all have the same value chosen for Subject.

When you go through the generation process in figure 4.13, you make a particular
choice at each node as you go down the tree. You end up with the sequence of choices
shown in figure 4.14. You end up with one particular possible world. What's the probability of this possible world? The answer comes from the chain rule, one of the rules
of inference you'll learn in part 3. According to this rule, the probability of a possible
world is the product of the choices made in generating that world. In our example,
for the world Subject = Landscape, Size = Medium, Brightness = Bright, the probability is $0.2 \times 0.5 \times 0.7 = 0.07$. It's not hard to prove that the probabilities you get for all
possible worlds will add up to 1. Therefore, a Bayesian network defines a probability
distribution over possible worlds.

Now you see how a Bayesian network specifies a process for generating values of
variables. If you think about a program in an ordinary programming language, it also
specifies a process for generating values of variables, except that that process doesn't
involve random choices. A probabilistic program is like an ordinary program, except
that the process for generating values of variables includes random choices. A prob-

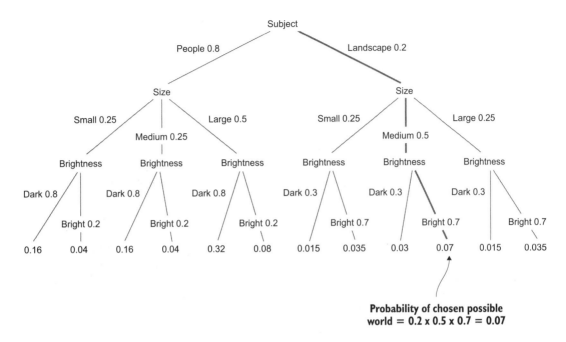

Figure 4.14 **A sequence of choices and its probability**

abilistic program is like a Bayesian network, except that programming language constructs are used to describe the generation process. And because you have a programming language at your disposal, you have many more possibilities than are available in a Bayesian network. You can have rich control flow like loops and functions, and complex data structures like sets and trees. But the principle is the same: the program defines a process for generating the values of all of the variables.

As you go through a probabilistic program, you generate a value for each variable by using its definition, based on the values of the variables it depends on. After the program has terminated, you've generated a value for a set of variables. This set of variables, along with their generated values, constitutes a possible world. As in a Bayesian network, the probability of this possible world is the product of the probabilities of each of the random choices.

There's a big difference between probabilistic programs and Bayesian networks, however, in that the set of variables that's assigned values in a program can differ from run to run. To see this, consider the following Figaro program:

```
Chain(Flip(0.5), (b: Boolean) => if (b) Constant(0.3) else Uniform(0, 1))
```

The `Constant(0.3)` element will be created only if `Flip` has the value `true`, while the `Uniform(0, 1)` element will be created only if `Flip` is `false`. There's no possible run of the program in which both elements are created and assigned values. Nevertheless, each run of the program results in a possible world with a well-defined probability. And, although it's somewhat harder to prove, it turns out that the probabilities of these possible worlds still add up to 1. Therefore, a probabilistic program defines a probability distribution over possible worlds.

> **CAVEAT** In a programming language, it's possible to write programs that don't terminate, and the same is true for probabilistic programming languages. If the random process defined by a probabilistic program has a positive probability of not terminating, it doesn't define a valid probability distribution over possible worlds. Imagine a probabilistic program that defines a recursive function that keeps on calling itself without stopping; the process defined by this program doesn't terminate.

At this point, you should have a good idea of what a probabilistic model is and how to use it, as well as how a probabilistic program can represent all of the ingredients of a probabilistic model. Before ending this chapter, you need to consider one more technical point, which is how to use continuous variables in a probabilistic model.

4.5 *Models with continuous variables*

The examples of probabilistic models you've seen so far have used discrete variables. A discrete variable is one whose values are well separated, like enumerations and integers, whereas a continuous element is one whose values have no separation, like real numbers. Chapter 2 hinted at the fact that continuous variables are treated differently from discrete variables and promised to provide a full explanation later. Here's that explanation.

The challenge with continuous elements is that it's hard to define a probability distribution over all values of a continuous element. Let's consider any interval of real numbers. If you assign positive probability to all numbers in the interval, the total probability will be infinite. This is true no matter how small the interval. So how do you define the probabilities of continuous variables? This section provides the answer.

To make things concrete, I'll use as an example the beta-binomial model. This useful model is used in many applications. In chapter 3, you used this model to indicate the number of unusual words in an email. This section details the beta-binomial model to illustrate the concepts you've learned in the chapter so far. This model contains a continuous variable, so I'll explain how to represent this variable, and along with it explain continuous variables in general.

4.5.1 *Using the beta-binomial model*

The model is called *beta-binomial* because it uses a beta distribution and a binomial distribution working together. Let's see where these distributions show up in a simple example. Suppose you have a biased coin, so it doesn't come out heads or tails with the same probability. Your goal is to predict the probability that a toss will come out heads, given observations of previous coin tosses. Imagine that you observe the outcome of 100 tosses and want to query the probability that the 101st toss will be heads.

First, you define the variables. For this example, you'll use the following three:

- The bias of the coin, called Bias.
- The number of the first 100 tosses that came out heads, called NumberOf-Heads. This is an integer variable that takes a value between 0 and 100.
- The result of the 101st toss, called $Toss_{101}$.

For the dependency model, you use the Bayesian network in figure 4.15. Remember, although you infer the bias from the number of heads, the dependencies in the model can go in the opposite direction of inference. Causally, the bias of the coin determines the result of each coin toss, which in turn drives the number of heads, so the edge goes from Bias to NumberOfHeads.

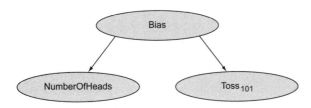

Figure 4.15 Bayesian network for the coin-toss example. The first 100 tosses are summarized in a single variable representing the number of heads.

You might be wondering why there's no edge from NumberOfHeads to $Toss_{101}$. After all, the number of heads in the first 100 tosses provides information relevant to the 101st toss. The reason is that all that information is mediated by the bias of the coin. The first 100 tosses tell you about the bias of the coin, which is then used to predict $Toss_{101}$. If you already knew the bias, the first 100 tosses wouldn't provide any additional information. In other words, $Toss_{101}$ is conditionally independent of NumberOf-Heads, given Bias.

Now you can choose functional forms. You'll have one functional form for each variable. Let's start with $Toss_{101}$. This is a toss of a coin that comes out either heads or tails. This is one of the simplest forms possible. It requires only that you specify the probability of coming out heads or tails. In our case, the probability of heads is given by the value of the Bias variable. With probability equal to Bias, the coin comes out heads, and with probability equal to 1 – Bias, it comes out tails. In Figaro, you can use a compound `Flip`, where the probability is given by the bias.

Next, you need a functional form that characterizes the probability that a particular number of coin tosses come out heads, when there are 100 tosses in total, given that the probability of each toss is equal to the value of Bias. You saw in chapter 2 that the right functional form for this is a binomial distribution. In a binomial distribution, you repeatedly run the same experiment that can have one of two outcomes. It specifies a probability distribution over the number of times a certain outcome happens. In our example, it'll tell us the probability of observing a specific number of heads in 100 tosses.

In general, the binomial distribution depends on two parameters: the number of trials (100 in our case), and the probability that any particular trial has the desired outcome (in this case, turning up heads). If you know this probability, you can immediately compute the probability of a certain number of heads—say, 63. In our example, however, this probability is given by the value of the Bias variable.

You need a functional form for Bias. You can probably guess, from the name of the model, that you'll use a beta distribution for the bias. In general, the beta-binomial model is the name for a probabilistic model containing a binomial variable representing the number of successful outcomes of a trial whose probability of success is given by a beta variable.

So you know that the bias has a beta distribution. But what exactly does that mean? How can you have a probability distribution over a continuous variable?

4.5.2 *Representing continuous variables*

The value of Bias is a real number between 0 and 1, so it's a continuous variable. Continuous variables need a different method for specifying probability distributions. For example, suppose you believe that a painting's height is somewhere between 50 cm and 150 cm, and that you don't believe any one height to be more likely than the others. Therefore, the range is 50 cm to 100 cm, and you believe the probability to be uniform across that range. You might want to know the probability that the height is exactly 113.296 cm. The problem is that there are infinitely many possible heights. If any possible height had positive probability, say 0.2, and you believe that all heights have the same probability, then there will be infinitely many heights with probability 0.2, so the total probability of all heights between 50 cm and 150 cm would be infinite. But you know the total probability must sum to 1.

The solution is that instead of considering the probabilities of individual heights, you look at *intervals*, or ranges, of heights. For example, if you ask the probability that the height is between 113 cm and 114 cm, you can say that it's 1 in 100, because this is 1 cm out of 100 equally likely centimeters. In fact, you can ask for the probability of any interval around 113.296 cm, no matter how small. For example, the probability of the interval from 113.2 cm to 113.3 cm is 1 in 1,000; and from 113.29 cm to 113.30 cm is 1 in 10,000, and so forth.

So for continuous variables, individual points usually have probability 0. Let's consider the bias of the coin. The probability that the bias is exactly 0.49326486… is 0, because there are infinitely many other points. But intervals containing points have positive probability. For example, the bias might be between 0.49326 and 0.49327.

There's a mathematical way to specify the probability of every interval, depicted in figure 4.16, using a *probability density function*, or PDF. A PDF is a way of specifying the probability of every interval. It works by providing the density of every point. If you have a small interval, the density might be approximately the same across the interval, so the probability of the interval is equal to this constant probability times the length of the interval. In figure 4.16, which shows a uniform PDF, the density is completely

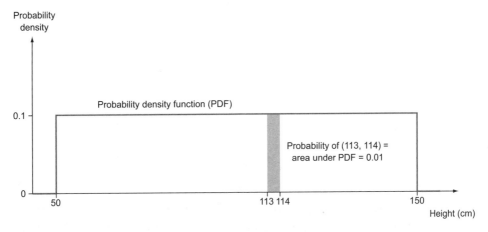

Figure 4.16 A probability density function (PDF): the probability of an interval is equal to the area under the PDF over the interval. (The figure is not to scale.)

flat at a value of 0.01, so the probability of the interval (113, 114) is equal to 0.01 times the length of the interval, which is 1, so the probability is 0.01. When the density function is completely flat, multiplying the constant density by the length of the interval gives you the area under the density curve contained in that interval. In general, the density might vary from one point to the next. The same principle applies where the probability of the interval is the area under the curve contained in the interval. If you remember your calculus, you'll recognize this area under the curve contained in an interval as being the integral of the density function over the interval. I'm not going to ask you to do any calculus in this book, or compute the area under any curve—Figaro takes care of that—but I do want to make sure that you understand that continuous distributions are a little different from other distributions, and that you know what a density function is.

Getting back to our example, you're looking for a functional form for Bias, and it needs to specify a PDF. You know that the bias must be between 0 and 1, because it's a probability, so the density must be 0 outside the interval (0, 1). It turns out that there's a good functional form for precisely this case, and it's the beta distribution. The beta distribution is used to model the probability that a particular trial has a certain outcome, when there are two possible outcomes. Figure 4.17 shows an example of a beta distribution. You can see that it's positive only between 0 and 1, and it has a single peak. You'll see in a minute how to characterize where that peak is and how pointy it is.

The reason beta is chosen to characterize the bias of the coin is that beta and binomial work well together. Specifically, if you have evidence about NumberOfHeads and your prior distribution for Bias is a beta distribution, then your posterior distribution for Bias after seeing the number of heads will also be a beta distribution. You'll see in part 3 that it's simple to predict the 101st toss in this way.

To summarize what you have so far, you have the following variables and their functional forms:

- Bias, characterized by a beta distribution
- NumberOfHeads, characterized by a binomial distribution, where the total number of trials is 100, and the probability of heads in each trial is the value of Bias
- $Toss_{101}$, characterized by `Flip`, where the probability of heads is the value of Bias

You can write a Figaro skeleton for our model:

```
val bias = Beta(?,?)
val numberOfHeads = Binomial(100, bias)
val toss101 = Flip(bias)
```

Now for the fourth step in specifying the model: choosing numerical parameters. Looking at our program skeleton, you see that the relevant parameters for `numberOf-Heads` and `toss101` are specified by the value of `bias`, which is already an element in the program. You have to specify only the parameters of `bias`. To do this, you have to understand the parameters of a beta distribution.

The beta distribution has many versions; figure 4.17 shows a particular one. Each version is characterized by two numerical parameters, named α and β. The version in the figure is `beta(2, 5)`, meaning that α has the value 2 and β has the value 5.

It turns out that there's a natural interpretation for α and β. They represent the number of times you've observed each type of outcome, plus 1. In our example, α is the number of heads that have been observed, plus 1, and β is the same for the number of tails. So the prior α and β parameters, before you've observed any coin tosses, represent

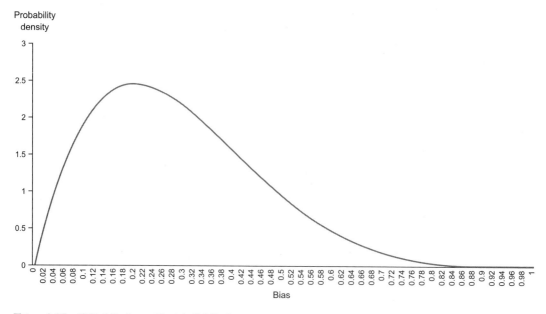

Figure 4.17 **PDF of the `beta(2, 5)` distribution.**

what you think you know about the coin in terms of imaginary previous coin tosses that have been observed. If you think you don't know anything, you have zero imaginary coin tosses, so you set α and β to 1. If you think, based on experience with similar coins, that this coin is more likely to land heads than tails, you can set α to be greater than β. And the more you trust this experience, the greater the magnitude of α and β will be.

For example, in figure 4.17, α is 2 and β is 5. Because β is larger than α, in your prior beliefs you tend to think that the bias is toward tails (the probability of heads is small), and indeed you see that the probability density of low values of the bias (< 0.5) is higher than that of high values (> 0.5). Also, starting with α = 2 and β = 5 implies that you imagine having already seen one head and four tails, so you're starting with some prior knowledge about the bias, which is reflected in the fact that the PDF isn't a flat line.

So there you have it. You've seen all four ingredients of a probabilistic model and how they're represented in a probabilistic program. You're now ready to dive into modeling techniques and design patterns. You'll begin in the next chapter with a detailed discussion of dependencies and two representational frameworks for describing them, Bayesian networks and Markov networks.

4.6 Summary

- Probabilistic models represent general domain knowledge as a probability distribution over possible worlds.
- You use evidence to rule out worlds that are inconsistent with the evidence and normalize the probabilities of the remaining worlds. Probabilistic programming systems use inference algorithms to take care of this.
- Building a probabilistic model requires specifying variables and their types, dependencies between the variables in the form of a network, and a functional form and numerical parameters for each variable.
- The functional form of a continuous variable is specified by a probability density function.
- The ingredients of a probabilistic model define a generative process for generating values of all of the variables.
- Probabilistic programs define generative processes by using programming languages.

4.7 Exercises

Solutions to selected exercises are available online at www.manning.com/books/practical-probabilistic-programming.

1 Consider a poker game with a five-card deck: ace of spades, king of spades, king of hearts, queen of spades, and queen of hearts. Each player gets one card. What are the possible worlds? Assuming the deck is fairly shuffled, what's the probability of each possible world?

2 In the same poker game, you observe evidence that one player has a picture card (king or queen). What's the probability that the other player has a spade?

3 Let's elaborate on the rules of this poker game. The game includes betting. Here are the betting rules:

Player 1 can bet or pass.

If player 1 bets:

– Player 2 can bet or fold.

If player 1 passes:

– Player 2 can bet or pass.

If player 2 bets:

– Player 1 can bet or fold.

The possible betting outcomes are (1) both players bet; (2) both players pass; (3) one bets and one passes. If both pass, neither player wins or loses anything. If one bets and one folds, the player that bets wins $1. If both bet, the player with the higher card wins $2. If both players have the same rank card, spades beats hearts.

You want to build a probabilistic model of this poker game. The goal of this model is to help you decide your action at any point in the game, based on a prediction of what will happen for each of the actions.

   a What are the variables in the model?
   b What are the dependencies between the variables?
   c What are the functional forms of these dependencies?
   d Which numerical parameters do you know for sure? Which do you have to estimate or learn from experience?

4 Write a Figaro program to represent the probabilistic model for this game. Assume certain values for the parameters that need to be estimated. Use the program to make the following decisions:

   a You're player 1 and were dealt the king of spades. Should you bet or pass?
   b You're player 2 and were dealt the king of hearts, and your opponent bets. Should you bet or fold?
   c Now, see if you can change the values of the estimated parameters in such a way that it would change your decision.

5 Describe three different sequences of choices through the generative process of your program from exercise 4. Using the parameters you used for the first version of the program, what's the probability of each sequence, with no evidence observed?

6 You suspect that your opponent isn't dealing the cards fairly. Specifically, you believe that with some unknown probability p, she's giving you the queen of hearts, while with the remaining probability $1 - p$, she's dealing the cards uniformly at random. You believe the probability that p is drawn from a Beta(1, 20) distribution. Out of 100 cards you've received, 40 are the queen of hearts. Use Figaro to compute the probability that your next card will be the queen of hearts.

5

Modeling dependencies with Bayesian and Markov networks

This chapter covers

- Types of relationships among variables in a probabilistic model and how these relationships translate into dependencies
- How to express these various types of dependencies in Figaro
- Bayesian networks: models that encode directed dependencies among variables
- Markov networks: models that encode undirected dependencies among variables
- Practical examples of Bayesian and Markov networks

In chapter 4, you learned about the relationships between probabilistic models and probabilistic programs, and you also saw the ingredients of a probabilistic model, which are variables, dependencies, functional forms, and numerical parameters. This chapter focuses on two modeling frameworks: Bayesian networks and Markov networks. Each framework is based on a different way of encoding dependencies.

Dependencies capture relationships between variables. Understanding the kinds of relationships and how they translate into dependencies in a probabilistic model is one of the most important skills you can acquire for building models. Accordingly, you'll learn all about various kinds of relationships and dependencies. In general, there are two kinds of dependencies between variables: directed dependencies, which express asymmetric relationships, and undirected dependencies, which turn into symmetric relationships. Bayesian networks encode directed dependencies, whereas Markov networks encode undirected dependencies. You'll also learn how to extend traditional Bayesian networks with programming language capabilities to benefit from the power of probabilistic programming.

After you understand the material in this chapter, you'll have a solid knowledge of the essentials of probabilistic programming. All probabilistic models boil down to a collection of directed and undirected dependencies. You'll know when to introduce a dependency between variables, whether to make it directed or undirected, and, if it's directed, what direction it should take. Chapter 6 builds on this knowledge to create more-complex models using data structures, and chapter 7 will further extend your skills with object-oriented modeling.

This chapter assumes you have a basic knowledge of Figaro, as appears in chapter 2. In particular, you should have familiarity with `Chain`, which underlies directed dependencies, and conditions and constraints, which are the basis for undirected dependencies. You'll also use the `CPD` and `RichCPD` elements that appear in chapter 4. Don't worry if you don't remember these concepts; I'll remind you of them here when you see them.

5.1 Modeling dependencies

Probabilistic reasoning is all about using dependencies between variables. Two variables are *dependent* if knowledge of one variable provides information about the other variable. Conversely, if knowing something about one variable tells you nothing about the other variable, the variables are *independent*.

Consider a computer system diagnosis application in which you're trying to reason about faults in a printing process. Suppose you have two variables, Printer Power Button On and Printer State. If you observe that the power button is off, you can infer that the printer state is down. Conversely, if you observe that the printer state is down, you can infer that the power button might be off. These two variables are clearly dependent.

Dependencies are used to model variables that are related in some way. Many kinds of relationships between variables exist, but only two kinds of dependencies:

- *Directed dependencies* go from one variable to the other. Typically, these model a cause-effect relationship between the variables.
- *Undirected dependencies* model relationships between variables where there's no obvious direction of influence between them.

The next two subsections describe both kinds of dependencies in detail and give plenty of examples.

5.1.1 *Directed dependencies*

Directed dependencies lead from one variable to another and are typically used to represent cause-effect relationships. For example, the printer's power button being off causes the printer to be down, so a direct dependency exists between Printer Power Button On and Printer State. Figure 5.1 illustrates this dependency, with a directed edge between the two variables. (*Edge* is the usual term for an arrow between two nodes in a graph.) The first variable (in this case, Printer Power Button On) is called the *parent*, and the second variable (Printer State) is called the *child*.

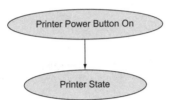

Figure 5.1 Directed dependency expressing cause-effect relationship

Why does the arrow go from cause to effect? A simple reason is that causes tend to happen before effects. More deeply, the answer is closely related to the concept of the generative model explored in chapter 4. Remember, a generative model describes a process for generating values of all of the variables in your model. Typically, the generative process simulates a real-world process. If a cause leads to an effect, you want to generate the value of the cause first, and use that value when you generate the effect. In our example, if you create a model of a printer, and imagine generating values for all of the variables in the model, you'll first generate a value for Printer Power Button On and then use this value to generate Printer State.

Now, it bears repeating that *the direction of a dependency isn't necessarily the direction of reasoning*. You can reason from the printer power button being off to the printer state being down, but you can also reason in the opposite direction: if the printer state is up, you know for sure that the power button isn't off. Many people make the mistake of constructing their models in the direction they intend to reason. In a diagnosis application, you might observe that the printer is down and try to determine its causes, so you'd reason from Printer State to Printer Power Button On. You might be tempted to make the arrow go from Printer State to Printer Power Button On. This is incorrect. The arrow should express the generative process, which follows the cause-effect direction.

I've said that directed dependencies typically model cause-effect relationships. In fact, cause-effect is just one example of a general class of asymmetric relationships between variables. Let's have a closer look at various kinds of asymmetric relationships—first, cause-effect relationships, and then other kinds.

VARIETIES OF CAUSE-EFFECT RELATIONSHIPS

Here are some kinds of cause-effect relationships:

- *What happens first to what happens next*—The most obvious kind of cause-effect relationship is between one thing that leads to another thing at a later time. For example, if someone turns the printer power off, then after that, the printer will be down. This temporal relationship is such a common characteristic of cause-effect relationships that you might think all cause-effect relationships involve time, but I don't agree with this.

- *Cause-effect of states*—Sometimes you can have two variables that represent different aspects of the state of the situation at a given point in time. For example, you might have one variable representing whether the printer power button is off and another representing whether the printer is down. Both of these are states that hold at the same moment in time. In this example, the printer power button being off causes the printer to be down, because it makes the printer have no power.

- *True value to measurement*—Whenever one variable is a *measurement* of the value of another variable, you say that the true value is a cause of the measurement. For example, suppose you have a Power Indicator Lit variable that represents whether the printer's power LED is lit. An asymmetric relationship exists from Printer Power Button On to Power Indicator Lit. Typically, measurements are produced by sensors, and there may be more than one measurement of the same value. Also, measurements are usually observed, and you want to reason from the measurements to the true values, so this is another example of the direction of the dependencies being different from the direction of reasoning.

- *Parameter to variable that uses the parameter*—For example, consider the bias of a coin, representing the probability that a toss will come out heads, and a toss of that coin. The toss uses the bias to determine the outcome. It's clear that the bias is generated first, and only then the individual toss. And when there are many tosses of the same coin, they're all generated after the bias.

ADDITIONAL ASYMMETRIC RELATIONSHIPS

The preceding cases are by far the most important and least ambiguous. If you understand these cases, you'll be 95% of the way to determining the correct direction of dependencies. Now let's go deeper by considering a variety of other relationships that, although obviously asymmetric, are ambiguous about the direction of dependency. I'll list these relationships and then describe a rule of thumb that can help you resolve the ambiguity.

- *Part to whole*—Often, the properties of part of an object lead to properties of the object as a whole. For example, consider a printer with toner and a paper feeder. Faults with either the toner or paper feeder, which are parts of the printer, can lead to faults with the printer as a whole. Other times, properties of the whole can determine properties of the part. For example, if the printer as a whole is badly made, both the paper feeder and the toner will likely be badly made.

- *Specific to general*—This one can also go both ways. A user can experience a printer problem in lots of ways, such as a paper jam or poor print quality. If the user experiences any of these specific problems, that user will experience the more general problem of a poor printing experience. In this case, the specific causes the general. On the other hand, imagine the process of generating an object. Typically, you generate the general properties of the object before refining them with specifics. For example, when generating a printer, you might first decide whether it's a laser or inkjet printer before generating its individual properties. Indeed, it doesn't make sense to generate the specific properties, which might be relevant for only a particular kind of printer, before you know what kind of printer it is.

- *Concrete/detailed to abstract/summary*—An example of a concrete-abstract relationship is between a score on a test and a letter grade. Many scores correspond to the same letter grade. Clearly, the teacher bases the letter grade on the test score, not the other way around, so the test score causes the letter grade. On the other hand, consider the process of generating a student and test results. You might first generate the abstract kind of student (for example, an A student or B student), and then generate the concrete test score.

Disambiguating cause-effect relationships

As you can see from the preceding examples, although it's clear that an asymmetric dependency exists in these cases, teasing out the direction of the dependency can be tricky. Here's an idea that can help. Imagine that someone is speaking a sentence in English to another person, as shown in the following illustration. The speaker has a certain meaning in mind for the whole sentence. From this meaning, the speaker generates words. This is a whole-part relationship, from the sentence to its words. Then the sentence is heard by somebody else. This person puts together the perceived meaning of the sentence from the words, creating a part-whole relationship.

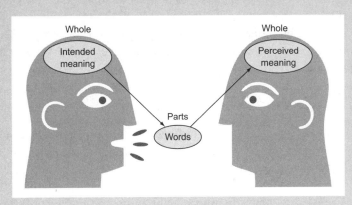

Communication of a sentence: the speaker's intended meaning of the whole sentence generates the words (parts), which in turn generate the hearer's perceived meaning of the whole sentence.

(continued)

If you look at this example closely, you can see that in the process of making the sentence, the meaning of the whole sentence is made before the individual words. But in the process of perceiving the sentence, the meaning of the sentence is perceived after the individual words. This isn't an ironclad rule, but often when you make something, first you make the general/abstract/whole thing and then refine it to produce the specific/concrete/detailed/many-parted thing. When you generate a printer, you first generate the general class of the whole printer. Then you generate the specific type of printer, and also detailed information about the components of the printer. Similarly, when generating the student, you first generate the abstract class of the student and then fill in the concrete test score. On the other hand, when you perceive and report something, you first perceive specific/concrete/detailed information about its parts, and then derive and summarize general/abstract properties about its whole. For example, the user who experiences a specific printer problem may summarize it in a general way, or a teacher grading a student will first observe the test score before reporting the letter grade. So here's the rule of thumb:

> *If you're modeling the making or definition of properties, dependencies go from the general, abstract, or whole concept to the specific, concrete, or parts. If you're modeling the perception and reporting of properties, dependencies go from the specific, concrete, or parts to the general, abstract, or whole.*

As I said earlier, if you understand the main cause-effect relationships, you'll get the directions right almost all of the time. In the exceptions to this rule, even experienced modelers can disagree on the appropriate direction of the dependencies. I hope that the rule of thumb I gave you will provide some guidance to help you build models.

DIRECTED DEPENDENCIES IN FIGARO

Remember the four ingredients of a probabilistic model? They're variables, dependencies, functional forms, and numerical parameters. Until now, you've assumed that the variables are given and focused on the dependencies. When you want to express these dependencies in Figaro, you need to provide a functional form and specify numerical parameters.

You can express directed dependencies in Figaro in a variety of ways. The general principle is to use a `Chain` of some sort as the functional form. Remember that `Chain` has two arguments:

- The parent element
- A chain function from a value of the parent element to a result element

`Chain(parentElement, chainFunction)` defines the following generative process: get a value for the parent from `parentElement`, then apply `chainFunction` to obtain `resultElement`, and finally get a value from `resultElement`.

When expressing a directed dependency by using `Chain`, the `parentElement` is, naturally, the parent. The chain function specifies a probability distribution over the child for each value of the parent. Figaro has a lot of constructs that use `Chain`, so in many cases you're using `Chain` even if it doesn't look like it.

Here are some equivalent examples, all expressing that if the printer power button is off, the printer will definitely be down, but if the power button is on, the printer could be up or down:

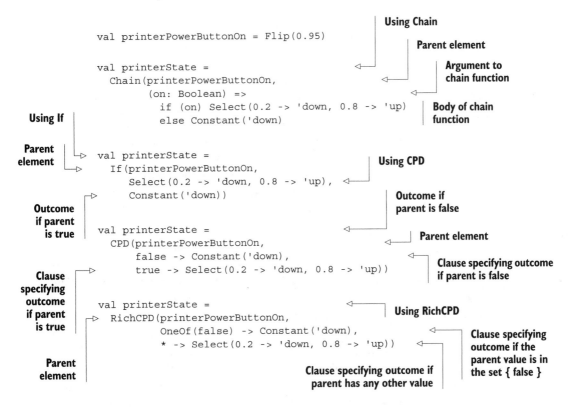

As mentioned earlier, one kind of asymmetric relationship is between a parameter and a variable that depends on the parameter, such as the bias of a coin and a toss of that coin. Again, this can be expressed using a `Chain` or using a compound version of an atomic element. Here are a couple of equivalent examples:

```
val toss = Chain(bias, (d: Double) => Flip(d))

val toss = Flip(bias)
```

5.1.2   Undirected dependencies

You've seen that directed dependencies can represent a variety of asymmetric relationships. Undirected dependencies model relationships between variables where there's no obvious direction between them. These kinds of relationships are called *symmetric relationships*. If you have variables that are correlated, but there's no obvious generative process whereby one variable is generated before the other, an undirected dependency might be appropriate. Symmetric relationships can arise in two ways:

- *Two effects of the same cause, where the cause isn't modeled explicitly*—For example, two measurements of the same value, when you don't have a variable for the value, or two consequences of the same event, when you don't have a variable for the event. Clearly, if you don't know the underlying value of an event, the two measurements or consequences are related. Imagine, in the printer scenario, that you have separate variables for the print quality and speed of printing. If you didn't have a variable representing the state of the printer, these two variables would be related, because they're two aspects of printing that might have the same underlying cause.

  You might ask, why don't we include a variable for the cause in our model? One possible answer is that the cause is much more complex than the effects and would be difficult to model accurately. In this chapter, you'll see an example of image reconstruction. The image is a two-dimensional effect of a complex three-dimensional scene. It might be harder to create a correct probabilistic model of three-dimensional scenes than to model the relationships between pixels in the image.

- *Two causes of the same known effect*—This one's interesting. Usually, there's no relationship between two causes of the same effect. For example, the paper feeder status of a printer and the toner level both influence the status of the printer as a whole, but the paper feeder status and toner level are independent. But if you learn that the printer isn't printing well, suddenly the paper feeder status and toner level become dependent. If you learn that the toner is low, that might lead you to believe that the reason the print quality is poor is due to low toner rather than obstructed paper flow. In this example, the overall printer status is the effect, and the toner level and paper feeder status are the possible causes, and the two causes become dependent when the effect is known. This is an example of an *induced dependency*, which you'll learn about in more detail in section 5.2.3. If you don't have a variable for the effect, this becomes a symmetric relationship between the two causes. But it's less usual to leave the common effect of the two causes out of the model.

EXPRESSING UNDIRECTED DEPENDENCIES IN FIGARO

You can express asymmetric relationships in Figaro in two ways: using constraints and using conditions. Each has an advantage and a disadvantage. The advantage of the constraints method is that it's conceptually simpler. But the numbers that go in the constraints are hardcoded and can't be learned in Figaro because they aren't accessible to a learning algorithm. The advantage of the method that uses conditions is that the numbers can be learned.

The basic principle behind the two approaches is similar. Section 5.5 describes how undirected dependencies are encoded in detail, but here's the short version.

When an undirected dependency exists between two variables, some joint values of the two variables are preferred to others. This can be achieved by assigning weights to the different joint values. A constraint encodes the weights by specifying a function from a joint value of the two variables to a real number representing the weight of that value. In the conditions approach, essentially the same information is encoded but in a more complex way.

For example, let's encode a relationship between two adjacent pixels in an image. These relationships have an "all else being equal" nature. For example, you might believe that, all else being equal, the two pixels are three times as likely to have the same color as they are to have different colors. In actuality, many relationships may affect the colors of the two pixels, so it's not actually three times as likely that they have the same color.

Here's how to express this relationship in Figaro using the constraints approach. Let's call the two pixel colors `color1` and `color2`. To keep the example simple, you'll assume that colors are Boolean. Remember that a constraint is a function from the value of an element to a `Double`. You need to create an element that represents the pair of `color1` and `color2` so you can specify a constraint on the pair. You can do this as follows:

```
import com.cra.figaro.library.compound.^^
val pair = ^^(color1, color2)
```

⤺ `^ ^` **is the Figaro pair constructor.**

Now you have to define the function that implements the constraint:

```
def sameColorConstraint(pair: (Boolean, Boolean)) =
  if (pair._1 == pair._2) 0.3; else 0.1
```

⤺ **The test checks whether the first component of the pair equals the second component.**

Finally, you apply the constraint to the pair of colors:

```
pair.setConstraint(sameColorConstraint _)
```

⤺ **The underscore indicates that you want the function itself and not to apply it.**

Figaro interprets the constraint exactly how you'd expect. All else being equal, a state in which the two components of the pair are equal (in other words, both colors are equal) will be three times as likely as one where they're unequal. These constraints come together in defining the probability distribution in the correct way, as defined in section 5.5. Unfortunately, however, the numbers 0.3 and 0.1 are buried inside the constraint function, so they can't be learned from data.

For the conditions approach, I'll show you how it works in code and then explain why it's correct. First, you define an auxiliary Boolean element, which you'll call `same-ColorConstraintValue`. You then define it so that the probability that it comes out true is equal to the value of the constraint. Finally, you'll add a condition that says that this auxiliary element must be `true`. This can be achieved using an observation:

```
val sameColorConstraintValue =
  Chain(color1, color2,
        (b1: Boolean, b2: Boolean) =>
          if (b1 == b2) Flip(0.3); else Flip(0.1))
sameColorConstraintValue.observe(true)
```

This code is equivalent to the constraints version. To see this, realize that a condition causes any value that violates the condition to have probability 0; otherwise, it has probability 1. The overall probability of any state is obtained by combining the probabilities resulting from the definition of elements and from conditions or constraints. For example, suppose that the two colors are equal. Using the definition of `Chain`, `sameColorConstraintValue` will come out `true` with probability 0.3 and `false` with probability 0.7. If `sameColorConstraintValue` comes out `true`, the condition will have probability 1, whereas if it's `false`, the condition will have probability 0. Therefore, the combined probability of the condition is $(0.3 \times 1) + (0.7 \times 0) = 0.3$. Similarly, if the two colors are unequal, the combined probability is $(0.1 \times 1) + (0.9 \times 0) = 0.1$. So you see that the colors being the same is three times as likely, all else being equal, as the colors being different. This is exactly the same result as the one you got with the constraint.

This construction using conditions is general enough to cover all asymmetric relationships. The advantage of this approach, as you can see, is that the numbers 0.3 and 0.1 are inside `Flip` elements, so you could make them depend on other aspects of the model. For example, suppose you wanted to learn the degree to which two adjacent pixels are more likely to be the same color than different. You can create an element, perhaps defined using a beta distribution, to represent the weight. You can then use this element inside the `Flip` instead of 0.3. Then, given data, you can learn a distribution over the value of the weight.

5.1.3   *Direct and indirect dependencies*

Before you move on to look at Bayesian and Markov networks, I want to make an important point. A typical probabilistic model has many pairs of variables, and so knowledge of one variable changes your beliefs about the other. By definition, these are all cases of a dependency between variables. But most of these dependencies are *indirect*: they don't go directly between two variables but instead go through some intermediary variables. To be precise, the reason knowledge about the first variable changes your beliefs about the second is because knowledge about the first variable changes your beliefs about the intermediary variables, which in turn changes your beliefs about the second variable.

For example, look at figure 5.2, which has three variables: Printer Power Button On, Printer State, and Number of Printed Pages. Clearly, Printer Power Button On and Number of Printed Pages have a dependency. If you know that the power button

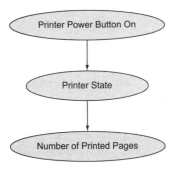

Figure 5.2 **Printer Power Button On has an indirect relationship with Number of Printed Pages that goes through the intermediary variable Printer State.**

is off, you'll believe that the number of printed pages is zero. But in the figure, the dependency from Printer Power Button On to Number of Printed Pages passes through an intermediary variable, which is Printer State. This means that the reason knowledge about Printer Power Button On changes your beliefs about Number of Printed Pages is that it first changes your beliefs about Printer State, and the changed beliefs about Printer State in turn change your beliefs about Number of Printed Pages. If you know the power button is off, that tells you that the printer is down, which leads you to believe that no pages will be printed.

> **TERMINOLOGY ALERT** Earlier I talked about directed and undirected dependencies, and now I'm talking about direct and indirect dependencies. Although the names are similar, they have different meanings. A *direct* dependency goes directly between two variables; its antonym is indirect, which goes through intermediary variables. A *directed* dependency has a direction from one variable to another, as opposed to an undirected dependency that has no direction. You can have a direct undirected dependency and an indirect directed dependency.

Let's look at another example, this time involving undirected dependencies. Earlier, I gave an example of adjacent pixels in an image that have an undirected dependency between them. What about nonadjacent pixels? Consider the example in figure 5.3. If you know that pixel 11 is red, that will lead you to believe that pixel 12 is likely to be red, which will in turn lead you to believe that pixel 13 is likely to be red. This is an obvious example of an indirect dependency, because knowledge about pixel 11 influences beliefs about pixel 13 only through the intermediary variable pixel 12.

It's important to recognize which dependencies in your domain are direct and which are indirect. In both Bayesian and Markov networks, you create a graph with

Figure 5.3 **Pixel 11 has an indirect relationship with pixel 13 that goes through the intermediary variable pixel 12.**

edges between variables to represent the dependencies. In a Bayesian network, these are directed edges, whereas in a Markov network, they're undirected. You draw an edge only for direct dependencies. If two variables have only an indirect dependency, you don't draw an edge between them.

Next, you'll look at Bayesian networks, which are models that represent directed dependencies, and then at Markov networks, which are models that represent undirected dependencies. I do want to point out, however, that just because there are separate modeling frameworks for directed and undirected dependencies doesn't mean you have to choose one or the other for your model. Other frameworks combine both kinds of dependencies in a single model. It's easy to do that in a probabilistic program: you use the generative definition of elements to encode directed dependencies, and add any constraints you want to express undirected dependencies.

5.2   *Using Bayesian networks*

You've seen that encoding relationships between variables is essential to probabilistic modeling. In this section, you'll learn about Bayesian networks, which are the standard framework for encoding asymmetric relationships using directed dependencies. You've already seen Bayesian networks in chapter 4, in the context of the Rembrandt example. This section provides a more thorough treatment, including a full definition and an explanation of the reasoning patterns you can use.

5.2.1   *Bayesian networks defined*

A Bayesian network is a representation of a probabilistic model consisting of three components:

- A set of variables with their corresponding domains
- A directed acyclic graph in which each variable is a node
- For each variable, a conditional probability distribution (CPD) over the variable, given its parents

SET OF VARIABLES WITH CORRESPONDING DOMAINS
The example in figure 5.4 shows three variables: Subject, Size, and Brightness. The domain of a variable specifies which values are possible for that variable. The domain of Subject is {People, Landscape}, the domain of Size is {Small, Medium, Large}, and the domain of Brightness is {Dark, Bright}.

DIRECTED ACYCLIC GRAPH
Directed means that each edge in the graph has a direction; it goes from one variable to another. The first variable is called the *parent*, and the second variable is called the *child*. In figure 5.4 Subject is a parent of both Size and Brightness. The word *acyclic* means that there are no cycles in the graph: there are no *directed cycles* that follow the direction of the arrows; you can't start at a node, follow the arrows, and end up at the same node. But you can have an *undirected cycle* that would be a cycle if you ignored

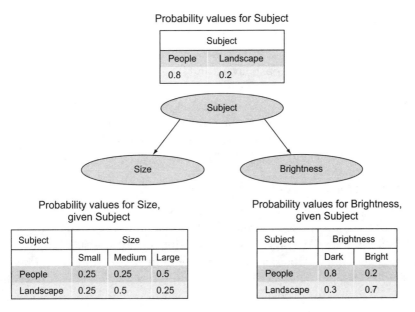

Probability values for Subject

Subject	
People	Landscape
0.8	0.2

Probability values for Size, given Subject

Subject	Size		
	Small	Medium	Large
People	0.25	0.25	0.5
Landscape	0.25	0.5	0.25

Probability values for Brightness, given Subject

Subject	Brightness	
	Dark	Bright
People	0.8	0.2
Landscape	0.3	0.7

Figure 5.4   A three-node Bayesian network

the directions of the edges. This concept is illustrated in figure 5.5. The graph on the left has a directed cycle A-B-D-C-A. In the graph on the right, the cycle A-B-D-C-A sometimes runs counter to the direction of the arrows, so it's an undirected cycle. Therefore, the graph on the left isn't allowed, but the graph on the right is allowed. This point is important, because later, when you allow undirected edges to express symmetric dependencies, you'll be allowed to have undirected cycles.

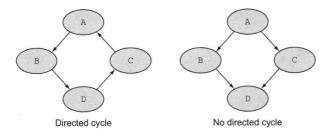

Directed cycle   No directed cycle

Figure 5.5   A directed cycle is a cycle that follows the arrows and ends up where it started.

CONDITIONAL PROBABILITY DISTRIBUTION OVER THE VARIABLE

A CPD specifies a probability distribution over the child variable, given the values of its parents. This CPD considers every possible assignment of values to the parents, when the value of a parent can be any value in its domain. For each assignment, it defines a probability distribution over the child. In figure 5.6, each variable has a CPD. Subject is a root of the network, so it has no parents. When a variable has no parents, the CPD specifies a single probability distribution over the variable. In this example, Subject takes the value People with probability 0.8 and Landscape with probability 0.2. Size has a parent, which is Subject, so its CPD has a row for each value of Subject. The CPD says that when Subject has value People, the distribution over Size makes Size have value Small with probability 0.25, Medium with probability 0.25, and Large with probability 0.5. When Subject has value Landscape, Size has a different distribution. Finally, Brightness also has parent Subject, and its CPD also has a row for each value of Subject.

5.2.2 *How a Bayesian network defines a probability distribution*

That's all there is to the definition of Bayesian networks. Now, let's see how a Bayesian network defines a probability distribution. The first thing you need to do is define the possible worlds. For a Bayesian network, a possible world consists of an assignment of values to each of the variables, making sure the value of each variable is in its domain. For example, <Subject = People, Size = Small, Brightness = Bright> is a possible world.

Next, you define the probability of a possible world. This is simple. All you have to do is identify the entry in the CPD of each variable that matches the values of the parents and child in the possible world. The process is illustrated in figure 5.6. For

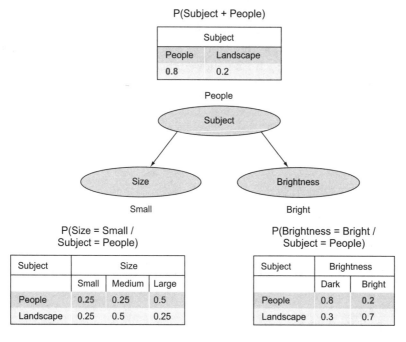

P(Subject = People, Size = Small, Brightness = Bright) = 0.8 x 0.25 x 0.2 = 0.04

Figure 5.6 Computing the probability of a possible world by multiplying the appropriate entries in each CPD

example, for the possible world <Subject = People, Size = Small, Brightness = Bright>, the entry for Subject is 0.8, which is from the column labeled Subject. For Size, you look at the row corresponding to Subject = People and the column corresponding to Size = Small and get the entry 0.25. Finally, for Brightness, you again look at the row corresponding to Subject = People and this time take the column labeled Bright to get the entry 0.2. Finally, you multiply all these entries together to get the probability of the possible world, which is $0.8 \times 0.25 \times 0.2 = 0.04$.

If you go through this process for every possible world, the probabilities will add up to 1, just as they're supposed to. This is always the case for a Bayesian network. So you've seen how a Bayesian network defines a valid probability distribution. Now that you understand exactly what a Bayesian network consists of and what it means, let's see how to use one to derive beliefs about some variables, given knowledge of other variables.

5.2.3 *Reasoning with Bayesian networks*

A Bayesian network encodes a lot of independencies that hold between variables. Recall that independence between two variables means that learning something about one variable doesn't tell you anything new about the other variable. From the preceding example, you can see that Number of Printed Pages and Printer Power Button On *aren't* independent. When you learn that no pages were printed, that reduces the probability that the power button is on.

Conditional independence is similar. Two variables are conditionally independent given a third variable if, *after the third variable is known,* learning something about the first variable doesn't tell you anything new about the second. A criterion called *d-separation* determines when two variables in a Bayesian network are conditionally independent of a third set of variables. The criterion is a little involved, so I won't provide a formal definition. Instead, I'll describe the basic principles and show you a few examples.

The basic idea is that reasoning *flows along a path* from one variable to another. In the example of figure 5.4, reasoning can flow from Size to Brightness along the path Size-Subject-Brightness. You saw a glimpse of this idea in section 5.1.3 on direct and indirect dependencies. In an indirect dependency, reasoning flows from one variable to another variable via other intermediary variables. In this example, Subject is the intermediary variable between Size and Brightness. In a Bayesian network, reasoning can flow along a path as long as the path isn't *blocked* at some variable.

In most cases, a path is blocked at a variable if the variable is observed. So if Subject is observed, the path Size-Subject-Brightness is blocked. This means that if you observe Size, it won't change your beliefs about Brightness if Subject is also observed. Another way of saying this is that Size is conditionally independent of Brightness, given Subject. In our model, the painter's choice of subject determines the size and the brightness, but after choosing the subject, the size and brightness are generated independently.

CONVERGING ARROWS AND INDUCED DEPENDENCIES

One other case may seem counterintuitive at first. In this case, a path is blocked at a variable if the variable is unobserved, and becomes unblocked if the variable is observed. I'll illustrate this situation by extending our example, as shown in figure 5.7. You have a new variable called Material, which could be oil or watercolor or something else. Naturally, Material is a cause of Brightness (perhaps oil paintings are brighter than watercolors), so the network has a directed edge from Material to Brightness. Here, you have two parents of the same child. This is called a *converging arrows* pattern, because edges from Subject and Material converge at Brightness.

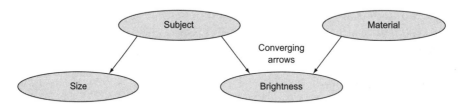

Figure 5.7   Extended painting example, including converging arrows between two parents of the same child

Now, let's think about reasoning between Subject and Material. According to the model, Subject and Material are generated independently. So this is true:

(1) Subject and Material are independent when nothing is observed.

But what happens when you observe that the painting is bright? According to our model, landscapes tend to be brighter than people paintings. After observing that the painting is bright, you'll infer that the painting is more likely to be a landscape. Let's say you then observe that the painting is an oil painting, which paintings also tend to be bright. This observation provides an alternative explanation of the brightness of our painting. Therefore, the probability that the painting is a landscape is discounted somewhat compared to what it was after you observed that the painting is bright but before you observed that it's an oil painting. You can see that reasoning is flowing from Material to Subject along the path Material-Brightness-Subject. So you get the following statement:

(2) Subject and Material aren't conditionally independent, given Brightness.

What you have here is the opposite pattern from the usual. You have a path that's blocked when the intermediary variable is unobserved, and becomes unblocked when the variable is observed. This kind of situation is called an *induced dependency*—a dependency between two variables that's induced by observing a third variable. Any converging arrows pattern in a Bayesian network can lead to an induced dependency.

A path between two variables can include both ordinary patterns and converging arrows. Reasoning flows along the path only if it's not blocked at any node on the

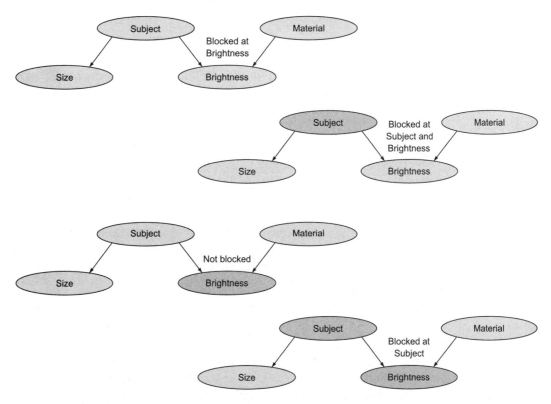

Figure 5.8 Examples of blocked and unblocked paths that combine an ordinary pattern with a converging arrows pattern. Each figure shows the path from Size to Material, with Subject and Brightness either unobserved or observed.

path. Figure 5.8 shows four examples for the path Size-Subject-Brightness-Material. In the top-left example, neither Subject nor Brightness is observed, and the path is blocked at Brightness because it has converging arrows. In the next example, on the right, Subject is now observed, so the path is blocked at both Subject and Brightness. In the next example, on the left, Subject is unobserved and Brightness is observed, which is precisely the condition required for the path not to be blocked at either Subject or Brightness. Finally, in the bottom right, Subject is observed in addition to Brightness, so the path is blocked there.

5.3 *Exploring a Bayesian network example*

Now that you've learned the basic concepts of Bayesian networks, let's look at an example of troubleshooting a printer problem. I'll first show you how to design the network and then show you all of the ways of reasoning with the network. I'll save a discussion of learning the parameters of the network for chapter 12, where you'll explore a useful design pattern for parameter learning.

5.3.1   *Designing a computer system diagnosis model*

Imagine that you're designing a help desk application for technical support. You want to help the tech support person identify the causes of faults as quickly as possible. You can use a probabilistic reasoning system for this application—given evidence, consisting of reports from the user and diagnostic tests, you want to determine the internal state of the system. For this application, it's natural to use a Bayesian network to represent the probabilistic model.

When you design a Bayesian network, you typically go through three steps: choosing the variables and their corresponding domains, specifying the network structure, and encoding the CPDs. You'll see how to do this in Figaro.

In practice, you don't usually go through all steps in a linear fashion, choosing all of the variables, building the entire network structure, and then writing down the CPDs. Usually, you'll build up the network a bit at a time, refining it as you go. You'll take that approach here. First, you'll build a network for a general print fault model and then drill down into a more detailed model of the printer.

GENERAL PRINT FAULT MODEL: VARIABLES

You want to model possible reports from the user, the faults that might be involved, and system factors that might lead to those faults. You'll introduce variables for all these things.

You start with a Print Result Summary. This represents the user's overall experience of the print result at a high level of abstraction. When the user first calls the help desk, that user may provide only a high-level summary like this. Three results are possible: (1) printing happens perfectly (you'll label this excellent); (2) printing happens, but isn't quite right (poor); (3) no printing happens at all (none).

Next, you consider various concrete aspects of the print result. These are Number of Printed Pages, which could be zero, some of the pages, or all of the pages; Prints Quickly, a Boolean variable indicating whether printing happens in a reasonable time; and Good Print Quality, another Boolean variable. One reason for modeling each of these aspects individually is that they differentiate between different faults. For example, if no pages print, it might be because the network is down. But if some but not all of the pages print, the problem is less likely to be the network and more likely to be user error.

So you consider all elements of the system that might influence the printing result. These include the Printer State, which could be good, poor, or out; the Software State, which could be correct, glitchy, or crashed; the Network State, which could be up, intermittent, or down; and User Command Correct, which is a Boolean variable.

GENERAL PRINT FAULT MODEL: NETWORK STRUCTURE

Considering the variables you've defined, there are three groups: the abstract Print Result Summary, the various concrete aspects of the print result, and the system states that influence the print result. Accordingly, it makes sense to design the network in three layers. What should be the order of the layers?

Cause-effect relationships exist between the system state variables and concrete print result variables. For example, the Network State being down is a cause of a failure to Print Quickly. In addition, concrete-abstract relationships exist between the individual print result variables and the overall Print Result Summary. In section 5.1.1, I said that these relationships could go in either direction. In our application, you're modeling the user's experience and reporting of the print result, so according to the rule of thumb I introduced there, the right direction is to go from the concrete print result variables to the abstract summary. So the order of layers in our network is (1) system state variables, (2) concrete print result variables, (3) Print Result Summary.

The network structure is shown in figure 5.9. You can see the three layers, but there's not always an edge from every variable in one layer to variables in the next layer. This is because some of the print result variables depend on the state of only some of the system components. For example, whether the print quality is good depends on the state of the printer but not on the network. Likewise, the speed of printing according to our model depends only on the network and the software. Whether these statements are correct is up for debate; the main point is that in any application, arguments can be made to remove some of the edges. The benefit of removing edges is smaller CPDs.

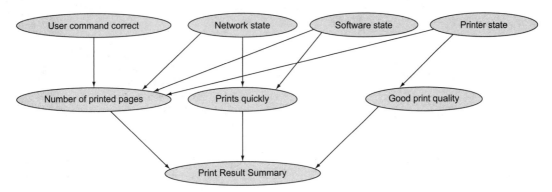

Figure 5.9   Network structure for the general print fault part of our computer system diagnosis model

GENERAL PRINT FAULT MODEL: CPDS
I'll show you the CPD design through Figaro code, making sure to explain the most interesting items. Section 5.1.1 showed you various ways CPDs can be defined in Figaro. You'll use a variety of them here.

![Listing 5.1] **Listing 5.1   Implementing the general print fault model in Figaro**

This comes from the detailed printer model coming next. →

```
val printerState = …

val softwareState =
  Select(0.8 -> 'correct, 0.15 -> 'glitchy, 0.05 -> 'crashed)
val networkState =
  Select(0.7 -> 'up, 0.2 -> 'intermittent, 0.1 -> 'down)
val userCommandCorrect =
  Flip(0.65)
```
For root variables, we have atomic CPDs like Select or Flip.

```
val numPrintedPages =
  RichCPD(userCommandCorrect, networkState,
        softwareState, printerState,
        (*, *, *, OneOf('out)) -> Constant('zero),
        (*, *, OneOf('crashed), *) -> Constant('zero),
        (*, OneOf('down), *, *) -> Constant('zero),
        (OneOf(false), *, *, *) ->
          Select(0.3 -> 'zero, 0.6 -> 'some, 0.1 -> 'all),
        (OneOf(true), *, *, *) ->
          Select(0.01 -> 'zero, 0.01 -> 'some, 0.98 -> 'all))
```
numPrintedPages uses RichCPD to represent the dependency on the user command and the network, software, and printer states.

```
val printsQuickly =
  Chain(networkState, softwareState,
        (network: Symbol, software: Symbol) =>
          if (network == 'down || software == 'crashed)
                Constant(false)
          else if (network == 'intermittent || software == 'glitchy)
                Flip(0.5)
          else Flip(0.9))
```
printsQuickly uses Chain to represent the dependency on network and software states.

```
val goodPrintQuality =
  CPD(printerState,
      'good -> Flip(0.95),
      'poor -> Flip(0.3),
      'out -> Constant(false))
```
goodPrintQuality uses a simpleCPD to represent the dependency on the printer state.

```
val printResultSummary =
  Apply(numPrintedPages, printsQuickly, goodPrintQuality,
        (pages: Symbol, quickly: Boolean, quality: Boolean) =>
          if (pages == 'zero) 'none
          else if (pages == 'some || !quickly || !quality) 'poor
          else 'excellent)
```
Because it's fully determined by its parents, printResult-Summary uses Apply.

This code uses several techniques to represent the probabilistic dependence of a child on its parents:

- numPrintedPages uses RichCPD, which implements the following logic: If the printer state is out, or the network state is down, or the software is crashed, zero pages will be printed, regardless of the state of other parents. Otherwise, if the user issues the wrong command, it's unlikely all of the pages will be printed, but if the user issues the right command, it's highly likely that all pages will be printed.

- `printsQuickly` uses `Chain` to implement the following logic: If the network is down or software is crashed, it definitely won't print quickly. Otherwise, if either the network is intermittent or the software is glitchy, printing quickly is a toss-up. If both the network and software are in good states, it will usually print quickly (but not guaranteed).

- `goodPrintQuality` uses a simple `CPD`. If the printer is out, there definitely won't be good-quality printing. If the printer is in a poor state, there probably won't be good-quality printing. Even if the printer is in a good state, good-quality printing isn't guaranteed (because that's the way printers are).

- `printSummary` is a deterministic variable: It's fully determined by its parents without any uncertainty. You can use `Apply` instead of `Chain` for a deterministic variable.

DETAILED PRINTER MODEL

This section goes through the detailed printer model more quickly, because many of the principles are the same. The network structure is shown in figure 5.10. Three factors influence the printer state: Paper Flow, Toner Level, and Printer Power Button On. The model adds a new kind of variable, which you haven't seen, an indicator or measurement. Paper Jam Indicator On is a measurement of the Paper Flow, and Toner Low Indicator On is a measurement of the Toner Level. As discussed in section 5.1.1, the relationship between a true value and its measurement is a kind of cause-effect relationship, so you have an edge from Paper Flow to Paper Jam Indicator On and from Toner Level to Toner Low Indicator On.

Here's the code defining the CPDs, which is mostly straightforward.

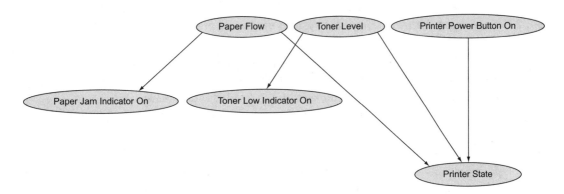

Figure 5.10   Network structure for detailed printer model

Listing 5.2   Detailed printer model in Figaro

```
val printerPowerButtonOn = Flip(0.95)
val tonerLevel = Select(0.7 -> 'high, 0.2 -> 'low, 0.1 -> 'out)        <─┐
val tonerLowIndicatorOn =
    If(printerPowerButtonOn,                        Recall that a single-quote
        CPD(paperFlow,                              character ' indicates the
            'high -> Flip(0.2),                          Scala Symbol type.
            'low -> Flip(0.6),
            'out -> Flip(0.99)),
        Constant(false))
val paperFlow = Select(0.6 -> 'smooth, 0.2 -> 'uneven, 0.2 -> 'jammed)

val paperJamIndicatorOn =
    If(printerPowerButtonOn,              A CPD nested inside an If. If printer
        CPD(tonerLevel,                   power button is on, toner low
            'high -> Flip(0.1),           indicator depends on toner level. If
            'low -> Flip(0.3),            power button is off, toner indicator
            'out -> Flip(0.99)),          will be off because there's no power,
        Constant(false))                  regardless of the toner level.

val printerState =
    Apply(printerPowerButtonOn, tonerLevel, paperFlow,
        (power: Boolean, toner: Symbol, paper: Symbol) => {        Printer state is
            if (power) {                                           a deterministic
                if (toner == 'high && paper == 'smooth) 'good      summary of
                else if (toner == 'out || paper == 'out) 'out      the factors that
                else 'poor                                         make it up.
            } else 'out
        })
```

To summarize the example, the full Bayesian network structure is shown in figure 5.11. You can also see the entire program in the book's code under chap05/PrinterProblem.scala.

5.3.2   *Reasoning with the computer system diagnosis model*

This section shows how to reason with the computer system diagnosis model you just built. The Figaro mechanics of reasoning are simple, but the reasoning patterns you get out of it are interesting and illustrate the concepts introduced in section 5.2.3. All of the reasoning patterns in this section are divided into separate steps in the code for the chapter. Comment out the steps you don't want to execute, to highlight each step as it's presented.

QUERYING A PRIOR PROBABILITY

First, let's query the probability that the printer power button is on, without any evidence. This is the prior probability. You can use the following code:

```
val answerWithNoEvidence =                                     Compute
    VariableElimination.probability(printerPowerButtonOn, true) P(Printer
println("Prior probability the printer power button is on = " + Power Button
    answerWithNoEvidence)                                       On = true)
```

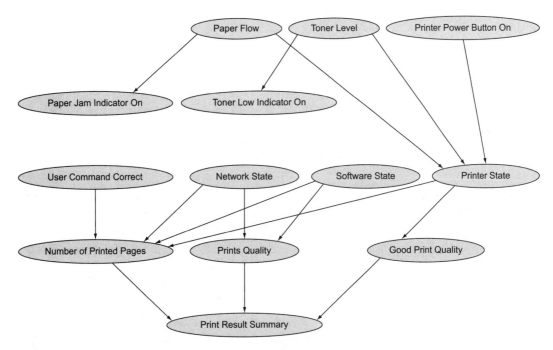

Figure 5.11   **The full network for the computer system diagnosis example**

This prints the following result:

```
Prior probability the printer power button is on = 0.95
```

If you look back at the model, you'll see that `printerPowerButtonOn` is defined using the following line:

```
val printerPowerButtonOn = Flip(0.95)
```

You can see that the answer to the query is exactly what you'd get if you ignored the entire model except for this definition. This is an example of a general rule: the network downstream from a variable is relevant to the variable only if it has evidence. In particular, for prior probabilities, there's no evidence, so you don't care about the downstream network.

QUERYING WITH EVIDENCE
What happens if you introduce evidence? Let's query the model for the probability that the printer power button is on, given that the print result is poor, implying there was some result, but it wasn't what the user wanted. You can use the following code:

```
printResultSummary.observe('poor)
val answerIfPrintResultPoor =
  VariableElimination.probability(printerPowerButtonOn, true)
println("Probability the printer power button is on given a poor "
  + "result = " + answerIfPrintResultPoor)
```

> **Compute P(Printer Power Button On = true | Print Result = poor)**

This prints the following result:

```
Probability the printer power button is on given a poor result = 1.0
```

This might be surprising! The probability is higher than if you didn't have any evidence about printing. If you think about the model, you can understand why. A poor printing result can happen only if at least some of the pages are printed, which won't be the case if the power is off. Therefore, the probability the power is on is 1.

Now let's query with the evidence that nothing is printed:

```
printResultSummary.observe('none')
val answerIfPrintResultNone =
  VariableElimination.probability(printerPowerButtonOn, true)
println("Probability the printer power button is on given empty "
  + "result = " + answerIfPrintResultNone)
```

Compute P(Printer Power Button On = true | Printer Result = none)

Now the result is as follows:

```
Probability the printer power button is on given empty result =
0.8573402523786461
```

This is as you expect. The power button being off is a good explanation for an empty print result, so its probability increases based on the evidence.

INDEPENDENCE AND BLOCKING

Section 5.2.3 introduced the concept of a blocked path and the relationship of this concept to conditional independence. This concept can be illustrated with three variables: Print Result Summary, Printer Power Button On, and Printer State. In figure 5.11, you see that the path from Printer Power Button On to Print Result Summary goes through Printer State. Because this isn't a converging arrows pattern, the path is blocked if Printer State is observed. Indeed, this is the case, as you'll see now:

```
printResultSummary.unobserve()
printerState.observe('out')
val answerIfPrinterStateOut =
  VariableElimination.probability(printerPowerButtonOn, true)
println("Probability the printer power button is on given " +
    "out printer state = " + answerIfPrinterStateOut)
```

Compute P(Printer Power Button On = true | Printer State = out)

```
printResultSummary.observe('none')
val answerIfPrinterStateOutAndResultNone =
  VariableElimination.probability(printerPowerButtonOn, true)
println("Probability the printer power button is on given " +
    "out printer state and empty result = " +
    answerIfPrinterStateOutAndResultNone)
```

Compute P(Printer Power Button On = true | Printer State = out, Print Result Summary = none)

This prints the following:

```
Probability the printer power button is on given out printer state =
0.6551724137931032
Probability the printer power button is on given out printer state and empty
result = 0.6551724137931033
```

You can see that learning that the print result is empty doesn't change the probability that the printer power button is on, after you already know that the printer state is out. This is because Print Result Summary is conditionally independent from Printer Power Button On, given Printer State.

REASONING BETWEEN DIFFERENT EFFECTS OF THE SAME CAUSE

All of the reasoning paths you've seen so far have gone straight up the network. You can also combine both directions when reasoning. It's easy to see this when you consider what a measurement tells you about the value it's measuring, and what that can inform in turn. In our example, Toner Low Indicator On is a child of Toner Level, and Toner Level is a parent of Printer State. If the toner level is low, it's less likely that the printer state is good. Meanwhile, the toner low indicator being on is a sign that the toner level is low. It stands to reason that if you observe that the toner low indicator is on, it should reduce the probability that the printer state is good. You can see that this is the case with the following code:

```
printResultSummary.unobserve()
printerState.unobserve()
val printerStateGoodPrior =
  VariableElimination.probability(printerState, 'good)
println("Prior probability the printer state is good = "
      + printerStateGoodPrior)
```
Compute P(Printer State = good)

```
tonerLowIndicatorOn.observe(true)
val printerStateGoodGivenTonerLowIndicatorOn =
  VariableElimination.probability(printerState, 'good)
println("Probability printer state is good given low toner "
      + "indicator = " + printerStateGoodGivenTonerLowIndicatorOn)
```
Compute P(Printer State = good | Toner Low Indicator On = true)

This prints the following:

```
Prior probability the printer state is good = 0.39899999999999997
Probability the printer state is good given low toner indicator =
0.23398328690807796
```

You can see that the probability that the printer state is good decreases when you observe the low toner indicator, as expected.

REASONING BETWEEN DIFFERENT CAUSES OF THE SAME EFFECT: INDUCED DEPENDENCIES

As discussed in section 5.2.3, reasoning between different causes of the same effect is different from other kinds of reasoning, because it involves converging arrows, which lead to an induced dependency. For an example, let's use Software State and Network State, which are both parents of Prints Quickly. First, you'll get the prior probability that the software state is correct:

```
tonerLowIndicatorOn.unobserve()
val softwareStateCorrectPrior =
  VariableElimination.probability(softwareState, 'correct)
println("Prior probability the software state is correct = " +
      softwareStateCorrectPrior)
```
Compute P(Software State = correct)

This prints the following:

```
Prior probability the software state is correct = 0.8
```

Next, you'll observe that the network is up and query the software state again:

```
networkState.observe('up')
val softwareStateCorrectGivenNetworkUp =
  VariableElimination.probability(softwareState, 'correct)
println("Probability software state is correct given network up = " +
        softwareStateCorrectGivenNetworkUp)
```

Compute P(Software State = correct | Network State = up)

This prints the following:

```
Probability software state is correct given network up = 0.8
```

The probability hasn't changed, even though there's a clear path from Network State to Software State via Prints Quickly! This shows that in general, two causes of the same effect are independent. This is intuitively correct: the network being up has no bearing on whether the software state is correct.

Now, if you know that the printer isn't printing quickly, that's different. If you see the printer printing slowly, our model provides two possible explanations: a network problem or a software problem. If you observe that the network is up, it must be a software problem. You can see this with the following code:

Compute P(Software State = correct | Prints Quickly = false)

```
networkState.unobserve()
printsQuickly.observe(false)
val softwareStateCorrectGivenPrintsSlowly =
  VariableElimination.probability(softwareState, 'correct)
println("Probability software state is correct given prints "
        + "slowly = " + softwareStateCorrectGivenPrintsSlowly)
```

Compute P(Software State = correct | Prints Quickly = false, Network State = up)

```
networkState.observe('up')
val softwareStateCorrectGivenPrintsSlowlyAndNetworkUp =
  VariableElimination.probability(softwareState, 'correct)
println("Probability software state is correct given prints "
        + "slowly and network up = "
        + softwareStateCorrectGivenPrintsSlowlyAndNetworkUp)
```

Running this code prints the following:

```
Probability software state is correct given prints slowly =
0.6197991391678623
Probability software state is correct given prints slowly and network up =
  0.39024390243902435
```

Learning that the network is up significantly reduces the probability that the software is correct. So Software State and Network State are independent, but they aren't conditionally independent given Prints Quickly. This is an example of an induced dependency.

To summarize:

- When reasoning from an effect X to its indirect cause Y, X isn't independent of Y, but becomes conditionally independent, given Z, if Z blocks the path from X to Y.
- The same holds when reasoning from a cause to an indirect effect or between two effects of the same cause.
- For two causes X and Y of the same effect Z, the opposite is true. X and Y are independent, but not conditionally independent, given Z, as a result of the induced dependency.

That wraps up the computer system diagnosis example. You've seen a fairly substantial network with some interesting reasoning patterns. In the next section, you'll move beyond traditional Bayesian networks.

5.4   Using probabilistic programming to extend Bayesian networks: predicting product success

This section shows how to extend the basic Bayesian network model to predict the success of a marketing campaign and product placement. The purpose of this example is twofold: first, to show the power of using programming languages to extend Bayesian networks, and second, to illustrate how Bayesian networks can be used not only to infer causes of observed events but also to predict future events. As with the computer system diagnosis example, I'll first show how to design the model and express it in Figaro and then how to reason with the model.

5.4.1   Designing a product success prediction model

Imagine that you have a new product, and you want to make the product as successful as possible. You could achieve this in various ways. You could invest in the product's packaging and other things that might make it appealing to customers. You could try to price it in such a way that people would be more likely to buy it. Or you could promote the product by giving away free versions in the hope that people will share them with their friends. Before you choose a strategy, you want to know the relative importance of each factor.

This section describes the framework of a model you could use for this application. I say *framework*, because this is just a skeleton of the model you would build if you were doing this for real, but it's enough to make the point. The model presented here is a simple Bayesian network with just four nodes, but the types of the nodes and the CPDs are rich and interesting.

The model has four variables, as shown in figure 5.12:

- Target Social Network is a variable whose type is a social network. This is one way a programming language lets you go beyond ordinary Bayesian networks, where variables are just Booleans, enumerations, integers, or real numbers.

The CPD of this variable randomly generates the network based on the popularity of the target. As for the popularity itself, because it's a control variable, you model it as a known constant rather than a variable. But if you wanted to, you could introduce uncertainty about the popularity and make it a variable itself.

- Target Likes is a Boolean variable indicating whether the target likes the product, which is a function of the product quality. Again, the product quality is a known constant, but you could have made it a variable that depends on investment.

- Number Friends Like is an integer variable, but its CPD traverses the Target Social Network to determine the number of friends who are shown the product and who like it. This is a much richer CPD than has traditionally been available in Bayesian networks.

- Number Buy is an integer variable. Its model is simply defined by considering that each person who likes the product will buy it with a probability that depends on its affordability, a control variable whose value is a known constant. Therefore, the number of people who buy the product is a binomial.

Here's the Figaro code for this model. I'll describe how the code works on a high level and then present details of the model.

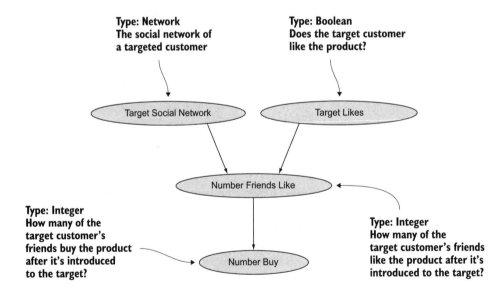

Figure 5.12   Product success prediction network

Listing 5.3 Product success prediction model in Figaro

Create a Model class that takes the known control parameters as arguments

```
class Network(popularity: Double) {
    val numNodes = Poisson(popularity)
}

class Model(targetPopularity: Double, productQuality: Double,
            affordability: Double) {

    def generateLikes(numFriends: Int,
                      productQuality: Double): Element[Int] = {

        def helper(friendsVisited: Int, totalLikes: Int,
                   unprocessedLikes: Int): Element[Int] = {
            if (unprocessedLikes == 0) Constant(totalLikes)
            else {
                val unvisitedFraction =
                    1.0 - (friendsVisited.toDouble - 1) / (numFriends - 1)
                val newlyVisited = Binomial(2, unvisitedFraction)
                val newlyLikes =
                    Binomial(newlyVisited, Constant(productQuality))
                Chain(newlyVisited, newlyLikes,
                    (visited: Int, likes: Int) =>
                        helper(friendsVisited + unvisited,
                               totalLikes + likes,
                               unprocessedLikes + likes - 1))
            }
        }

        helper(1, 1, 1)
    }

    val targetSocialNetwork = new Network(targetPopularity)

    val targetLikes = Flip(productQuality)

    val numberFriendsLike =
        Chain(targetLikes, targetSocialNetwork.numNodes,
            (l: Boolean, n: Int) =>
                if (l) generateLikes(n, productQuality)
                else Constant(0))

    val numberBuy =
        Binomial(numberFriendsLike, Constant(affordability))
}
```

Define a Network class with a single attribute defined by a Poisson element (see text)

Define a recursive process for generating the number of people who like the product (see text)

The target social network is defined to be a random network, based on the target's popularity.

Whether the target likes the product is a Boolean element based on the product quality.

If the target likes the product, calculate the number of friends using generateLikes. If she doesn't, she doesn't tell friends about it, so the number is 0.

The number of friends who buy the product is a binomial (see text).

Three details of the code need additional explanation: the `Poisson` element used in the `Network` class, the `generateLikes` process, and the definition of `numberBuy`. Let's first talk about the `Poisson` element and the `numberBuy` logic and then get to the `generateLikes` process, which is the most interesting part of the model.

- A *Poisson element* is an integer element that uses what is known as the *Poisson distribution*. The Poisson distribution is typically used to model the number of occurrences of an event in a period of time, such as the number of network failures in a month or the number of corner kicks in a game of soccer. With a little creativity, the Poisson distribution can be used to model any situation where you want to know the number of things in a region. Here, you use it to model the number of people in someone's social network, which is different from the usual usage but still a reasonable choice.

The Poisson element takes as an argument the average number of occurrences you'd expect in that period of time, but allows for the number to be more or less than the average. In this model, the argument is the popularity of the target; the popularity should be an estimate of the average number of people you expect to be in the target's social network.

- Here's the logic for the number of people who buy the product. Each person who likes the product will buy it with a probability equal to the value of the affordability parameter. So the total number of people who buy is given by a binomial, in which the number of trials is the number of friends who like the product, and the probability of buying depends on the affordability of the product. Because the number of people who like the product is itself an element, you need to use the compound binomial that takes elements as its arguments. The compound binomial element requires that the probability of success of a trial also be an element, which is why the affordability is wrapped in a `Constant`. A `Constant` element takes an ordinary Scala value and produces the Figaro element that always has that value.

- The purpose of the `generateLikes` function is to determine the number of people who like the product after giving it to a target whose social network contains the given number of people. This function assumes that the target herself likes the product; otherwise, the function wouldn't be called at all. The function simulates a random process of people promoting the product to their friends if they like the product. The `generateLikes` function takes two arguments: (1) the number of people in the target's social network, which is an `Integer`, and (2) the quality of the product, which is a `Double` between 0 and 1.

The precise logic of the `generateLikes` function isn't critical, because the main point is that you can use an interesting recursive function like this as a CPD. But I'll explain the logic, so you can see an example. Most of the work of `generateLikes` is done by a helper function. This function keeps track of three values:

- `friendsVisited` holds the number of people in the target's social network who have already been informed about the product. This starts at 1, because initially the target has been informed about the product.

- `totalLikes` represents the number of people, out of those who have been visited so far, who like the product. This also starts at 1, because you assume that the target likes the product for `generateLikes` to be called.

- `unprocessedLikes` represents the number of people who like the product for whom you've not yet simulated promoting the product to their friends.

I'll explain the logic of the helper function through the following code.

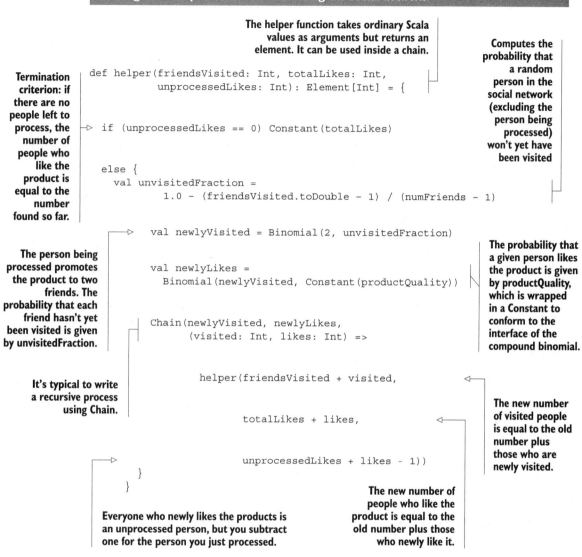

Listing 5.4   Helper function for traversing the social network

The helper function takes ordinary Scala values as arguments but returns an element. It can be used inside a chain.

Computes the probability that a random person in the social network (excluding the person being processed) won't yet have been visited

Termination criterion: if there are no people left to process, the number of people who like the product is equal to the number found so far.

The person being processed promotes the product to two friends. The probability that each friend hasn't yet been visited is given by unvisitedFraction.

It's typical to write a recursive process using Chain.

The probability that a given person likes the product is given by productQuality, which is wrapped in a Constant to conform to the interface of the compound binomial.

The new number of visited people is equal to the old number plus those who are newly visited.

Everyone who newly likes the products is an unprocessed person, but you subtract one for the person you just processed.

The new number of people who like the product is equal to the old number plus those who newly like it.

```scala
def helper(friendsVisited: Int, totalLikes: Int,
        unprocessedLikes: Int): Element[Int] = {

  if (unprocessedLikes == 0) Constant(totalLikes)

  else {
    val unvisitedFraction =
        1.0 - (friendsVisited.toDouble - 1) / (numFriends - 1)

    val newlyVisited = Binomial(2, unvisitedFraction)

    val newlyLikes =
        Binomial(newlyVisited, Constant(productQuality))

    Chain(newlyVisited, newlyLikes,
        (visited: Int, likes: Int) =>

          helper(friendsVisited + visited,

              totalLikes + likes,

              unprocessedLikes + likes - 1))
  }
}
```

This example uses more programming and Scala skills, but the essential modeling techniques are similar to Bayesian networks. The main point is to imagine a process by which a possible world is generated. In this example, you saw one relatively simple process of propagating a product through a social network; a richer process could easily be encoded.

5.4.2 *Reasoning with the product success prediction model*

Because you've designed the model for predicting success, the typical usage would be to set values for the control constants and predict the number of people who buy the product. Because the number of people is an `Integer` variable that could have a wide range, you're not really interested in predicting the probability of a particular value. Rather, you want to know the average value you can expect. This is known as the *expectation* of the value.

In probability theory, expectation is a general concept. The expectation takes a function defined on a variable and returns the average value of that function. An example is shown in figure 5.13. You start with a probability distribution over values of any type; in this example, the values are `Integers`. You then apply a function to each value to produce a `Double` value. In this example, the function converts each `Integer` to a `Double` representation of the `Integer`. Next, you take the weighted average of these `Double` values, where each `Double` value is weighted by its probability. This means that you multiply each `Double` value by its probability and add the results.

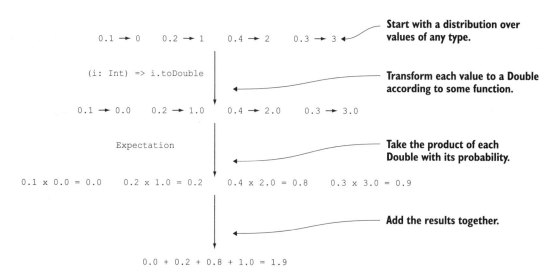

Figure 5.13 Computing the expectation of a distribution over an `Integer`-valued element. The values of the element are first converted to `Doubles`. Then you take the average of these `Doubles`, where each `Double` is weighted by its probability.

In our example of predicting product success, you want to compute the expectation of the number of people who buy the product, which is an `Integer` variable. You can use the following line in Figaro to do this:

```
algorithm.expectation(model.numberBuy, (i: Int) => i.toDouble)
```

Here, `algorithm` is a handle on the inference algorithm you're using. This application uses an importance sampling algorithm, which is a particularly good algorithm for predicting the outcome of a complex generative process. Because you need a handle on the algorithm, you need to use slightly more-complex code than before to run inference, as is explained in the following code snippet. The entire process of taking in the control constants and computing the expected number of people who buy the product is accomplished by a function called `predict`:

```
def predict(targetPopularity: Double, productQuality: Double,
            affordability: Double): Double = {

  val model =
    new Model(targetPopularity, productQuality, affordability)

  val algorithm = Importance(1000, model.numberBuy)

  algorithm.start()

  val result =
    algorithm.expectation(model.numberBuy, (i: Int) => i.toDouble)

  algorithm.kill()

  result
}
```

Create a new instance of our product prediction model, using the given control constants

Create an instance of the importance sampling algorithm. 1000 is the number of samples to use, while model.numberBuy indicates what we want to predict.

Run the algorithm

Clean up and free resources taken by the algorithm

Compute the expectation of the number of people who buy the product

If you're trying to understand the effect of various controls on the number of people who buy the product, you'll want to run this `predict` function many times with different inputs. You might produce a result like this:

```
Popularity  Product quality Affordability Predicted number of buyers
100         0.5             0.5               2.0169999999999986
100         0.5             0.9               3.7759999999999962
100         0.9             0.5               29.21499999999997
100         0.9             0.9               53.13799999999996
10          0.5             0.5               0.7869999999999979
10          0.5             0.9               1.4769999999999976
10          0.9             0.5               3.3419999999999885
10          0.9             0.9               6.066999999999985
```

You can conclude a couple of things from this table. The number of buyers appears to be roughly proportional to the affordability of the product. But there's a disproportionate dependence on the product quality: for every case of popularity and affordability, the number of buyers when the product quality is 0.9 is at least several times as high as when the quality is 0.5. When the popularity is 100, it's about 15 times as high. There appears to be an interaction between the popularity and product quality, where the popularity places a limit on the number of people who will be reached when the quality is high. When the quality is low, the popularity doesn't matter as much.

In this example, you've seen Figaro used as a simulation language. Predicting what will happen in the future is typically what simulations do, and this is the use case described here. You could just as easily use the model for reasoning backward. For example, after you hand out the product to some people and observe how many other people they influenced to buy the product, you could estimate the quality of the product. This could be a valuable alternative use of the model.

5.5 *Using Markov networks*

The preceding sections have been concerned with Bayesian networks, which encode directed dependencies. It's time to turn your attention to undirected dependencies. The counterpart to Bayesian networks for undirected dependencies is Markov networks. I'll explain the principles behind Markov networks using a typical image-recovery application. I'll then show you how to represent and reason with the image-recovery model in Figaro.

5.5.1 *Markov networks defined*

A Markov network is a representation of a probabilistic model consisting of three things:

- *A set of variables*—Each variable has a domain, which is the set of possible values of the variable.
- *An undirected graph in which the nodes are variables*—The edges between nodes are undirected, meaning they have no arrow from one variable to the other. This graph is allowed to have cycles.
- *A set of potentials*—These potentials provide the numerical parameters of the model. I'll explain what potentials are in detail in a moment.

Figure 5.14 shows a Markov network for an image-recovery application. There's a variable for every pixel in the image. This figure shows a 4×4 array of pixels, but it's easy

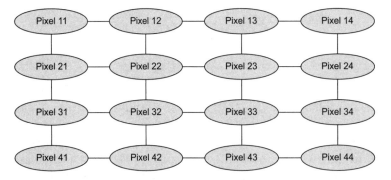

Figure 5.14   A Markov network for a pixel image

to see how it can be generalized to any size image. In principle, the value of a pixel could be any color, but for the sake of example, let's say it's a Boolean representing whether the pixel is bright or dark. There's an edge between any pair of pixels that are adjacent either horizontally or vertically. Intuitively, these edges encode the fact that, all else being equal, two adjacent pixels are more likely to have the same value than different values.

This "all else being equal" qualifier is important to understand the meaning of this model. If you ignore the edge between two pixels for a moment and consider the individual probability distribution over each of the pixels, it might be likely that they are, in fact, different. For example, based on everything else you know, you might believe that pixel 11 is bright with probability 90% and that pixel 12 is bright with probability 10%. In this case, it's highly likely that pixel 11 and pixel 12 are different. But the edge between pixel 11 and pixel 12 makes them *more likely to be the same than they would otherwise have been.* It adds a piece of knowledge that they're likely to be the same. This knowledge counterweighs the other knowledge that they're likely to be different, but it might not completely change the overall conclusion. The specific knowledge expressed by the edge between pixel 11 and pixel 12 is represented by the potential on that edge. Now let's see exactly how potentials are defined.

POTENTIALS

How are the numerical parameters of a Markov network defined? In a Bayesian network, each variable has a CPD. In a Markov network, it's not as simple. Variables don't own their numerical parameters. Instead, functions called *potentials* are defined on sets of variables. When there's a symmetric dependency, some joint states of the variables that are dependent on each other are more likely than others, all else being equal. The potential specifies a weight for each such joint state. Joint states with high weights are more likely than joint states with low weights, all else being equal. The relative probability of the two joint states is equal to the ratio between their weights, again, all else being equal.

Mathematically, a potential is simply a function from the values of variables to real numbers. Only positive real numbers or zero are allowed as the values of a potential. Table 5.1 shows an example of a unary potential over a single pixel for the image-recovery application, and table 5.2 shows a binary potential over two pixels.

Table 5.1 A unary potential over a single pixel. This potential encodes the fact that, all else being equal, a pixel is lit with probability 0.4.

Pixel 31	Potential value
F	0.6
T	0.4

Table 5.2   A binary potential over two adjacent pixels. This potential encodes the fact that, all else being equal, the two pixels are nine times as likely to have the same value as different values.

Pixel 31	Pixel 32	Potential value
F	F	0.9
F	T	0.1
T	F	0.1
T	T	0.9

How do potential functions interact with the graph structure? There are two rules:

- A potential function can mention only variables that are connected in the graph.
- If two variables are connected in the graph, they must be mentioned together by some potential function.

In our image-recovery example, every variable will have a copy of the unary potential in table 5.2, and every pair of adjacent pixels, either horizontally or vertically, will have a copy of the binary potential in table 5.2. You can see that the two rules are respected by this assignment of potentials.

HOW A MARKOV NETWORK DEFINES A PROBABILITY DISTRIBUTION

You've seen how a Markov network is defined. How does it define a probability distribution? How does it assign a probability to every possible world so that the probabilities of all possible worlds add up to 1? The answer isn't quite as simple as for Bayesian networks but also isn't too complicated.

Just as in a Bayesian network, a possible world in a Markov network consists of an assignment of values to all of the variables, making sure that the value of each variable is in its domain. What's the probability of such a possible world? Let's build it up piece by piece by using an example.

To keep things simple, let's consider a 2 × 2 array of pixels with the following assignment of values: pixel 11 = true, pixel 12 = true, pixel 21 = true, pixel 22 = false. You'll look at all potentials in the model and their potential values for this possible world. For the unary potentials, you have the values in table 5.3. Pixels that are true

Table 5.3   Potential values for unary potentials for example possible world

Variable	Potential value
Pixel 11	0.4
Pixel 12	0.4
Pixel 21	0.4
Pixel 22	0.6

have potential value 0.4, while the one pixel that's false has potential value 0.6. Table 5.4 shows the potential values from the four binary pixels. The cases where the two pixels have the same value have potential value 0.9, whereas the other two cases have potential value 0.1. This covers all potentials in the model.

Table 5.4 Potential values for binary potentials for example possible world

Variable 1	Variable 2	Potential value
Pixel 11	Pixel 12	0.9
Pixel 21	Pixel 22	0.1
Pixel 11	Pixel 21	0.9
Pixel 12	Pixel 22	0.1

Next, you multiply the potential values from all of the potentials. In our example, you get $0.4 \times 0.4 \times 0.4 \times 0.6 \times 0.9 \times 0.1 \times 0.9 \times 0.1 = 0.00031104$. Why do you multiply? Think about the "all else being equal" principle. If two worlds have the same probability except for one potential, then the probabilities of the worlds are proportional to their potential value according to that potential. This is exactly the effect you get when you multiply the probabilities by the value of this potential. Continuing this reasoning, you multiply the potential values of all of the potentials to get the "probability" of a possible world.

I put "probability" in quotes because it's not actually a probability. When you multiply the potential values in this way, you'll find that the "probabilities" don't sum to 1. This is easily fixed. To get the probability of any possible world, you normalize the "probabilities" computed by multiplying the potential values. You call these the *unnormalized probabilities*. The sum of these unnormalized probabilities is called the *normalizing factor* and is usually denoted by the letter Z. So you take the unnormalized probabilities and divide them by Z to get the probabilities. Don't worry if this process sounds cumbersome to you; Figaro takes care of all of it.

A surprising point comes out of this discussion. In a Bayesian network, you could compute the probability of a possible world by multiplying the relevant CPD entries. In a Markov network, you can't determine the probability of any possible world without considering all possible worlds. You need to compute the unnormalized probability of every possible world to calculate the normalizing factor. For this reason, some people find that representing Markov networks is harder than Bayesian networks, because it's harder to interpret the numbers as defining a probability. I say that if you keep in mind the "all else being equal" principle, you'll be able to define the parameters of a Markov network with confidence. You can leave computing the normalizing factor to Figaro. Of course, the parameters of both Bayesian networks and Markov networks can be learned from data. Use whichever structure seems more appropriate to you, based on the kinds of relationships in your application.

5.5.2   *Representing and reasoning with Markov networks*

There's one way Markov networks are definitely simpler than Bayesian networks: in the reasoning patterns. A Markov network has no notion of induced dependencies. You can reason from one variable to another variable along any path, as long as that path isn't blocked by a variable that has been observed. Two variables are dependent if there's a path between them, and they become conditionally independent given a set of variables if those variables block all paths between the two variables. That's all there is to it.

Also, because all edges in a Markov network are undirected, there's no notion of cause and effect or past and future. You don't usually think of tasks such as predicting future outcomes or inferring past causes of current observations. Instead, you simply infer the values of some variables, given other variables.

REPRESENTING THE IMAGE-RECOVERY MODEL IN FIGARO

In the image-recovery application, you'll assume that some of the pixels are observed and the rest are unobserved. You want to recover the unobserved pixels. You'll use the model described in the previous section, which specifies both the potential value for each pixel being on and the potential value for adjacent pixels having the same value. Here's the Figaro code for representing the model. Remember that in section 5.1.2, I said there are two methods for specifying symmetric relationships, a constraints method and a conditions method. This code uses the constraints method:

```
val pixels = Array.fill(10, 10)(Flip(0.4))      ◁──┐  Set the unary constraint
                                                     on each variable

def setConstraint(i1: Int, j1: Int, i2: Int, j2: Int) {
  val pixel1 = pixels(i1)(j1)                          Set the binary
  val pixel2 = pixels(i2)(j2)                          constraint on a
  val pair = ^^(pixel1, pixel2)                        pair of variables
  pair.addConstraint(bb => if (bb._1 == bb._2) 0.9; else 0.1)    given their
}                                                                 coordinates

for {
  i <- 0 until 10
  j <- 0 until 10                             Apply the binary
} {                                           constraint to all pairs
  if (i <= 8) setConstraint(i, j, i+1, j)     of adjacent variables
  if (j <= 8) setConstraint(i, j, i, j+1)
}
```

A few notes on this code are in order:

- In the definition of pixels, `Array.fill(10, 10)(Flip(0.4))` creates a 10×10 array and fills every element of the array with a different instance of `Flip(0.4)`. All of the different pixels are defined by different `Flip` elements, which is important because they can all have different values.
- You might be wondering why a `Flip` element is used at all for the unary potentials rather than a constraint. For a unary potential, defining it in the usual

Figaro way or using a constraint has the same effect. In this case, the `Flip` will come out `true` with probability 0.4 and `false` with probability 0.6. These probabilities will be multiplied into the unnormalized probability of a possible world, just as if they had been specified through a constraint.

In fact, every Figaro element has to be defined in the usual way, using some type of element constructor, even if you're using Figaro to encode a Markov network. If your element doesn't have a unary constraint, this ordinary Figaro constructor should be neutral and not favor any possible world over another. You could use `Flip(0.5)` or a `Uniform` element to achieve this.

- In the definition of `setConstraint`, `^^` is the Figaro pair constructor. So `^^(pixel1, pixel2)` creates an element whose value is the pair of values of the elements `pixel1` and `pixel2`.

- In the `for` comprehension, `0 until 10` is Scala for the integers 0 to 10, exclusive; in other words, the integers 0, 1, …, 9. If you wanted to say 0 to 10 inclusive, you would use `0 to 10`.

- This `for` comprehension also shows an example of a nested loop. In other languages, this would have been written using one `for` loop inside another. In Scala, you can put both loops in the same `for` header.

REASONING WITH THE IMAGE-RECOVERY MODEL

You want to use the image-recovery model to infer the values of unobserved pixels, given the observed pixels. You need three things: a way to ingest and process the evidence, a way to compute the most likely states of pixels, and a way to view the results. Let's look at these one at a time.

Process evidence. If you have a 10×10 array of pixels, you might have data that's a 10×10 array of characters, where each character is 0 for off, 1 for on, or ? for unknown. You can process this data by using the following simple `setEvidence` function:

```scala
def setEvidence(data: String) = {
  for { n <- 0 until data.length } {
    val i = n / 10
    val j = n % 10
    data(n) match {
      case '0' => pixels(i)(j).observe(false)
      case '1' => pixels(i)(j).observe(true)
      case _ => ()
    }
  }
}
```

Uses Scala pattern matching, which in this case is a lot like a switch statement in other languages. The `_` indicates a default case. So no observation will be made on a '?'.

Compute the most likely state of pixels: This example introduces a new kind of query you haven't considered before. In the past, you've wanted to estimate the posterior probabilities of elements. This time, you're interested in the most likely values of elements (the values with highest probability). But you're not interested in the most likely values of elements individually, without regard to the other elements; rather, you want the most likely joint assignment of values to all of the variables. You want to know what the most likely possible world is.

This query is known in Figaro as a *most probable explanation* (MPE) query, because you want to know the world that's the most probable explanation of the data. The algorithms for MPE queries are different from the probability computation algorithms you've seen so far, although they're related. In this example, you'll use a version of the belief propagation designed for computing the MPE. This algorithm is known as MPE-BeliefPropagation. Belief propagation is an iterative algorithm, and you can control the number of iterations with a parameter. In this case, you'll use 10 iterations. You can create an instance of the MPEBeliefPropagation algorithm and tell it to run in this way:

```
val algorithm = MPEBeliefPropagation(10)
algorithm.start()
```

Viewing the results: This is simply a matter of going through all of the pixels, getting their most likely values, and printing them accordingly. You can obtain the most likely value of an element by using the mostLikelyValue method of MPEBeliefPropagation. Here's the code:

```
for {
  i <- 0 until 10
} {
  for { j <- 0 until 10 } {
    val mlv = algorithm.mostLikelyValue(pixels(i)(j))
    if (mlv) print('1') else print('0')
  }
  println()
}
```

To run the model, you need to provide it with some input. Ordinarily, this would be read from a file or provided programmatically by another module. To keep this example simple, you can define the input directly in the program, as follows:

```
val data =
  """00?000?000
     0?010?0010
     110?010011
     11??000111
     11011000?1
     1?0?100?10
     00001?0?00
     0010??0100
     01?01001?0
     0??000110?""".filterNot(_.isWhitespace)

setEvidence(data)
```

Scala's """ constructor allows you to create long strings that span multiple lines. You filter out all whitespace characters to produce a string of 100 characters.

When run on this data, the program outputs the following:

```
0000000000
0001000010
1100010011
1100000111
1101100011
1000100010
0000100000
0010000100
0100100100
0000001100
```

That's all there is to Markov networks. This has been a long chapter, but you've learned a lot. Now you know all of the main principles of probabilistic models and can write probabilistic programs for a variety of applications. The next few chapters build on and elaborate the material in this chapter to give you even more power in writing programs. You'll start in the next chapter by looking at how to use Scala and Figaro containers to build larger and more-structured models.

5.6 Summary

- Probabilistic modeling is all about encoding relationships between variables. Symmetric relationships produce directed dependencies, whereas asymmetric relationships produce undirected dependencies.
- Directed dependencies lead from a cause to an effect. There are a variety of cause-and-effect relationships.
- Bayesian networks encode directed dependencies by using a directed acyclic graph.
- The direction of the arrows in a Bayesian network isn't necessarily the direction of reasoning. Bayesian networks can be used to reason in all directions in the network.
- Markov networks encode undirected dependencies by using an undirected graph.
- If you can identify the types of relationships between variables in your model and use them to write your programs, you won't go far wrong.

5.7 Exercises

Solutions to selected exercises are available online at www.manning.com/books/ practical-probabilistic-programming.

1 For each of the following pairs of variables, decide whether the dependency between them should be directed or undirected, and if directed, which way the arrow should go.

   a A player's poker cards and the player's bet
   b Player 1's poker cards and player 2's poker cards
   c My mood and today's weather

d My mood and whether I've had breakfast

e The temperature in my living room and the house thermostat setting

f The temperature in my living room and the thermometer reading in the living room

g The temperature in my living room and the temperature in the kitchen

h The topic of a news article and the contents of the article

i The summary of a news article and the contents of the article

2 For each of the following sets of variables, draw a Bayesian network over the variables.

   a Player 1's poker cards, player 2's poker cards, player 1's bet, and player 2's subsequent bet

   b My mood on waking up, my mood at 10 a.m., today's weather, and whether I've had breakfast

   c The temperature in my living room, the temperature in the kitchen, the house thermostat setting, the thermometer reading in the living room, and the thermometer reading in the kitchen

   d The topic of a news article, the summary of the article, the contents of the article, and the comments on the article

3 Your task is to design a Bayesian network to model the process of cooking soup. The goal of this network is to help you decide what ingredients to use and how much of each ingredient, as well as cooking variables such as the amount of heat and time, in order to optimize various food qualities such as spiciness and creaminess.

   a What are the variables in your model?

   b Draw a Bayesian network structure over these variables.

   c Choose Figaro functional forms for each of your variables.

   d Populate your functional forms in Figaro with numerical parameters.

   e Use your Figaro model to answer queries such as how long you should cook the soup with a given set of ingredients to ensure optimal creaminess.

4 A match of tennis consists of a number of sets, each of which consists of a number of games. The first player to win two sets wins the match. The first player to win six games wins a set. (Let's ignore tie breakers, but after doing exercise 5, you'll be able to model them.) Players alternate serving for a game at a time. Write a Figaro program that takes two arguments—the probability that each player wins a game in which he's the server—and predicts the winner of the match.

5 Now elaborate your tennis model to model individual points. Within a game, the players try to get points. The first player to get four points wins the game, unless both players get to three points. In that case, the first player to move two points ahead of his opponent wins the game. Write a Figaro program that takes

two arguments as before, except that now they're the probability that each player wins a point in which he's the server. Again, your program should predict the winner of the match.

6 Now you can further elaborate the tennis model to model individual points as rallies. Players could have variables such as serving ability, speed, and error proneness. Your model can be as detailed as you like, including the positions of the players and the ball at each shot in the rally.

7 My house has central air conditioning controlled by a thermostat downstairs. The top floor is usually hotter than the ground floor. Create a Markov network representing the temperature throughout the house (ignoring the thermostat for now). Write a Figaro model to represent the network. Use the model to compute the probability that the top floor is at least 80 degrees Fahrenheit, given that the ground floor is 72 degrees Fahrenheit.

8 Now add the thermostat to the model as well as the outside temperature and whether any windows are open. This model will combine directed and undirected dependencies, so it won't be a pure Markov network, but it's easy enough to make this combination in Figaro. Write the Figaro program and use it to help decide whether I should open the window on the top floor.

9 Consider the spam filter application from chapter 3. In that application, every email was treated as independent. Now suppose you have multiple emails from the same sender. Their spam status will be highly correlated.

  a Create a Markov network to capture these correlations.
  b The Bayesian network for each spam email is shown in figure 3.8. Replicate this network in the Markov network from exercise 9a. Again, this is a combined directed and undirected network.

Note: Although I've said that the class of an object determines its properties causally, which is the approach used in the spam filter, in some cases it makes sense to go in the opposite direction. This is the case when all of the features are always observed, as is the case with the spam filter. In this case, it can be wasteful to model the probability distribution over the observed features explicitly. Instead, a model can be created where the features of each email determine the class of an email. The classes of the email are then related by the Markov network from exercise 9a. This kind of model, known as a *conditional random field*, is widely used in natural language understanding and computer vision applications.

I'm not going to go into details of conditional random fields here, but I'll note, for those who are familiar with them, that they can easily be represented in Figaro. The trick is to make sure that the observed email features aren't Figaro elements but rather Scala variables that help determine the distribution over the element representing whether the email is spam. Any learnable parameters of the model will, of course, be Figaro elements, and they can interact with the Scala variables representing the features to determine the spam probability.

6

Using Scala and Figaro collections to build up models

This chapter covers

- How to use collections to organize probabilistic models

- The difference between Scala collections and Figaro collections, the roles of each, and how to use them together

- Common modeling patterns that can be expressed using collections, including hierarchical Bayesian modeling, modeling situations with an unknown number of objects, and models defined over a continuous region

In the preceding two chapters, you've gained a solid foundation in probabilistic modeling. This chapter focuses on the *programming* aspect of probabilistic programming and shows you ways that the features of a programming language can help you build probabilistic models. In particular, you're going to focus on collections.

Collections are one of the most useful features of high-level programming languages, because they let you organize many items of the same type and treat them as a group. For example, if you're working with lots of integers, you can put them in an array and then write a loop to go through all entries in the array, multiply them by 2, and add them. Or, in functional programming terms, you can write a `map` function to multiply every entry in the array by 2 and a `fold` function to perform the addition. The same holds for probabilistic programming; if you have many variables of the same type, you can put them in a collection and operate on them with functions such as `map` and `fold`.

You can do this in two ways in Figaro. The first is to use ordinary Scala collections. If you're an experienced programmer, you'll no doubt be familiar with collections such as arrays, lists, sets, maps, and so on. Scala provides an extensive collections library, which is at your service for organizing elements and building probabilistic programs.

Figaro also provides a collections library, which adds powerful capabilities for working with many elements. You can do things with Figaro collections that you can't easily do with ordinary Scala collections. On the other hand, Scala collections provide variety that Figaro collections don't have, so both are useful for working with probabilistic models.

You'll start out by looking at using ordinary Scala collections. Then you'll look at Figaro collections, what you can do with them, and how and when to use Scala collections and/or Figaro collections in a program. In the last two sections of the chapter, you'll look at two powerful uses of Figaro collections: using variable-size arrays to model situations with an unknown number of objects, and defining probabilistic models over a continuous region of time or space.

> **NOTE** Because this chapter focuses on programming, it has a lot of code. The chapter includes seven full programs, which you can find in the code for the book. Familiarity with Scala collections will be helpful, although the code doesn't use any particularly sophisticated features. Also, you should be comfortable with the Bayesian network concepts presented in chapter 5.

6.1 Using Scala collections

The examples you've seen so far have had one of everything. In the Rembrandt example, you had one painting, which had one subject, one size, and one brightness. What if you want to work with many things—for example, a model with many paintings, each of which might have more than one subject?

In programming, you use collections to hold many things of the same type that are processed together. For example, you might have an array of numbers. You could use this array to apply an operation to every number in the array or to add all of the numbers. The ability to loop over all of the numbers in the array instead of writing them all out greatly shortens the program and provides flexibility, because you can change the size of the array in just one place. Without the array, you'd have to unroll the loop completely, and it would be harder to use the same code for different-size arrays in the same program.

Using Scala collections provides the same kind of advantages for probabilistic programming. I'll provide examples of several typical patterns for which Scala collections are useful, starting with situations in which many variables of the same type all depend on a single variable.

6.1.1   *Modeling dependence of many variables on a single variable*

Let's look at a classical example, which you first encountered in chapter 4. You have a coin of dubious origin. The coin may be biased, and you don't know the probability that it'll come out heads on any given toss. You want to estimate the bias of the coin (the probability that it'll come out heads). You also want to be able to predict subsequent coin tosses.

Figure 6.1 shows a Bayesian network for this situation. The root node is Bias. This is a real-valued variable that represents the probability that any given toss will be heads. The figure shows nodes for 101 tosses, but the same network could be used for any number of tosses. For each toss, the probability it comes out heads is equal to the value of Bias. You can imagine observing the first 100 tosses and predicting the 101st.

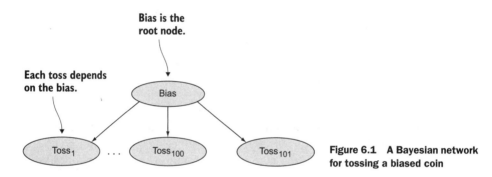

Figure 6.1   A Bayesian network for tossing a biased coin

REPRESENTING THE COIN-TOSS MODEL IN FIGARO

This example can easily be represented in Figaro by using a Scala array for all previously observed coin tosses. Our program will read in a command-line argument consisting of H and T characters, which will represent the previously observed tosses. You can get the size of the array from this argument. Here's the code for the model:

```
val outcomes = args(0)
val numTosses = outcomes.length

val bias = Beta(2,5)
val tosses = Array.fill(numTosses)(Flip(bias))      ◁—
val nextToss = Flip(bias)
```

Create an array of size numTosses in which each item is a different instantiation of Flip(bias). Each element of this array represents a separate coin toss.

To model the bias, you use a `Beta` element. In chapter 3, when you designed the spam filter, you used the `Beta` element to model the occurrence of a word in an email. I mentioned that the `Beta` element works well with `Flip` and `Binomial`, so using a `Beta` for the bias of a coin is appropriate. See the following sidebar for more details on the relationship between `Beta` and `Flip`.

Next, you create an array of coin tosses to represent all previously seen tosses. You use Scala's `Array.fill` method, which creates an array of a given number of items and provides a definition for each item. This definition is evaluated separately for every item in the array. So each item is a separate instantiation of `Flip(bias)`—a separate coin flip whose probability of coming out heads is `bias`. Finally, you create one more coin flip for the next toss you're trying to predict.

Conjugate priors and why Beta works with Flip

The standard name for `Flip` in probability theory is the *Bernoulli distribution*. The beta distribution is called the *conjugate prior* of the Bernoulli distribution. This means that if you have a `Beta` variable and a Bernoulli variable, and the `Beta` variable represents the probability that the Bernoulli variable comes out true, then conditioning the `Beta` variable on the outcome of the Bernoulli variable results in another `Beta` variable.

It's time to look more closely at the two arguments of the `Beta` element. The first argument, called α, represents an imaginary number of heads you've already seen, plus 1. The second, called β, is the same thing for tails. In your example, you're using `Beta(2,5)`, meaning that you're imagining having already seen one head and four tails even before learning. (By the way, the reason you add 1 to the number of heads and tails is mathematical convention; it makes the prediction of the next toss simple, as you'll see in a couple of paragraphs.) This enables you to encode the fact that you have some prior beliefs about the bias even before seeing any data. If you have no prior beliefs, you can use `Beta(1,1)`.

Now, suppose you observe a toss that comes out heads. You increment α by 1 to get the posterior. Similarly, if the toss comes out tails, you increment β by 1. In general, if you observe *h* heads and *t* tails, you increment α by *h* and β by *t*. So if the prior is `Beta(2, 5)` and you observe three heads and two tails, the posterior is `Beta(5,7)`. This is why the beta distribution is the conjugate prior of the Bernoulli distribution.

It's also easy to predict whether the next toss comes out heads when the bias is a beta distribution. The probability of this happening is $\alpha / (\alpha + \beta)$, so 5/12 for `Beta(5,7)`.

The calculations in this example are simple, and you don't need a programming language to complete them. But the calculations can get much more complicated, and you can't usually compute posterior distributions and make predictions using a simple formula like this. Also, you don't usually have to use conjugate priors in Figaro. Nevertheless, it makes sense to use a conjugate prior where you can, because it's a sensible way to represent your prior knowledge about a parameter.

Using a Scala array also makes it easy to assert evidence. Recall that `outcomes` was read from the command line and consists of H and T characters, one for every toss. You can use the following code to observe the appropriate outcome on each of the previously observed tosses:

```
for {
  toss <- 0 until numTosses
} {
  val outcome = outcomes(toss) == 'H'
  tosses(toss).observe(outcome)
}
```

RUNNING INFERENCE USING AN ANYTIME ALGORITHM

You've created the model and asserted evidence, so it's now time to run inference. This chapter presents a new way of running inference that gives you precise control over the amount of time the inference runs: using anytime algorithms. An *anytime algorithm*, as the name suggests, is an algorithm that you can run for any amount of time and that produces the best answer it can in the given time. You can tell it exactly how long you want it to run, and it'll do its best.

Using an anytime algorithm in Figaro is similar to using an ordinary algorithm. You create an instance of the algorithm and tell it to start. Anytime algorithms in Figaro run in a separate thread, so you can do whatever you like while the algorithm is running. Typically, you sleep for the specified amount of time you want the algorithm to run. Then you query the algorithm to get the information you want. Finally, you kill the algorithm. It's important to kill anytime algorithms because that releases the thread; otherwise, the algorithm will continue to take resources.

Here's the code to run inference on our coin-toss model using importance sampling. Importance sampling has both an ordinary *one-time* version, which runs once to completion when it starts, and an anytime version. Many of the other Figaro algorithms also have one-time and anytime versions. In one-time importance sampling, you have to tell the algorithm how many samples to take. In anytime importance sampling, you don't tell it how many samples to take, because it'll take as many as it can in the available time.

```
val algorithm = Importance(nextToss, bias)          ⟵    Create a version of importance
algorithm.start()                                        sampling with the goal of querying
Thread.sleep(1000)          ⟵  Wait 1000               nextToss and bias. Figaro knows
algorithm.stop()               milliseconds           it's the anytime version because
                                                       there's no argument for the
println("Average bias = " + algorithm.mean(bias))     number of samples.
println("Probability of heads on next toss = " +
        algorithm.probability(nextToss, true))

algorithm.kill()          ⟵  Release all
                             resources
```

When run on the argument `HTHHHHHTHTHHHHTHHHHHH`, this code runs for 1 second and produce output like this:

```
Average bias = 0.6641810675997326
Probability of heads on next toss = 0.6414832927224574
```

6.1.2 *Creating hierarchical models*

This section shows you how to use sequences of sequences to extend the preceding example in a hierarchical way. Imagine that you have a toss of a coin, which is one of many coins in a bag, which is one of many bags in a box, and so on. To keep things simple, you'll model tosses of coins that come from the same bag, using two levels of sequences, but it'll be easy to see how this generalizes to any number of levels.

In the previous section, you saw how the property of a toss (namely, whether it came up heads) depended on a property of the coin (namely, its bias). In this section, the coin's bias depends on a property of the bag. Specifically, some of the coins in the bag are fair, meaning that they come up heads exactly 50% of the time, but the rest are biased. The bag has a property that represents the probability that any given coin in the bag will be fair.

A Bayesian network for this example is shown in figure 6.2. This network has three layers, corresponding to each of the levels of the hierarchy. The first layer represents the bag, with the FairProbability variable. The second layer represents the individual coins with their biases. This network has three coins, but it could easily be extended to any number of coins. The third layer contains the tosses of each coin. Each toss has two subscripts, representing the coin number and the toss number. Each toss depends on the bias of the appropriate coin. Different coins can have different numbers of tosses; in this network, the third coin has three tosses and the first two have two each.

This situation can be captured by using two levels of sequences. The first level has two sequences containing Figaro elements relating to particular coins: whether the

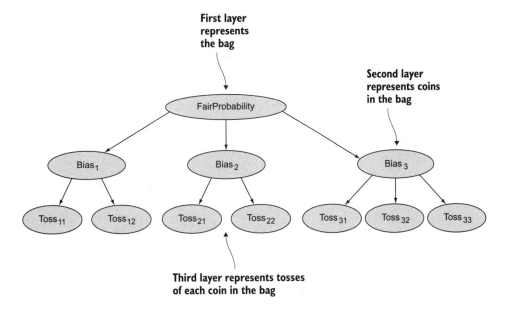

Figure 6.2 Bayesian network for hierarchical model

coin is fair, and what its bias is. For each coin, the second level has a sequence containing Figaro elements representing the tosses of the coin. Scala sequences can be created easily by using `for` comprehensions.

The code for the model is as follows. This code expects a number of command-line arguments, one for each observed coin. Each command-line argument contains H and T characters for the individual observed coin tosses, as in the previous example:

```
val numCoins = args.length

val fairProbability = Uniform(0.0, 1.0)

val isFair =
  for { coin <- 0 until numCoins }
  yield Flip(fairProbability)

val biases =
  for { coin <- 0 until numCoins }
  yield If(isFair(coin), Constant(0.5), Beta(2,5))

val tosses =
  for { coin <- 0 until numCoins }
  yield {
    for { toss <- 0 until args(coin).length }
    yield Flip(biases(coin))
  }
```

> Creates a sequence of length numCoins in which each item is a Flip(fairProbability) element

> For each coin, if the coin is fair, its bias is definitely 0.5; otherwise it's Beta(2, 5).

> Produces a sequence of toss sequences, one for each coin

> Given a coin, produces a sequence of Flip(biases(coin)) elements whose length is the number of tosses of the coin, read from the command line

Now you can use a simple two-dimensional `for` comprehension to assert the evidence:

```
for {
  coin <- 0 until numCoins
  toss <- 0 until args(coin).length
} {
  val outcome = args(coin)(toss) == 'H'
  tosses(coin)(toss).observe(outcome)
}
```

Finally, you can run inference as follows:

```
val algorithm = Importance(fairProbability, biases(0))
algorithm.start()
Thread.sleep(1000)
algorithm.stop()

val averageFairProbability = algorithm.mean(fairProbability)
val firstCoinAverageBias = algorithm.mean(biases(0))
println("Average fairness probability: " + averageFairProbability)
println("First coin average bias: " + firstCoinAverageBias)

algorithm.kill()
```

Given the arguments HTHHT H THHH HHT, this code produces output like the following:

```
Average fairness probability: 0.7079517451620699
First coin average bias: 0.4852371044437457
```

6.1.3 *Modeling simultaneous dependence on two variables*

In the preceding section, you saw how tosses of a coin depended on the bias of the coin, which in turn depended on the fair probability of the bag. This is a hierarchical organization. An alternative is to have a variable depend on two other variables simultaneously without any hierarchy between the variables. For the last example of using Scala collections, you'll see how to model this kind of situation by using two-dimensional arrays, where one variable depends on two other variables, each of which is one of a collection. For example, sales of a product in a region may depend on the quality of the product and the brand's penetration of the region. Here, you have an array of products, an array of regions, and a two-dimensional array of sales, each of which depends on the appropriate product and region.

> **NOTE** This section shows two-dimensional arrays. In reality, you could have any number of dimensions. Because these are Scala arrays, this is the same as in ordinary programming.

A Bayesian network for this situation in shown in figure 6.3. This network should be simple to understand. It has three product-quality variables, two region-penetration variables, and six sales variables, one for each combination of product quality and region penetration.

Despite the simplicity of the network, the reasoning that can be done in this network is sophisticated, especially if the sales are observed and you're trying to infer product quality and region penetration. For example, sales of product 1 can provide information about the quality of product 2. To see how this works, suppose sales of

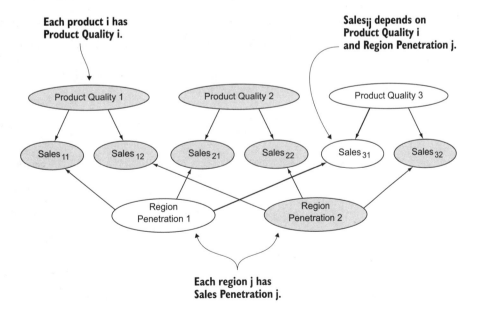

Figure 6.3 Bayesian network for two-dimensional sales model

product 1 are high in region 1. This might lead you to believe that region 1's penetration is high. Now, if sales of product 2 are low in region 1, you might conclude that product 2 has low quality. On the other hand, if sales of product 1 had also been low in region 1, you'd be less inclined to conclude that product 2 has low quality, because you'd believe that region 1 has low penetration.

If you remember what you learned in chapter 5 about reasoning patterns in Bayesian networks, you'll see that the path $Sales_{11}$—Region Penetration 1—$Sales_{21}$—Product Quality 2 is active. The only intermediate variable on this path that's observed is $Sales_{21}$. But the path has converging arrows at this variable, meaning that the path isn't blocked by this variable when it's observed. Meanwhile, Region Penetration 1 is unobserved, and the path doesn't have converging arrows at Region Penetration 1, so it's also not blocked there. Therefore, the path is active.

You can conclude that all of the variables are linked together when sales are observed in the model. When you run inference, you'll infer the quality of all of the products and the penetration of all regions simultaneously. This kind of inference process is known as *collective inference*, and it's a typical kind of reasoning performed in probabilistic programming.

TWO-DIMENSIONAL SALES MODEL IN FIGARO

It's easy to represent this situation in Figaro by using two-dimensional arrays. I'll show the whole code, because you've seen the ingredients already.

Listing 6.1   Two-dimensional sales model

```
import com.cra.figaro.library.atomic.continuous.Beta
import com.cra.figaro.language.Flip
import com.cra.figaro.algorithm.sampling.Importance

object Sales {
  def main(args: Array[String]) {
    val numProducts = args.length
    val numRegions = args(0).length

    val productQuality = Array.fill(numProducts)(Beta(2,2))
    val regionPenetration = Array.fill(numRegions)(Beta(2,2))

    def makeSales(i: Int, j: Int) =
      Flip(productQuality(i) * regionPenetration(j))
    val highSales =
      Array.tabulate(numProducts, numRegions)(makeSales _)

    for {
      i <- 0 until numProducts
      j <- 0 until numRegions
    } {
      val observation = args(i)(j) == 'T'
      highSales(i)(j).observe(observation)
    }
```

The command-line arguments are a number of strings, one for each product. Each string has one character for each region; the strings should have the same length.

Array.tabulate(numProducts, numRegions) creates a two-dimensional array, where each item is generated based on the corresponding product and region indices. Each item is a Flip where the probability is the appropriate product quality times the appropriate region penetration.

The sales observations are taken from the command line; a T indicates high sales for the corresponding product and region. The appropriate evidence is asserted on each highSales element.

```
val targets = productQuality ++ regionPenetration
val algorithm = Importance(targets:_*)
algorithm.start()
Thread.sleep(1000)
algorithm.stop()
```

Create an anytime Importance sampling algorithm in which the query targets are all of the product quality and region penetration elements

```
for { i <- 0 until numProducts } {
  println("Product " + i + " quality: " +
          algorithm.mean(productQuality(i)))
}
for { j <- 0 until numRegions } {
  println("Region " + j + " penetration: " +
          algorithm.mean(regionPenetration(j)))
}

  algorithm.kill()
  }
}
```

Print the average inferred product quality and region penetration of every product and region

Now you've seen three practical models that can be represented using Scala collections. It's time to increase your modeling prowess by learning how to use Figaro collections.

6.2 Using Figaro collections

In the previous section, you learned how Scala collections can help you create a variety of interesting models that involve many variables of a particular kind. This section introduces Figaro collections. A *Figaro collection* is a data structure that holds many Figaro elements of the same kind. You're probably thinking that that sounds an awful lot like a Scala collection—why do you also need Figaro collections?

6.2.1 Understanding why Figaro collections are useful

Figaro collections are special because they know that the things they contain are elements, which define probability distributions over values. They let you reach inside the elements and work with operations on the values. Figure 6.4 illustrates how this works.

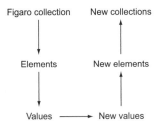

Figure 6.4 A Figaro collection contains elements, which define probability distributions over values. Figaro collections let you apply operations to these values, which can be used to produce new elements and new collections.

This capability lets you do lots of useful things, including these:

- If c is a Figaro collection of `Integer` elements, `c.map((i: Int) => i * 2)` will produce a new Figaro collection. For each element e in the original collection, there will be an element equivalent to `Apply(e, (i: Int) => i * 2)` in the new collection. So the new collection consists of `Integer` elements. Each element corresponds to the process of starting with an element in the original collection, generating its value, and multiplying it by 2. For example, if c is the Figaro collection containing the two elements `Uniform(2, 3)` and `Constant(5)`, then `c.map((i: Int) => i * 2)` is the Figaro collection containing the elements `Apply(Uniform(2, 3), (i: Int) => i * 2)` and `Apply(Constant(5), (i: Int) => i * 2)`. In practice, this means that the collection contains two elements, one of which is uniformly distributed over 4 (2 * 2) and 6 (3 * 2), and the other of which is constantly 10 (5 * 2).

- If c is a Figaro collection of double elements, `c.chain((d: Double) => Flip(d))` will produce a new Figaro collection, in which for each element e of the original collection, there's an element `Chain(e, (d: Double) => Flip(d))` in the new collection. The first collection is a collection of parameters, and the second is a collection of `Flip`s, where each `Flip` depends on the corresponding parameter. For example, if c contains the elements `Beta(2, 1)` and `Beta(1, 2)`, the two elements in the resulting collection will be equivalent to `Flip(Beta(2, 1))` and `Flip(Beta(1, 2))` (remembering that a compound `Flip` is shorthand for the `Chain`).

- If c is a Figaro collection of `Integer` elements, `c.exists((i: Int) => i < 0)` returns a Boolean element representing whether any of the elements in the collection have a negative value. Similarly, `c.count((i: Int) => i < 0)` returns the number of such elements.

- You can apply any fold or aggregation operation on a container. If you're experienced with Scala, you're probably familiar with operations such as `foldLeft`. For example, if c is a Figaro collection of `Integer` elements, you can use `c.foldleft(_ + _)` to create an element representing the sum of the values of elements in the collection. Let's take the example where c is a Figaro collection with the two elements `Uniform(2,3)` and `Constant(5)`. Two sums are possible: 2 + 5 = 7 and 3 + 5 = 8. Because 2 and 3 each have probability 1/2 in the first element, these two sums also have probability 1/2. So `c.foldleft(_ + _)` is an element that's uniformly distributed over 7 and 8.

- A variety of other operations on Figaro containers are available—see the Scaladoc for details.

This is the main reason Figaro collections are useful. Other important reasons include the following:

- They allow you to represent situations involving an unknown number of objects by using variable-size collections.

- They also enable you to represent situations involving infinitely many variables, or even a continuum of variables.

You'll learn more about these later in the chapter.

6.2.2 Revisiting the hierarchical model with Figaro collections

For your first example of Figaro collections, you'll revisit the hierarchical model involving tosses of coins drawn from a bag, and see how to represent it using Figaro collections. This model uses what is probably the simplest kind of Figaro collection: `FixedSizeArray`. As its name indicates, `FixedSizeArray` contains a fixed number of elements, each of which is generated in some way. As shown in figure 6.5, the `FixedSizeArray` constructor takes two arguments: the number of elements and an element generator. The element generator is a function that takes an `Integer` argument, representing an index into the array, and returns an element that may depend on the index. The code in figure 6.5 creates a Figaro collection consisting of 10 elements, where the `i`th element (starting from 0) is equal to `Flip(1.0 / (i + 1))`.

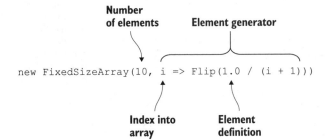

Figure 6.5 Structure of a fixed-size array construction

Because you've already seen the hierarchical model, I'll show the code with the changes highlighted in bold. To illustrate the use of Figaro containers, I've extended the example slightly to allow the command-line arguments to also contain ? characters, indicating that the outcome of the coin toss wasn't observed. You can then query whether any of the tosses of a particular coin came out heads.

Listing 6.2 Hierarchical model using Figaro containers

```
import com.cra.figaro.language.{Flip, Constant}
import com.cra.figaro.library.atomic.continuous.{Uniform, Beta}
import com.cra.figaro.library.compound.If
import com.cra.figaro.algorithm.sampling.Importance
import com.cra.figaro.library.process.FixedSizeArray        ⟵  com.cra.figaro.library
                                                                .process is the
                                                                package containing
                                                                Figaro's collections
object HierarchicalContainers {                                 library.
  def main(args: Array[String]) {
    val numCoins = args.length

    val fairProbability = Uniform(0.0, 1.0)
```

The variable tosses is a Scala sequence (one for each coin) where every item is a Figaro collection, in which every element is a Flip whose probability of coming out heads is the bias of the appropriate coin.

In this fixed-size array, every element is Flip(fairProbability), regardless of the index.

```scala
val isFair =
    new FixedSizeArray(numCoins + 1, i => Flip(fairProbability))

val biases = isFair.chain(if (_) Constant(0.5) else Beta(2,5))

val tosses =
    for { coin <- 0 until numCoins } yield
    new FixedSizeArray(args(coin).length, i => Flip(biases(coin)))

val hasHeads =
    for { coin <- 0 until numCoins } yield
    tosses(coin).exists(b => b)

for {
    coin <- 0 until numCoins
    toss <- 0 until args(coin).length
} {
    args(coin)(toss) match {
        case 'H' => tosses(coin)(toss).observe(true)
        case 'T' => tosses(coin)(toss).observe(false)
        case _  => ()
    }
}

val algorithm = Importance(fairProbability, hasHeads(2))
algorithm.start()
Thread.sleep(1000)
algorithm.stop()
println("Probability at least one of the tosses of the third " +
        "coin was heads = " +
        algorithm.probability(hasHeads(2), true))
algorithm.kill()
    }
}
```

For each coin, this creates a new element that's either Constant(0.5) or Beta(2, 5), depending on the value of isFair(coin).

For each coin, hasHeads(coin) is an element representing whether any of the tosses of the coin came out heads. See text for a breakdown of tosses(coin) .exists(b => b).

Observing the evidence is done in almost the exact same way as before. tosses(coin) is a FixedSizeArray, and you can use tosses(coin)(toss) to get an element just as in a Scala array.

The line that needs most explanation is `tosses(coin).exists(b => b)`. Let's break it down. First, `tosses` is defined using this code:

```scala
for { coin <- 0 until numCoins } yield
new FixedSizeArray(args(coin).length, i => Flip(biases(coin)))
```

The for...yield construct creates a Scala sequence, in which you have a fixed-size array for every coin. The number of elements in this fixed-size array is equal to the number of tosses of the coin, which is given by the corresponding command-line argument. Each element is a Flip with the bias of this coin. Therefore, `tosses(coin)` is a fixed-size array.

exists is a method on Figaro collections that creates a new element representing whether any of the elements in the collection has a value that satisfies a given predicate. In this case, the predicate is b => b, which is the function that takes a value b and returns the same value. Because the coin tosses are Boolean, b is a Boolean, and this predicate returns true precisely when the value of the element is true (when the coin toss came out heads). So tosses(coin).exists(b => b) returns an element whose value is true when any of the tosses of the appropriate coin came out true.

Now that you've seen a first example of Figaro collections, let's explore further the relationship between Scala collections and Figaro collections.

6.2.3   *Using Scala and Figaro collections together*

Now that you've seen how to work with Figaro collections by using operations defined on the values of elements, you might be wondering whether Scala collections are useful at all in Figaro. They are—because there are more kinds of Scala collections than Figaro collections, and many methods are defined on Scala collections that aren't defined on Figaro collections. As long as you don't need to work with collections by using operations defined on values, you're better off sticking with Scala collections.

CONVERTING TO AND FROM SCALA AND FIGARO COLLECTIONS

Sometimes you need both. You might need the flexibility of Scala collections together with the ability to use operations on values. Fortunately, it's easy to convert from Scala collections to Figaro collections, and vice versa. Here are some ways Figaro lets you convert between Scala and Figaro collections:

- *The* Container *constructor*—In Figaro, a Container is the general class of a collection containing a finite number of elements. A Container constructor is provided that takes a variable number of arguments, each of which is an element over the same value type. This constructor returns a Figaro collection with these elements. You could write Container(toss1, toss2, toss3) to create a Figaro collection consisting of these three tosses.

  If your Scala collection is a kind of sequence (it implements the Seq trait, such as an array or list), you can convert it to a variable number of arguments by using the :_* construct. So if tosses = List(toss1, toss2, toss3), then Container(tosses:_*) is the same as the Figaro collection in the previous paragraph. If your collection is something like a set, which isn't a sequence, you can first convert it to a sequence by using the toList method, and then use the :_* construct—for example, Container(Set(toss1, toss2, toss3).toList:_*). Any Scala collection that implements the Traversable trait, which covers most collections, can be converted to a list in this way, and in turn converted into a Figaro collection.

- *Enumerating the elements in a* Container—If you have a Figaro Container (a finite collection), you can turn it into a Scala Seq of elements by using the elements method. So `Container(toss1, toss2, toss3).elements` will return a Scala `Seq` containing `toss1`, `toss2`, and `toss3`. You can then turn this `Seq` into whatever Scala collection you want, such as a list or a set.

■ *Producing a mapping from indices to elements*—The core definition of a Figaro collection is a mapping from values in an index set to elements. You'll explore this concept more in section 6.4, when you consider infinite processes in which the index set consists of real numbers. For a `FixedSizeArray`, the index set comprises the integers from 0 to the number of elements minus 1. For `Container`, the index set is finite. Therefore, you can easily turn the `Container` into an explicit Scala `Map` from indices to values. This is achieved through the `Container`'s `toMap` method.

EXAMPLE: SALES PREDICTION

To illustrate how to use Scala and Figaro collections together, let's extend the sales example from section 6.1.3. As before, you have a number of products, each with a product quality; and a number of regions, each with a degree of region penetration. You'll observe the sales of each product in each region last year and predict the sales of each product in each region in the coming year. You'll further predict the number of new people your company might hire to support each product line and each region's sales force.

You'll start, as before, with one-dimensional Scala arrays of products and regions, and two-dimensional Scala arrays of sales:

```
val productQuality = Array.fill(numProducts)(Beta(2,2))
val regionPenetration = Array.fill(numRegions)(Beta(2,2))
def makeSales(i: Int, j: Int) =
    Flip(productQuality(i) * regionPenetration(j))
val highSalesLastYear =
    Array.tabulate(numProducts, numRegions)(makeSales _)
val highSalesNextYear =
    Array.tabulate(numProducts, numRegions)(makeSales _)
```

This is a complete model of all products, regions, and both last year's and next year's sales and can be used to predict next year's sales based on last year's. For this purpose, Scala collections are sufficient, and if you don't need the extra power of Figaro collections, you shouldn't use them. But you also want to predict the number of new hires per product and per region, and for that, you need Figaro collections. The following code creates a Scala array, with one item for each product, in which each item is a Figaro `Container` containing the elements representing the predicted sales of the corresponding product in all regions:

```
def getSalesByProduct(i: Int) =
  for { j <- 0 until numRegions } yield highSalesNextYear(i)(j)
val salesPredictionByProduct =
  Array.tabulate(numProducts)(i => Container(getSalesByProduct(i):_*))
```

Now, here's where you use the Figaro collections to predict the number of hires. First, for each product, you'll create an element representing the number of regions in which that product will have high sales next year. You achieve this as follows:

```
val numHighSales =
  for { predictions <- salesPredictionByProduct }
  yield predictions.count(b => b)
```

numHighSales is a Scala array, with one item for each product, and each item is a Figaro `Integer` element. The reason `salesPredictionByProduct` was made an array of Figaro collections is so that, for each predictions collection in `salesPredictionBy-Product`, you can call `predictions.count(b => b)` to get an element representing the number of products for which you predict high sales. This would be challenging to do using other methods and is easy with the Figaro collection.

Now, for each product, you'll create an element representing the number of hires for that product, which depends on `numHighSales` for that product. As usual in Figaro, these kinds of dependencies are created using `Chain`. I'll show you two equivalent ways of doing this, one using Scala collections and one using Figaro collections. First, using Scala collections:

```
val numHiresByProduct =
  for { i <- 0 until numProducts }
  yield Chain(numHighSales(i), (n: Int) => Poisson(n  + 1))
```

This creates a Scala array of `Chain` elements. Now, using Figaro collections:

```
val numHiresByProduct =
  Container(numHighSales:_*).chain((n: Int) => Poisson(n + 1))
```

This creates a Figaro `Container` of `Chain` elements.

That's it for the model. The code for asserting evidence and running inference is essentially the same as before. One subtlety is worth mentioning. Because the query targets are the elements in the `numHiresByProduct`, for the version in which `numHires-ByProduct` is a Figaro `Container`, you need to get its elements to pass them to the importance sampling algorithm. This is achieved with the following:

```
val targets = numHiresByProduct.elements
val algorithm = Importance(targets:_*)
```

Let's reflect on this example. Both Scala and Figaro collections had important roles to play. On the one hand, multidimensional arrays are convenient and easy to use in Scala. You could create a Figaro `Container` with a two-dimensional index set, but it would be much more cumbersome. On the other hand, the count aggregation is easy to do with Figaro containers, but would be much more difficult in Scala. In fact, you'd probably have to reimplement Figaro's logic for doing the aggregation, which isn't trivial.

Now that you've learned the fundamentals of using Figaro collections, let's look at more exotic, but still useful, kinds of collections.

6.3 Modeling situations with an unknown number of objects

Until now, our Figaro collections have contained a fixed number of objects. Although you can combine multiple Figaro collections in the same situation, to this point the total set of objects they contain will be the same. In many situations, the number of objects is unknown and is variable. For these situations, Figaro provides variable-size arrays. I'll first describe the kinds of situations in which variable-size arrays are useful, then present the Figaro `VariableSizeArray` data structure, and finally provide an example of variable-size arrays in action.

6.3.1 Open-universe situations with an unknown number of objects

Imagine you're implementing a highway traffic–surveillance system. Your goal is to monitor the flow of vehicles along the highway and predict when traffic jams might occur. You have video cameras placed at strategic points. To accomplish your goal, you need to do two things. First, you need to infer the vehicles passing at each point, including identifying when the same vehicle passes two different cameras. Second, you need to predict future vehicles that will arrive on the highway and the traffic jams that will result.

Both tasks require reasoning about an unknown number of objects. When you're inferring the vehicles currently on the highway, you don't know the number of vehicles, and your video images don't give you a perfect indication of that number. Sometimes, multiple vehicles might be merged in the image, and some vehicles might not be detected at all. And when you're predicting future traffic jams, you certainly don't know exactly how many vehicles there will be.

A situation in which you don't know the number of objects is known as an *open-universe situation* (see the accompanying sidebar for an explanation of the name). An open-universe situation is characterized by two properties:

- You don't know the exact number of objects, such as the number of vehicles. This is called *number uncertainty*.
- You're uncertain about the identity of the objects. For example, you might be uncertain whether two vehicle images at different sites belong to the same vehicle. This is called *identity uncertainty*.

This section focuses on number uncertainty, which is addressed by variable-size arrays. Figaro can also handle situations with identity uncertainty, but you'll have to wait until the next chapter to see an easy way to do that.

Open-universe modeling

Use of the term *open universe* in probabilistic programming comes from Stuart Russell and his group, who introduced it for their probabilistic programming language BLOG, which is primarily designed to represent and reason about open-universe situations. The term originally comes from logic, where *closed world* or *closed universe* means that you assume that only objects that are explicitly mentioned or directly derivable from your model exist.

If you're familiar with the logic programming language Prolog, you'll know that Prolog practices negation by failure: if it can't prove something to be true, it's assumed to be false. For example, if you're trying to prove that a green vehicle exists in your image, and you're unable to prove it based on the vehicles you know about, then you assume that no such vehicle exists. You don't have to prove that there's no other green vehicle that you don't happen to know about. Negation by failure is a form of closed-universe reasoning.

In contrast, full first-order logic is open universe. To prove that there's no green vehicle in your image, you have to prove that there can't possibly be such a vehicle, even if you don't know about it. Modeling open-universe situations is something probabilistic programming languages enable you to do that's hard to do in other probabilistic reasoning frameworks.

6.3.2 *Variable-size arrays*

Figaro's approach to open-universe modeling is to use variable-size arrays. A variable-size array takes two arguments: an element whose value is the size of the array, and an element generator, which is similar to the element generator for a fixed-size array. Figure 6.6 shows an example of constructing a variable-size array. The first argument to the `VariableSizeArray` constructor is an `Integer` element representing the number of elements in the array. The second argument is the element generator, which is a function from an array index to an element definition. In figure 6.6, each element in the array is defined by a `Beta`, so it's a `Double` element.

What happens when you construct a variable-size array? Technically, a variable-size array isn't a single array at all, but rather represents a random variable whose value could be one of many arrays, each of a different length, depending on the value of the

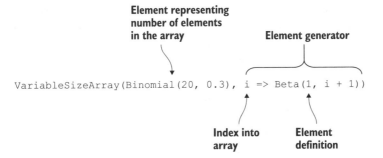

Figure 6.6 Structure of a variable-size array construction

number argument. When you invoke `VariableSizeArray`, you're creating a `Make-Array` element to represent this random variable. All operations on variable-size arrays are applied to this `MakeArray` element. Under the hood, Figaro makes sure that `Make-Array` is implemented as efficiently as possible to ensure the maximum amount of data sharing between the arrays of different size. In particular, shorter arrays are prefixes of longer arrays and use the same elements. As a programmer, all this is taken care of for you, and you don't have to worry about it, but I want to make sure you know what `MakeArray` is because you might encounter this type.

6.3.3 *Operations on variable-size arrays*

What can you do with a variable-size array? Pretty much everything you can do with a fixed-size array, but important differences exist. In the following examples, `vsa` represents a variable-size array whose items are String elements. Here are some operations on variable-size arrays:

- *Getting the element at an index*—In principle, `vsa(5)` will get the element at index 5 (the sixth element in the array). But this can be dangerous. You should be sure the array will always have at least six elements to call this method. Otherwise, you're liable to get an `IndexOutOfRangeException`.

- *Safely getting an optional element at an index*—For this reason, Figaro provides a safer way to get at the element at an index. `vsa.get(5)` returns `Element[Option[String]]`. This is a Scala type that could be `Some[String]`, if there's a string, or `None` if there's no string. `vsa.get(5)` represents the following random process:
  - Choose the number of elements according to the number argument.
  - Get the fixed-size array of the appropriate size.
  - If the array has a least six elements, let s be the value of the element at index 5. Return `Some(s)`.
  - Otherwise, return `None`.

  You see that in either case, the random process produces `Option[String]`. So the process is represented by an `Element[Option[String]]`. You can use an `Element[Option[String]]` in various ways. You could pass it, for example, to an `Apply` element that does something interesting if the argument is `Some(s)`, and produces a default value if the argument is `None`.

- *Map the variable-size array through a function on values*—This is similar to fixed-size arrays, except that now Figaro reaches inside the variable-size array to the fixed-size arrays it points to, and then reaches inside the fixed-size arrays to the values. For example, `vsa.map(_.length)` produces a new variable-size array, in which each string is replaced by its length.

- *Chain the variable-size array through a function that maps values to elements*—Again, this is similar to a fixed-size array, and again Figaro reaches inside the variable-size array to the fixed-size arrays and chains each of the elements in the fixed-size arrays through the function. For example, `vsa.map((s: String) => discrete.Uniform(s:_*))` creates a variable-size array in which each element contains a random character from the corresponding string. In this example, `s:_*` turns the string into a sequence of characters, and `discrete.Uniform (s:_*)` selects a random member from the sequence.

- *Folds and aggregates*—All of the folds and aggregates that are offered for fixed-size arrays are also available for variable-size arrays. For example, `vsa.count (_.length > 2)` returns an `Element[Int]` representing the number of strings in the array whose length is greater than 2. You can understand this as randomly choosing a fixed-size array according to the number argument, and then counting the number of strings in that array whose length is greater than 2. Again, consult the Scaladoc to see all folds and aggregates that are defined.

6.3.4 Example: predicting sales of an unknown number of new products

In this example, you'll imagine that you're planning the research and development (R&D) investment of your company in the coming year. Higher R&D investment leads to more new products being developed, which leads to higher sales. But at the time of making the investment, you don't know exactly how many new products will be developed for a given level of investment.

Therefore, you use a variable-size array to represent the new products. The model is defined as follows:

1 It takes as argument `rNDLevel`, which is a `Double` representing the level of R&D investment.

2 The `numNewProducts` element, which represents the number of new products that are developed as a result of R&D, is an `Integer` element defined by `Geometric(rNDLevel)`. A `Geometric` element characterizes a process that goes on for a number of steps. After each step, the process can terminate or it can go on to the next step. The probability of going on to the next step is provided by the parameter of the `Geometric` element (in this case, `rNDLevel`). The value of the process is the number of steps before termination. The probabilities of the number of steps decrease geometrically by a factor of `rNDLevel` each time. The higher the `rNDLevel`, the longer the process is likely to go on, and the more new products will be developed.

3 You create a variable-size array called `productQuality`, representing the quality of each of the new products. The number argument of this variable-size array is `numNewProducts`. The element generator is the function that maps an index `i` to `Beta(1, i + 1)`. In section 6.1.1, you learned that the expected value of `Beta(1, i + 1)` is $1 / (i + 2)$, so the product quality tends to decrease as more new products are developed, representing a diminishing return on R&D investment.

4 Next, you turn the product quality into a prediction of the sales of each product. This takes place in two steps. First, you generate the raw sales by using a `Normal` element centered on the product quality. But a `Normal` element can

have negative values, and negative sales are impossible, so in the second step, you truncate the `Normal` element and give it a lower bound of 0. These two steps are accomplished by using the `chain` and `map` methods of `VariableSizeArray`.

5 Finally, you get the total sales by folding the `sum` function through the product-Sales variable-size array.

The full code for the model is shown here:

```
val numNewProducts = Geometric(rNDLevel)
val productQuality =
  VariableSizeArray(numNewProducts, i => Beta(1, i + 1))
val productSalesRaw = productQuality.chain(Normal(_, 0.5))
val productSales = productSalesRaw.map(_.max(0))
val totalSales = productSales.foldLeft(0.0)(_ + _)
```

In this example, probabilistic programming lets you implement a rich process in just a few lines of code. Next, you'll learn the fundamental concepts that make Figaro collections work and see how they're applied to infinite collections.

6.4 *Working with infinite processes*

This section shows how to use Figaro collections defined over an infinite space. Your first question might be, how can you possibly have a collection with an infinite number of elements in a finite amount of memory? And how can you work with such a collection in a finite amount of time?

The answer is that the elements in the collection are defined only implicitly. You never access infinitely many elements. But they're all available to you should you need them.

> **WARNING** This section contains advanced material. Feel free to skip it on first reading; you won't need it for the rest of the book. But do return to it if you want to get deeply into Figaro collections and appreciate their power.

The `Process` trait is Figaro's general representation of collections, which could be finite or infinite. The following pages explain how a process can implicitly represent many elements and how you can work with a process. Then you'll see an example of a process defined over points in time.

6.4.1 *The Process trait*

In Figaro, a *process* is an implicit representation of a collection of elements defined over an index set. By *implicit*, I mean that given any index, you can get the element at that index. Arrays are naturally defined this way; given any integer index within the bounds, you can get the element at that index. But for Figaro processes, the index can be any type you like. So the `Process` trait is parameterized by two types: the index type, and the value type, representing the type of values of elements in the process.

The essential method that needs to be defined for `Process[Index, Value]` is generate. In its simplest form, `generate` takes an index of type `Index` and returns `Element[Value]`. When you call the `generate` method, it should create and return the appropriate element for the given index.

You shouldn't call `generate` directly when you use a process. You've seen earlier that if p is a fixed-size array, `p(5)` gets the element of p at index 5. There's no need to call `generate`. In fact, `p(5)` is safer than an explicit call to `generate`. Calling `p(5)` will result in a call to `generate` to produce an element, which is cached, to make sure you get the same element each time. If you call `generate` directly, you'll get a different element each time you call it with the same index, which probably isn't what you want.

> **NOTE** In Scala, `p(5)` is shorthand for `p.apply(5)`. The `Process` trait has an `apply` method that calls `generate` and caches the result, enabling you to call `p(5)` to get the element you want.

Another form of `generate` lets you get the elements for many indices at once. This one is special, and illustrates a way in which Figaro collections can be different from ordinary collections. In a Figaro process, dependencies might exist between the elements at different indices. For example, suppose you have a process representing the amount of rainfall at various locations in a region. Clearly, the elements representing rainfall at nearby locations should be dependent on each other. If you get the elements one at a time, you won't capture these dependencies, but if you get the elements at all of the locations you're interested in together, you can generate the dependencies between them.

This second form of `generate` takes as an argument a list of indices. It returns `Map[Index, Element[Value]]`, a mapping from indices to elements. This map should contain the element corresponding to each of the indices in its argument. Behind the scenes, `generate` will also produce elements representing the dependencies between the elements for the indices, although these aren't put in the map. For example, if you have a process containing the rainfall at different locations, then calling `generate` with a set of locations will produce the elements representing the rainfall at those locations, as well as elements representing the dependencies between the rainfall at those locations. You'll see how this works in an example shortly.

The `Process` trait has one other method that needs to be defined. Not every possible index of type `Index` is a valid index in the process that has an element associated with it. For example, in an array, only integers from 0 to the size of the array minus 1 are valid indices. The `Process` trait has a method called `rangeCheck` that takes an index argument and returns a Boolean indicating whether the index is in range and valid. When you use the process's `apply` method to get an element, it first checks whether the index is in range; if not, it throws an `IndexOutOfRangeException`.

Containers revisited

Section 6.2 indicated that `Container` is the general superclass representing finite collections in Figaro. Now that you've seen the more general `Process` trait, it's time to revisit `Container`. A `Container` is a process that has provided a particular finite sequence of indices. Only indices in that sequence are valid. A `Container` has `generate` methods to get one or many elements, just like a process.

Because the number of elements is finite, you can define folds and aggregates on `Containers`. A fold operation requires going through all elements in the collection. This can be done only if the collection is finite. Therefore, the general `Process` trait doesn't support folds or aggregates. But the `Process` trait does support `map` and `chain` operations, just like `Containers`.

`FixedSizeArray` is a subclass of `Container`. It's special in two ways. First, the sequence of valid indices is integers from 0 up to the size of the array minus 1. Second, the elements in `FixedSizeArray` are assumed to be independent. Whether you generate a single element or many elements together, each element is generated using the element generator, and no additional elements are generated to encode dependencies.

6.4.2 *Example: a temporal health process*

The final example of the chapter uses a temporal process representing a value that varies over time. The process models the health of a patient over time. There are two approaches to modeling a temporal process. One is to set up discrete time points at regular intervals (for example, every minute) and define a random variable to represent the health of the patient at each discrete time point. The second is to treat time as continuous, with a health variable defined at every time point. This lets you access the health variables at exactly the time points you want. I'll take this second approach to illustrate Figaro's infinite processes.

   You'll define a `HealthProcess` object that's a `Process` whose indices are doubles representing time points and whose elements are Boolean elements representing whether the patient is healthy at each point in time. The declaration of `HealthProcess` is as follows:

```
object HealthProcess extends Process[Double, Boolean]
```

You need to implement three methods: (1) The version of `generate` that produces an element for a single time point; (2) the version of `generate` that produces elements for multiple time points, along with their dependencies; and (3) `rangeCheck`.

   Let's start with `rangeCheck` because it's simplest. Let's assume that this process has a start time, which will be time 0. Any time that's 0 or greater will be valid. So `rangeCheck` is defined by the following:

```
def rangeCheck(time: Double) = time >= 0
```

Next, let's implement the `generate` method that produces the health of a patient at a single point in time. When you look at a single time point in isolation, the health variable is a simple `Flip`. But let's suppose that you don't know the `Flip` probability and want to learn it. You can introduce a parameter called `healthyPrior` to represent this probability. `healthyPrior` and the single element `generate` are defined as follows:

```
val healthyPrior = Uniform((0.05 to 0.95 by 0.1):_*)
def generate(time: Double): Element[Boolean] = Flip(healthyPrior)
```

For `healthyPrior`, a discrete `Uniform` element is used that chooses between the values 0.05, 0.15, ..., 0.95.

Now for the most interesting part. You want to implement a `generate` function that can produce the elements for a set of time points along with the dependencies between them. How should you model the dependencies between time points? One natural model is that nearby time points are likely to have the same health value. The degree to which this is true depends on how close the time points are to each other. You'll assume that the influence of one time point on the next decreases exponentially with the distance between the time points. You'll use a parameter called `health-ChangeRate` to represent the speed with which the health status changes over time, and you'll learn this parameter from the data.

So you're going to create two sets of elements. The first set is the elements for the time points, which are created using the single time point `generate` method. The second set encodes dependencies between each successive pair of time points. You go through the ordered sequence of time points, and for each pair, create an element that encodes the fact that successive time points are more likely to have the same health status than different health statuses. The strength of this constraint will depend on the distance between the time points and will be modulated by `healthChangeRate`:

Sort the times so we can always assume they are in order

Produce the map from time indices to health status elements

Go through the times, in order, processing each successive pair

Create an element encoding the dependency between the health status at successive time points

```
def generate(times: List[Double]): Map[Double, Element[Boolean]] = {
  val sortedTimes = times.sorted

  val healthy = sortedTimes.map(time => (time, generate(time))).toMap

  def makePairs(remaining: List[Double]) {
    if (remaining.length >= 2) {
      val time1 :: time2 :: rest = remaining

      val probChange =
        Apply(healthChangeRate,
              (d: Double) => 1 - math.exp(- (time2 - time1) / d))
      val equalHealth = healthy(time1) === healthy(time2)
      val healthStatusChecker =
        If(equalHealth, Constant(true), Flip(probChange))
      healthStatusChecker.observe(true)

      makePairs(time2 :: rest)
    }
  }
}
```

```
  makePairs(sortedTimes)
  healthy
}
```

Here's how you create the element encoding the dependency between the health statuses at successive time points. You'll model it as an undirected dependency. Recall from chapter 5 that Figaro provides two ways to encode undirected dependencies. The simpler method uses a constraint. But that doesn't allow you to learn the parameters characterizing the dependency, and you want to learn `healthChangeRate`. So you'll use the other method, which is to create a Boolean element whose probability of being `true` depends on the two health statuses, and observe that the element has value `true`. Here's what you have as inputs:

- `healthy(time1)`—The health status at the first time point
- `healthy(time2)`—The health status at the second time point
- `healthChangeRate`—The rate at which health status tends to change

The preceding code creates an element named `healthStatusChecker` that you'll observe to be `true`. If `healthy(time1)` and `healthy(time2)` are equal, `healthStatus-Checker` will definitely be `true`. This is equivalent to saying that when `healthy(time1)` and `healthy(time2)` are equal, the constraint value is 1. If `healthy(time1)` and `healthy(time2)` are unequal, the probability `healthStatusChecker` is `true` depends on the distance between `time2` and `time1`. Intuitively, the larger the distance between `time2` and `time1`, the more likely the health status has changed. According to the definition of `probChange`, the probability the health status *hasn't* changed is exponentially decreasing in `time2 - time1` divided by the value of `healthChangeRate`. So the probability that the health status *has* changed gets closer to 1 the larger the time difference.

6.4.3   *Using the process*

That's it for defining the process. Now it's time to use it. To do that, you'll assume that you're given data containing the health status at a number of time points. You want to query the health status at other time points. You also want to query the learned `healthyPrior` and `healthChangeRate` based on the data.

The crucial step is to generate the elements for all time points you're interested in, including the time points in both the data and the query, in one go. That way, all necessary dependencies will be created. If you generated elements for the data and the query separately, you wouldn't get any dependencies between them, and you wouldn't be able to use the data to predict the health at the query times.

This example uses variable elimination for inference. Variable elimination works efficiently in this model and is an exact inference algorithm, so it's the best choice here. But Figaro's variable elimination works only when variables have a finite number of choices. This is why `healthyPrior` and `healthChangeRate` were modeled with a discrete, finite set of choices. Here's the code for generating the required elements, asserting evidence, running inference, and getting the answers to queries:

```
val data = Map(0.1 -> true, 0.25 -> true, 0.3 -> false,
               0.31 -> false, 0.34 -> false, 0.36 -> false,
               0.4 -> true, 0.5 -> true, 0.55 -> true)
```
> **The data maps time points to observed health status.**

```
val queries = List(0.35, 0.37, 0.45, 0.6)
val targets = queries ::: data.keys.toList
val healthy = generate(targets)
```
> **Generate elements for all data and query points**

```
for { (time, value) <- data } {
  healthy(time).observe(value)
}
```
> **Assert the evidence. healthy, which was returned by generate, is a map from time points to elements.**

```
val queryElements = queries.map(healthy(_))
val queryTargets = healthyPrior :: healthChangeRate :: queryElements
val algorithm = VariableElimination(queryTargets:_*)
algorithm.start()
```
> **Run inference on the target elements. Again you use the healthy map to get the relevant elements.**

```
for { query <- queries } {
  println("Probability the patient is healthy at time " + query + " = " +
          algorithm.probability(healthy(query), true))
}
println("Expected prior probability of healthy = " +
        algorithm.mean(healthyPrior))
println("Expected health change rate = " +
        algorithm.mean(healthChangeRate))
algorithm.kill()
```

This example is a bit more advanced than the previous ones in this chapter. Fixed-SizeArray takes care of all of the work of defining rangeCheck and the two versions of generate. But if you need to roll up your own custom process or container, now you know how to do it.

That wraps it up for this chapter. You started with some relatively simple but useful design patterns and gradually moved to more powerful and far-reaching concepts. In the next chapter, you'll learn how to use Figaro to create object-oriented probabilistic models, which will further enhance your ability to create practical models.

6.5 Summary

- Just as in ordinary programming, collections let you organize many objects and use the same code to operate on all of them.
- Scala collections provide useful and powerful organizing structures for Figaro elements, enabling you to create models with hierarchical or multidimensional dependencies.
- Figaro collections provide additional capabilities for organizing elements while providing you with the ability to reach inside the elements and manipulate the values, enabling operations such as folds and quantifiers.

- In addition, Figaro collections let you model open-universe situations with an unknown number of objects.
- Figaro processes let you model collections over an infinite set of indices, such as time or space.

6.6   Exercises

Solutions to selected exercises are available online at www.manning.com/books/practical-probabilistic-programming.

1 In your town, there are three elementary schools. Each school has classes from first grade through sixth grade. Each class has 30 students. Each student takes exams in mathematics. The score of the student on each exam depends on the ability of the student and the skill of the teacher. Write a probabilistic program to represent this situation and infer the skills of the teachers from the test results. Write this program using Scala collections.

2 You're taking your family to an amusement park. There are seven rides, each of which is either thrilling or gentle. Each ride also has a quality, which can be high, medium, or low. Whether a ride is thrilling or gentle is observed, but the quality is not. You have three children, ages 16, 11, and 7. The degree to which a child likes a ride depends on their age, the quality of the ride, and whether it's thrilling or gentle; older children tend to prefer more thrilling rides, and all children prefer higher-quality rides. Your 16-year-old has been to the amusement park before and has told you which rides he likes. Use Scala collections to write a program to predict whether your 11- and 7-year-old will enjoy each ride.

3 In golf, each hole has a *par*, which is a target number of shots to get the ball in the hole. Par is usually 3, 4, or 5. Assume that a golfer has a skill level s that determines probabilistically how many shots he or she will take to get the ball in the hole. The skill level s is a real number uniformly distributed between 0 and $8/13$. Specifically, the probability of using a given number of shots is defined by the following table.

Par – 2	Par – 1	Par	Par + 1	Par + 2
$\frac{s}{8}$	$\frac{s}{2}$	s	$\frac{4}{5} \times \left(1 - \frac{13s}{8}\right)$	$\frac{1}{5} \times \left(1 - \frac{13s}{8}\right)$

Create a data structure representing a golf course with 18 holes of various pars. Write a Figaro program to represent a player's playing a round of golf.

a Use the program to predict the probability that the player's score will be greater than 80, given an unknown skill level.

b Use the program to answer the same query, given that the skill level is at least 0.3.

c Use the program to infer the probability that the player's skill level is at least 0.3, given that the total score is 80.

4 In the game Minesweeper, you need to detect mines in a grid. Every square in a grid can be in one of four states: (1) known mine, (2) known safe, (3) unknown mine, (4) unknown safe. Each of the known safe squares contains a number indicating the number of mines (known or unknown) in the eight squares adjacent to it horizontally, vertically, or diagonally. Write a probabilistic program that takes a Minesweeper grid and predicts the probability of a mine in each of the unknown squares.

5 You own a candy store and are trying to predict how many pieces of candy you will sell on a given day. Assume that the number of children who come to your store on a given day is `Binomial(100, 0.1)`. Each child buys candy with probability 0.5, and if a child buys candy, the number of pieces is uniformly chosen from 1 to 10. Use a variable-size array to predict the total number of pieces sold on a given day.

6 Again, you own a candy store, but now children come into the store together and their purchasing decisions influence each other. Specifically, if one child buys candy, another child is more likely to also buy candy. The amount of candy a child buys, given that he or she buys candy, is unchanged. Assume that the number of groups of children who come to the store on a given day is `Binomial(40, 0.1)`, and each group contains a number of children uniformly chosen from 1 to 5. Create a Figaro process to capture the logic of this situation and use it to predict the total number of pieces sold on a given day.

Object-oriented
probabilistic modeling

7

This chapter covers

- Using object-oriented (OO) programming techniques to organize complex probabilistic models

- Combining OO techniques with concepts from relational databases, using objects and relationships between objects to create flexible models

- Figaro constructs for OO modeling, including element collections and references

- Using Figaro constructs to represent uncertainty about object types and relationships

In the previous chapter, you learned all about how collections can be used to structure probabilistic programs. This chapter continues with the theme of using common programming language constructs to build probabilistic programs. The theme of this chapter is using object-oriented programming techniques to represent probabilistic models. Object orientation is a powerful programming technique in general, and, as you'll learn, it's particularly appropriate for probabilistic modeling, because it's natural to describe a situation in terms of objects in that situation and relationships between the objects. Scala is a particularly appropriate programming language as the basis for probabilistic programming, because it's both functional and object-oriented. This is one of the main reasons Scala was chosen as the language for embedding Figaro.

The chapter starts with basic object-orientation concepts as they're applied to probabilistic programming. You'll see the use of classes, instances, subclasses, and inheritance, and the way these enable you to put together programs by using objects as the building blocks. Section 7.2 presents relational probabilistic models, in which relationships between objects take center stage. After you start working with relationships, it becomes natural to consider situations where you don't know what the relationships are. This is called *relational uncertainty*, and is the main topic of section 7.3. You'll learn about Figaro features that enable representing and reasoning about relational uncertainty. In addition to relational uncertainty, you'll learn how to use these features to model type uncertainty, where you're unsure about the type of an object.

This chapter assumes you're comfortable with concepts from previous chapters. In particular, you should be familiar with the basics of Figaro from chapter 2 as well as modeling dependencies by using Bayesian networks and Markov networks from chapter 5. In addition, you should be familiar with object-oriented programming features from languages such as Java or Scala. In general, I don't use Scala-specific features like traits, although I do use Scala objects, so if you're comfortable with Java, you should be able to understand the object-oriented programming constructs in this chapter.

7.1 Using object-oriented probabilistic models

You're most likely familiar with OO programming and the benefits that result, but I want to get concrete and specific about what I view as the most important benefits here. During the course of the chapter, I emphasize how these benefits apply to probabilistic programming.

To see the motivation for using OO techniques for probabilistic programming, let's revisit the corner-kick example from chapter 1. To remind you, we're modeling a corner kick in a game of soccer, taking into account information such as the skill of the attacking and defending teams, environmental conditions such as the wind, and so on. This situation can be modeled using an OO approach in a natural way. Players are objects. Players belong on teams, which are also objects. Players do things like move or kick the ball. Different kinds of players, like center forwards and goalies, can be modeled using subclasses of the `Player` class. Players interact with other players, as well as the ball, which is also an object. The environment, which can also be modeled as an object, also interacts with the ball and the players.

Object-oriented programming has two main advantages:

- *Providing structure to complex programs*—Objects are coherent units that capture a set of data and behaviors. An object provides a uniform interface to these data and behaviors, and the internals of the object are encapsulated from the rest of the program. This allows the programmer to modify the internals of the object in a modular way, without affecting the rest of the program. For example, a full goalie model might involve a lot of variables and dependencies at a high level of detail, but only a few of those, such as skill at diving for the ball, might influence the rest of the model.

- *Enabling reuse of code*—First, the same class code, with all its internal structure, can be reused for all instances of the class. The same player model can be used for many players on the same team. Second, inheritance makes it possible to reuse common aspects of different classes. For example, a center forward and a goalie can share many variables and dependencies in common.

These same advantages naturally apply to probabilistic programming. But object orientation is arguably even more appropriate for probabilistic models. In probabilistic programming, we're building models of the real world, and the real world naturally can be described in terms of objects.

This section first discusses basic concepts such as classes, instances, attributes, and subclasses, and their application to probabilistic modeling. Then it presents two examples based on the printer example from chapter 5. The first example shows you how to change a flat Bayesian network into an object-oriented model. The second example shows you how to then reuse code to model different kinds of printers in the same network.

7.1.1   *Understanding elements of object-oriented modeling*

In an object-oriented program, you have classes that describe general data and behaviors, and instances of those classes that contain specific data and instantiations of those behaviors. For example, you might have a general *class* of printer and then a specific printer that's an *instance* of that class. The printer class describes general behavior of printers, whereas a printer instance has data and behaviors that are specific to that printer and that are derived from the class behaviors.

> **NOTE**   The term *object* is sometimes used to refer to a class and sometimes an instance. Scala also has an `object` keyword, which defines an instance of a singleton class (a class whose only instance is this particular instance). Because of this confusion, I avoid using the word *object* from now on and use *class* and *instance*, which are unambiguous.

What does this mean for a probabilistic program? The following:

- *A probabilistic class model defines a general process for generating the values of random variables.* For example, a printer class model describes a general process for generating whether the power is on, whether the paper is stuck, the overall state of the printer, and so on.

- *An instance is a specific instantiation of this general class model that describes a process to generate the values of random variables that pertain to this specific instance.* For example, a printer instance uses its class model to describe a process to generate values for variables representing whether this particular printer's power is on, this printer's paper is stuck, and the overall state of this printer.

To represent probabilistic classes and instances in Figaro, you can use ordinary Scala classes and instances. You give the Scala class attributes whose values are elements. For example, in a Scala class to represent a printer, you might have attributes for power-ButtonOn, paperFlow, and state. Each of these is defined to be an element. In Scala, the attribute of a class represents a general definition. Each instance of the class has a particular attribute that's defined by this element. For example, if you have a printer instance named myPrinter, it has attributes myPrinter.powerButtonOn, myPrinter .paperFlow, and myPrinter.state. These attributes are ordinary Scala variables that are defined to be Figaro elements. So you've defined a generative process over the values of the attributes of myPrinter. The following code snippet shows the definition of a Printer class with these three attributes and the definition of a particular instance of the class named myPrinter, which has these specific attributes. myPrinter.power-ButtonOn is an element Flip(0.95), myPrinter.paperFlow is a Select element, and so on.

```
class Printer {
  val powerButtonOn = Flip(0.95)
  val paperFlow = Select(0.6 -> 'smooth, 0.2 -> 'uneven, 0.2 -> 'jammed)
  val state = // etc.
}
val myPrinter = new Printer
```

Another way of putting this is that a set of probabilistic class definitions provides general definitions of random processes that can be reused many times for different instances. This is like ordinary OO programming, in which a class model can be reused for many different instances. If you have printer, network, and software classes, you can reuse these for different instances of printer, network, and software. These instances can be in any configuration you like. For example, you could have different printers working with different software. You may even have different instantiations of the same class within the same program, such as multiple printers on a network.

Because Scala supports subclassing and inheritance, you can use subclasses and inheritance for Figaro models too. This enables you to reuse parts of class definitions for multiple classes. For example, you could have different kinds of printers, such as a laser printer and an inkjet printer. These different kinds of printers can share behaviors in common, such as the propensity for paper jams, while being different in other behaviors, like being out of toner, which is specific to laser printers. The familiar concepts of subclasses, inheritance, and overriding enable you to represent this kind of situation easily.

7.1.2 *Revisiting the printer model*

Those are the basic concepts. Now let's see them in action. You'll use the printer program from chapter 5. Figure 7.1 reproduces the Bayesian network for this problem.

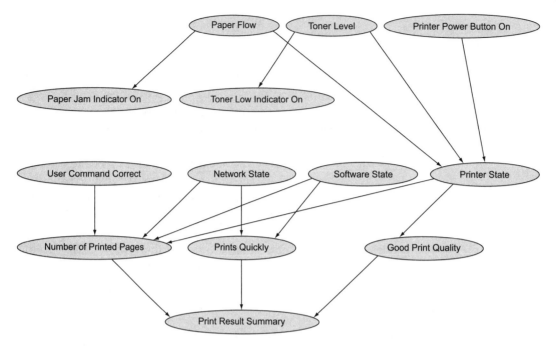

Figure 7.1   Printer Bayesian network, reproduced from chapter 5. Notice how this network is "flat," with all variables existing on the same level, and no structure. Intuitively, the top part of the network corresponds to properties of the printer, but this structure isn't readily apparent in the network.

The Bayesian network describes a user who calls a help desk with a printer problem. The user describes a summary of the print result, which is a function of the number of pages printed, whether the printer prints quickly, and the print quality. In turn, these depend on the user command and the state of the computer network, software, and printer. The Bayesian network then goes into more detail about the printer, modeling whether the power button is on, the paper flow, and the toner level.

This model is a natural candidate for object orientation. First, you have the printer. Six variables in the network are related to the printer, and the only one that's relevant to the rest of the model is Printer State. If you use a printer class, all of the rest of the variables will be encapsulated inside the class. Likewise, although you have only a single node for the user, network, and software in this particular network, these might also be more complex and contain some encapsulated internal state. Finally, you can have an object representing the overall print experience.

You can turn your printer model into an object-oriented Bayesian network by grouping all related variables, as shown in figure 7.2. Here, the six variables pertaining to the printer have been grouped into the Printer class. Likewise, the four nodes relating to the print experience are put in a Print Experience class. I've also chosen to put the user, network, and software each in its own class. Although each has only one

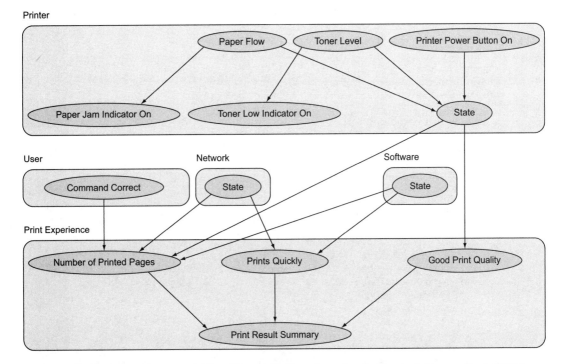

Figure 7.2 **Object-oriented representation of the printer Bayesian network. The shaded boxes group related variables. The label at the top left of these boxes is the name of the class. Notice how this model provides the structure that wasn't apparent in the Bayesian network of figure 7.1.**

variable in this particular model, putting each in a separate class enables you to modify the class at a later stage and add more structure without breaking the overall model. This is a common reason to use an object-oriented style.

The code to represent the printer problem in an object-oriented way is shown next. The code is simple, and the style should be familiar to anyone who's used object-oriented programming. There's not much here that's new to probabilistic programming. The code shows a three-step process:

1 Define the class models.
2 Create instances of those classes.
3 Reason with the instances.

In this example, the instances have been used to infer whether the printer's power button is on, given the summary of the print experience, but they could be used to support any reasoning pattern, just like an ordinary Bayesian network.

The code listing for this problem is divided into three parts. The first part presents class models for the printer, software, network, and user. These class models are the same as before, except that the variables are now placed inside class definitions. Here's the code.

Listing 7.1 Printer problem using object-orientation: class models
---

```scala
package chap07

import com.cra.figaro.language._
import com.cra.figaro.library.compound._
import com.cra.figaro.algorithm.factored.VariableElimination

object PrinterProblemOO {
  class Printer {
    val powerButtonOn = Flip(0.95)
    val tonerLevel = Select(0.7 -> 'high, 0.2 -> 'low, 0.1 -> 'out)
    val tonerLowIndicatorOn =
      If(powerButtonOn,
          CPD(tonerLevel,
              'high -> Flip(0.2),
              'low -> Flip(0.6),
              'out -> Flip(0.99)),
          Constant(false))
    val paperFlow = Select(0.6 -> 'smooth, 0.2 -> 'uneven, 0.2 -> 'jammed)
    val paperJamIndicatorOn =
      If(powerButtonOn,
          CPD(paperFlow,
              'smooth -> Flip(0.1),
              'uneven -> Flip(0.3),
              'jammed -> Flip(0.99)),
          Constant(false))
    val state =
      Apply(powerButtonOn, tonerLevel, paperFlow,
            (power: Boolean, toner: Symbol, paper: Symbol) => {
              if (power) {
                if (toner == 'high && paper == 'smooth) 'good
                else if (toner == 'out || paper == 'out) 'out
                else 'poor
              } else 'out
            })
  }

  class Software {
    val state = Select(0.8 -> 'correct, 0.15 -> 'glitchy, 0.05 -> 'crashed)
  }

  class Network {
    val state = Select(0.7 -> 'up, 0.2 -> 'intermittent, 0.1 -> 'down)
  }

  class User {
    val commandCorrect = Flip(0.65)
  }
```

Next, here's the definition of the `PrintExperience` class. This class uses the previous four classes as its arguments and refers to variables inside those classes in its definition.

Listing 7.2 Printer problem: `PrintExperience` class

A print experience involves a particular printer, software, network, and user,
so the PrintExperience class takes instances of those classes as arguments.

```
class PrintExperience(printer: Printer, software: Software, network:
    Network, user: User) {

  val numPrintedPages =
    RichCPD(user.commandCorrect, network.state, software.state,
    printer.state,
        (*, *, *, OneOf('out)) -> Constant('zero),
        (*, *, OneOf('crashed), *) -> Constant('zero),
        (*, OneOf('down), *, *) -> Constant('zero),
        (OneOf(false), *, *, *) -> Select(0.3 -> 'zero, 0.6 -> 'some, 0.1
    -> 'all),
        (OneOf(true), *, *, *) -> Select(0.01 -> 'zero, 0.01 -> 'some, 0.98
    -> 'all))
  val printsQuickly =
    Chain(network.state, software.state,
        (network: Symbol, software: Symbol) =>
            if (network == 'down || software == 'crashed) Constant(false)
            else if (network == 'intermittent || software == 'glitchy)
    Flip(0.5)
            else Flip(0.9))
  val goodPrintQuality =
    CPD(printer.state,
        'good -> Flip(0.95),
        'poor -> Flip(0.3),
        'out -> Constant(false))
  val summary =
    Apply(numPrintedPages, printsQuickly, goodPrintQuality,
        (pages: Symbol, quickly: Boolean, quality: Boolean) =>
        if (pages == 'zero) 'none
        else if (pages == 'some || !quickly || !quality) 'poor
        else 'excellent)

}
```

The print experience depends on particular attributes of the printer, software, network, and user. These are referred to by putting the name of the instance, then a '.', then the name of the attribute. For example, "printer.state" refers to the attribute named "state" of the instance named "printer."

After all of the classes have been defined, you can create instances of these classes and hook them up. This defines a process for generating values of the attributes of these instances; in other words, a particular probabilistic model. You can then provide evidence and ask queries about specific attributes.

Listing 7.3 Printer problem: creating instances and querying the model

```
val myPrinter = new Printer
val mySoftware = new Software
val myNetwork = new Network
val me = new User
val myExperience = new PrintExperience(myPrinter, mySoftware,
    myNetwork, me)
```

Create instances of the classes. myExperience is related to myPrinter, mySoftware, myNetwork, and me by the PrintExperience constructor.

```scala
    def step1() {
      val answerWithNoEvidence =
        VariableElimination.probability(myPrinter.powerButtonOn, true)
      println("Prior probability the printer power button is on = " +
        answerWithNoEvidence)
    }

    def step2() {
      myExperience.summary.observe('poor)
      val answerIfPrintResultPoor =
        VariableElimination.probability(myPrinter.powerButtonOn, true)
      println("Probability the printer power button is on given a poor result =
        " + answerIfPrintResultPoor)
    }

    def main(args: Array[String]) {
      step1()
      step2()
    }
  }
```

Queries and evidence involve particular attributes of the instances.

That's it for the basic printer model. Next, let's elaborate the model by including multiple printers in the same situation.

7.1.3   *Reasoning about multiple printers*

So far, you've seen how object orientation can be used to structure models and provide the benefits of encapsulation. One of the main strengths of object-oriented programming is the way it enables you to reuse code. It has two mechanisms of reuse: multiple instances of the same class within the same model, and multiple subclasses of the same class with slightly different definitions.

This section shows how to implement both of these reuse mechanisms using Scala. First, let's look at defining multiple subclasses of the same class. Imagine you have two kinds of printers: laser printers and inkjet printers. Both kinds of printers share a power button and a paper-feed mechanism, but each has characteristics of its own. You can use subclassing and inheritance in the standard way to get the effect you want.

Listing 7.4 provides the code for the Printer class and its two subclasses, Laser-Printer and InkjetPrinter. Printer is an abstract class in which the state attribute has no definition; it's supplied by the subclasses. This class defines three attributes whose definition is common to all printers. This design has two benefits. First, it enables code reuse between LaserPrinter and InkjetPrinter. Second, it defines a common interface for printers that the rest of the model can depend on. If myPrinter is an instance of a subclass of Printer, it can be relied on to have a state attribute.

Listing 7.4 **Printer** class hierarchy

This class is abstract because it contains a state attribute with no definition.

Reused code that's common to all printers

```
abstract class Printer {

  val powerButtonOn = Flip(0.95)
  val paperFlow =
    Select(0.6 -> 'smooth, 0.2 -> 'uneven, 0.2 -> 'jammed)
  val paperJamIndicatorOn =
    If(powerButtonOn,
       CPD(paperFlow,
           'smooth -> Flip(0.1),
           'uneven -> Flip(0.3),
           'jammed -> Flip(0.99)),
       Constant(false))

  val state: Element[Symbol]
}
```

Common interface that declares an attribute all printers have. Concrete subclasses must implement this attribute.

Attributes specific to the LaserPrinter subclass

```
class LaserPrinter extends Printer {
  val tonerLevel = Select(0.7 -> 'high, 0.2 -> 'low, 0.1 -> 'out)
  val tonerLowIndicatorOn =
    If(powerButtonOn,
       CPD(tonerLevel,
           'high -> Flip(0.2),
           'low -> Flip(0.6),
           'out -> Flip(0.99)),
       Constant(false))

  val state =
    Apply(powerButtonOn, tonerLevel, paperFlow,
          (power: Boolean, toner: Symbol, paper: Symbol) => {
            if (power) { //
              if (toner == 'high && paper == 'smooth) 'good
              else if (toner == 'out || paper == 'out) 'out
              else 'poor
            } else 'out
          }
    )
}
```

Attributes specific to the InkjetPrinter subclass

Separate implementations of the common interface

```
class InkjetPrinter extends Printer {
  val inkCartridgeEmpty = Flip(0.1)
  val inkCartridgeEmptyIndicator =
    If(inkCartridgeEmpty, Flip(0.99), Flip(0.3))
  val cloggedNozzle = Flip(0.001)

  val state =
    Apply(powerButtonOn, inkCartridgeEmpty,
          cloggedNozzle, paperFlow,
          (power: Boolean, ink: Boolean,
           nozzle: Boolean, paper: Symbol) => {
            if (power && !ink && !nozzle) {
              if (paper == 'smooth) 'good
              else if (paper == 'uneven) 'poor
              else 'out
```

```
            } else 'out                    ↑ Separate implementations
        }                                   | of the common interface
    )
}
```

That's how you create multiple object models that share some code and a common interface. Because LaserPrinter and InkjetPrinter are both subclasses of the same Printer class, instances of LaserPrinter and InkjetPrinter can be used as arguments to PrintExperience, which expects a Printer. In fact, you can have two instances of PrintExperience, one with a LaserPrinter and one with an Inkjet-Printer, in the same model. These two instances might share the same user, network, or software. Here's what this looks like:

```
val myLaserPrinter = new LaserPrinter
val myInkjetPrinter = new InkjetPrinter
val mySoftware = new Software
val myNetwork = new Network
val me = new User
val myExperience1 =
  new PrintExperience(myLaserPrinter, mySoftware, myNetwork, me)
val myExperience2 =
  new PrintExperience(myInkjetPrinter, mySoftware, myNetwork, me)
```

Now you can reason about the common elements across these two experiences: the software, network, and user. Here's an example of what you can do:

```
def step1() {
  myExperience1.summary.observe('none)
  val alg =
    VariableElimination(myLaserPrinter.powerButtonOn, myNetwork.state)
  alg.start()
  println("After observing that printing with the laser printer " +
    "produces no result:")
  println("Probability laser printer power button is on = " +
    alg.probability(myLaserPrinter.powerButtonOn, true))
  println("Probability network is down = " +
    alg.probability(myNetwork.state, 'down))
  alg.kill()
}
def step2() {
  myExperience2.summary.observe('none)
  val alg =
    VariableElimination(myLaserPrinter.powerButtonOn, myNetwork.state)
  alg.start()
  println("\nAfter observing that printing with the inkjet printer " +
    "also produces no result:")
  println("Probability laser printer power button is on = " +
    alg.probability(myLaserPrinter.powerButtonOn, true))
  println("Probability network is down = " +
    alg.probability(myNetwork.state, 'down))
  alg.kill()
}
```

When this program is run, it prints the following:

```
After observing that printing with the laser printer produces no result:
Probability laser printer power button is on = 0.8573402523786461
Probability network is down = 0.2853194952427076

After observing that printing with the inkjet printer also produces no result:
Probability laser printer power button is on = 0.8978039844824163
Probability network is down = 0.42501359502427405
```

The logic behind this result is that after observing that the inkjet printer also fails to print, it's less likely that the problem the first time around was with the laser printer (which would mean the inkjet printer was also faulty), and more likely that it was something else, such as the network. So the probability that the laser printer's power button is on goes up, as does the probability that the network is down.

To close off this section, let's imagine now that you don't know what kind of printer you have. You know it's either a laser printer or an inkjet printer, but you don't know which. This is called *type uncertainty*, and it requires some extra machinery to handle, which you'll learn in section 7.3. Before you can get into type uncertainty, however, you need to generalize from object-oriented models to models with general kinds of relationships. These are called *relational probability models* and are the subject of the next section.

7.2 *Extending OO probability models with relations*

Imagine you're trying to model users on a social media site like Facebook and want to infer their interests and relationships by observing their posts and comments. Social media is, by definition, relational. It's all about relationships between people. Natural relationships also exist between people and their posts and comments. In addition, there's a relationship between a post and a comment to that post. There's natural OO structure in this domain, with classes for people, posts, and comments, but to model this domain successfully, you need to use a relational probability model.

A relational probability model is nothing more than an OO model in which relationships are made an explicit and central part of the representation. Over the last few years, a number of languages for relational probability models have been developed, such as Probabilistic Relational Models and Markov Logic. This section doesn't present any particular language, but rather a general programming style that combines features of many languages.

To describe how to design and implement a relational probability model, I'll proceed in three steps. First, I'll show how to describe a general model using class probability models. Then, I'll show how to describe a specific situation using this general model. Finally, I'll show how to implement all of this in Figaro.

7.2.1 *Describing general class-level models*

In a relational probability model, the class probability models serve two purposes:

- To describe the structure of the model, including the classes in the model, their attributes, and relationships between classes
- To define the probabilistic dependencies, functional forms, and numerical parameters that govern the probabilistic model

It's easiest to understand relational probability models by first looking at the structure of the model. Figure 7.3 shows the structure of a model for our social media application.

- The model has four classes: Person, Connection, Post, and Comment
- A class has attributes. There are two kinds of attributes.
  - Simple attributes, shown as ovals, represent random variables over values of some type. For example, a Person has an Interest, which is a random variable over strings. A Post has a Topic, which is also a variable over strings. A Connection has a Type, which could be family, close friend, or acquaintance. A Comment has a Match attribute, which is a variable over a Boolean indicating whether a match exists between the interest of the commenter and the topic of the post.

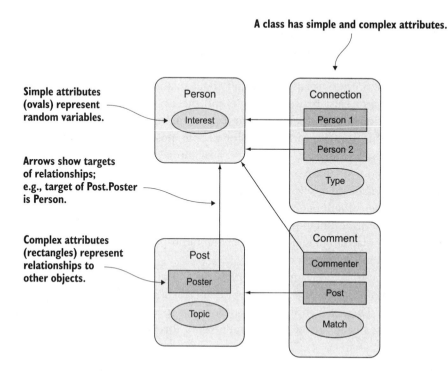

Figure 7.3   Structure of a relational probability model

– Complex attributes, shown as rectangles, define relationships to other objects. For example, the Post class has a Poster attribute that naturally represents the person who posted the post. For any instance of Post, the value of the Poster attribute will be an instance of Person. Therefore, the Poster attribute defines a relationship between instances of Post and instances of Person.

After you have the relational structure, the next step is to define the probabilistic bits of the representation. The main thing you need to do is define the dependencies. Let's think first on the instance level. The guiding principle is that *an attribute of an instance can depend on other attributes of that instance or on attributes of related instances.* For example, if you have a particular instance of Post called Post 1 and an instance of Person called Amy, such that the value of Post 1.Poster is Amy, then Post 1.Topic can depend on Amy.Interest.

Those are the kinds of dependencies you want to get on the instance level. How do you encode them on the class level? Simple! You just draw an arrow from the Interest attribute of the Person class to the Topic attribute of the Post class. Figure 7.4 shows

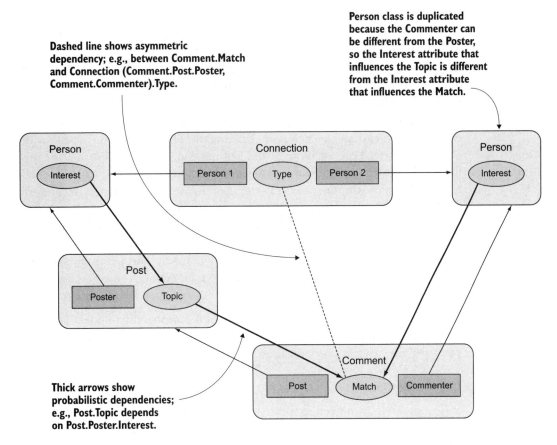

Figure 7.4　Probabilistic dependencies in the social media relational probability model

the probabilistic dependencies for our social media model. The probabilistic dependencies are overlaid thickly over the relational structure from figure 7.3, so you can see them clearly. This example includes both directed dependencies, shown as thick arrows, and an undirected dependency, shown as a thick dashed line.

After you've specified the dependencies, you can specify the functional forms and numerical parameters. There's nothing unusual about this, and you can use the same methods you've used previously. As you may recall from chapter 5, the directed dependencies in a Bayesian network are specified using conditional probability distributions, whereas the undirected dependencies in a Markov network are encoded using potentials. Recall that a potential is a function that's defined over a set of variables and assigns a non-negative real number to each combination of values of the variables.

Our example has the following:

- For Person.Interest, because it has no parents, you'll have a probability distribution over the possible interests.
- For Connection.Type, again it has no parents, so you'll have a probability distribution over the possible connection types.
- For Post.Topic, you have a CPD given Post.Poster.Interest that specifies that the topic of a post usually matches the interest of the poster.
- For Comment.Match, you have a CPD given Comment.Post.Topic and Comment.Commenter.Interest. A deterministic CPD specifies that a match exists if the post's topic and commenter's interest coincide.
- You also have a potential over whether the comment matches and the connection type between the poster and commenter. The connection type can be identified as the Type attribute of the Connection, in which Person 1 is Comment.Post.Poster and Person 2 is Comment.Commenter. You call this attribute Connection(Comment.Post.Poster, Comment.Commenter).Type. For any instance *c* of Comment, you identify the two instances of Person who are the *c*.Post.Poster and *c*.Commenter. You then identify the Connection instance that connects these two people and get that Connection's Type attribute. So the potential is defined over that attribute and *c*.Match. The potential says that the Comment is highly likely to match if the connection type is acquaintance, but less so if the connection type is close friend, and even less so for family.

That wraps up the class-level definitions of a relational probability model. The next step is to create instances and specify relationships between them. I'll show how this defines a probability distribution over the attributes of the instances.

7.2.2 *Describing a situation*

To describe a situation, you need to specify exactly what the instances are of each class in the situation and how they're connected. For example, with our social media model, the situation might be specified by table 7.1.

Table 7.1 Specification of the instances in the social media model and the relationships between them. The first table specifies three instances of Person. The second table specifies three instances of Post, and for each instance, the value of the Poster complex attribute. The third table specifies four instances of Comment, and for each instance, the values of the Post and Commenter attributes.

Person
Amy
Brian
Cheryl

Post	Poster
Post 1	Amy
Post 2	Brian
Post 3	Amy

Comment	Post	Commenter
Comment 1	Post 1	Brian
Comment 2	Post 1	Cheryl
Comment 3	Post 2	Amy
Comment 4	Post 3	Cheryl

You don't need to specify Connection instances, as these are derived automatically. For every instance c of Comment, you automatically derive Connection(c.Post.Poster, c.Commenter). For Comment 1, Post.Poster is Amy and Commenter is Brian, so you derive Connection(Amy, Brian). Similarly, for Comments 2 and 3, you derive Connection(Amy, Cheryl) and Connection(Brian, Amy).

For Comment 4, you also derive Connection(Amy, Cheryl). This is the same Connection instance as the one derived for Comment 2. This is an important point. You want to infer things from both of Cheryl's comments to Amy's points. If you used different Connection instances for each comment, you wouldn't be able to infer from the combination of the comments to the connection type. By using the same Connection instance, you make sure that all comments by Cheryl on Amy's posts are used to infer the type of the connection. (On the other hand, in our model, Connection(Amy, Brian) is different from Connection(Brian, Amy). This is a design choice; you've chosen to regard connections as asymmetric. You could easily model connections as symmetric, in which case you'd have a single Connection instance for both Comment 1 and Comment 3.)

DERIVING THE PROBABILISTIC MODEL FOR THE SITUATION

One of the main benefits of using class probability models is that the probabilistic model for a situation is derived automatically; you don't have to work it out for yourself. But it's important to understand how it works. You proceed in the usual way. First, you decide on the variables describing the situation. Next, you specify the dependencies. Finally, you specify the functional forms and numerical parameters characterizing each of these dependencies.

For the variables, after these instances and relationships have been specified, they automatically define a set of simple attributes for all instances in the situation, each of which becomes a variable in the model. In this example, these are as follows:

- Amy.Interest, Brian.Interest, Cheryl.Interest
- Post 1.Topic, Post 2.Topic, Post 3.Topic
- Comment 1.Match, Comment 2.Match, Comment 3.Match, Comment 4.Match
- Connection(Amy, Brian).Type, Connection(Amy, Cheryl).Type, Connection (Brian, Amy).Type

For each of these attributes, you can identify the attributes that it depends on from the general class-level model. This lets you build a graph showing the dependencies in this situation, shown in figure 7.5. For example, according to the model of the Person class, Person.Interest has no parents, so the same is true of Amy.Interest, Brian.Interest, and Cheryl.Interest. According to the Post class model, the parent of Post.Topic is Post.Poster.Interest. This means that on the instance level, the parent of Post 1.Topic is Amy.Interest, the parent of Post 2.Topic is Brian.Interest, and the parent of Post 3.Topic is Amy.Interest again.

Now let's consider Comment 1.Match. According to the class models, Comment .Match has two parents, Comment.Post.Topic and Comment.Commenter.Interest. In addition, it has an undirected edge to Connection(Comment.Post.Poster, Comment.Commenter).Type. For this specific instance Comment 1 of Comment, Comment 1.Post is Post 1, Comment 1.Commenter is Brian, and Comment 1.Post.Poster is Amy. Therefore, Comment 1.Match has two parents, Post 1.Topic and Brian.Interest. It also has an undirected edge to Connection(Amy, Brian).Type. You see exactly these edges in the Bayesian network. It's a similar story for the other instances of Comment.

The graph of dependencies is, strictly speaking, neither a Bayesian network nor a Markov network, because it contains both directed and undirected edges. Nevertheless, it should be reasonably easy to understand the probabilistic model it defines. The

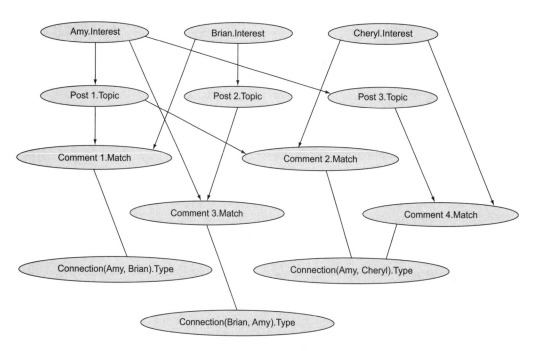

Figure 7.5 Graph of dependencies for the social media example. This network is constructed automatically from the class-level model of figure 7.3 using the situation specification of table 7.1. For each class-level simple attribute, there's a set of variables in the network, one for each instance of the class. As you can imagine, these networks quickly get hairy as you move beyond a few instances.

portion of the graph involving directed edges can be understood as an ordinary Bayesian network. The undirected edges impose additional constraints on the network, just like using Figaro constraints. In fact, that's how it will be implemented in Figaro in the next section.

After you understand the graph of dependencies, the numerical parameters for the situation are derived naturally from the class-level model. For example, the CPD of Post 1.Topic given Amy.Interest is derived from the class-level CPD of Post.Topic given Post.Poster.Interest. Similarly, the constraint on Comment 1.Match and Connection(Amy, Brian).Type is derived from the class-level potential over Comment.Match and Connection(Comment.Post.Poster, Comment.Commenter).Type.

At this point, you have all of the ingredients to define a joint probability distribution over the values of all simple attributes of all instances in the situation. To summarize, then, a relational probability model is a way of describing a probabilistic model over the attributes of instances in a situation. It provides two major benefits over building the model described in the graph of figure 7.4 directly. These are precisely the two main benefits of object orientation highlighted at the beginning of the chapter:

- By describing the application domain using objects and relationships, you provide structure to potentially complex situations. The graph of figure 7.4 isn't too bad, but it involves only three users, three posts, and four comments. Imagine that there were thousands of users, posts, and comments. Trying to build and maintain this network would be a horrible task. But our class-level model of figure 7.3 stays the same no matter how many instances there are. True, you have to specify the instances and relationships as in table 7.1, but this is a much easier task. Lots of relational database tools enable you to organize many instances and the relationships between them.
- Class models can be applied to many instances with different relationships. This is a powerful reuse mechanism, because you can use the same class-level definition of the probabilistic model for many situations.

Okay, now that you've seen what a relational probability model is and how it defines a probability distribution, it's time to see how to implement one by using probabilistic programming.

7.2.3 Representing the social media model in Figaro

It turns out to be easy to represent a relational probability model in Figaro. You've already seen the concepts in the object-oriented printer model from section 7.1.2, and the model of social media is similar.

To start, you create class models with attributes in the same way as before. In our example, you can make the complex attributes arguments to the classes. So you have the following:

```
class Person() {
  val interest = Uniform("sports", "politics")
}
```

```
class Post(val poster: Person) {
  val topic = If(Flip(0.9), poster.interest, Uniform("sports", "politics"))
}
```

> **NOTE FOR ADVANCED USE** In our example, you could make `poster` an argument of `Post` because the post depends on the poster, but the poster doesn't depend on the post. So you can generate the poster and then generate the post. If the poster also depended on the post, you couldn't make `poster` an argument of `Post`, because the poster can't be generated before the post. You have two solutions to this. One is to use Scala's lazy evaluation, so that the post could depend on the poster, but attributes of the poster won't be evaluated until they're needed. The other is to give `Post` an internal attribute called `poster`, which is initially `null`, and have the value of this attribute set later, before calling Figaro's inference algorithms. As long as all references to `poster` happen inside `Chain` elements (in our example, inside the `If`, which is syntactic sugar for `Chain`), the `poster` elements won't be needed until inference, by which time the value of the `poster` attribute will have been set correctly.

You can define the other two classes in a similar way. There's one thing you need to be careful about for the `Connection` class. Connections are derived from two people. You want to be able to call `connection(person1, person2)` to get the connection between the two people. You need to make sure that when you call `connection(person1, person2)` multiple times, you get the same connection every time. Figaro provides an easy way to do this using its `memo` function, which is found in the `com.cra.figaro.util` package, which ensures that a function returns the same value every time when called on the same arguments. Here's how it works:

```
import com.cra.figaro.util.memo
class Connection(person1: Person, person2: Person) {
  val connectionType = Uniform("acquaintance", "close friend", "family")
}
def generateConnection(pair: (Person, Person)) =
  new Connection(pair._1, pair._2)
val connection = memo(generateConnection _)
```

For `Comment`, you use a combination of directed and undirected dependencies. You've seen how to do this sort of thing before. Following is the code. `===` (three equals signs) is Figaro equality. It's a Boolean element whose value is `true` if the values of its two arguments are equal.

```
class Comment(val post: Post, val commenter: Person) {
  val topicMatch = post.topic === commenter.interest
  val pair =
    ^^(topicMatch, connection(post.poster, commenter).connectionType)
  def constraint(pair: (Boolean, String)) = {
    val (topicMatch, connectionType) = pair
    if (topicMatch) 1.0
    else if (connectionType == "family") 0.8
```

```
      else if (connectionType == "close friend") 0.5
      else 0.1
    }
  pair.addConstraint(constraint _)
}
```

Next, you specify some evidence:

```
    post1.topic.observe("politics")
    post2.topic.observe("sports")
    post3.topic.observe("politics")
```

Finally, you answer some queries:

```
println("Probability Amy's interest is politics = " +
  VariableElimination.probability(amy.interest, "politics"))
println("Probability Brian's interest is politics = " +
  VariableElimination.probability(brian.interest, "politics"))
println("Probability Cheryl's interest is politics = " +
  VariableElimination.probability(cheryl.interest, "politics"))
println("Probability Brian is Amy's family = " +
  VariableElimination.probability(connection(amy, brian).connectionType,
                                  "family"))
println("Probability Cheryl is Amy's family = " +
  VariableElimination.probability(connection(amy, cheryl).connectionType,
                                  "family"))
println("Probability Cheryl is Brian's family = " +
  VariableElimination.probability(connection(brian, cheryl).connectionType,
                                  "family"))
```

This program prints the following:

```
Probability Amy's interest is politics = 0.9940991345397325
Probability Brian's interest is politics = 0.10135135135135132
Probability Cheryl's interest is politics = 0.7692307692307692
Probability Brian is Amy's family = 0.5472972972972974
Probability Cheryl is Amy's family = 0.4205128205128205
Probability Cheryl is Brian's family = 0.3333333333333333
```

Notice how Amy is most likely to be interested in politics because she's posted twice on politics. Cheryl is also likely to be interested in politics, even though she hasn't posted, because she's commented on two of Amy's posts on politics. Brian, on the other hand, posted on sports, so he's probably not interested in politics. On the other hand, Brian commented on one of Amy's posts on politics, so he's likely to be Amy's family, because he's probably not interested in politics. Finally, because Cheryl never commented on Brian's posts, the probability that Cheryl is Brian's family is the same as it was originally, 1/3.

7.3   *Modeling relational and type uncertainty*

Let's elaborate on our social media example. Suppose, at any given time, some topics are hot, which makes them more likely to be posted. You can model this by making topics objects instead of strings, creating a `Topic` class with a `hot` attribute. The `topic` attribute of the `Post` class will now be a complex attribute that points to the `Topic` class. So far, so good.

Now suppose you don't know the topic of a given post p. Maybe you're using natural language processing to identify the topic, and your algorithms aren't perfect. You have uncertainty about the value of `p.topic`, which is a complex attribute. In other words, you have uncertainty about the relationship between the post and its topic, which could be one of a number of instances of `Topic`. This kind of situation is called *relational uncertainty*. It's also sometimes called *reference uncertainty*, because you don't know to which object `p.topic` refers.

Similarly, going back to the printer example, you might not know what type of printer you have. Maybe you're working at a help desk and a user has called in and not told you what kind of printer he's using. Technically, this means that the class of the printer argument to the `PrintExperience` object is unknown. This situation is known as *type uncertainty*. Type uncertainty is a special case of relational uncertainty, because you can handle it by creating putative printers of each possible class, with uncertainty over which is the printer.

Conceptually, relational uncertainty and type uncertainty are simple to understand, but it turns out that some extra machinery is needed to handle them in Figaro. This machinery, called *element collections and references*, is useful for various purposes. In this chapter, you'll see the number-one purpose, which is handling relational uncertainty. In the next chapter, you'll see another important purpose, which is working with dynamic models. This section first presents the basics of element collections and references, and then shows you how to implement the social media example with the unknown topic, and finally the printer example with type uncertainty.

7.3.1   *Element collections and references*

You probably don't know this yet, but every Figaro element has a name and belongs to an element collection. An *element collection* is a Figaro collection in which an element is indexed by a string, which is its name. The reason you don't know this yet is that, by default, you don't have to specify the name and element collection of an element. By default, an element's name is the empty string `""`. Also, there's a default element collection that every element goes into, unless told otherwise. Up to this point in the book, you've had no reason to give an element a special name or put it in any element collection other than the default, so I haven't introduced these concepts until now. But for relational uncertainty, you need them.

Element collections are useful because they give you a way to identify elements other than through Scala variables. If ec is an element collection, you can get the element associated with the name n using `ec.get(n)`. Sometimes, this is the only way for you to get a handle on this element. When you're writing your program, you might not know which element will have the name n when you need it. This is like compile time versus runtime type checking. Sometimes, you can't fully determine the type of a variable at compile time, so you have to perform a runtime check. In the same way, you might not know how to get at a particular element at compile time, and element collections give you a way to get the variable dynamically at runtime.

If you think about it, this can give you a way to handle relational uncertainty. You're unsure about the value of the topic attribute of Post. The topic has an attribute named hot, which is an element. What you want to be able to do is refer to topic.hot from within the Post class. But you can't do this using Scala, because topic isn't a specific instance of Topic! Instead, what you'll do is make Post and Topic element collections and use get("topic.hot") to get at the element you need.

Now, you might be asking, how does this work, because topic.hot isn't a name? It's the concatenation of two names. The first name, topic, is the name of an element in the Post element collection. In this case, it's an Element[Topic] whose value represents the particular topic of the post. The second name, hot, is the name of an element in the Topic element collection. This concatenation of names is called a *reference*. Figure 7.6 shows how to parse this reference. The main point is that each subsequent name in the reference is defined in an element collection that's a possible value of the previous element.

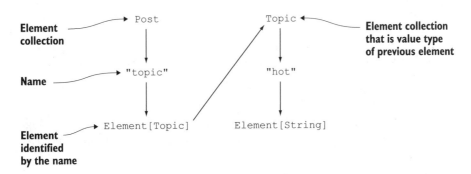

Figure 7.6 Parsing the topic.hot reference

How should you understand references? Let's think about them in a principled way as defining random processes. Suppose that there are two possible topics, sports and politics. Each of these is an instance of the Topic class. Topic is an element collection, and it has an attribute hot whose name is "hot". (In general, there's no requirement for the Figaro name of an attribute to be the same as the name of the Scala variable, but it often makes sense.) post1 is an instance of Post, which is also an element collection, with poster and topic attributes. The name of the topic attribute is "topic". Calling post1.get("topic.hot") defines a random process, which goes through the steps visualized in figure 7.7.

Remember that an element in Figaro represents a random process? You can use an element to represent the random process defined by post1.get("topic.hot"). Getting a reference in an element collection is implemented precisely this way, as it

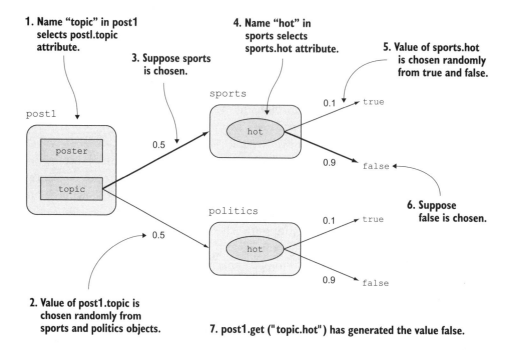

1. Name "topic" in post1 selects post1.topic attribute.

3. Suppose sports is chosen.

4. Name "hot" in sports selects sports.hot attribute.

5. Value of sports.hot is chosen randomly from true and false.

6. Suppose false is chosen.

2. Value of post1.topic is chosen randomly from sports and politics objects.

7. post1.get ("topic.hot") has generated the value false.

Figure 7.7   A reference as a random process that generates values. In this diagram, the process generates a value for the reference `topic.hot` in the element collection `post1`.

returns the element representing the random process. You can use this element in your models just as you would any other element. The nice thing is that Figaro takes care of chasing down the reference and all its possible resolutions under the hood, and you don't have to worry about it at all.

One subtle point needs to be mentioned. What if the Topic class also had an attribute named important, and a dependency existed between this attribute and the attribute named hot? Suppose now that you create an element representing post1.get ("topic.hot") and another one representing post1.get("topic.important"). In any given possible world, topic is either sports or politics; it can't be both. In any possible world, the resolution of topic in post1 has to come out the same way, whether you're getting the important or hot element out of it. This introduces a dependency between post1.get("topic.hot") and post1.get("topic.important"). This is what you'd intuitively expect, and Figaro's algorithms handle this case correctly.

7.3.2   *Social media model with relational uncertainty*

With that machinery in hand, you're ready to tackle the social media model again, this time with uncertainty over the topics of posts. You start out by creating a Topic class:

```
class Topic() extends ElementCollection {
    val hot = Flip(0.1)("hot", this)
}
```

The first line says that an instance of Topic is also an ElementCollection, meaning that elements can be given names and placed in it. The second line creates a Flip(0.1) element, gives it the name hot, and puts it in element collection this. Within the context of the Topic class, the this keyword refers to this specific instance of Topic. So any given instance of Topic will be an element collection, and there will be an element named hot in that element collection that's a Flip(0.1).

This is the first time you've encountered these two extra arguments to the Flip constructor. These arguments are optional and can usually be omitted. You need them only if you want to give your element a name or put it in a specific element collection. But if you just want to give it a name, or just want to put it in a specific element collection, you also have to specify the other optional argument. Flip isn't the only constructor that provides these optional arguments. In general, all of Figaro's built-in element constructors allow you to specify a name and element collection for the element.

Now you can define two instances of the Topic class:

```
val sports = new Topic()
val politics = new Topic()
```

A Person has an interest that's an unknown Topic. Here, the attribute interest is an Element[Topic]:

```
class Person() {
  val interest = Uniform(sports, politics)
}
```

A Post is also an ElementCollection. It has an attribute named topic. This is an Element[Topic] that depends on poster.interest:

```
class Post(val poster: Person) extends ElementCollection {
  val topic =
    If(Flip(0.9), poster.interest,
        Uniform(sports, politics))("topic", this)
}
```

Now, the reference topic.hot is used in the Comment class. The logic is that people will comment on hot topics even if they're not usually interested in them. So a comment is appropriate if either the topic matches the commenter's interest or the topic is hot. Here's the relevant code from the Comment class:

```
class Comment(val post: Post, val commenter: Person) {
  val isHot = post.get[Boolean]("topic.hot")

  val appropriateComment =
    Apply(post.topic, commenter.interest, isHot,
    (t1: Topic, t2: Topic, b: Boolean) => (t1 == t2) || b)
  // add the undirected constraint on appropriateComment and the connection
  // type as before
}
```

If you look at the preceding definition of isHot, notice that you have to specify the value type of the element (Boolean, in this case). In fact, you generally do have to specify the value type. There's no way for the Scala compiler to know, just from the name of the element, what the value type of the element is. But to be able to use isHot, you have to know its value type. Specifying the value type as a type argument to get, in square brackets, tells the Scala compiler what it needs.

That covers the model. You can create instances and relationships exactly as you did before—I won't show the code again. I will show you how to assert evidence about a complex attribute. It's exactly the same as for a simple attribute. You can write post1.topic.observe(politics) to observe that the value of the topic attribute is the politics instance of Topic.

You can also query for the value of a complex attribute. This model supports some interesting queries and inference. Let's start with the following queries, which show how you can query for the interests of people and topics of posts, which are instances of the Topic class:

```
println("Probability Amy's interest is politics = " +
  VariableElimination.probability(amy.interest, politics))
println("Probability post 2's topic is sports = " +
  VariableElimination.probability(post2.topic, sports))
println("Probability post 3's topic is sports = " +
  VariableElimination.probability(post3.topic, sports))
println("Probability Amy is Brian's family = " +
  VariableElimination.probability(connection(brian, amy).connectionType,
                                  "family"))
```

This prints the following result:

```
Probability Amy's interest is politics = 0.9656697011762803
Probability post 2's topic is sports = 0.24190044937009825
Probability post 3's topic is sports = 0.06958146174469142
Probability Amy is Brian's family = 0.3791735849751334
```

Now let's observe that the sports topic is hot (sports.hot.observe(true)) and run the same queries. This prints the following:

```
Probability Amy's interest is politics = 0.9609178093049061
Probability post 2's topic is sports = 0.3729396845525878
Probability post 3's topic is sports = 0.0900555124038995
Probability Amy is Brian's family = 0.33670840928905443
```

Note that the probability has increased that post 2's and 3's topics are sports. This might be surprising, because in the Post class model, the hotness of the topics doesn't enter into the choice of topic. But here's the reasoning: You previously observed that post 1's topic is politics. Amy posted post 1, so her interest is most likely to be politics. You also know that Brian posted post 2 and Amy commented on it. Because people tend to comment more on topics that match their interests, unless they're hot, you believed it was likely that post 2's topic was politics. But now you know that sports is hot. As a result, it could well be the case that post 2's topic is sports, and the reason Amy commented on it is because sports is hot, not because she's interested in sports. This is why the probability increases that post 2's topic is sports. Similar reasoning holds for post 3.

Now, let's think about why the probability decreases that Amy is Brian's family. You know Amy is most likely interested in politics. Post 2 has two possibilities: either it's about politics, in which case you don't need an explanation for why Amy commented on it, or it's about sports, in which case you do need an explanation. Two alternative explanations are that Amy is Brian's family or that sports is hot. Before you observed that sports is hot, you had about a 38% belief that Amy is Brian's family. Observing that sports is hot provides an alternative explanation, and therefore discounts the explanation that Amy is Brian's family, making that probability decrease. This is an example of something you saw in chapter 5 about Bayesian networks: induced dependencies. A priori, Amy being Brian's family and the hotness of sports are independent. There's no reason why the two should be connected. But after you observe that Amy is likely to be interested in politics and Amy commented on Brian's post, they become connected. This is a classic example of the reasoning pattern known as *explaining away*, where there are two alternative explanations for the same observation, and observing one explanation discounts the other explanation.

7.3.3 *Printer model with type uncertainty*

Now that you've seen how to implement a model with relational uncertainty, let's look at type uncertainty using the printer model with a printer of unknown type. The principles are similar: you use element collections and references. You create multiple printer instances, one for each possible type, and create an element whose value is one of the printer instances to represent the unknown printer.

This example has two new wrinkles that you didn't see in the previous section. First, you'll be asserting evidence on and querying elements whose identity is uncertain. So you use `get` within the query and observation. This is simple enough.

The second wrinkle is that you're not going to fundamentally change the original definition of `PrintExperience`, which took `Printer` as an argument. You don't have a specific printer—instead, you have an `Element[Printer]` representing an unknown printer, and you have to create a `PrintExperience` and access its attributes. You'll use Figaro's `Apply` to achieve this. Given an unknown printer, represented by an `Element[Printer]`, you use `Apply` to create an `Element[PrintExperience]`, where the `PrintExperience` is based on whatever printer the printer is.

In fact, you'll see that the model is changed minimally, in only five lines. More changes are found in the way the model is instantiated and queried, but that's where you want the changes, ideally. Here are the five changes to the model:

1 `object PrinterProblemTypeUncertainty extends ElementCollection {`

We place the entire model in an element collection.

2 `abstract class Printer extends ElementCollection {`

A printer is an element collection.

3 `val powerButtonOn = Flip(0.95)("power button on", this)`

powerButtonOn, which is an attribute you'll query, is given a name and placed in the element collection of the printer to which it belongs.

4 `class PrintExperience(printer: Printer, software: Software, network:`
`Network, user: User) extends ElementCollection {`

A print experience is also an element collection.

5 `val summary = Apply(…)("summary", this)`

You'll observe evidence about the print summary, so you give it a name and put it in the print experience element collection.

That's it. Now you describe a specific situation. Here's where the type uncertainty comes in. You proceed as follows. First you define `myPrinter` to be a random choice among printers of different types, give `myPrinter` a name, and put it in the element collection of the entire model:

```
val myPrinter =
  Select(0.3 -> new LaserPrinter,
         0.7 -> new InkjetPrinter)("my printer", this)
```

Next, you create instances of `Software`, `Network`, and `User`, just like before:

```
val mySoftware = new Software
val myNetwork = new Network
val me = new User
```

Finally, to create `myExperience`, you use `Apply` and the existing `PrintExperience` class, which takes a particular printer, software, network, and user as arguments. Again, you give `myExperience` a name and put it in the top-level element collection:

```
val myExperience =
  Apply(myPrinter,(p: Printer) =>
    new PrintExperience(p, mySoftware, myNetwork, me))("print experience",
                                                       this)
```

Now you're ready to assert evidence and ask some queries. You're going to observe evidence on the summary of the print experience. But `myExperience` is an `Element [PrintExperience]`, so how do you get at its summary? You use a reference, of course! You gave the summary element a name and put it in the `PrintExperience` element collection, and you gave `myExperience` a name and put it in the top-level element collection so you could do this. Here's what it looks like in code:

```
val summary = get[Symbol]("print experience.summary")
summary.observe('none)
```

Based on the evidence that nothing was printed, you'll query two things. One is whether the printer's power button is on. Again, myPrinter is an element, so you can't query it directly, but you can use a reference:

```
val powerButtonOn = get[Boolean]("my printer.power button on")
```

The second query is more interesting. Imagine that you're at the help desk wondering what type of printer the user has. After the user starts telling you things about the print experience, you might develop hypotheses about the type of printer. You can query your model for the type of the printer based on the evidence. You use Scala's runtime type-checking method isInstanceOf to achieve this. Specifically, you can define an element whose value is true if the myPrinter is a laser printer as follows:

```
val isLaser =
  Apply(myPrinter, (p: Printer) => p.isInstanceOf[LaserPrinter])
```

Now you can run inference and answer queries to get a result like this:

```
After observing no print result:
Probability printer power button is on = 0.8868215502107177
Probability printer is a laser printer = 0.23800361000850662
```

The prior probability of a printer being a laser printer was 0.3. Now that you've observed a bad print experience, the probability has decreased. According to our model, laser printers are more reliable than inkjet printers, so a bad print experience is more likely to happen with an inkjet printer.

I hope you can see that modeling objects and relationships, including relational and type uncertainty, enables you to describe interesting and rich situations and perform sophisticated kinds of reasoning. Along with the collections described in the previous chapter, the object-oriented and relational modeling paradigms described in this chapter give you the full power to create probabilistic models using techniques that are familiar to you from ordinary programming. The next chapter describes how to model and reason about an important special case—a dynamic model of a situation that changes over time.

7.4 Summary

- Object-oriented and relational programming paradigms enable you to structure complex models and reuse model components effectively.
- In these paradigms, you specify class models with attributes and probabilistic dependencies, functional forms, and numerical parameters.
- At the instance level, these define a probabilistic distribution over all attributes of all instances; you can assert evidence on and query these attributes.
- Element collections and references provide a mechanism in Figaro to access elements whose identity isn't known at compile time.

■ To represent relational or type certainty, you create an element whose value is an unknown element collection and use a reference to refer to attributes of that element collection.

7.5   *Exercises*

Solutions to selected exercises are available online at www.manning.com/books/practical-probabilistic-programming.

1 Your firm has five departments: Research and Development, Production, Sales, Human Resources, and Finance. Build an object-oriented probabilistic model that captures the influences between these departments. Use the model to answer queries about the health of the firm based on the state of the departments.

2 You're modeling the popularity of movies. Each movie has multiple actors, and each actor plays in multiple movies. Each actor has a variable representing how much that actor is liked by the populace. The popularity of a movie depends on how much the actors are liked. Given a dataset of movies, their actors, and their popularity, predict the popularity of a new movie with a given set of actors.

3 In your college, students can take courses in different subjects. The same instructor can teach multiple subjects, and the same subject can be taught by multiple instructors. The grade of a student in a course depends on three factors: the ability of the student, the difficulty of the subject, and the quality of the instructor. Write a relational probabilistic model to represent this situation. Using a dataset consisting of students, the courses they took, their instructors, and their grades, infer the ability of a target student, the difficulty of a target subject, and the quality of a target instructor.

4 Continuing on from exercise 3, you're a student planning which courses to take next semester. Unfortunately, the instructors haven't been published, but you can assume that the instructor for a given course will be one of the previous instructors. Use relational uncertainty to represent this situation and predict your grade in a target course.

5 Consider a vehicle surveillance application. Multiple kinds of vehicles exist, such as truck, car, and motorcycle. Each vehicle has properties such as size and color. The distribution over these variables is different for each kind of vehicle. You have a camera that takes pictures of vehicles entering your property and an image analysis algorithm that estimates the size and color of the vehicle. The estimated size and color are dependent on, but not necessarily identical to, the true size and color. Use a relational model with type uncertainty to represent this situation. Using this model, infer the type of a given vehicle based on its estimated size and color.

Modeling dynamic systems

8

Over the past few chapters, you've learned a good deal about using probabilistic programming to build probabilistic models. At this point, you have many techniques in your pocket, including modeling dependencies, functions, collections, and object-oriented modeling. This chapter builds on these techniques to model a particularly important kind of system: *a dynamic system whose state varies over time.*

After presenting the general concept of dynamic probabilistic models in section 8.1, section 8.2 builds up the concepts through a series of examples, starting from the simplest time series and ending with systems in which the structure of the state of the system can change over time. At first, the chapter assumes that the dynamic system runs for a fixed length of time, but section 8.3 relaxes this assumption, enabling modeling systems that go on indefinitely. This requires a new Figaro concept, the *universe*. You'll see how to use Figaro universes to model and reason about ongoing systems.

8.1   *Dynamic probabilistic models*

In chapter 1, you looked at the problem of reasoning about a corner kick in a game of soccer. Three kinds of queries could be answered with a probabilistic reasoning system:

- Predicting the outcome of a corner kick, given factors such as the wind, height of the center forward, and so on
- Inferring properties that may have led to the observed outcome, such as the skill level of the goalie
- Using the outcome of one corner kick to infer properties that can influence the outcome of a second corner kick, and then predicting the second corner kick accordingly

In this chapter, you'll move from modeling individual corner kicks as isolated events to modeling an entire soccer match as a sequence of connected events. A soccer match is an example of a *dynamic system*. This means two things:

- A soccer match has a *state* at every point in time. This state can include things such as the score, who has possession, and how confident each team is feeling.
- The state at any point in time is *dependent on earlier states*. For example, in a soccer match, the score at any point in time is dependent on the previous score and whether a goal was just scored; the possession is dependent on the previous possession, because a team in possession has a chance to maintain possession; and the confidence of a team also depends on their previous confidence, because confidence doesn't usually fluctuate wildly and suddenly.

Putting these two points together produces the following definition: a *dynamic system* is a system that has a state at every point in time, and those states at different time points are dependent.

Many examples of dynamic systems exist. Weather is clearly a dynamic system, because today's weather is dependent on the weather of previous days. Similarly, the performance of a business is a dynamic system; the state consists of various quantities such as revenues and profits, and the values of these quantities over time are connected. A third example is the traffic on a highway; the state might be the number of cars in each lane, and clearly the number of cars at one time point depends on the number at earlier time points.

You'll be looking at creating probabilistic models of dynamic systems. Such models are called *dynamic probabilistic models*. In a dynamic probabilistic model, the state is represented by random variables. For example, for the performance of a business, you might have variables representing the levels of revenues and profits at any given time point. These variables are called *state variables*. The probabilistic model defines probabilistic dependencies between the values of state variables at different time points.

A dynamic probabilistic model can be used in ways that correspond to the ways of using an ordinary static probabilistic model:

- *Predicting the state of the system at a future time point, taking into account the current state and the dependencies between states over time.* For example, you might predict the final score of the soccer match by considering the current score and confidence of the teams.

- *Inferring the past causes of the current state.* For example, if your team lost the soccer match, you can try to determine which decisions during the game led to the bad result.

- *Monitoring the state of the system over time, based on observations that you get over time.* For example, you might continually estimate the confidence and quality of the two teams based on what you observe to be happening on the field over time. You can then use these estimates to predict what will happen in the rest of the game.

All three of these capabilities would be tremendously useful to a soccer manager. In fact, dynamic systems are so important and ubiquitous that a whole set of techniques has been developed for dynamic probabilistic models. Probabilistic programming systems can represent many of the established frameworks for dynamic probabilistic models, such as the hidden Markov models and dynamic Bayesian networks introduced in the next section, and go beyond them by including features such as rich data structures and control flow. Without further ado, let's look at some of these frameworks and how you express them using probabilistic programming.

8.2 Types of dynamic models

This section presents various kinds of dynamic models. You'll start with the most basic kind of model, which is a Markov chain, and then consider a widely used extension, hidden Markov models. Then you'll look at dynamic Bayesian networks, which, as the name implies, are an extension of Bayesian networks to dynamic models. All of these are standard frameworks that existed before probabilistic programming. They all assume that the structure of the model is the same at every time point. Probabilistic programming lets you go beyond these frameworks, however, and describe models whose structures vary over time, as you'll see in section 8.2.4.

8.2.1 Markov chains

A dynamic system is one with a state that varies over time, such that the states at different times are dependent. A *Markov chain* is the simplest kind of dynamic system, characterized by two things: First, the state consists of a single variable. Second, the state variable at each point in time depends probabilistically on the variable at the previous point in time, but not on any prior state variables.

Figure 8.1 shows an example of a Markov chain for a soccer match. In this model, the state consists of a single variable, representing which team has possession at a particular time point in the match. For convenience, you might say that the time points represent minutes of the match, but they could be any subdivision of the match.

Figure 8.1   A Markov chain. The state at a time point consists of a single variable, which depends on the variable at the previous time. Possession(1) depends directly on Possession(0), Possession(2) depends directly on Possession(1), and so on through to Possession(n) depending directly on Possession(n – 1).

If you look at figure 8.1, you'll see that the arrows go sequentially from one state to the next, which indicates the following:

- Possession(1) depends directly on Possession(0).
- Possession(2) depends directly only on Possession(1) and not on Possession(0).
- Any influence of Possession(0) on Possession(2) is mediated by Possession(1).

Another way of saying this is that Possession(2) is *conditionally independent* of Possession(0), given Possession(1). The same holds true for future time points: *the possession at any point in time is conditionally independent of the possession at all earlier times, given the possession at the immediately previous time.* This statement is an example of a property called the *Markov assumption.*

> **MARKOV ASSUMPTION**   A dynamic probabilistic model satisfies the *Markov assumption* if the state at any time point depends only on the directly previous state; the state at any time point is conditionally independent of all earlier states given the directly previous state.

SPECIFYING A MARKOV CHAIN

To create a Markov chain, you need to do several things:

1   Decide on the set of values for the state variable. These consist of all of the values of the variable that you consider to be relevant at any point in time. You generally want to be careful here and not include more values than is necessary. As you'll see in a moment, the size of the Markov chain representation is quadratic in the number of values of the state variable, so you want to avoid it getting too large. For example, you might have a Markov chain for a soccer match in which the state variable represents the score differential. In principle, this differential could grow large—if a goal could be scored in any minute, the final score could be 90 to 0! But in practice, large score differentials are rare, and furthermore, the difference between leading by 5 and leading by 15 is inconsequential because it's rare for a team in a professional soccer match to

overcome a five-goal deficit. So you might restrict the score differential to the range –5 to +5.

2 Do one of the following:

- Specify an initial value for the Markov chain. This means the value of the first state variable. For example, the score differential at the start of a soccer match is 0.

- Specify a distribution over the initial value. This is needed if you don't know the exact value. For example, the possession at the start of the game depends on the coin toss, so the probability of each team having possession is 0.5.

3 Specify the transition model. The transition model defines how the state at one time point depends on the state at the previous time point. In figure 8.1, the transition model specifies the probability of Possession(1) given Possession(0), and the probability of Possession(2) given Possession(1), and so on. In symbols, the transition model specifies $P(\text{Possession}(t) \mid \text{Possession}(t-1))$ for any $t \geq 1$.

In step 3, I made the assumption that the transition probabilities at all different time points are exactly the same. This assumption isn't strictly required for all Markov chains, but is practical and used in most applications. Using this assumption, you can define the Markov chain by using a simple loop.

One thing you'll find with dynamic models is that they can become expensive to work with. The complexity of representing and reasoning about dynamic models depends crucially on the number of states. In a Markov chain, the number of parameters in the transition model is quadratic in the number of values of the state variable. In our example, the transition model specifies $P(\text{Possession}(t) \mid \text{Possession}(t-1)$. This is a conditional probability distribution that can be defined by a table that specifies a probability for all possible values of Possession($t-1$) and Possession(t). The number of entries in this table is the square of the number of possible values of the Possession variable.

USING MARKOV CHAINS IN FIGARO

If you know the total number of time steps in advance, it's easy to specify a Markov chain in Figaro. If you don't know the total number of time steps and the system could go on indefinitely, more-advanced techniques are needed, which are described in section 8.3. But if you know the total number of time steps, you can write a simple loop.

Here's the code to define the Markov chain from figure 8.1.

Listing 8.1 Markov chain specification

```
val length = 90                                    Length of the chain

val ourPossession: Array[Element[Boolean]] =       Array of state variables,
  Array.fill(length)(Constant(false))              one for each time step

ourPossession(0) = Flip(0.5)                        Sets the distribution for the
                                                    initial state of the sequence
```

```
for { minute <- 1 until length } {
  ourPossession(minute) =
    If(ourPossession(minute - 1), Flip(0.6),   Flip(0.3))
}
```

Transition model defining a distribution for each state variable based on the one before in the sequence

You first set the length of the sequence to 90 minutes. You then create an array with one element, representing a Boolean state variable indicating whether your team has possession, for every time point from 0 through 89. The Scala method `Array.fill` creates an array whose length is given by the first `length` argument, and in which each value is initialized to be the `Constant(false)` element. This initial value is unimportant because you'll overwrite it explicitly in a moment.

Next, you define a distribution over whether your team has possession at time point 0. You've chosen it to be defined by `Flip(0.5)`, so you have possession at the initial time point with probability 0.5.

Next comes a loop that goes through all of the time points 1 through 89. At each time point, it defines whether you have possession at that time point based on whether you had possession at the previous time point. Specifically, if you did have possession, you continue to have it with probability 0.6, but if you didn't have possession, you take it with probability 0.3.

You can query this Markov model for the probability distribution over the state variable at any time point, given observations at any time points. For example, suppose you want to query the probability that you have possession at time step 5. You can first ask for the probability before observing any evidence by calling

```
VariableElimination.probability(ourPossession(5), true)
```

This returns 0.428745 for the prior probability you have possession at time step 5.

You can then observe that you had possession at time step 4 using

```
ourPossession(4).observe(true)
```

The same query now returns 0.6. You can see that the probability has increased, given the knowledge that you had possession at the previous time step. In fact, the probability is exactly the probability of keeping possession in one time step.

Now, what happens if you observe that you also had possession at time step 3? Querying the model returns the answer 0.6 again for the probability that you have possession at time step 5. The new observation hasn't changed the probability. This is because of the Markov assumption: whether you have possession at time step 5 is independent of whether you had possession at step 3, given whether you had possession at step 4.

You can also observe that you also had possession at time step 6. This illustrates that you can reason not only forward through the Markov chain to predict the future, but also backward to infer previous states from future observations. After adding this observation, the probability that you had possession at time step 5 goes up to 0.75.

Finally, you observe that you also had possession at time step 7. The answer remains 0.75 (within rounding error). This is another instance of the Markov assumption. Whether you had possession in minute 7 adds no new information to minute 5 after minute 6 is known.

Markov chains are the simplest case of dynamic probabilistic models but provide the basis for more-powerful models. The next few subsections elaborate on these models step by step.

8.2.2 Hidden Markov models

A *hidden Markov model* (HMM) is an extension of a Markov chain in which two variables exist at each time point, one representing a "hidden" state and the other representing an observation. Figure 8.2 shows an example of an HMM. The hidden state represents whether your team is confident at each time point. You can never truly know whether your team is confident; you have to infer it based on what's happening on the pitch. This is why it's a hidden state. The observation, which you can directly observe, is whether you have possession.

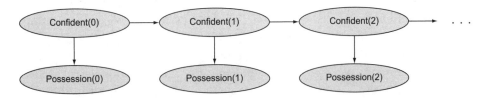

Figure 8.2 A hidden Markov model. Confident is a hidden state variable, and Possession represents an observation. The hidden state variables make a Markov chain, and the observation depends only on the hidden state at that time point.

From figure 8.2, you can see that an HMM satisfies two assumptions:

- The hidden states form a Markov chain that satisfies the Markov assumption.
- The observation at a point in time depends only on the hidden state at that point in time. The observation is independent of all previous hidden states and observations, given the hidden state at that time point.

This also implies that the hidden state at a particular time point is independent of all previous observations *given the previous hidden state.* But an important point must be made here. The previous hidden state is, by assumption, hidden, so you won't usually know it for certain. The current hidden state *isn't* independent of previous observations if you don't know the previous hidden state. For example, in figure 8.2, Possession(0) isn't independent of Confident(2) if you don't observe Confident(0) or Confident(1).

These points are essential to understanding why HMMs are a useful and powerful representation. The preceding two assumptions are important for making the HMM representation compact and making inference efficient. At the same time, they don't prevent you from using the *entire* observation sequence to infer the hidden states.

SPECIFYING AN HMM IN FIGARO

After you know how to specify a Markov chain, specifying an HMM isn't much more complex. You need to do the following:

1 Define the set of values of the hidden state variable. In our example, Confident might be a Boolean variable. Because the hidden state variables form a Markov chain, the size of the representation will be quadratic in the number of values of the hidden state variable.

2 Define the set of values of the observation variable. In our example, Possession might also be a Boolean variable representing whether our team has possession at a particular time point. Because the observation variable depends on the hidden state but not on previous observations, the size of the representation will be proportional to the number of values of the hidden state times the number of values of the observation.

3 Define a probability distribution over the initial hidden state. This is known as the *initial model*. In our example, this specifies P(Confident(0)).

4 Define the *transition model* for the hidden state variables, representing the conditional distribution over the state variable at one time point given the previous time point. In our example, this specifies P(Confident(t) | Confident($t-1$)).

5 Define the *observation model* that specifies the conditional probability distribution over the observation variable at any time point, given the hidden state variable at that time point. In our example, this specifies P(Possession(t) | Confident(t)).

The following listing shows how these steps are realized in code.

Listing 8.2 HMM specification

```
val length = 90

val confident: Array[Element[Boolean]] =
  Array.fill(length)(Constant(false))
val ourPossession: Array[Element[Boolean]] =
  Array.fill(length)(Constant(false))

confident(0) = Flip(0.4)

for { minute <- 1 until length } {
  confident(minute) = If(confident(minute - 1), Flip(0.6), Flip(0.3))
} //
```

Sets the distribution for the initial hidden state of the sequence

Array of hidden state variables, one for each time step

Array of observation variables, one for each hidden state variable

Transition model defining a distribution for each hidden state variable based on the one before in the sequence

```
for { minute <- 0 until length } {
  ourPossession(minute) = If(confident(minute), Flip(0.7), Flip(0.3))
} //
```

**Observation model defining a distribution for
each observation variable given its
corresponding hidden state variable**

When you infer the hidden state at a time point from observations, you can consider
three kinds of observation: the current observation, previous observations, and future
observations. *Future observations* sounds paradoxical; how can you possibly observe the
future? What I mean is that you can infer the hidden state in an earlier time point
based on observations that were received from that time point up to the present.
From the point of view of that earlier time point, these are future observations.

As discussed earlier, all observations need to be taken into account to infer the hidden state, not just the current and most immediate neighboring observations. This
can be demonstrated by the following series of queries on our program.

Listing 8.3   HMM queries

```
println("Probability we are confident at time step 2")
println("Prior probability: " +
  VariableElimination.probability(confident(2), true))
ourPossession(2).observe(true)
println("After observing current possession at time step 2: " +
    VariableElimination.probability(confident(2), true))
ourPossession(1).observe(true)
println("After observing previous possession at time step 1: " +
  VariableElimination.probability(confident(2), true))
ourPossession(0).observe(true)
println("After observing previous possession at time step 0: " +
  VariableElimination.probability(confident(2), true))
ourPossession(3).observe(true)
println("After observing future possession at time step 3: " +
  VariableElimination.probability(confident(2), true))
ourPossession(4).observe(true)
println("After observing future possession at time step 4: " +
  VariableElimination.probability(confident(2), true))
```

When run, this program prints the following:

```
Probability we are confident at time step 2
Prior probability: 0.42600000000000005
After observing current possession at time step 2: 0.6339285714285714
After observing previous possession at time step 1: 0.6902173913043478
After observing previous possession at time step 0: 0.7046460176991151
After observing future possession at time step 3: 0.7541436464088398
After observing future possession at time step 4: 0.7663786503335885
```

You see that every observation adds to your belief that you are confident at time step 2.

8.2.3   *Dynamic Bayesian networks*

Although HMMs are powerful in that they enable you to infer hidden state from a sequence of observations, they're still a simple representation that uses only two variables at every time point. In general, there might be many variables you're interested in, and they might be dependent on each other in a variety of ways. *Dynamic Bayesian networks* (DBNs) are a generalization of HMMs that serve this need. They operate on the same principle as HMMs of modeling a sequence of variables over time, but there can be many variables and they can be dependent on each other in interesting ways.

Figure 8.3 shows an example DBN for a soccer match. As the name implies, a DBN is like a Bayesian network, and consists of similar content.

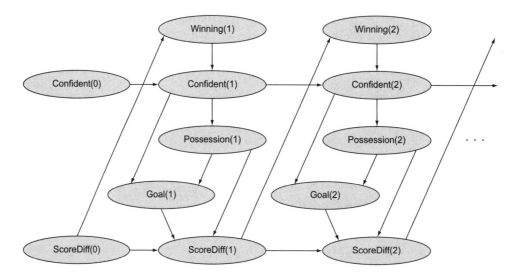

Figure 8.3   A dynamic Bayesian network. Several variables exist at each point in time. A variable at a time point can depend on other variables at that time point or on variables at the previous time point.

A DBN has the following content:

1   A set of state variables at each time point. In figure 8.3, these are the following variables:
   - Winning, representing which team is currently winning the match
   - Confident, representing whether your team is confident
   - Possession, representing whether your team has possession
   - Goal, representing whether a goal is scored at that time point
   - ScoreDiff, representing the score differential between the two teams

2   For each variable, a set of possible values. In our example:
   - Winning could be "us", "them", or "none"
   - Confident is Boolean

- Possession is Boolean
- Goal is Boolean
- ScoreDiff is an integer from –5 to 5

3 A transition model, consisting of the following:

- For each variable, a set of parents. These parents could be other variables at the same time step or variables at the previous time step. The only restrictions on the parents are (1) edges can't cross more than one time step, and (2) the edges can't make directed cycles, just as in a Bayesian network. In our example, you have the following dependencies:
  - Whether you're Winning at one time point depends on the ScoreDiff at the previous time point.
  - Whether you're Confident at one time point depends on who is currently Winning and whether you were previously Confident.
  - Whether you have Possession depends on whether you're currently Confident.
  - Whether a Goal is scored (by either team) depends on whether you have Possession and on your Confidence.
  - The new ScoreDiff is determined by the previous ScoreDiff, whether a Goal was scored, and who scored the goal if it was scored, determined by whether you had Possession.

- For each variable, a conditional probability distribution (CPD) that specifies, for each variable, the probability distribution over the variable for each value of the parents. In our example, the CPDs are as follows:
  - Winning is determined by the previous ScoreDiff in the obvious way.
  - The CPD of Confident specifies that you're more likely to be Confident if you're Winning and if you were previously Confident.
  - The CPD of Possession specifies that you're more likely to have Possession if you're Confident.
  - The CPD of Goal makes a Goal more likely if the team that has possession also has favorable confidence. That means that if you have Possession and are Confident, or you don't have Possession and aren't Confident, a Goal is more likely to be scored.
  - The new ScoreDiff is a deterministic function of the previous ScoreDiff, whether a Goal was scored, and whether you had Possession (which determines whether you or they scored the goal).

4 An initial model that specifies a probability distribution over variables at the initial time point. Typically, this is an ordinary Bayesian network over the initial variables. But you need the distribution only over variables that have an effect on the next time point to get the DBN going. In our DBN, these are the variables Confident(0) and ScoreDiff(0).

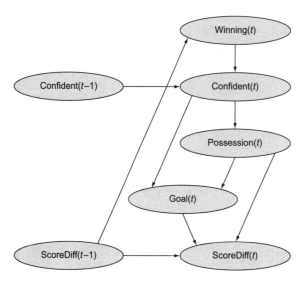

Figure 8.4   A two-time-step Bayesian network (2TBN) for our example. The 2TBN shows the variables at time step *t* and their dependence on time step *t* – 1.

As you can see from this list, the main content of the DBN specification is in the transition model. Typically, rather than show the sequence of variables over time, as in figure 8.3 (which shows variables at times 0, 1, 2, and so forth), it's typical to show the relationship between a time step and the previous time step. This relationship is called a *two time-step Bayesian network*, or 2TBN for short. Figure 8.4 shows the 2TBN for our running example.

As you can see from the figure, a 2TBN is similar to an ordinary Bayesian network in which the variables are the state variables of the DBN at time steps *t* and *t* – 1. The only difference is that the variables at time step *t* – 1 have no parents and no CPDs; only the dependencies and distributions of the variables at time step *t* are defined. The 2TBN is an encoding of the transition model of the DBN previously described, and is the usual way the DBN is depicted.

SPECIFYING DBNS IN FIGARO

You already know how to specify both ordinary Bayesian networks and HMMs in Figaro. Because DBNs are a combination of these two frameworks, you have the necessary techniques to specify DBNs.

Listing 8.4   Implementation of the DBN in figure 8.3 in Figaro

```
val length = 91
val winning: Array[Element[String]] = Array.fill(length)(Constant(""))
val confident: Array[Element[Boolean]] =
  Array.fill(length)(Constant(false))
val ourPossession: Array[Element[Boolean]] =
  Array.fill(length)(Constant(false))
val goal: Array[Element[Boolean]] =
  Array.fill(length)(Constant(false))
val scoreDifferential: Array[Element[Int]] =
  Array.fill(length)(Constant(0))
```

Create arrays of the
five state variables
at each point in time

Create Figaro elements to represent the initial values of confident and scoreDifferential

The loop defines the transitions at every time point. The transition model specifies how the five state variables depend on the previous state of confident and score-Differential. Each variable can also depend on earlier variables in the loop. For example, confident depends on winning at the same time point.

```
confident(0) = Flip(0.4)
scoreDifferential(0) = Constant(0)

for { minute <- 1 until length } {
  winning(minute) =
    Apply(scoreDifferential(minute - 1), (i: Int) =>
           if (i > 0) "us" else if (i < 0) "them" else "none")
  confident(minute) =
    CPD(confident(minute - 1), winning(minute),
        (true, "us") -> Flip(0.9),
        (true, "none") -> Flip(0.7),
        (true, "them") -> Flip(0.5),
        (false, "us") -> Flip(0.5),
        (false, "none") -> Flip(0.3),
        (false, "them") -> Flip(0.1))
  ourPossession(minute) = If(confident(minute), Flip(0.7), Flip(0.3))
  goal(minute) =
    CPD(ourPossession(minute), confident(minute),
        (true, true) -> Flip(0.04),
        (true, false) -> Flip(0.01),
        (false, true) -> Flip(0.045),
        (false, false) -> Flip(0.02))
  scoreDifferential(minute) =
    If(goal(minute),
        Apply(ourPossession(minute), scoreDifferential(minute - 1),
              (poss: Boolean, diff: Int) =>
                 if (poss) (diff + 1).min(5) else (diff - 1).max(-5)),
        scoreDifferential(minute - 1))
}
```

You can use this DBN model for a variety of queries. For example, you can predict the future of the match based on the current state or infer the previous state that led to the current outcome. One practical use for a soccer coach (or a gambler) is to predict who will win the match. If you query the preceding program for the final score-Differential variable, you get that the probability of winning the match is about 0.4. But if you observe that your team scored a goal in the fourth minute, that probability goes up to about 0.73.

8.2.4 *Models with variable structure over time*

The three kinds of models you've seen so far—Markov chains, hidden Markov models, and dynamic Bayesian networks—are standard stuff. They consist of a fixed set of variables with fixed structure. Probabilistic programming gives you the ability to work with more-advanced models in which the structure of the state can vary over time.

For example, imagine a restaurant owner who wants to know how full her restaurant will be on a given night; this might help her decide various things like how much food to make, whether to encourage her patrons to linger or leave quickly, and so on. The restaurant is a dynamic system involving guests arriving, eating their dinners, and leaving. The state of the system might consist of the number of guests currently at the restaurant and the amount of time they've been there, as well as the number of people waiting to be seated. Because the number of guests changes over time, the structure of the state varies. Furthermore, you don't know in advance what the structure will be at any point in time; at any given time point, you must consider many possible structures.

USING PROBABILISTIC PROGRAMMING TO MODEL SYSTEMS WITH VARIABLE STRUCTURE

The easiest way to model this kind of system using probabilistic programming is to create a set of state variables whose types are data structures that can vary. In our example, shown in figure 8.5, you might have two state variables:

- Seated represents the guests who are currently seated at the restaurant and the amount of time they've been there. Its data type is a list of integers. The length of the list is the current number of guests seated, and each integer represents the amount of time a particular guest has been seated.
- Waiting represents the number of guests currently waiting to be seated. It's a simple integer.

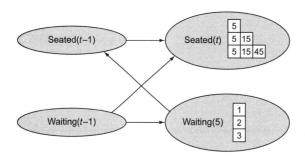

Figure 8.5 A dynamic model with variables whose structures change over time. Three possible values of each state variable are shown. The possible values of the Seated variable are arrays of variable length.

After you've set up the model using these state variables of rich data types, the model becomes like a DBN, and you can encode it similarly. But some extra techniques are needed to deal with the variables over rich data types. Let's build up the model bit by bit.

To start, you'll set the capacity of the restaurant and the number of steps you're going to run the model. For simplicity, assume that the restaurant has ten tables of equal size, and each group of guests occupies one table, so the capacity is 10. In addition, assume that you'll be reasoning in time steps of 5 minutes each, for a period of 1 hour, so the number of steps is 12.

```
val numSteps = 12
val capacity = 10
```

For each of the two state variables previously described, an array will represent the value of that variable over time, where each variable has the appropriate type. So each of the seated variables is an Element[List[Int]], and waiting is an Element[Int]:

```
val seated: Array[Element[List[Int]]] =
  Array.fill(numSteps)(Constant(List()))
val waiting: Array[Element[Int]] = Array.fill(numSteps)(Constant(0))
```

This example assumes that the restaurant owner is starting at a particular point in the evening with a known state, so you'll set the initial values of the state variables to their known values by using Figaro's `Constant` construct. At the initial time point, the restaurant is already full and three people are waiting.

```
seated(0) = Constant(List(0, 5, 15, 15, 25, 30, 40, 60, 65, 75))
   waiting(0) = Constant(3)
```

REPRESENTING THE TRANSITION MODEL

Now for the interesting part: the transition model. You'll write it in two steps. First, you'll write the skeleton of the transition model, and then you'll fill in the details. Here's the skeleton.

Listing 8.5 Dynamic model with variable structure—code skeleton

```
def transition(seated: List[Int], waiting: Int):                    Define a transition function
  (Element[(List[Int], Int)]) = {                                   that takes the previous state
  // details go here                                                variables, and returns a joint
  ^^(allSeated, newWaiting)                                         probability distribution over
}                                                                   the new state variables

for { step <- 1 until numSteps } {
  val newState =                                                    Produce the joint distribution over the
    Chain(seated(step - 1), waiting(step - 1),                      new state variables from the distributions
      (l: List[Int], i: Int) => transition(l, i))                   over the previous state variables

  seated(step) = newState._1                                        Extract the new state variables
  waiting(step) = newState._2                                       from this joint distribution
}
```

Let's look closely at this code, because it shows a general pattern. You might be wondering whether the word *chain* in *Markov chain* has anything to do with Figaro chains. A close connection does exist. We haven't paid close attention to it until now, but the chaining of state variables from one time step to the next can be accomplished by Figaro's `Chain`. Remember that `Chain` takes a probability distribution over a parent, and a CPD from the parent to a child, and produces a probability distribution over the child. In a Markov chain, the parent is a variable such as `possession(t - 1)`, and the child is a variable such as `possession(t)`, and the CPD is the transition model that gives the probability distribution over `possession(t)`, given `possession(t - 1)`. So to get the distribution over `possession(t)`, you can write this:

```
Chain(possession(t - 1), transitionModel)
```

This code uses similar logic. You have the state at time `step - 1`, consisting of `seated(step - 1)` and `waiting(step - 1)`. The transition function is a function that takes a particular value of `seated` and `waiting` and produces an element over the next state, which is a pair of a `List[Int]` (for `seated`) and an `Int` (for `waiting`). You use `Chain` to get the element over the next state from the current state.

The next state is an element over the pair of seated and waiting values. It defines a joint distribution over the seated and waiting variables at the new time step. In the transition function, this element is constructed by using Figaro's `^^` constructor, which creates elements over pairs (or larger tuples) from individual elements. In this transition function, these are the elements allSeated and newWaiting. You'll see in a moment how these are generated.

Finally, the result of the chain is an element over a pair. You want to get the individual seated and waiting elements out of this pair. This is achieved using Figaro's `_1` and `_2` extractor operations. `_1` takes an element over a pair and creates an element over the first component, and similarly for `_2`.

Now here's the transition function in detail.

Listing 8.6   Dynamic model with variable structure—detailed transition function

```
def transition(seated: List[Int], waiting: Int):
  (Element[(List[Int], Int)]) = {
  val newTimes: List[Element[Int]] =
    for { time <- seated }
    yield Apply(Flip(time / 80.0),
                (b: Boolean) => if (b) -1 else time + 5)

  val newTimesListElem: Element[List[Int]] = Inject(newTimes:_*)

  val staying = Apply(newTimesListElem,
                      (l: List[Int]) => l.filter(_ >= 0))

  val arriving = Poisson(2)
  val totalWaiting = Apply(arriving, (i: Int) => i + waiting)

  val placesOccupied =
    Apply(staying, (l: List[Int]) => l.length.min(capacity))
  val placesAvailable =
    Apply(placesOccupied, (i: Int) => capacity - i)
  val numNewlySeated =
    Apply(totalWaiting, placesAvailable,
          (tw: Int, pa: Int) => tw.min(pa))

  val newlySeated =
    Apply(numNewlySeated, (i: Int) => List.fill(i)(0))
  val allSeated =
    Apply(newlySeated, staying,
          (l1: List[Int], l2: List[Int]) => l1 ::: l2)

  val newWaiting = Apply(totalWaiting, numNewlySeated,
                         (tw: Int, ns: Int) => tw - ns)

  ^^(allSeated, newWaiting)
}
```

newTimes is a list of Element[Int]. You need to turn it into an Element [List[Int]], which is achieved by Inject.

Determine the number of people who arrive at the restaurant and the resulting number that are waiting

Determine the new amount of time each guest is at the table. −1 indicates that they're leaving, which happens with probability time / 80.

Determine the number of people who are leaving by removing all those whose seated time is less than 0

Determine the number of waiting people that can be newly seated

Determine the new list of seated guests

Determine the new number of waiting guests

Return an element over a pair of the new list of seated guests and number of waiting guests

Because this code mostly uses Figaro features you've already seen, I won't explain it in gory detail. But one feature is worth mentioning: Figaro's `Inject` element can turn a list of elements into an element of lists. What does that mean? Suppose you have a list consisting of three `Element[Int]`s. One possible set of values is that the first is 5, the second is 10, and the third is 15. You can make this into a list consisting of the values 5, 10, and 15. In this case, the value of `Inject(1)` will be `List(5, 10, 15)`.

Why is this useful? Some operations in our model, namely, determining the new amount of time a guest is seated and whether the guest is leaving, are applied to individual elements. Other operations, such as determining the list of guests who are staying, are applied to the list of guests as a whole. You need an element over lists, and `Inject` gives you that.

REASONING WITH THE MODEL

There's not too much to say about running inference on this model, as it's similar to the types of dynamic probabilistic models you've seen previously. Again, you can use the model to predict the future or infer past causes of observed events. Section 8.3 shows you how to use the exact same model to monitor the state of the restaurant over time.

In general, you probably won't use a factored algorithm such as variable elimination or belief propagation for these variable structure models. The number of possible values of the state variables is enormous. In the restaurant example, each possible seated time is a number between 0 and 75 that's divisible by 5. (Once the seated time reaches 75, the guest will definitely leave at the next time step.) This produces 16 possible values. The number of possible lists of 10 seated times is 16^{10}. You also need to consider cases where the number of guests is less than 10. This results in far too many possibilities to enumerate.

Therefore, a sampling algorithm will work better. This example uses importance sampling to predict the number of people waiting to get into the restaurant at the end of the next hour. Here's some code to do that:

```
val alg = Importance(10000, waiting(numSteps - 1))
alg.start()
println(alg.probability(waiting(numSteps - 1), (i: Int) => i > 4))
```

Running this code produces a value around 0.4693, which means that with probability around 47%, more than four people will be waiting at the end of the hour.

You've now seen a variety of dynamic probabilistic models, from simple to advanced. A limitation of all of the programs I've shown so far is that you have to define the number of time steps in advance. The next section shows you how this restriction can be lifted.

8.3 *Modeling systems that go on indefinitely*

The goal in this section is to define dynamic probabilistic models that can go on for any length of time. These models can be used to monitor the state of the system in an ongoing fashion based on evidence that's accumulated over time. The mechanics for achieving this aren't difficult, but you'll need a new Figaro concept, the *universe*.

8.3.1   *Understanding Figaro universes*

In chapter 7, you learned about element collections. An *element collection* is a data structure in which elements can be accessed by name. A *universe* is a special type of element collection that also provides services that are useful to inference algorithms, such as memory management and dependency analysis. As a result, inference algorithms usually operate on a universe.

Up until now, the concept of *universe* has been completely invisible to you, and most of the time you don't have to think about it. But every element belongs to a universe. *There's always a default universe*, and, unless you specify otherwise, your element is placed in the default universe.

The concepts of element collection and universe are closely related. Here are some things to remember:

- Every universe is an element collection, but not every element collection is a universe.
- Every element collection is associated with a universe. In the case of an element collection that is also a universe, the associated universe is itself.
- When you place an element in an element collection, its universe is the universe associated with the element collection.

Remember that you place an element in an element collection by supplying optional name and element collection arguments. For example, if you write this:

```
Flip(0.5)("coin", collection)
```

the element `Flip(0.5)` is given the name `coin` and placed in the element collection identified by `collection`. Because a universe is an element collection, you can place an element directly in a universe by supplying the universe as the second optional argument, for example:

```
Flip(0.5)("coin", universe)
```

There's always a current default universe. When you don't provide optional name and element collection arguments when creating an element, both its element collection and its universe become this default universe. This default universe is held in the Scala variable `Universe.universe` in the `com.cra.figaro.language` package.

Algorithms also operate on a universe. Unless otherwise specified, this is the current default universe. A different universe can be specified by providing an optional additional argument in its own argument list. For example, `VariableElimination (target)` creates a variable elimination algorithm on the default universe with the given target. `VariableElimination(target)(u2)` creates a variable elimination algorithm on universe u2 with the given target. The one-line inference shortcuts such as `Variable-Elimination.probability` always operate on the default universe.

You can get a new universe in two ways. One is to call

```
new Universe
```

which creates a fresh universe with no elements in it. The other is to call

```
Universe.createNew()
```

which, in addition to creating a fresh universe, also sets the default universe to this new universe. This provides a convenient way to start working with a new universe, put your new elements in this universe, and have your algorithm run on this universe. For example, you could write the following:

```
Universe.createNew()
val x = Beta(1, 2)
val y = Flip(x)
println(VariableElimination.probability(y, true))
```

The elements x and y will be placed in the new universe, and the variable elimination algorithm will be run on it.

Everything that was said here about universes also applies when you're running Figaro in the interactive Scala interpreter. All elements you create will go in a universe, which is the default universe unless otherwise specified. If you want to forget your previous interactions and start from scratch, enter `Universe.createNew()`. All your new elements will be put in the newly created default universe, and all old elements will be ignored.

8.3.2 Using universes to model ongoing systems

To represent a dynamic probabilistic model with no time limit in Figaro, you create a universe for every time step that contains all of the variables at that time step. The model is normally specified in two pieces:

- An initial universe
- A function from one universe to the next universe

These two pieces define a dynamic probabilistic model, shown in figure 8.6, as follows:

1 Begin with a probability distribution over the initial state at time 0 as specified by all elements in the initial universe.
2 Apply the function to the initial universe to get a time 1 universe. The elements in the new universe define a probability distribution over the time 1 state.
3 Apply the function to the time 1 universe to get a time 2 universe. The elements in the new universe define a probability distribution over the time 2 state.
4 Continue for as long as desired.

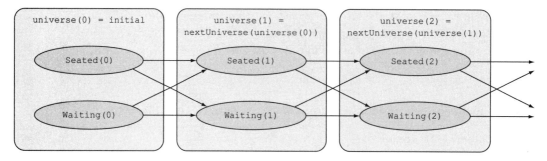

Figure 8.6   Progression of a dynamic model through a series of universes. Each universe contains the state variables at a given time point. The first universe is defined by the initial model, and subsequent universes are created by applying the nextUniverse function to the previous universe.

Any element in a time step that directly influences an element at the next time step must be given a name. This name enables the program to refer to the element in the previous universe. In the restaurant example, the number of guests waiting for a seat at the end of a time step influences the state at the next time step. You need to give the element representing this number the name waiting.

Now, the transition function takes the previous universe as an argument. Let's say this universe is contained in a Scala variable named previous. You can write

```
previous.get[Int]("waiting")
```

to get the element named waiting in the previous universe. Notice that you had to tell Scala the value type of this element (Int), because otherwise the get method would have no idea what kind of element to return.

Any element that you want to query or observe also needs to be given a name. That way, you can refer to the element consistently at every time step. With that introduction, here's a skeleton of the way to represent the ongoing restaurant model.

Listing 8.7   Implementation of the nextUniverse function

Define a function from the previous universe to the next universe

```
def transition(seated: List[Int], waiting: Int):
  (Element[(List[Int], Int, Int)]) = {
    // details are the same as before
    ^^(allSeated, newWaiting, arriving)
}
```

The transition function is unchanged, except that you also include the number of people arriving in the returned element because you'll observe it.

```
def nextUniverse(previous: Universe): Universe = {
  val next = Universe.createNew()
  val previousSeated = previous.get[List[Int]]("seated")
  val previousWaiting = previous.get[Int]("waiting")
  val state = Chain(previousSeated, previousWaiting, transition _)
```

Create the new universe, make it the default, and assign it to a Scala variable

Get the previous state variables from the previous universe

Use Chain to get the element representing the new state

```
    Apply(state, (s: (List[Int], Int, Int)) => s._1)("seated", next)
    Apply(state, (s: (List[Int], Int, Int)) => s._2)("waiting", next)
    Apply(state, (s: (List[Int], Int, Int)) => s._3)("arriving", next)
    next    <┐
}           │
```

Return the next universe

Get the elements representing the individual state variables out of this element and give each a name in the next universe

As you can see from this code, not much has changed from the previous time-limited version of this model. In particular, the transition function, which contains the essential logic, is almost unchanged. The most significant new aspect of the code is that you use names to identify the elements representing the state variables in each universe. You get these elements by name from the previous universe and give them a name when you put them in the new universe.

That's all there is to representing the model. Now let's see how to create an application to monitor the state of the system in an ongoing fashion.

8.3.3   Running a monitoring application

Your goal is to begin with an initial belief about the state of the system and repeatedly update your beliefs about the state, given evidence that you receive at every time step. Specifically, you want to execute the following process, depicted in figure 8.7:

1 Begin with a distribution over the state of the system at time 0.
2 Incorporate observations received at time 1 to produce a distribution over the state of the system at time 1.
3 Incorporate observations received at time 2 to produce a distribution over the state of the system at time 2.
4 Repeat for as long as desired.

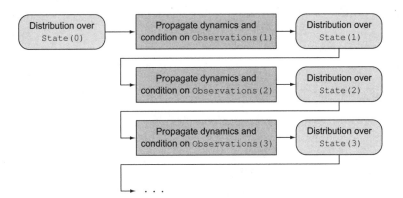

Figure 8.7   The filtering process. Figaro maintains a probability distribution over the state of the system at each time point. From one time point to the next, Figaro takes into account the dynamics of the model and conditions on the new observations to produce a probability distribution over the new state.

This process goes by various names, including monitoring, state estimation, and filtering. All are different names for the same thing. Algorithms for achieving this process are often called *filtering algorithms*, and this is the name used in Figaro. Probably the most popular filtering algorithm is called *particle filtering*. This is a sampling algorithm that represents the distribution over the state of the system at each time point by using a set of samples or "particles." Details about the particle-filtering algorithm can be found in chapter 12.

To create a particle-filtering algorithm in Figaro, you pass it three arguments:

- The initial universe
- The function that takes the previous universe to the next universe
- The number of particles to use at every time step

In our restaurant example, you create the algorithm as follows:

```
val alg = ParticleFilter(initial, nextUniverse, 10000)
```

The next step is the same as for other Figaro algorithms: you start the algorithm by using `alg.start()`. For a particle filter, this produces the probability distribution over the initial state.

Most of the work of the particle filter is accomplished by the `advanceTime` method, which advances the system from one time step to the next while taking into account the new evidence. In this example, you call the following:

```
alg.advanceTime(evidence)
```

The way the evidence is specified is different from what you've seen before. Throughout the book, you've seen evidence specified by adding conditions or constraints to elements. You can't do that here, because you have no direct handle on the elements representing the state of the system at any time point; they're internal to the `next-Universe` function. Instead, you refer to these elements by name. So you have to tell the particle filter the names of the elements you have evidence for as well as the nature of that evidence.

For example, you can specify a piece of evidence as follows:

```
NamedEvidence("arriving", Observation(3))
```

This is an instance of the `NamedEvidence` class, which pairs a name (`arriving`) with a piece of evidence (in this case, the observation that the element named `arriving` has value 3). The piece of evidence could also be a more general condition or constraint. The argument to the particle filter's `advanceTime` method is a list of these `Named-Evidence` items, which specify all evidence newly received at the time point.

In our restaurant example, let's assume that the restaurant owner intermittently observed the number of people arriving at the restaurant in a time step. So she may or may not get evidence at any particular time step. You can accomplish this in Scala by making her get an `Option[Int]`, which could be `None` or could be a particular observed

number of people. You then translate this optional observation into the argument to
advanceTime. Here's the code to do that:

```
val evidence = {
  arrivingObservation(time) match {
    case None => List()
    case Some(n) => List(NamedEvidence("arriving", Observation(n)))
  }
}
alg.advanceTime(evidence)
```

After calling advanceTime, you can query the state of the system at the current time
point. The particle filter provides several methods, such as currentProbability,
currentExpectation, and currentDistribution, to do this. Again, because you
don't have a handle on specific elements, you refer to elements being queried by
name. For example, to get the probability that more than four people are waiting,
you can write

```
alg.currentProbability("waiting", (i: Int) => i > 4)
```

To get the expected (average) number of guests seated at the restaurant, you can call

```
alg.currentExpectation("seated", (l: List[Int]) => l.length)
```

To summarize, here are the steps you take to run a particle filter, given the initial universe and the function that takes the previous universe and returns the next universe:

1 Create the particle filter.
2 Start the particle filter to get the initial distribution.
3 Do the following for each time step:

    a Collect the evidence at that time step.
    b Call advanceTime with that evidence to get the distribution over the new state.
    c Query the new distribution.

You can see these steps in action in the code for this chapter provided with the book,
which produces output like this:

```
Time 1: expected customers = 9.6498, expected waiting = 1.2325
Time 2: expected customers = 9.2651, expected waiting = 0.7388
Time 3: expected customers = 9.3622, expected waiting = 1.2295
Time 4: expected customers = 9.4169, expected waiting = 1.7192
Time 5: expected customers = 9.6011, expected waiting = 2.0629
Time 6: expected customers = 9.5866, expected waiting = 2.4307
Time 7: expected customers = 8.9794, expected waiting = 1.3958
Time 8: expected customers = 9.489, expected waiting = 2.2148
Time 9: expected customers = 9.5205, expected waiting = 2.5118
Time 10: expected customers = 9.5373, expected waiting = 2.8227
Time 11: expected customers = 9.5656, expected waiting = 3.1624
Time 12: expected customers = 9.4327, expected waiting = 2.6614
```

You can see how the program is monitoring the number of seated and waiting customers over time. You've accomplished your goal. You've built a model of a complex dynamic system and are able to monitor the state of this system over time.

This concludes the part of this book on modeling techniques. The presentation has focused on the most important ideas and the most common use cases. At this point, you should have enough knowledge to use Figaro for most of your applications and to understand all aspects of the Scaladoc related to modeling.

> **NOTE** I haven't tried to cover every feature of Figaro comprehensively. The Scaladoc provides a description of the full functionality of Figaro. If anything is unclear to you, please send an email to figaro@cra.com; we're always eager to improve our documentation.

The next part of the book shows you how probabilistic inference works, which will help you get the most out of your models.

8.4 Summary

- A dynamic system consists of state that varies over time; the states at different time points are dependent.
- Many dynamic probabilistic models implement the Markov assumption that the current state is conditionally independent of all earlier states, given the directly previous state.
- Even though a hidden Markov model implements the Markov assumption, all previous evidence must be considered when inferring the current state, because the previous state is unobserved.
- A dynamic Bayesian network is like an extension of a hidden Markov model that has multiple state variables; by making the types of these variables rich data structures, you can model systems with structure that varies over time.
- Monitoring or filtering is the process of keeping track of the state of the system over time, given observations that are received; this process is achieved by using algorithms such as particle filtering.
- Filtering in Figaro is accomplished by creating an initial universe and a function that maps the previous universe to the next universe.
- When filtering in Figaro, elements that influence the next time step, as well as evidence and query elements, are referred to by name.

8.5 Exercises

Solutions to selected exercises are available online at www.manning.com/books/practical-probabilistic-programming.

1 In a game of table tennis, the first player to 21 points wins. Alice and Bob are playing a game of table tennis, and Alice is slightly better, so she has a 52% chance of winning each point. Model a table tennis game by using a Markov chain and use it to estimate the probability that Bob will win the game.

2 Now let's try a variant on exercise 1. The relative skill levels of Alice and Bob are unknown, and at the beginning of the game we assume that the probability of Alice winning a point is Beta(2, 2). This can also be modeled as a Markov chain, except that the transition probabilities depend on an unknown parameter. Use the model to compute the probability that Bob will win the game, given that the current score is 11 to 8 in favor of Alice.

3 Let's model the progression of a student through a series of 10 chapters of increasing difficulty. Each chapter has a test. The score of the student on the test depends on how much she learned from the chapter. In addition, the chapters build on one another, so how much the student learns from one chapter depends on how much she learned from the previous. Model this situation by using a hidden Markov model and predict the probability that the student will pass the last test successfully given that she has passed the first three tests.

4 Use a DBN to create a simple economic model of a firm. The DBN has three variables: investment, profit, and capital. At any time step, capital is equal to the previous capital plus new profit minus new investment. The amount of profit at any time step is uncertain, but tends to be higher with higher Investment. Consider different policies where the level of Investment at a given time point is equal to a fixed fraction of the amount of capital at the previous time point. For a given fixed starting amount of capital, predict the amount of capital after 10 time steps for different investment policies.

5 Let's create a simple model of the evolution of a network over time. At each point in time, one of the following two things happens: With probability 0.1, a new node is added to the network and randomly connected to an existing node. With probability 0.9, two existing nodes have their edge status flipped (if they previously didn't have an edge between them, the edge is added; otherwise, the edge is removed).

  Using a given initial network, create a Figaro model for the evolution of the network over 100 time steps. Predict the number of edges in the network after 100 steps.

6 Let's create a model of the success of a new song in the pop charts. As a song is released, more and more people become exposed to it, so it grows in popularity. At some point, most of the people who would be interested in the song have already been exposed to it, so fewer buy, and it goes down the charts.

  We'll create a model with five variables. Quality represents the overall quality of the song; Newly Exposed is the number of people who first hear the song in a given week; Total Exposed is the total number of people who have heard the song; Newly Bought is the number of people who buy the song in a given week; and Total Bought is the total number of people who have bought the song so far. The Quality doesn't change over time, while the Total Bought is the previous Total Bought plus the Newly Bought, and similarly for Total Exposed. Newly Bought depends on the Quality and Newly Exposed; the more people are newly exposed, the more will buy the song, but this depends also on the song quality. Finally, Newly Exposed depends on both Total Exposed and Newly Bought; the more people have already heard the song, the fewer there are to hear it new; on the other hand, the more people who buy the song in a given week, the more air time it gets on the radio, so the more people are exposed to it.

Because there's no time limit on the amount of time a song stays in the charts, we have to use Figaro universes to create an ongoing model. Newly Bought is an observed variable. We'll query Total Exposed. Write a Figaro program to express this model.

a Generate data from this model. Use particle filtering, with no evidence, to create a sequence of numbers of Newly Bought. Stop when Newly Bought falls below a certain threshold (corresponding to the song falling off the charts).

b Now, using your generated data, observe Newly Bought and estimate the Total Exposed over time.

Part 3

Inference

So you've written a probabilistic program. How do you use it? You need to apply an inference algorithm. To get the most out of probabilistic programming, you need to understand inference algorithms and how best to use them. Part 3 of the book is all about inference. Chapter 9 provides basic concepts in probabilistic inference. Then chapters 10 through 13 describe a variety of inference algorithms. The chapters strike a balance between theoretical descriptions of the algorithms and practical considerations in using the algorithms, along with examples of how they're applied in the real world.

You'll learn that there are two main families of inference algorithms: factored algorithms and sampling algorithms. Grasping the principles behind these two families will help you understand most of the algorithms you'll encounter in probabilistic programming. Accordingly, chapter 10 focuses on factored algorithms and chapter 11 on sampling algorithms. Chapter 12 shows how you can adapt the same algorithms you learn in chapters 10 and 11 to answer a variety of queries. Finally, chapter 13 shows two advanced but very important types of inference: reasoning about dynamic systems and learning the numerical parameters of a model.

The three rules
of probabilistic inference

9

This chapter covers

- Three important rules for working with probabilistic models:
  - The chain rule, which lets you build complex models out of simple components
  - The total probability rule, which lets you simplify a complex probabilistic model to answer simple queries
  - Bayes' rule, with which you can draw conclusions about causes from observations of their effects
- The basics of Bayesian modeling, including how to estimate model parameters from data and use them to predict future cases

---

In part 2 of this book, you learned all about writing probabilistic programs for a variety of applications. You know that probabilistic programming systems use inference algorithms operating on these programs to answer queries, given evidence. How do they do that? That's what this part of the book is all about. It's important that you know about this, so you can design models and choose algorithms that support fast and accurate inference.

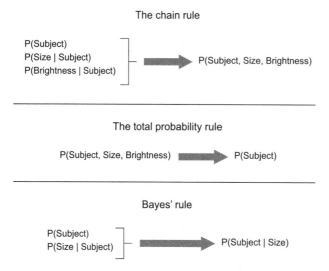

Figure 9.1   Inputs and output of each of the three rules of probabilistic inference. The chain rule lets you turn a set of conditional probability distributions into a joint probability distribution. The total probability rule lets you take a joint probability distribution over a set of variables and produce a distribution over a single variable. Bayes' rule lets you "invert" a conditional probability distribution over an effect, given a cause, into a conditional probability distribution over the cause, given the effect.

This chapter begins with the basics of inference: the three rules of probabilistic inference. The inputs and output of each of the three rules is summarized in figure 9.1:

- First you'll learn about the chain rule, which lets you go from simple (local conditional probability distributions over individual variables) to complex (a full joint probability distribution over all variables).
- The total probability rule, described in section 9.2, goes from complex (a full joint distribution) back to simple (a distribution over a single variable).
- Finally, Bayes' rule, described in section 9.3, is probably the most famous rule of inference. Bayes' rule lets you "flip" the direction of the dependencies, turning a conditional distribution over an effect, given a cause, into a distribution over a cause, given an effect. Bayes' rule is essential to incorporating evidence, which is often an observation of an effect, and inferring a cause.

These three rules of inference can be used to answer queries.

Before diving into the new material, let's recap some definitions from chapter 4 that you need in this chapter:

- *Possible worlds*—All states you consider possible
- *Probability distribution*—An assignment of a probability between 0 and 1 to each possible world, such that all of the probabilities add up to 1
- *Prior probability distribution*—The probability distribution before seeing any evidence
- *Conditioning on the evidence*—The process of applying evidence to a probability distribution

- *Posterior probability distribution*—The probability distribution after seeing the evidence; the result of conditioning
- *Conditional probability distribution*—Rule that specifies a probability distribution over one variable for every combination of values of some other variables
- *Normalizing*—The process of proportionally adjusting a set of numbers so they add up to 1

NOTE For each of the rules, a sidebar presents generic mathematical definitions. These are useful if you want a deeper understanding; and if you're comfortable with the mathematical notation, this more abstract discussion can help cement the principles. If not, feel free to skip these sidebars. The main thing is that you understand why and how the rule is used.

9.1 The chain rule: building joint distributions from conditional probability distributions

As you may recall, chapter 4 covered how a probabilistic model defines a probability distribution over possible worlds, as well as the ingredients of probabilistic models: variables, dependencies, functional forms, and numerical parameters. I hinted that the chain rule is the essential mechanism that turns these ingredients into a probability distribution over possible worlds. I promised you a full discussion of the chain rule in part 3, and now it's time for that discussion.

How does the chain rule define a probability distribution over possible worlds? In other words, *how does it specify a number between 0 and 1 for each possible world?* Let's revisit our Rembrandt example from chapter 4. Let's start with the variables Subject, Size, and Brightness, and assume you're given the dependency model where Size and Brightness both depend on Subject but not on each other. You're also given a specification of a probability distribution over Subject; a CPD of Size, given Subject; and a CPD of Brightness, given Subject. These ingredients are summarized in figure 9.2. (For Subject, which doesn't depend on anything, I use the same CPD table notation as the other variables, except that there are no conditioning variables and only one row.)

Now, a possible world specifies a value for each of the variables Subject, Size, and Brightness. *How do you get the probability of a possible world?* For example, what's P(Subject = People, Size = Large, Brightness = Dark)? According to the chain rule, this is simple. *You find the correct entries in the CPD tables and multiply them together.* So, in this case,

P(Subject = People, Size = Large, Brightness = Dark) =

P(Subject = People) × P(Size = Large | Subject = People) × P(Brightness = Dark | Subject = People) =

0.8 × 0.5 × 0.8 =

0.32

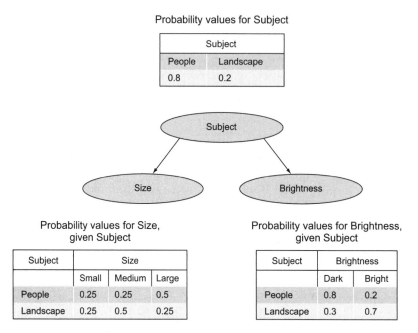

Probability values for Subject

Subject	
People	Landscape
0.8	0.2

Probability values for Size, given Subject

Subject	Size		
	Small	Medium	Large
People	0.25	0.25	0.5
Landscape	0.25	0.5	0.25

Probability values for Brightness, given Subject

Subject	Brightness	
	Dark	Bright
People	0.8	0.2
Landscape	0.3	0.7

Figure 9.2   Bayesian network structure and CPDs for the chain rule example

You can use the same formula for all possible values of Subject, Size, and Brightness, and get the result shown in table 9.1. This result is called a *joint probability distribution* over Subject, Size, and Brightness, because it specifies the probability of each joint value of these three variables.

Table 9.1   Joint probability distribution resulting from applying the chain rule to the CPDs in figure 9.1. You multiply P(Subject) by P(Size | Subject) and P(Brightness | Subject). The probabilities add up to 1.

Subject	Size	Brightness	Probability
People	Small	Dark	0.8 × 0.25 × 0.8 = 0.16
People	Small	Bright	0.8 × 0.25 × 0.2 = 0.04
People	Medium	Dark	0.8 × 0.25 × 0.8 = 0.16
People	Medium	Bright	0.8 × 0.25 × 0.2 = 0.04
People	Large	Dark	0.8 × 0.5 × 0.8 = 0.32
People	Large	Bright	0.8 × 0.5 × 0.2 = 0.08
Landscape	Small	Dark	0.2 × 0.25 × 0.3 = 0.015
Landscape	Small	Bright	0.2 × 0.25 × 0.7 = 0.035
Landscape	Medium	Dark	0.2 × 0.5 × 0.3 = 0.03

Table 9.1   Joint probability distribution resulting from applying the chain rule to the CPDs in figure 9.1. You multiply P(Subject) by P(Size | Subject) and P(Brightness | Subject). The probabilities add up to 1.

Subject	Size	Brightness	Probability
Landscape	Medium	Bright	$0.2 \times 0.5 \times 0.7 = 0.07$
Landscape	Large	Dark	$0.2 \times 0.25 \times 0.3 = 0.015$
Landscape	Large	Bright	$0.2 \times 0.25 \times 0.7 = 0.035$

The truth is, I've cheated a little bit. The standard chain rule for three variables says that for the third variable, you need to condition its probability on both the first two variables. So rather than

P(Subject = People, Size = Large, Brightness = Dark) =

P(Subject = People) × P(Size = Large | Subject = People) × P(Brightness = Dark | Subject = People)

you should be computing

P(Subject = People, Size = Large, Brightness = Dark) =

P(Subject = People) × P(Size = Large | Subject = People) × P(Brightness = Dark | Subject = People, Size = Large)

That would be the officially correct statement of the chain rule. But I'm taking advantage of specific knowledge I have about the dependencies, namely that Brightness doesn't depend on Size, only Subject. Brightness is conditionally independent of Size, given Subject:

P(Brightness = Dark | Subject = People, Size = Large) =

P(Brightness = Dark | Subject = People)

So I can legitimately simplify the chain rule the way I have. Anytime you have a Bayesian network and want to use the chain rule to define the full probability distribution over all variables, you can *always* simplify the rule so that each variable depends only on its parents in the network. On the other hand, if Brightness wasn't conditionally independent of Size, given Subject, you'd have to use the longer form. Bayesian networks and the chain rule go hand in hand. A Bayesian network specifies exactly the form of the chain rule to use in building up the joint distribution.

That's all there is to the chain rule, a simple but crucial rule in probabilistic modeling. The chain rule is essential to understanding not only Bayesian networks but also generative models in general. Because probabilistic programs are encodings of generative models, now that you understand the chain rule, you have a fundamental understanding of the probabilistic model defined by a probabilistic program.

The generic chain rule

This chain rule is a generic principle that applies to any dependency model and any set of CPDs for the variables, in whatever functional form. As long as each variable has a CPD that specifies a probability distribution over its values for any possible values of the variables it depends on, you can get the probability of any joint assignment to all variables by multiplying the correct numbers in the CPDs.

In mathematical notation, you start with two variables X and Y, such that Y depends on X. You're given $P(X)$, a probability distribution over the values of X, and $P(Y \mid X)$, the CPD of Y given X. The chain rule takes these two ingredients $P(X)$ and $P(Y \mid X)$, and turns them into a probability distribution $P(X,Y)$ over X and Y jointly. For every possible value x of X and y of Y, the chain rule is defined by this simple formula:

$$P(X = x, Y = y) = P(X = x)P(Y = y \mid X = x)$$

> **NOTATION ALERT** It's standard practice to use uppercase letters like X and Y to represent variables, and lowercase letters like x and y for values.

You have a convenient way to indicate that this formula holds for *every* value x and y:

$$P(X,y) = P(X)P(Y \mid X)$$

This easy-to-remember formula is shorthand for many formulas about specific values x and y.

What if you have more than two variables? The chain rule generalizes to any number of variables. Suppose you have variables X_1, X_2, ..., X_n. In the standard statement of the chain rule, you don't make any independence assumptions, so each variable depends on all variables that precede it. The full chain rule, using shorthand notation, is as follows:

$$P(X_1, X_2, ... X_n) = P(X_1)P(X_2 \mid X_1)P(X_3 \mid X_1, X_2) ... P(X_n \mid X_1, X_2, ... X_{n-1})$$

Let's see what this formula says. It says that to get the joint probability distribution over X_1, X_2, ... X_n, you start with X_1 and get its probability, and then you look at X_2, which depends on X_1, and get its appropriate probability out of its CPD. Then you get the probability of X_3, which depends on X_1 and X_2, from its CPD, continuing recursively until finally, you get the appropriate probability of X_n, which depends on all previous variables, from its CPD. This formula, by the way, is the reason for the name *chain rule*. You compute a joint probability distribution from a chain of conditional distributions.

Our multivariable chain rule formula didn't make any assumptions about dependencies, especially not independence relationships. Adding independence information can significantly simplify the formula. Instead of including all previous variables on the right-hand side of the "|" for a given variable, you need to include only the variables it directly depends on in the dependency model. For example, let's consider the three variables Subject, Size, and Brightness. If you were to follow formula (3), you'd get

P(Subject, Size, Brightness) = P(Subject) P(Size | Subject) P(Brightness | Subject, Size)

(continued)

But according to the network, Brightness doesn't depend on Size, only Subject. So you can simplify this formula to

P(Subject, Size, Brightness) = P(Subject) P(Size | Subject) P(Brightness | Subject)

And indeed, this is the formula used to compute table 9.1.

9.2 The total probability rule: getting simple query results from a joint distribution

The chain rule lets you build a joint distribution out of simple CPDs, say, a joint distribution over Subject, Size, and Brightness. Typically, your query will be about a particular variable or small number of variables. For example, you might want to infer the identity of a painter based on observations of a painting. Suppose you have a joint distribution over all of the variables. How do you get a probability distribution over a single variable? The principle is simple: the probability of any value of the variable is equal to the sum of probabilities of all joint assignments to all variables that are consistent with that value.

You already saw this basic principle in chapter 4: *the probability of any fact is the sum of the probabilities of possible worlds consistent with that fact.* So to get the probability that Subject = Landscape, you add the probabilities of all possible worlds consistent with Subject = Landscape. Because each world consists of a joint assignment of values to all variables, including Subject, you look for the worlds in which the value assigned to Subject is Landscape. This simple principle usually goes by the fancy name of the *law of total probability,* but I prefer to call it the more mundane *total probability rule.*

The use of the total probability rule is illustrated in figure 9.3. You start with the prior probability distribution shown in the top of the figure. You then condition on the evidence that Size = Small to obtain the posterior distribution in the middle. You use the usual two steps: first, you cross out all assignments of values to the variables inconsistent with the evidence that Size = Small, and then you normalize the remaining probabilities so that they sum to 1. On the bottom of the figure, you use the total probability rule to compute the probability that the painting is a landscape, given the evidence. You add the probabilities of all rows in which the value of the Subject variable is Landscape.

Notice how the posterior probability of a row in which the value of Size is anything other than Small is 0. This is always the case, because you cross out worlds inconsistent with the evidence and set their probability to 0. So, in fact,

P(Subject = Landscape, Brightness = Dark | Size = Small)

is equal to

P(Subject = Landscape, Brightness = Dark, Size = Small | Size = Small)

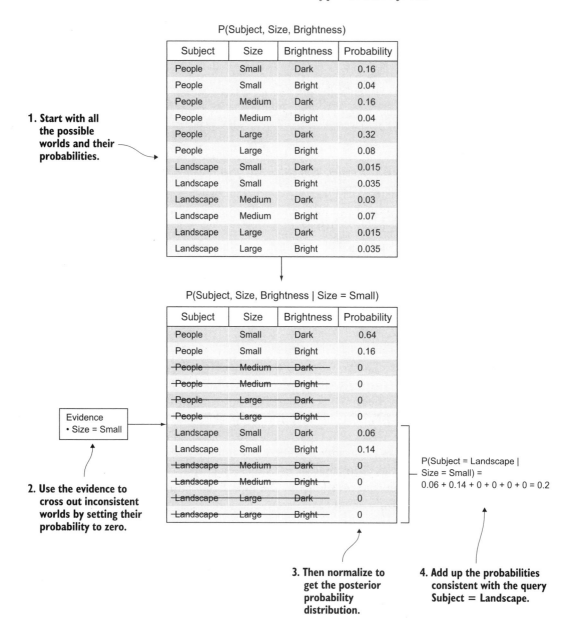

1. Start with all the possible worlds and their probabilities.

P(Subject, Size, Brightness)

Subject	Size	Brightness	Probability
People	Small	Dark	0.16
People	Small	Bright	0.04
People	Medium	Dark	0.16
People	Medium	Bright	0.04
People	Large	Dark	0.32
People	Large	Bright	0.08
Landscape	Small	Dark	0.015
Landscape	Small	Bright	0.035
Landscape	Medium	Dark	0.03
Landscape	Medium	Bright	0.07
Landscape	Large	Dark	0.015
Landscape	Large	Bright	0.035

P(Subject, Size, Brightness | Size = Small)

Subject	Size	Brightness	Probability
People	Small	Dark	0.64
People	Small	Bright	0.16
People	Medium	Dark	0
People	Medium	Bright	0
People	Large	Dark	0
People	Large	Bright	0
Landscape	Small	Dark	0.06
Landscape	Small	Bright	0.14
Landscape	Medium	Dark	0
Landscape	Medium	Bright	0
Landscape	Large	Dark	0
Landscape	Large	Bright	0

Evidence
• Size = Small

2. Use the evidence to cross out inconsistent worlds by setting their probability to zero.

P(Subject = Landscape | Size = Small) = 0.06 + 0.14 + 0 + 0 + 0 + 0 = 0.2

3. Then normalize to get the posterior probability distribution.

4. Add up the probabilities consistent with the query Subject = Landscape.

Figure 9.3   Using the total probability rule to answer a query. The total probability of a value of a variable is the sum of probabilities of all joint assignments consistent with the value.

You can see that P(Subject = Landscape | Size = Small), which is the sum of two rows in the middle table in figure 9.3, can be expressed by the following summation:

P(Subject = Landscape | Size = Small) =

P(Subject = Landscape, Brightness = Dark | Size = Small) + P(Subject = Landscape, Brightness = Bright | Size = Small)

A concise way of writing this summation uses the Greek letter Σ, which is the standard mathematical notation for addition:

P(Subject = Landscape | Size = Small) =

Σ_b P(Subject = Landscape, Brightness = b | Size = Small) (1)

On the right-hand side of this equation, b stands for any possible value of Brightness, and Σ_b means you add the following terms for all possible values of Brightness. We say we're "summing out" Brightness. Now, formula (1) holds for any possible values of Subject and Size, so you can use the snappy shorthand from the previous section:

P(Subject | Size) = Σ_b P(Subject, Brightness = b | Size)

The generic total probability rule

Now that you've seen the total probability rule applied to our example, you're ready to see the general mathematical definition. It's the same simple principle, but the notation is a little messier. You have a joint probability distribution over a set of variables, and you want to sum out some of those variables to get a distribution over the other variables. For example, you might have a joint distribution over Color, Brightness, Width, and Height. You want a distribution over Color and Brightness and to sum out Width and Height. Now, your joint distribution over all of the variables may be conditioned on some other set of variables, such as Rembrandt and Subject. To keep the formulas short, you'll use the initial of each variable. Also, let's assume that the possible values of Width and Height are small and large. According to the total probability rule

P(C = yellow, B = bright | R = true, S = landscape) =

P(C = yellow, B = bright, W = small, H = small | R = true, S = landscape) +

P(C = yellow, B = bright, W = small, H = large | R = true, S = landscape) +

P(C = yellow, B = bright, W = large, H = small | R = true, S = landscape) +

P(C = yellow, B = bright, W = large, H = large | R = true, S = landscape)

(continued)

You can write this in mathematical notation. Let's call the variables that you want the distribution $X_1,\dots,X_n$, and the variables to be summed out $Y_1,\dots,Y_m$. Let's call the variables you're conditioning on $Z_1,\dots,Z_l$. The total probability rule says that for any values $x_1,\dots,x_n$ of $X_1,\dots,X_n$ and $z_1,\dots,z_l$ of $Z_1,\dots,Z_l$:

$$P(X_1 = x_1,\dots,X_n = x_n \mid Z_1 = z_1,\dots,Z_1 = z_l) =$$

$$\Sigma_{y1}\,\Sigma_{y2}\dots\Sigma_{y3}\,P(X_1 = x_1,\dots,X_n = x_n, Y_1 = y_1,\dots,Y_m = y_m \mid Z_1 = z_1,\dots,Z_1 = z_1)$$

All this is saying is that to get the conditional probability that the target variables $X_1,\dots,X_n$ have values $x_1,\dots,x_n$, you take the sum of all cases in the full conditional distribution over all variables in which the values of the target variables match the values $x_1,\dots,x_n$.

Because this formula holds for all values $x_1,\dots,x_n$ and $z_1,\dots,z_l$, you can use the same shorthand as in section 2.1 and write

$$P(X_1,\dots,X_n \mid Z_1,\dots,Z_1) = \Sigma_{y1}\,\Sigma_{y2}\dots\Sigma_{ym}\,P(X_1,\dots,X_n, Y_1 = y_1,\dots,Y_m = y_m \mid Z_1,\dots,Z_1)$$

Another notational trick makes the total probability rule an easy formula to remember. If you have a set of variables $X_1,\dots,X_n$, you can summarize them all with a boldface X. So X is shorthand for $X_1,\dots X_n$. Likewise, you can use a bold lowercase x as shorthand for the values $x_1,\dots,x_n$.

> **NOTATION ALERT**   It's common to use nonbold, italic letters like X and x for individual variables or values, and boldface X and x for sets of variables or values.

So for specific values x and z, you have

$$P(\mathbf{X} = \mathbf{x} \mid \mathbf{Z} = \mathbf{z}) = \Sigma_y\,P(\mathbf{X} = \mathbf{x}, \mathbf{Y} = \mathbf{y} \mid \mathbf{Z} = \mathbf{z})$$

Generalizing over all values x and z, you finally get the pithy formula

$$P(\mathbf{X} \mid \mathbf{Z}) = \Sigma_y P(\mathbf{X}, \mathbf{Y} = \mathbf{y} \mid \mathbf{Z})$$

This summarizes the total probability rule.

There's a technical term you might encounter when you start with a joint distribution over a set of variables and you sum out some of the variables to get a probability distribution over the remaining variables. This resulting distribution is called the *marginal distribution* over the remaining variables, and the process of summing out variables to get the marginal distribution over other variables is called *marginalization*. Most typically, you sum out all but one of the variables and end up with the marginal distribution over a single variable.

Now you've covered two of the three rules of probabilistic inference. Let's turn our attention to the last, and possibly the most interesting one.

9.3   *Bayes' rule: inferring causes from effects*

The final piece of the puzzle in reasoning about probabilistic models is Bayes' rule, named after Rev. Thomas Bayes, an eighteenth-century mathematician who first discovered how to infer knowledge about causes from observations about effects. *Bayes' rule lets you compute the conditional probability of a cause, given its effect, by combining the prior probability of the cause (before you know anything about the effect) and the probability of the effect, given the cause.*

9.3.1   *Understanding, cause, effect, and inference*

Bayes' rule is related to the notions of cause and effect, which in turn are related to the dependencies in your model. In an ordinary program, when one variable X uses the value of another variable Y in its definition, changing the value of Y can result in a change to X. So, in a sense, Y is a cause of X. In the same way, if you're building a probabilistic model where X depends on Y, Y is often a cause of X. For example, consider Subject and Brightness. You modeled Brightness as depending on Subject, and typically a painter might decide what type of painting to paint before deciding how bright it should be. So in this sense, Subject is a cause of Brightness.

I'm using the word *cause* a little loosely here. A more accurate description is to say that you're modeling the *generative process* of the data. In this process, you imagine the painter first choosing the subject, and then based on that, choosing the brightness. So the painter first generates a value for the Subject variable, which then gets passed to the generation of the value of the Size variable. When a model follows a generative process, you loosely use the words *cause* and *effect* when the value of one variable is being used by another.

Figure 9.4 shows a slightly more elaborate example of a generative process, described by a Bayesian network. In this example, the first variable that gets generated is whether the painting is by Rembrandt or not, because the identity of the painter influences everything about the painting. Then the painter chooses the Subject, which in turn helps determine the Size and Brightness. The reason Size depends on both Rembrandt and Subject is that landscapes by different painters might tend to have different sizes; similarly for Brightness.

The right-hand side of figure 9.4 makes an important point. Although the generative process follows the arrows in the model, inference about the model can go in any direction. In fact, in this example, our goal is to decide whether the painting is a Rembrandt, so the inference will go in the opposite direction from the generative process. I've emphasized this point throughout the book; the direction of the arrows in the network isn't necessarily the direction in which you expect to do inference. Don't let the way you typically reason about a domain (for example, "I look at the painting's brightness to decide who the artist is") guide the way you structure the network. Instead, think about the generative process. In most cases, following the generative process results in the simplest and clearest model. You can infer in any direction you want.

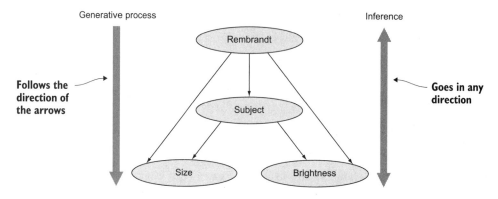

Figure 9.4   Network arrows often follow the generative process, but inference can be in any direction.

Okay, so I've said you can infer in the opposite direction from the arrows in the network. How do you do that? Bayes' rule is the answer! Let's look at the two-variable example in figure 9.5. Here, the network follows the natural generative process in which Subject determines Size. You're given, as ingredients, P(Subject) and P(Size | Subject). First, let's think about inference in the forward direction, following the generative process. Suppose you observe that Subject = Landscape, and you want to query the posterior probability of Size. You can get it directly from P(Size | Subject). If you want to infer an effect from evidence about a cause, you have that information immediately available.

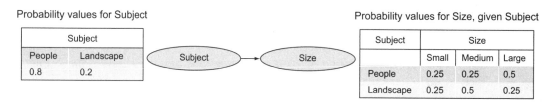

Figure 9.5   Two-variable model for the Bayes' rule example

But often you observe evidence about an effect, and you want to infer something about a possible cause of that effect. You want to invert the model, because you want to get P(Subject | Size), which is the probability of the cause, given the effect. Bayes' rule makes this possible.

9.3.2   *Bayes' rule in practice*

The operation of Bayes' rule is simple. I'll show how it works first and then explain each of the steps. The full process is illustrated in figure 9.6. You start with the model from figure 9.5. Then you observe evidence that Size = Large. You want to compute a posterior probability distribution over Subject given this evidence—you want to compute P(Subject | Size = Large). Here's what you do:

1 Calculate P(Subject = People) P(Size = Large | Subject = People) = 0.8 × 0.5 = 0.4, and P(Subject = Landscape) P(Size = Large | Subject = Landscape) = 0.2 × 0.25 = 0.05. These numbers are shown in the middle table of figure 9.6.

2 Normalize this table to get the answer you want. The normalizing factor is 0.4 + 0.05 = 0.45. So, P(Subject = People | Size = Large) = 0.4 / 0.45 = 0.8889, and P(Subject = Landscape | Size = Large) = 0.05 / 0.45 = 0.1111. This answer is shown in the bottom table of figure 9.6.

Now, why does this work? You have the ingredients for this process in the chain rule and the total probability rule. You're going to construct the joint probability distribution from the CPD ingredients by using the chain rule, as you learned in section 9.1. Then you'll apply the chain rule again, this time in the opposite direction.

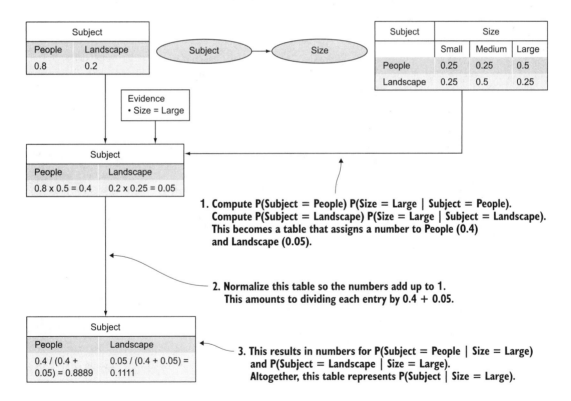

Figure 9.6   Bayes' rule in operation

Finally, you'll use the total probability rule to complete the calculation. Here are the steps:

1 Take P(Subject) and P(Size | Subject) and apply the chain rule to get P(Subject, Size) = P(Subject) P(Size | Subject).
2 Using the chain rule, but breaking things up in the inverse direction, you can write P(Size, Subject) = P(Size) P(Subject | Size).
3 Because P(Subject, Size) and P(Size, Subject) are equal, you can put 1 and 2 together to get P(Size) P(Subject | Size) = P(Subject) P(Size | Subject).
4 Divide by P(Size) on both sides of this equation to get

$$P(\text{Subject}|\text{Size}) = \frac{P(\text{Subject})P(\text{Size}|\text{Subject})}{P(\text{Size})}$$

You now have the answer to your query, P(Subject | Size) on the left-hand side. This is the formula typically referred to as Bayes' rule, but it's not yet in usable form, because it includes P(Size), which you don't have, so there's one more step.

1 Use the total probability rule and the chain rule to express P(Size) in terms you know. First, use the total probability rule to write P(Size) = Σ_s P(Subject = s, Size). Then, use the chain rule to write P(Subject = s, Size) = P(Subject = s) P(Size | Subject = s). Finally, combine those to get P(Size) = Σ_s P(Subject = s) P(Size | Subject = s).
2 You get your final answer:

$$P(\text{Subject}|\text{Size} = \text{Large}) = \frac{P(\text{Subject})P(\text{Size} = \text{Large}|\text{Subject})}{\Sigma_s P(\text{Subject} = s)P(\text{Size} = \text{Large}|\text{Subject} = s)}$$

You can see how this answer relates to the two steps illustrated in figure 9.6. The first step computes the numerator P(Subject) P(Size = Large | Subject) for each of the two possible values of Subject. Now, take a look at the denominator. You add P(Subject = s) P(Size | Subject = s) for each possible value s of Subject. But this is just the quantity you computed in the first step for each value of Subject. The denominator adds together all of the quantities you computed in the first step. So you need to divide each of these quantities by their total. This is another way of saying that you normalize those quantities, which you do in step 2.

Although Bayes' rule is simple, there's more to learn about it. Bayes' rule provides the basis for the Bayesian modeling framework, which is the subject of the next section. That section also goes into more depth on how Bayes' rule works, and provides a sidebar on the generic Bayes' rule.

9.4 *Bayesian modeling*

Bayes' rule provides the basis for a general approach to modeling, in which you infer knowledge about causes from observations of their effects, and then apply that knowledge to other potential effects.

This section demonstrates Bayesian modeling by using the coin-toss scenario you first encountered in chapter 2. Based on the results of 100 coin tosses (the effects of the model), you'll do the following:

- Use Bayes' rule to infer the bias of the coin (the cause of the effects)
- Demonstrate several methods to predict the result of the 101st coin toss
  - The maximum a posteriori (MAP) method
  - The maximum likelihood estimation (MLE) method
  - The full Bayesian method

Figure 9.7 reproduces the Bayesian network for the example where you're trying to predict the toss of the 101st coin, based on the outcome of the first 100 tosses. You have three variables: the Bias of the coin, the NumberOfHeads in the first 100 tosses, and the outcome of $Toss_{101}$. Bias is generated first, and then all of the coin tosses depend on Bias. If Bias is known, the coin tosses are independent. Remember, when I say that Bias is generated first, I'm describing the generative process, not that Bias is *known* first. This is yet another example indicating that the order in which variables are generated isn't necessarily the order of inference. In our example, Bias is generated first, but inference goes from NumberOfHeads to Bias.

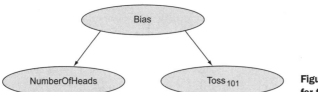

Figure 9.7 Bayesian network for the coin-toss example

You're using the beta-binomial model, so Bias is characterized by a beta distribution, whereas NumberOfHeads is characterized by a binomial distribution that depends on Bias. As a reminder:

- The binomial variable characterizes the number of times a random process comes out a certain way, out of a total number of attempts. In our example, a binomial is used to characterize the number of times a coin toss comes out heads. A binomial variable is parameterized by the probability that each attempt comes out the right way.
- This probability is the bias of the coin. If you knew the bias of the coin, this could be a specific value. But in this scenario, you don't know the bias, and you're trying to estimate it based on the outcomes of the coin tosses. Therefore,

you model the bias by using a random variable. Specifically, you use the beta distribution, which is a continuous distribution, to model this bias. For a continuous distribution, you use a *probability density function* (PDF) instead of specifying the probability of each value. A beta distribution has two parameters, α and β. α can intuitively be understood as representing the number of heads you've previously seen, plus one. Similarly for β and tails. As mentioned in chapter 4, you use the beta distribution because it works well with the binomial. You'll see why in this section.

The outcome of any future coin toss is given by a `Flip`, in which the probability it comes out heads is equal to Bias. As is implied by the Bayesian network, the future coin toss depends directly only on the bias. If the bias is known, the other coin tosses don't add any information. But if the bias is unknown, the first 100 coin tosses provide information about the bias that can then be used to predict the 101st coin toss.

9.4.1 *Estimating the bias of a coin*

How do you use this model to predict a future coin toss based on the outcome of the first 100? This is where Bayesian modeling comes in. In Bayesian modeling, you can use Bayes' rule to infer a posterior probability distribution over the bias from observing the number of tosses that came out heads. You can then use this posterior distribution to predict the next toss.

This process is shown in figure 9.8. If you observe thousands of tosses and 40% of them come out heads, you might infer that the bias is probably close to 0.4. If you don't have as many tosses, the inference will be less confident. These inferences are the direct result of applying Bayes' rule. Getting back to our example, if you see 63 heads in 100 coin tosses, you can compute a posterior distribution over Bias given that NumberOfHeads = 63, and then use this to predict Toss_{101}.

To achieve this, you start with a prior distribution for Bias. The beta distribution is characterized by two parameters, α and β. Let's call the parameters of the prior beta

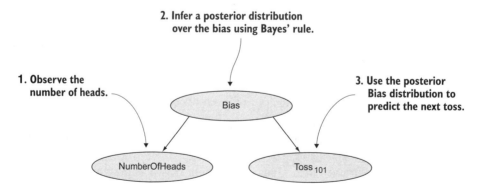

Figure 9.8   Order of inference in the biased coin example

distribution for Bias α_0 and β_0. Remember from chapter 2 that α_0 and β_0 represent the number of imaginary heads and tails you've seen prior to observing any real tosses, plus one. To get the posterior distribution, you add the actual number of heads and tails to those imaginary numbers. For example, suppose you start with beta$(2, 5)$. This means that you imagine having seen 1 head and 4 tails (because α_0 is the number of imagined heads plus one, and similarly for β_0). You then observe 63 heads and 37 tails. The posterior distribution over the bias is given by beta$(65, 42)$. If you call the parameters of the posterior beta distribution α_1 and β_1, you have the simple formula

$$\alpha_1 = \alpha_0 + \text{number of observed heads}$$

$$\beta_1 = \beta_0 + \text{number of observed tails}$$

> **NOTE** In practice, you don't have to make these calculations yourself. A probabilistic programming system's algorithms will take care of everything for you. You specify that you want to use a beta-binomial model, and it will make all necessary calculations. But it's important that you understand the principles behind how the systems work, which is why you're spending time on it here.

Figure 9.9 shows this beta$(65, 42)$ distribution, superimposed on the original beta$(2, 5)$. You can see a couple of things. First, the peak of the distribution has moved to the right, because the fraction of heads in the actual observations (63 out of 100) is more than in the imaginary observations you started with (1 out of 5). Second, the peak has become sharper. Because you have 100 additional observations, you're much more confident in your assessment of the bias.

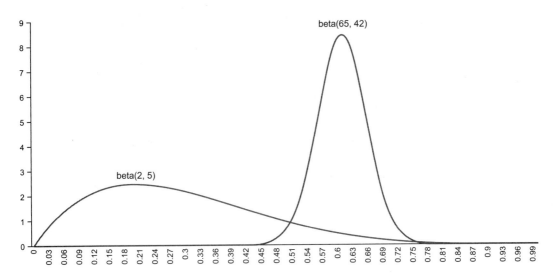

Figure 9.9 **Inferring the bias of the coin from a sequence of observations. Here, you've observed 63 heads and 37 tails and added them to the alpha and beta parameters. The posterior PDF beta(65, 42) is superimposed over the prior PDF beta(2, 5).**

This simple formula of adding outcomes to create the new beta-binomial model you got for the posterior distribution is the result of applying Bayes' rule. In applying Bayes' rule to the coin-toss example, you deal with three quantities:

- p(Bias = b): The prior probability density of the value b of Bias. (A lowercase p is used in this notation and below to emphasize that the quantity is a probability density, not a probability.)
- P(NumberOfHeads = 63 | Bias = b): The probability of observing that Number-OfHeads = 63, given that the value of Bias is b. This probability is known as the *likelihood* of b given the data.
- p(Bias = b | NumberOfHeads = 63): The posterior probability density of the value b of the Bias.

Because this example deals with a continuous variable (the bias), it's slightly more complicated than the example in section 9.3.2 about the painting. I'll repeat the conclusion of that example here, so you can see how it also works for the biased coin example. In section 9.3.2, you got the following expression for the probability distribution over the subject of the painting, given evidence about the size:

$$P(\text{Subject}|\text{Size} = \text{Large}) = \frac{P(\text{Subject})P(\text{Size} = \text{Large}|\text{Subject})}{\Sigma_s P(\text{Subject} = s)P(\text{Size} = \text{Large}|\text{Subject} = s)}$$

Let's focus on the denominator. It adds the values of the numerator for all possible values of Subject. It's a normalizing factor that ensures that (a) the left-hand side is always proportional to the numerator on the right-hand side, and (b) the left-hand side values sum to 1. You summarize this formula by using the following notation:

$$P(\text{Subject} | \text{Size} = \text{Large}) \propto P(\text{Subject})P(\text{Size} = \text{Large} | \text{Subject})$$

The symbol $\propto$ means that the left-hand side *is proportional to* the right-hand side, where the constant of proportionality is $1/\Sigma_s P(\text{Subject} = s) P(\text{Size} = \text{Large} | \text{Subject} = s)$. The left-hand side is the posterior probability distribution over Subject. The first term on the right-hand side is the prior distribution. The second term, the probability of observing specific data about the Size for a given value of Subject, is the likelihood. Therefore, the preceding formula can be summarized as follows:

Posterior $\propto$ Prior x Likelihood

This formula is broken down in figure 9.10. If there's one formula you should remember about Bayesian modeling, it's this one. Although you saw it specifically for the painting example, it's a general principle that holds for applications of Bayes' rule. To get the actual posterior of the particular value b, you compute the right-hand side of this equation for every possible value of b, and add all of the results to get the total B.

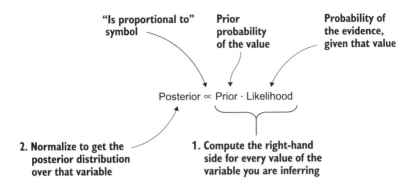

Figure 9.10 Structure of the Bayesian modeling formula

This total B is the normalizing factor. You then divide the Prior times the Likelihood by B to get the Posterior.

If you're talking about a continuous variable, as in our example, this normalizing process can be difficult, because it requires integrating over all possible values of b. Returning to our coin-tossing example, Bayes' rule says that

$$p(\text{Bias} = b | \text{NumberOfHeads} = 63) =$$

$$\frac{P(\text{Bias} = b)P(\text{NumberOfHeads} = 63 | \text{Bias} = b)}{\int_0^1 P(\text{Bias} = x)P(\text{NumberOfHeads} = 63 | \text{Bias} = x)\,dx}$$

Using our "proportional to" notation, you can rewrite this as follows:

$$p(\text{Bias} = b \mid \text{NumberOfHeads} = 63) \propto P(\text{Bias} = b)P(\text{NumberOfHeads} = 63 \mid \text{Bias} = b)$$

Once again, the posterior is proportional to the prior times the likelihood. Although this last equation is simple, it does hide an integral that can be difficult to estimate. Fortunately, in the case of the beta-binomial model, a simple solution to this equation exists, which you've already seen at the beginning of this section. You add the number of observed successes and failures to the parameters of the beta distribution. This is why the beta and binomial work well together. If you take any arbitrary continuous distribution and try to pair it with the binomial, you'll end up with an integration problem that doesn't have an easy solution. But when you pair a beta with the binomial, you get an easy answer.

Working with probabilistic programming systems, you'll never have to compute these integrals yourself. Probabilistic programming systems can often use approximation algorithms to deal with these difficult integration problems, so you're not restricted to working with functional forms that fit together particularly well. Nevertheless, when you have such a form available to you, it's best to use it.

NOTE In chapter 6, you first encountered the technical term *conjugate prior* to describe a prior distribution that works well with a distribution that depends on the parameter. Technically, this means that the posterior distribution has the same form as the prior distribution. Using this term, the beta distribution is the conjugate prior of the binomial, because the posterior distribution over the parameter is also a beta distribution. When you have a conjugate prior distribution, the integration in Bayes' rule has an easy solution. This is why conjugate distributions are used frequently in Bayesian statistics. But when using probabilistic programming, you're not limited to conjugate distributions.

The generic Bayes' rule

Now that you've learned more about Bayes' rule, in particular the proportionality relationship, it's time to explain the generic Bayes' rule. As with the total probability rule, Bayes' rule can be generalized to any number of variables, and can include conditioning variables. Following the notation of section 9.2, you have three sets of variables: $X_1,...,X_n$ (the "causes"), $Y_1,...,Y_m$ (the "effects"), and $Z_1,...,Z_l$ (the conditioning variables). You're given $P(X_1,...,X_n \mid Z_1,...,Z_l)$, the prior probability of the causes, conditioned on the conditioning variables, and $P(Y_1,...,Y_n \mid X_1,...,X_m, Z_1,...,Z_l)$, the conditional probability of the effects given the causes, again conditioned on the conditioning variables. You want the probability of the causes, given the effects, once again conditioned on the conditioning variables. This is $P(X_1,...,X_n \mid Y_1,...,Y_m, Z_1,...,Z_l)$. Bayes' rule says that

$$P(X_1,...,X_n \mid Y_1,...,Y_m, Z_1,...,Z_l) =$$

$$\frac{P(X_1,...,X_n \mid Z_1,...,Z_l)P(Y_1,...,Y_n \mid X_1,...,X_m, Z_1,...,Z_l)}{\Sigma_{x_1}...\Sigma_{x_n} P(X_1 = x_1,...,X_n = x_n \mid Z_1,...,Z_l)P(Y_1,...,Y_n \mid X_1 = x_1,...,X_n = x_n, Z_1,...,Z_l)}$$

I promised that in this section, I'd make the notation for this formula simpler. Because the denominator is the normalizing factor, you can use our "is proportional to" shorthand to make the equation much easier to understand:

$$P(X_1,...,X_n \mid Y_1,...,Y_m, Z_1,...,Z_l) \propto P(X_1,...,X_n \mid Z_1,...,Z_l)P(Y_1,...,Y_n \mid X_1,...,X_m, Z_1,...,Z_l)$$

This is the same as our Posterior $\propto$ Prior × Likelihood equation except that the posterior is a joint distribution over multiple cause variables, the likelihood also considers multiple effect variables, and other variables (the *Z* variables) influence the causes and effects.

Finally, recall that you can use boldface letters like *X*, *Y*, and *Z* for sets of variables. Bayes' rule can then be summarized in the succinct formula

$$P(X \mid Y,Z) \propto P(X \mid Z)P(Y \mid X,Z)$$

where *X* refers to all causes, *Y* refers to all effects, and *Z* refers to all conditioning variables. This pithy formula is the best way to remember the generic Bayes' rule.

Now you've learned how to estimate Bias. The next step is to use it to predict Toss_{101}.

9.4.2 *Predicting the next coin toss*

Okay, you've gotten a posterior distribution over Bias in the form of a beta distribution. How do you predict the next coin toss? There are three common ways to do this, all of which turn out to be simple for the beta-binomial model. As mentioned earlier, they are as follows:

- The maximum a posteriori (MAP) method
- The maximum likelihood estimation (MLE) method
- The full Bayesian method

You'll look at each method in turn.

USING THE MAXIMUM A POSTERIORI METHOD

In the first method, called *maximum a posteriori (MAP) estimation,* you compute the value of Bias that has the highest posterior probability density. This value, which maximizes the prior times the likelihood, is called the *most likely value* of the Bias. You then use this value of the Bias to predict the next coin toss.

The MAP process is described in figure 9.11. The first step is to compute a posterior distribution over the Bias by using the approach of the previous section. You start with a prior of beta(2, 5), observe 63 heads and 37 tails, and obtain a posterior of beta(65, 42). In the next step, you compute the value of the Bias that's the peak of beta(65, 42). Looking back at figure 9.9, this is the point on the x-axis for which the value of beta(65, 42) is highest. In other words, you want the mode of beta(65, 42). It turns out there's a simple formula for this:

$$\text{mode}(\text{beta}(\alpha,\beta)) = \frac{\alpha - 1}{\alpha + \beta - 2}$$

In our example, the mode is equal to $(65 - 1)/(65 + 42 - 2)$, which is approximately 0.6095. Now you assume that Bias is equal to 0.6095, and compute the probability that Toss_{101} is heads, given the data of 63 heads and 37 tails. The functional form for Toss_{101} says that the probability that the toss comes out heads is equal to the value of Bias, which you assumed is 0.6095. So your answer is 0.6095.

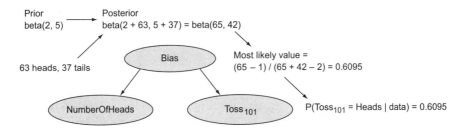

Figure 9.11   Predicting the next coin flip using the MAP method

USING THE MAXIMUM LIKELIHOOD ESTIMATION

The second method is a commonly used special case of the MAP estimation process called *maximum likelihood estimation* (MLE). In MLE, you choose the parameter values that "fit the data" the best, without regard to any prior. The MLE method is sometimes considered non-Bayesian, but it also fits into the Bayesian framework if you assume that every possible value of Bias has the same prior. So the formula

Posterior $\propto$ Prior $\times$ Likelihood

collapses to

Posterior $\propto$ Likelihood

Therefore, the most likely value of the posterior is the value that maximizes the likelihood, hence the name *maximum likelihood estimation.*

The maximum likelihood method is illustrated in figure 9.12. This is similar to the MAP method shown in figure 9.11, except that you start with a prior of beta(1, 1), which assigns the same probability density to every value between 0 and 1. If you recall that the parameters of the prior are the imaginary number of heads and tails you've seen, plus one, you'll see that this prior represents the case where you don't imagine having seen any heads or tails. You then go through the same sequence of calculations, resulting in a prediction of 0.63. This result is no coincidence. You observed 63 out of 100 tosses resulting in heads. The value of the Bias that's most consistent with these observations is that there's exactly a 0.63 chance of any coin toss resulting in heads. So you see that the maximum likelihood estimate chooses the parameter value that best fits with the data, whereas the MAP estimate counterbalances the data with the prior.

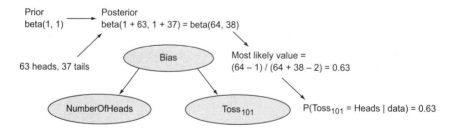

Figure 9.12   Predicting the next coin toss using the maximum likelihood method

USING THE FULL BAYESIAN METHOD

The third approach to predicting the next coin toss is sometimes called the *full Bayesian method*, because instead of estimating a single value of the Bias, it uses the full posterior distribution over Bias. The process is illustrated in figure 9.13. It starts in the same way as the MAP method, by computing the posterior distribution over Bias. To use this distribution to predict $Toss_{101}$, you use the formula for $P(Toss_{101} = Heads \mid Data)$ shown in the figure. This formula is derived by applying the total probability rule and the chain rule. The main thing to notice is that it involves integration, because Bias is a continuous variable. Just as for estimating the posterior parameter value, this integration can be difficult to work with. But the beta-binomial model is again easy. It turns out that if the posterior is $beta(\alpha_1, \beta_1)$, then the probability that the next toss is heads is

$$\frac{\alpha_1}{\alpha_1 + \beta_1}$$

So in our example, the probability of heads is $65 / (65 + 42) = 0.6075$. And, to close the loop, this simple formula for the probability of heads is why you add 1 to the count of heads and tails in the parameters of the beta distribution: so that you end up with a simple formula for the probability of the next coin toss coming up heads.

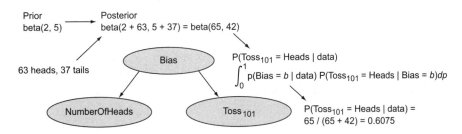

Figure 9.13 Predicting the next coin toss using the full Bayesian method

COMPARING THE METHODS

Having seen these three methods, let's compare them:

- *The MLE method* provides the best fit to the data, but is also liable to overfit the data. Overfitting is a problem in machine learning whereby the learner fits the pattern found in the data too closely, in a way that's unable to be generalized. This can especially be a problem with only a few coin tosses. For example, if there are only 10 coin tosses and 7 of them come out heads, should you immediately conclude that the bias is 0.7? Even a fair coin will come out heads 7 times out of 10 a fair percentage of times, so the coin tosses don't provide conclusive evidence that the coin isn't fair.

  The MLE method has two advantages that make it popular. First, it tends to be relatively efficient, because it doesn't require integrating over all parameter values to predict the next instance. Second, it doesn't require specifying a prior, which can be difficult when you don't have any basis for one. Nevertheless, the susceptibility to overfitting can be a significant problem with this method.

■ *The MAP method* can be a good compromise. Including a prior can serve two purposes. One is to encode prior beliefs that you have. The other is to counteract overfitting. For example, if you start with a beta(11, 11) prior, you aren't biasing the results toward heads or tails in any way, but the effect of the data will be dampened by adding 10 imaginary heads and tails to the result. To see this, suppose you toss the coin 10 times and 7 of them come up heads. Remember that a beta(11, 11) prior means that you've seen 10 imaginary heads and 10 imaginary tails. Adding 7 more heads and 3 more tails gives you 17 heads and 13 tails in total. So the MAP estimate for the bias is 17 / (17 + 13) = 17/30 ≈ 0.5667. You can also see this from the formula for the mode of a beta distribution given earlier, which is

$$\frac{\alpha - 1}{\alpha + \beta - 2}$$

With seven heads and three tails, the posterior is beta(18, 14), so the mode is 17/30. Even though 70% of your data is heads, your posterior belief in heads is still only slightly more than 0.5, and a lot less than 0.7 for the MLE method. In addition to being able to counter overfitting, the MAP method is also relatively efficient, because it doesn't require integrating over all parameter values. But it does require specifying a prior, which can be difficult.

■ *The full Bayesian approach*, where feasible, can be superior to the other approaches, because it uses the full distribution. In particular, when the mode of the distribution isn't representative of the full distribution, the other approaches can be misleading. For a beta distribution, this isn't a serious issue; the MAP and full Bayesian predictions are close to each other in our example. Specifically, with a beta(11, 11) prior and seven observed heads and three observed tails, you get a beta(18, 14) posterior. The Bayesian estimate of the probability that the next toss will be 18 / (18 + 14) = 18/32 = 0.5625, or just slightly less than the MAP estimate. For other distributions, especially those with multiple peaks, however, the full Bayesian approach can produce significantly better estimates than the MAP approach. Even the MAP approach, which uses a prior, will settle on one of the peaks, and completely ignore an important part of the distribution. But the Bayesian approach is more difficult to execute computationally.

Probabilistic programming systems vary in the range of approaches they support. Most typically, they support full Bayesian reasoning. Because full Bayesian reasoning often requires integration, these systems use approximation algorithms. Some probabilistic programming systems also support maximum likelihood and MAP estimation for specific models, which can be more computationally efficient. In particular, Figaro provides both full Bayesian and MAP algorithms. Chapter 12 shows you how to use these approaches practically in Figaro.

So now you know the basic rules of inference, and you understand how Bayesian modeling uses Bayes' rule to learn from data and use the learned knowledge for future predictions. In the forthcoming chapters, you'll learn specific algorithms for inference. Two main families of inference algorithms are used in probabilistic programming: factored algorithms and sampling algorithms. These two families are the subjects of the next two chapters.

9.5 *Summary*

- The chain rule lets you take the conditional probability distributions of individual variables and construct a joint probabilistic model over all variables.
- The total probability rule lets you take a joint probabilistic model over a set of variables and reduce it to get a probability distribution over individual variables.
- The network arrows in a probabilistic model typically follow the process by which the data is generated, but inference in the model can go in any direction. Bayes' rule lets you do this.
- Bayesian modeling uses Bayes' rule to infer causes from observations of their effects, and uses those inferences to predict future outcomes.
- In Bayesian inference, the posterior probability of a value of a variable is proportional to the prior probability of the value times the likelihood of the value, which is the probability of the evidence given the value.
- In the MAP estimation approach, the most likely posterior value of a parameter is used to predict future instances.
- In the MLE approach, the prior is ignored, and the parameter value that maximizes the likelihood is used for prediction. This is the simplest approach but can overfit the data.
- In the full Bayesian approach, the full posterior probability distribution over the parameter value is used to predict future instances. This is the most accurate approach but can be computationally difficult.

9.6 *Exercises*

Solutions to selected exercises are available online at www.manning.com/books/practical-probabilistic-programming.

1 Consider the detailed printer model from the printer diagnosis example, shown in the Bayesian network in figure 5.11 (in chapter 5). Consider the following case:

- Printer Power Button On = true
- Toner Level = low
- Toner Low Indicator On = false
- Paper Flow = smooth
- Paper Jam Indicator On = false
- Printer State = poor

  a Write the probability of this case using the full chain rule, where each variable is conditioned on all preceding variables.

  b Simplify this expression by taking into account independence relationships in the network.

  c Write an expression for the joint probability distribution that applies in a general way to all cases, without specifying specific values of variables.

2 For the network in exercise 1:

  a Write an expression for the probability that Printer Power Button On = true.

  b Write an expression for the probability that Printer Power Button On = true and Printer State = poor.

3 Assume that 1 in 40 million US citizens become president of the United States.

  a Assume that 50% of presidents are left-handed, compared to 10% of the general population. What is the probability someone became the president of the United States, given that he or she is left-handed?

  b Now assume that 15% of US presidents went to Harvard, compared to 1 in 2,000 for the general population. What is the probability that someone became the president of the United States, given that he or she went to Harvard?

  c Assuming left-handedness and going to Harvard are conditionally independent, given whether someone became president, what's the probability that someone became the president of the United States, given that he or she is left-handed and went to Harvard?

Factored inference algorithms

This chapter covers

- The basics of factored inference, definition of factors, and operations on factors
- The variable elimination algorithm
- The belief propagation algorithm

Now that you understand the basic rules of probabilistic inference, you'll spend the next two chapters learning about some of the inference algorithms used in probabilistic programming. This will give you better insight into which algorithm works best for a particular problem and how to design a model sympathetic to that algorithm.

There are two main types of inference algorithms:

- *Factored algorithms* work by operating on data structures called *factors* that capture the probabilistic model being reasoned about.
- *Sampling algorithms* work by creating examples of possible worlds from the probability distribution and using those examples to answer queries.

You'll look at sampling algorithms in the next chapter. This chapter covers factored algorithms by looking at the following:

- The factor data structure and the way it represents a probabilistic model and a query. You'll see that this is tied closely to the chain rule and the total probability rule you learned about in the preceding chapter.

- The *variable elimination (VE) algorithm.* This is an *exact algorithm,* meaning that it computes the exact probability of the query, given the evidence as defined by your model. Because it's exact, it's great to use if your model supports it, but it can also be slow to execute.

- The *belief propagation (BP) algorithm.* This is usually an *approximation algorithm.* It can be fast, and most of the time it returns an answer that's close to the right answer, but not always.

- The trade-offs in accuracy and speed between exact and approximate algorithms and how to design a probabilistic model to fit the type of algorithm you're using.

To explain the concepts in this chapter, I draw heavily on the Bayesian network and Markov network material from chapter 5. The Figaro modeling techniques used in chapter 5 are relatively basic, so feel free to review it before you cover chapters 6 through 8. You should also be comfortable with the rules of inference from chapter 9, especially the chain rule and the total probability rule.

10.1   *Factors*

The idea of *factoring* a probability distribution is similar to the idea of factoring an integer. If you have an integer such as 15, you can factor it into 3×5, so 3 and 5 are factors of 15. In the same way, you can factor a probability distribution into its constituent factors. In this section, you'll first learn what these factors are. Then you'll see how to factor a probability distribution into factors by using the chain rule. Finally, you'll see how to express the answer to a query with factors by using the total probability rule.

10.1.1   *What is a factor?*

First, I'll give you the general definition of a factor, and then explain how it fits into a probabilistic model. A *factor* is a representation of a function from the value of a set of variables to a real number. Although different factor representations are possible, in this book a factor is represented by a table.

Table 10.1 shows a factor over the two variables Subject and Size. The factor has a column for each of the variables. The factor also has a column on the right containing real numbers. Each row of the factor corresponds to a particular combination of values of the variables. For example, the first row corresponds to the values Subject = People and Size = Small. The factor assigns the real number 0.25 to these values.

Table 10.1 A factor over two variables, Subject and Size. Each row corresponds to particular values of the variables and assigns a real number to those values.

Subject	Size	
People	Small	0.25
People	Medium	0.25
People	Large	0.5
Landscape	Small	0.25
Landscape	Medium	0.5
Landscape	Large	0.25

Why are factors useful in probabilistic reasoning? Let's go back to our first principles:

- A probability distribution assigns a number between 0 and 1 to every possible world.
- In a probabilistic model defined by a set of variables, a possible world consists of a value for each variable.

A probability distribution is a function that, given a value for each variable in the model, assigns a number between 0 and 1. That means a distribution can be represented by a factor. You can therefore think of a probability distribution as a table, with a row for every possible assignment to the variables. As a running example, we'll use the painting scenario from earlier chapters with the variables Subject, Size, and Brightness. To remind you, the Bayesian network for this example, along with the conditional probability distributions (CPDs), is shown in figure 10.1.

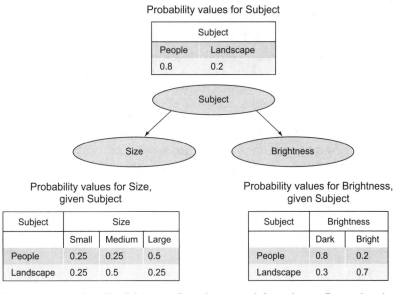

Probability values for Subject

Subject	
People	Landscape
0.8	0.2

Probability values for Size, given Subject

Subject	Size		
	Small	Medium	Large
People	0.25	0.25	0.5
Landscape	0.25	0.5	0.25

Probability values for Brightness, given Subject

Subject	Brightness	
	Dark	Bright
People	0.8	0.2
Landscape	0.3	0.7

Figure 10.1 Subject-Size-Brightness Bayesian network from chapter 5 reproduced

Each of the CPDs in this network can be represented in a factor, just like table 10.1. In fact, table 10.1 represents P(Size | Subject), the CPD for Size given Subject in figure 10.1. For example, according to the CPD, P(Size = Small | Subject = People) is 0.25. Accordingly, in table 10.1, the number associated with the row Subject = People, Size = Small is 0.25. Table 10.2, meanwhile, shows the factor corresponding to P(Subject). Because Subject has no parents, there's only one column for the Subject variable. Finally, table 10.3 shows the factor corresponding to P(Brightness | Subject), which mentions the variables Brightness and Subject.

Table 10.2   Factor corresponding to P(Subject)

Subject	
People	0.8
Landscape	0.2

Table 10.3   Factor corresponding to P(Brightness | Subject)

Subject	Brightness	
People	Dark	0.8
People	Bright	0.2
Landscape	Dark	0.3
Landscape	Bright	0.7

When you're thinking about the cost of representing and using a factor, the number of rows in the factor is important. You can use a simple formula for the number of rows in a factor: you multiply the number of values of each of the variables in the factor. For example, table 10.2 has a row for every possible value of Subject, making two rows. In table 10.1, there's a row for every combination of values of Subject and Size. There are 2 × 3 such combinations, making six rows in all.

> **NOTE** Although the factors you've seen so far have been CPDs, factors are more general than CPDs. During the course of an algorithm such as variable elimination, a variety of factors are created that don't correspond to CPDs. They can represent any function, from the value of variables to a real number, no matter its origin. In addition, although the value of the function represented by the factor is always a real number, it doesn't have to be a probability. In fact, it doesn't have to be between 0 and 1. For example, in a Markov network, the factors are derived from potentials, which can be greater than 1.

Now you understand what a factor is. But what does it have to do with factoring a probability distribution?

10.1.2 *Factoring a probability distribution by using the chain rule*

The first key to understanding factors and factored algorithms is the chain rule, which you saw in chapter 9. Recall that the chain rule lets you compute the joint probability of an assignment to many variables as a product of conditional probabilities. The chain rule is closely associated with Bayesian networks and is essential to the definition of the probability distribution defined by the Bayesian network.

For example, consider just the two variables Subject and Brightness. The chain rule says that to compute the probability that the painting is a bright painting of people, you use the following formula:

P(Subject = People, Brightness = Bright) =

P(Subject = People) P(Brightness = Bright | Subject = People) =

$0.8 \times 0.2 = 0.16$

Where do you get these numbers 0.8 and 0.2? You can find them in the factors. Specifically, 0.8 comes from the factor for P(Subject) shown in table 10.2, in the row where Subject has the value People. Similarly, 0.2 comes from the factor for P(Brightness | Subject) shown in table 10.3, in the row where Subject has the value People, and Brightness has the value Bright.

You can make a similar calculation for all values of Subject and Brightness, getting the numbers from the appropriate rows of the two factors. Figure 10.2 shows the result of multiplying two factors, which is known as the *factor product*. The essential concept of the factor product is that you multiply together the numbers associated with rows in which the variables have equal values. But some variables appear in only one or the other factor, not both. A row in the result factor will mention (a) all variables appearing in both factors, (b) all variables appearing in just the first factor, and (c) all variables appearing in just the second factor. To get the number associated with a row in the result factor, you find the row in the first factor with the same (a) and (b) variables, and the row in the second factor with the same (a) and (c) variables. You

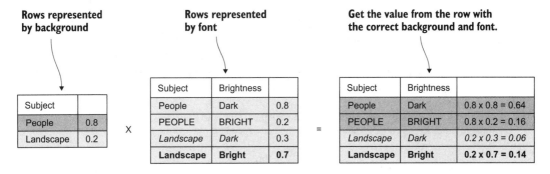

Figure 10.2   Factor product. The rows are coded to show where the numbers in the result factor come from. For example, the row in the result factor for (People, Bright) comes from the row for People (Dark background) in the first input and for (People, Bright) (all caps) in the second input.

then multiply the numbers associated with those two rows. Let's see this in detail using the factors for P(Subject) and P(Brightness | Subject). To multiply these two factors, you proceed as follows:

1 Create a new factor whose variables are all variables appearing in either of the two inputs. The rows in this factor correspond to all combinations of values of these variables. In our example, the variables are Subject and Brightness, and there are rows for (People, Dark), (People, Bright), (Landscape, Dark), and (Landscape, Bright).

   For each row in the result factor—for example, (People, Bright)—find the row in the first input that's consistent with this row and get the number from that row. In our example, the value of Subject in the result row is People, so we need to find the row for Subject = People in the input. The figure is coded. The row with Subject = People in the input has a Dark background, so the row for (People, Bright) in the result factor also has a Dark background. You get the number 0.8.

2 Do the same for the second factor: find the row that's consistent with the row in the result factor and get the number from that row. In this case, the row for (People, Bright) in the second factor has all caps font. You get the number 0.2.

Now that you know how to multiply two factors, you can multiply however many factors you want. In chapter 9, you saw that the probability distribution defined by a Bayesian network can be expressed using the chain rule. To keep the formulas short, I'll use the following shorthand:

- J for Subject
- Z for Size
- B for Brightness

In our example, you can write

$$P(J, Z, B) = P(J) \, P(Z \mid J) \, P(B \mid J)$$

This equation doesn't specify particular values for Subject, Size, and Brightness. The equation applies to all values of these variables. Because P(Subject), P(Size | Subject), and P(Brightness | Subject) are all factors, this equation says that the joint probability distribution over Subject, Size, and Brightness can be expressed as the product of three factors. This is shown in table 10.4.

Table 10.4   Joint probability distribution over Subject, Size, and Brightness calculated as the product of three factors. Each row gets numbers from the corresponding rows in the input factors.

Subject	Size	Brightness	
People	Small	Dark	$0.8 \times 0.25 \times 0.8 = 0.16$
People	Small	Bright	$0.8 \times 0.25 \times 0.2 = 0.04$

Table 10.4 Joint probability distribution over Subject, Size, and Brightness calculated as the product of three factors. Each row gets numbers from the corresponding rows in the input factors. *(continued)*

Subject	Size	Brightness	
People	Medium	Dark	$0.8 \times 0.5 \times 0.8 = 0.32$
People	Medium	Bright	$0.8 \times 0.25 \times 0.2 = 0.08$
People	Large	Dark	$0.8 \times 0.25 \times 0.8 = 0.16$
People	Large	Bright	$0.8 \times 0.5 \times 0.2 = 0.04$
Landscape	Small	Dark	$0.2 \times 0.25 \times 0.3 = 0.015$
Landscape	Small	Bright	$0.2 \times 0.5 \times 0.7 = 0.035$
Landscape	Medium	Dark	$0.2 \times 0.25 \times 0.3 = 0.015$
Landscape	Medium	Bright	$0.2 \times 0.25 \times 0.7 = 0.035$
Landscape	Large	Dark	$0.2 \times 0.5 \times 0.3 = 0.03$
Landscape	Large	Bright	$0.2 \times 0.25 \times 0.7 = 0.07$

You've seen that the number of rows in a factor is the product of the number of values of each variable. So in this factor representing the joint distribution, Subject has two values, Size has three, and Brightness has two, making a total of $2 \times 3 \times 2 = 12$ rows. In general, the number of rows will be exponential in the number of variables. This implies that as you get beyond small networks, the factor representing the joint distribution becomes huge, far too big to represent and reason with.

When you take an integer and express it as the product of smaller integers, you're factorizing the integer. The same goes for probability distributions. And, just as for integers, it can be easier to do multiplication and division using factors, which are much smaller than the full integer; the same goes for probability distributions. It's much easier to do probabilistic inference using factors over a small set of variables than using the full joint distribution, which is exponential in the number of variables. This explains why factors are so important for probabilistic inference.

10.1.3 *Defining queries with factors by using the total probability rule*

So far, you've seen how a joint probability distribution can be expressed as the product of factors. The next step is to express the answer to a query by using factors. The key to this is the total probability rule.

QUERIES WITHOUT EVIDENCE

To start, let's assume there's no evidence. You're interested in getting the probability distribution over a particular variable, say Brightness. You start with the joint probability distribution; in our example, this is shown in table 10.4. The total probability rule tells us that if you're interested in the probability that Brightness takes on a particular value, say Bright, you add all of the cases in the joint probability distribution where

Brightness takes that value. This is shown in table 10.5, which shows the same joint probability distribution except that all rows where Brightness = Bright are in bold type. You get that the probability that Brightness = Bright is the sum of all of the numbers of all rows in which Brightness has the value Bright, which is all rows in bold type. You get that

P(Brightness = Bright) = 0.04 + 0.08 + 0.04 + 0.035 + 0.035 + 0.07 = 0.3

Table 10.5   Joint probability distribution over Subject, Size, and Brightness, with all rows corresponding to Brightness = Bright in bold type. P(Brightness = Bright) is the sum of numbers in all rows in bold type.

Subject	Size	Brightness	
People	Small	Dark	0.16
People	**Small**	**Bright**	**0.04**
People	Medium	Dark	0.32
People	**Medium**	**Bright**	**0.08**
People	Large	Dark	0.16
People	**Large**	**Bright**	**0.04**
Landscape	Small	Dark	0.015
Landscape	**Small**	**Bright**	**0.035**
Landscape	Medium	Dark	0.015
Landscape	**Medium**	**Bright**	**0.035**
Landscape	Large	Dark	0.03
Landscape	**Large**	**Bright**	**0.07**

You can do the same for Brightness = Dark by adding the numbers from all rows in which Brightness has the value Dark (all rows in light type). Putting together the two numbers, you get the factor in table 10.6.

Table 10.6   Factor representing the probability distribution over Brightness. Each row is the sum of numbers from the appropriate rows in the joint factor. The row for Brightness = Bright is shown in bold type to indicate that the numbers are drawn from the bold rows in table 10.5.

Brightness	
Dark	0.16 + 0.32 + 0.16 + 0.015 + 0.015 + 0.03 = 0.7
Bright	**0.04 + 0.08 + 0.04 + 0.035 + 0.035 + 0.07 = 0.3**

The operation you've performed goes by two common names. One is the *factor sum*. Don't be confused: sum doesn't mean that you're adding two factors, but that you're adding numbers in rows of a single factor to produce a new, simpler factor. When you perform the sum operation, you remove some of the variables from the resulting factor; in our example, you've removed Subject and Size. You say that you're *summing over* these variables. The other name you'll see sometimes is *marginalization*. The resulting probability distribution over Brightness is called the marginal probability, as opposed to the joint distribution you started with. I'll avoid using the term marginalization, but the concept of factor sum will be an important one as we go forward with factored inference.

You can write a mathematical formula to express this concept. The mathematical notation for factor sum is the Greek letter Σ. To express that you sum out Subject and Brightness from P(Subject, Size, Brightness), you write

$$P(B) = \Sigma_{J,Z} \, P(J, Z, B)$$

In the previous section, you saw that

$$P(J, Z, B) = P(J) \, P(Z \mid J) \, P(B \mid J)$$

Combining these two equations, you get

$$P(B) = \Sigma_{J,Z} \, P(J) \, P(Z \mid J) \, P(B \mid J)$$

You've expressed the answer to our query by using product and sum operations on factors. The expression that results is known as a *sum-of-products expression*. The numbers in the final factor will be the sum of numbers obtained by taking the product of numbers in the input factors. Factored inference algorithms manipulate sum-of-product expressions to answer queries.

QUERIES WITH EVIDENCE

What happens if you do have evidence? Let's say you've observed Brightness = Bright and you want to query the posterior probability of Subject. In other words, you want to compute P(Subject | Brightness = Bright). The easiest way to handle evidence is to introduce new factors encoding your evidence.

As you may recall from chapter 4, conditioning on evidence is performed by crossing out all possible worlds that are inconsistent with the evidence—giving them probability 0. This can be achieved by creating a factor that assigns 0 to states that are inconsistent with the evidence. In our example, to encode the evidence Brightness = Bright, you can introduce the factor in table 10.7.

Table 10.7 Factor encoding the evidence Brightness = Bright

Brightness	
Dark	0
Bright	1

What is the effect of this factor? When you multiply this factor by any other factor, any row in which Brightness has the value Dark will automatically get the number 0, whereas the number in other rows will be unaffected. In the joint distribution, you'll effectively cross out all rows in which Brightness has the value Dark, while leaving other worlds intact.

If you call this factor E_B, you get the following sum-of-products expression:

$$P(J, B = \text{Bright}) = \Sigma_{Z,B} \, P(J) \, P(B \mid J) \, P(Z \mid J) \, E_B(B)$$

Table 10.8 shows the joint probability distribution, which is the product of P(Subject), P(Brightness | Subject), P(Size | Subject), multiplied by the evidence factor E(Brightness = Bright). Note that all rows that are inconsistent with the evidence have an entry of 0; those rows are "crossed out."

Table 10.8 Joint probability distribution over Subject, Size, and Brightness, multiplied by the evidence factor for Brightness = Bright

Subject	Size	Brightness	
People	Small	Dark	$0.16 \times 0 = 0$
People	Small	Bright	$0.04 \times 1 = 0.04$
People	Medium	Dark	$0.32 \times 0 = 0$
People	Medium	Bright	$0.08 \times 1 = 0.08$
People	Large	Dark	$0.16 \times 0 = 0$
People	Large	Bright	$0.04 \times 1 = 0.04$
Landscape	Small	Dark	$0.015 \times 0 = 0$
Landscape	Small	Bright	$0.035 \times 1 = 0.035$
Landscape	Medium	Dark	$0.015 \times 0 = 0$
Landscape	Medium	Bright	$0.035 \times 1 = 0.035$
Landscape	Large	Dark	$0.03 \times 0 = 0$
Landscape	Large	Bright	$0.07 \times 1 = 0.07$

The next step is to perform the sum operation. You sum over the variables that don't appear in the query: Size and Brightness. For each value of Subject, you add all non-zero rows in the factor in table 10.8. The result is the factor in table 10.9, which represents P(Subject, Brightness = Bright).

Table 10.9 Sum over Size and Brightness of the factor in table 10.8

Subject	
People	$0.04 + 0.8 + 0.04 = 0.16$
Landscape	$0.035 + 0.035 + 0.07 = 0.14$

If you look carefully at the preceding factor, you'll see that it doesn't exactly answer your query. You want to get the conditional probability P(Subject | Brightness = Bright); for example, you want to know the probability that the painting is a people painting, given that the painting is bright. But the preceding factor gives you P(Subject, Brightness = Bright). This can tell you the probability that the painting is a people painting and the painting is bright.

This is easily fixed. The probability distribution P(Subject, Brightness = Bright) is the un-normalized answer to your query. You can see that the numbers in the factor in table 10.9 don't add up to 1, but they have a 16:14 proportion. To get the query answer, you normalize this factor, making the numbers add up to 1 while retaining the proportion, to obtain the final result in table 10.10.

Table 10.10   P(Subject | Brightness = Bright), obtained by normalizing the factor in table 10.9

Subject	
People	0.16 / (0.16 + 0.14) = 0.5333
Landscape	0.14 / (0.16 + 0.14) = 0.4667

So now you've seen what factors are, you've learned the product and sum operations on factors, and you've seen how the answer to a query can be expressed as a sum-of-products expression. At this point, it looks like you have to multiply all of the factors together and create the joint distribution to answer queries. But the size of the full joint distribution is exponential in the number of variables in the model. The main goal of factored inference algorithms, which you'll start learning about in the next section, is to avoid creating this full distribution and instead work with more-compact forms.

10.2   *The variable elimination algorithm*

In the preceding section, you saw that the answer to a query can be defined by a sum-of-products expression over factors. *Variable elimination* (VE) is an algorithm that manipulates this expression. The basic operation is simple: one at a time, you eliminate the nonquery variables from the expression by using simple algebra. That's why it's called *variable elimination*. Because VE uses only the rules of algebra to manipulate expressions, it's an exact inference algorithm.

Although variable elimination is fundamentally an algorithm based on algebra, it can also be understood graphically. The graphical view provides an intuitive explanation of the elimination process and is useful for understanding the algorithm's complexity. The algebraic view is important to understand the details of how the algorithm operates. Accordingly, I'll first provide the graphical view to help you get an overall understanding of the algorithm and then present the detailed algebraic view.

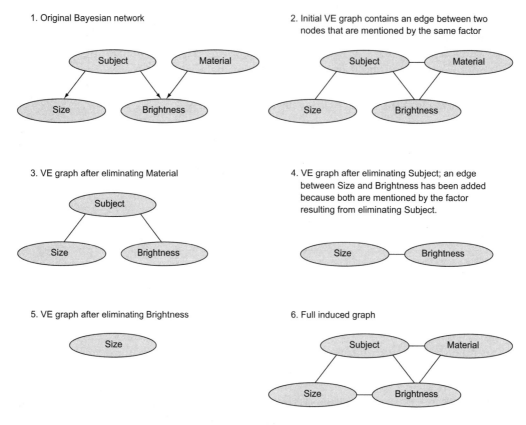

Figure 10.3   Building a VE graph through the process of eliminating variables

10.2.1 *Graphical interpretation of VE*

The graphical interpretation of VE is intuitive and can be explained in a few sentences and a picture. In VE, you have one or more query variables. You eliminate all variables other than the query variables in a certain order. When you eliminate a variable, you take the factors mentioning that variable and produce a new factor. The purpose of the graphs you create is to keep track of which variables appear in the same factor at any point in the computation.

Figure 10.3 shows a four-node Bayesian network containing the variables Subject, Size, Brightness, and Material. The query variable is Size, and you'll eliminate Material, Subject, and Brightness, in that order. This is an arbitrary choice of order. You can use any elimination order you like, but it does make a difference, as you'll see later.

Figure 10.3 illustrates the following steps:

1 Step 1 just copies over the original Bayesian network.
2 Given the original network, we start by constructing the initial VE graph. This graph contains a node for every node in the network, and an undirected edge

between any two nodes that are mentioned by the same factor. This includes an edge between every parent and child in the Bayesian network, as well as an edge between any two parents of the same child. For example, Subject and Material, which are both parents of Brightness, are both mentioned by the factor encoding the CPD of Brightness, so there's an edge between them.

3 Eliminate variables one by one. When eliminating a variable, add an edge between any two variables connected to the variable being eliminated, if they're not already connected. These two variables will both be mentioned by the factor created by eliminating the variable. Because they both appear in the same factor, they must be connected.

   In our example, Material is eliminated first. Because Subject and Brightness are already connected, no new edges need to be added.

4 Next, Subject is eliminated. Because Size and Brightness are both connected to Subject, they're connected to each other in the result.

5 The last variable to be eliminated is Brightness, with no new edges added, and just Size remains.

6 Finally, you put all edges that appeared in any of the graphs together into a single graph. This graph is called the graph induced by eliminating Material, Subject, and Brightness, or simply the *induced graph.*

TERMINOLOGY   When starting with a Bayesian network, the initial VE graph is known as the *moral graph.* The reason for this is that you get the moral graph by "marrying" nodes that are parents of the same child, by connecting them.

UNDERSTANDING THE COMPLEXITY OF THE ALGORITHM

This graphical interpretation is useful because it helps you understand the complexity of the algorithm. VE involves a lot of additions and multiplications. The number of additions and multiplications is closely related to the size of the factors that are created. The induced graph gives you a good handle on the size of the factors, because it tells you which variables appear in the same factor.

The analysis rests on the graphical notion of a clique. A *clique* is a set of nodes in a graph that are all connected to each other. If a set of nodes forms a clique in the induced graph, then all of those nodes must appear together in a factor at some point. In fact, it isn't hard to show that the maximum number of variables appearing in the same factor is exactly equal to the size of the largest clique in the induced graph.

For example, in the induced graph at the bottom right of figure 10.3, the variables Subject, Size, and Brightness are all connected to each other, so they form a clique. These variables all appear in the intermediate factor produced while eliminating Subject, after multiplying the factors mentioning Subject, but before summing out Subject from the result. Similarly, Subject, Material, and Brightness are all connected to each other and all appear in the CPD of Brightness. But Size and Material aren't connected, so Size, Subject, Brightness, and Material don't form a clique. Indeed, there's no factor mentioning both Size and Material at any point.

At this point, you know that the maximum number of variables appearing in a factor is the size of the largest clique. How large is that factor? Remember the formula: to get the number of rows in a factor, multiply together the number of values of each of the variables. The result is exponential in the number of variables. This leads to the following key result: *The complexity of VE using a given elimination order is exponential in the size of the largest clique in the graph induced by that elimination order.*

USING ALTERNATIVE ELIMINATION ORDERS

The preceding analysis followed a given elimination order. Does it matter which order you use? It turns out to make a big difference. The induced graph in figure 10.3 has two cliques of size 3, leading to a maximum clique size of 3.

Figure 10.4 shows the induced graphs resulting from two alternative orders. The one on the left has a maximum clique size of 4, because all of the variables are connected. This means that VE will be more expensive using that order. The order used on the right didn't result in adding any new edges. Although the maximum clique size is 3, just like our original order, there's only one clique of size 3, so VE using this order will be cheaper.

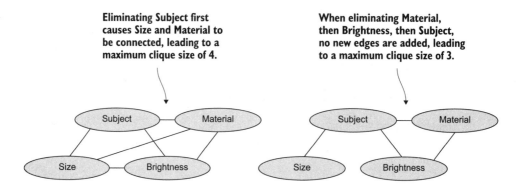

Figure 10.4 The induced graphs resulting from two alternative elimination orders. Left: Subject-Material-Brightness. Right: Material-Brightness-Subject.

This last elimination order is interesting because no new edges are added. When you add an edge, you force the variables you're connecting to appear in the same factor. This makes the factors bigger and makes inference more expensive. If you have an elimination order that doesn't add any edges, you can't possibly do better than that, because the factors you produce during the course of inference won't bring together any variables that weren't already contained together in some factor at the beginning.

The natural question arises whether there's always an elimination order that doesn't add any edges. The answer is related to a concept called *triangulation*. A graph is triangulated if all of its loops are "triangles"; the sidebar "Triangulated graphs" explains exactly what this means. If the initial VE graph is triangulated, there's at least one elimination order that doesn't require adding an edge. Conversely, if the initial

VE graph isn't triangulated, you have to add at least one edge no matter what elimination order you use. One way (but not the only way) to ensure that the initial VE graph is triangulated is to start with a network without any loops at all. Therefore: *If the initial VE graph has no loops, you can always eliminate nodes from the ends of the graph inward without adding any edges.*

Triangulated graphs

A graph is *triangulated* if all loops in the graph are made up of triangles. Technically, this means that there is no loop in a graph of length 4 or more that doesn't have a cross-cutting edge between two nonadjacent nodes. This is easier understood with a picture.

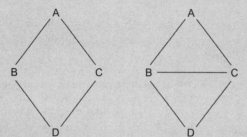

Triangulated graphs. The graph on the left contains a loop A-B-D-C that doesn't have a cross-cutting edge, so it's not triangulated. In the graph on the right, this loop has a cross-cutting edge B-C, so the graph is triangulated. Indeed, it's made up of triangles A-B-C and B-C-D.

Why does triangulation determine whether you can eliminate variables without adding an edge? If you look at the graph on the left, you can see that if you eliminate A or D first, you'll add the edge B-C, whereas if you eliminate B or C first, you'll add the edge A-D. No matter what you do, you have to add an edge. In the graph on the right, you can eliminate A first without adding an edge. At that point, you're left with the triangle B-C-D, all of which are connected, and you can eliminate in any order without adding edges.

This is a general principle. A nontriangulated graph has a loop of length 4 or more without a cross-cutting edge. The first time you eliminate a node in that loop, you'll have to add a cross-cutting edge. On the other hand, in a triangulated graph, there's always a node you can start elimination with, without adding an edge. Furthermore, after you eliminate that node, the graph will continue to be triangulated, so you can continue elimination without adding edges. The bottom line: there exists an elimination order that doesn't add edges if and only if the initial VE graph is triangulated.

What is the implication of this? If the graph is triangulated, the factors you produce during inference won't be any larger than the factors you started with. So if you were able to represent the model in the first place, you should be able to perform inference efficiently. On the other hand, if the graph isn't triangulated, you might end up creating much bigger factors during the course of inference.

Because the elimination order is so important, how do you find a good one? Unfortunately, this is a computationally difficult task, and the cost is generally exponential in the size of the largest clique under the best order. But you can use heuristics to come up with a good order. One popular heuristic uses the intuition that you want to avoid adding edges as much as possible. This heuristic chooses, at each point, the variable whose elimination would add the fewest edges to the graph. Figaro uses a variation on this heuristic, also taking into account the number of values of the variables involved.

10.2.2 VE as algebraic operations

This subsection explains the VE algorithm in detail. If you don't want to see all of the details, feel free to jump to the summary of the algorithm at the end.

To understand VE, let's work with a simple example. You want to compute P(Subject, Brightness = Bright), which is defined by the following sum-of-products expression:

$$P(J, B = \text{Bright}) = \Sigma_{Z,B} \ P(J) \ P(B \mid J) \ P(Z \mid J) \ E_B(B)$$

Let's write down the factor for P(J, B = Bright) with all of the calculations for each entry made explicit. The calculations are shown symbolically in table 10.11, while the numeric calculations are shown in table 10.12.

Table 10.11 Factor for P(Brightness) query with the calculations producing each entry made explicit. Because the evidence specifies that Brightness = Bright, any entry with Brightness = Dark will be set to 0, so you can handle the evidence factor by simply deleting those entries from the calculation.

Subject	
People	P(J = People) P(B = Bright | J = People) P(Z = Small | J = People) E_B(B = Bright) + P(J = People) P(B = Bright | J = People) P(Z = Medium | J = People) E_B(B = Bright) + P(J = People) P(B = Bright | J = People) P(Z = Large | J = People) E_B(B = Bright) + P(J = People) P(B = Dark | J = People) P(Z = Small | J = People) E_B(B = Dark) + P(J = People) P(B = Dark | J = People) P(Z = Medium | J = People) E_B(B = Dark) + P(J = People) P(B = Dark | J = People) P(Z = Large | J = People) E_B(B = Dark)
Landscape	P(J = Land.) P(B = Bright | J = Land.) P(Z = Small | J = Land.) E_B(B = Bright) + P(J = Land.) P(B = Bright | J = Land.) P(Z = Medium | J = Land.) E_B(B = Bright) + P(J = Land.) P(B = Bright | J = Land.) P(Z = Large | J = Land.) E_B(B = Bright) + P(J = Landscape) P(B = Dark | J = Land.) P(Z = Small | J = Land.) E_B(B = Dark) + P(J = Landscape) P(B = Dark | J = Land.) P(Z = Medium | J = Land.) E_B(B = Dark) + P(J = Landscape) P(B = Dark | J = Land.) P(Z = Large | J = Land.) E_B(B = Dark)

Table 10.12 The factor for P(Brightness) with each term replaced by a number derived from the CPDs. The numbers are encoded with different fonts to indicate which factor they come from. The small computer font numbers came from P(Subject), the bold numbers come from P(Brightness | Subject), the regular numbers come from P(Size | Subject), and the italicized numbers come from E_B(Brightness). This helps you keep track of the numbers as you do the calculations.

Subject	
People	$0.8 \times \mathbf{0.8} \times 0.25 \times \mathit{1} + 0.8 \times \mathbf{0.8} \times 0.25 \times \mathit{1} + 0.8 \times \mathbf{0.8} \times 0.5 \times \mathit{1} +$ $0.8 \times \mathbf{0.2} \times 0.25 \times 0 + 0.8 \times \mathbf{0.2} \times 0.5 \times 0 + 0.8 \times \mathbf{0.2} \times 0.25 \times 0$
Landscape	$0.2 \times \mathbf{0.3} \times 0.25 \times \mathit{1} + 0.2 \times \mathbf{0.3} \times 0.25 \times \mathit{1} + 0.2 \times \mathbf{0.3} \times 0.5 * \mathit{1} +$ $0.2 * \mathbf{0.7} * 0.25 * 0 + 0.2 * \mathbf{0.7} * 0.5 * 0 + 0.2 * \mathbf{0.7} * 0.25 * 0$

VE performs these calculations by eliminating variables you don't need in the answer, one at a time. In our example, you have to eliminate the variables Brightness and Size. Let's start by eliminating Brightness. You'll multiply the numbers from factors mentioning Brightness together, and you want to avoid also multiplying them with other numbers.

To achieve this, the first step is to move all numbers in the products so that numbers that come from factors mentioning Brightness move to the right, and numbers coming from other factors move to the left. In our example, the bold and italicized numbers come from P(Brightness | Subject) and E_B(Brightness), respectively, so they're moved to the right, and other numbers are moved to the left. This manipulation is legal because of the algebraic rule that a product is commutative, meaning that you can change the order of terms in a multiplication. The result is shown in table 10.13. Notice how the bold and italicized numbers, which come from P(Brightness | Subject) and E_B(Brightness), are moved to the right of each product.

Table 10.13   Our sum-of-products expression for P(Brightness), with numbers from factors mentioning Brightness moved to the right.

Subject	
People	$0.8 \times 0.25 \times \mathbf{0.8} \times \mathit{1} + 0.8 \times 0.25 \times \mathbf{0.8} \times \mathit{1} + 0.8 \times 0.5 \times \mathbf{0.8} \times \mathit{1} +$ $0.8 \times 0.25 \times \mathbf{0.2} \times \mathit{0} + 0.8 \times 0.5 \times \mathbf{0.2} \times \mathit{0} + 0.8 \times 0.25 \times \mathbf{0.2} \times \mathit{0}$
Landscape	$0.2 \times 0.25 \times \mathbf{0.3} \times \mathit{1} + 0.2 \times 0.25 \times \mathbf{0.3} \times \mathit{1} + 0.2 \times 0.5 \times \mathbf{0.3} \times \mathit{1} +$ $0.2 \times 0.25 \times \mathbf{0.7} \times \mathit{0} + 0.2 \times 0.5 \times \mathbf{0.7} \times \mathit{0} + 0.2 \times 0.25 \times \mathbf{0.7} \times \mathit{0}$

An important thing to notice is that although I showed you the numbers themselves being moved around, table 10.13 represents a sum-of-products expression on factors; specifically, as the next equation shows, you've moved P(B | J) and E_B(B) to the right of the factors that don't mention B.

$$P(J, B = Bright) = \Sigma_{Z,B}\ P(J)\ P(Z \mid J)\ P(B \mid J)\ E_B(B)$$

The next step is to use the distributive law of algebra, which says

$$a \times b + a \times c = a \times (b + c)$$

In our example, this means

$$0.8 \times 0.25 \times 0.8 \times 1 + 0.8 \times 0.25 \times 0.3 \times 0 = 0.8 \times 0.25 \times (0.8 \times 1 + 0.3 \times 0)$$

Using this law, you can rewrite the factor in table 10.13 as shown in table 10.14.

Table 10.14   **The factor resulting from taking the factor in table 10.13 and creating an inner summation that involves only the factors mentioning Brightness**

Subject	
People	$0.8 \times 0.25 \times (\mathbf{0.8} \times 1 + \mathbf{0.2} \times 0) +$ $0.8 \times 0.25 \times (\mathbf{0.8} \times 1 + \mathbf{0.2} \times 0) +$ $0.8 \times 0.5 \times (\mathbf{0.8} \times 1 + \mathbf{0.2} \times 0)$
Landscape	$0.2 \times 0.25 \times (\mathbf{0.3} \times 1 + \mathbf{0.7} \times 0) +$ $0.2 \times 0.5 \times (\mathbf{0.3} \times 1 + \mathbf{0.7} \times 0) +$ $0.2 \times 0.25 \times (\mathbf{0.3} \times 1 + \mathbf{0.7} \times 0)$

You've again performed an operation on factors. You've created an inner summation that involves only numbers coming from factors mentioning Size. These are the numbers you pushed to the right in the previous step; in our example, just the regular font numbers. In factor terms, you've now created the following sum-of-products expression:

$$P(J, B = Bright) = \Sigma_Z P(J) P(Z \mid J) \Sigma_B P(B \mid J) E_B(B)$$

The final step in eliminating Brightness is to go ahead and compute the inner sum of products, in other words, to compute $\Sigma_B P(B \mid J) E_B(B)$. The result of this computation is a factor. Because this computation starts with factors that mention Brightness and Subject, and you sum out Brightness, the resulting factor mentions only Subject. The factor is shown in table 10.15.

Table 10.15   **The factor resulting from computing $\Sigma_B P(B \mid J) E_B(B)$. The entries in this factor are shown in a fancy font.**

Subject	
People	$\mathbf{0.8} \times 1 + \mathbf{0.2} \times 0 = 0.8$
Landscape	$\mathbf{0.3} \times 1 + \mathbf{0.7} \times 0 = 0.8$

Let's give this factor the name F_B, which stands for the factor you get from eliminating Brightness. You can substitute this factor into equation 3 to get the expression in the following equation:

$$P(J) = \Sigma_Z P(J) P(Z \mid J) F_B(J)$$

And lo and behold, this is a sum-of-products expression that doesn't mention Brightness. You've successfully eliminated Brightness, and you didn't have to multiply all of the factors together to do it.

SUMMARY OF THE ALGORITHM

Although I've shown you this process in gory detail, it's simple. Here's the algorithm for eliminating a variable V from a sum-of-products expression S:

```
Eliminate(V, S) {
  Move all factors in S that mention V to the right
  Move the summation over V so that it encloses only those factors
  Compute the inner sum-of-products involving the factors that mention V
  Replace this sum-of-products in S with the resulting factor
}
```

That's also most of what there is to VE. Here's the essential VE algorithm:

```
VariableElimination(S) {
  Choose an elimination order O that contains all variables except the
      query variables
  For each variable V in O {
    Eliminate(V, S)
  }
}
```

10.3 Using VE

Now that you've seen how VE works, let's talk about how to use it practically. I'll first talk about the mechanics of using VE in Figaro, along with the different variations available. Then I'll talk about some general principles to use when designing your model for VE. Finally, I'll describe some real-world applications.

10.3.1 Figaro-specific considerations for VE

So far, you've looked at simple examples involving Bayesian networks. Probabilistic programs can be much more complicated than Bayesian networks, involving a much richer set of variables, data structures, control flow, and even recursion. Fortunately, Figaro handles all of this complexity for you.

The vanilla version of Figaro's VE is the VariableElimination algorithm we've been using a lot in this book. To recap, VE is run by passing the list of query targets to the VariableElimination constructor to create an algorithm, and then querying it afterward. For example:

Prints the mean value of element2, which is an Element [Double]

Prints the probability that the value of element1 = 0

Prints the probability that the value of element1 is greater than 0

```
val algorithm = VariableElimination(element1, element2)
algorithm.start()
println(algorithm.probability(element1, 0))
println(algorithm.probability(element1, (i: Int) => i > 0))
println(algorithm.distribution(element1).toList)
println(algorithm.mean(element2))
println(algorithm.expectation(element2, (d: Double) => d x d))
```

Prints the probability that distribution over element1. algorithm .distribution returns a stream, so you turn it into a list for printing

Prints the expectation of the square of element2

You've also seen one-line shortcuts:

```
VariableElimination.probability(element, 0)
VariableElimination.probability(element, (i: Int) -> i > 0)
```

Figaro's vanilla VE algorithm turns the probabilistic program into a giant Bayesian network. For this to succeed, the following condition has to hold: the number of variables that could possibly exist in the model is finite. This rules out some open-universe models, in which there's no upper bound on the number of objects. It also rules out recursive models when there's no bound on the number of recursions.

Also, VE is inherently a discrete algorithm and has trouble with continuous distributions. Figaro's solution to this is to sample a set of values for each atomic continuous element appearing in the model. Because you use only a small subset of the set of possible values, VE is no longer an exact algorithm when used in this way. But this may be good enough for your purposes, especially if you don't have too many continuous elements in your model.

If you want to stick to the standard algorithm, you can stop reading here and jump to the next section. But the Figaro team is constantly trying to advance the state of the art of probabilistic programming inference algorithms, and VE algorithms are no exception. If you're willing to dig a little deeper, you can benefit from these advances.

One Figaro alternative to VE, called *lazy VE*, relaxes the restriction on unbounded recursion. A full explanation of this algorithm is beyond the scope of this book, but I want to make you aware of its existence. The main intuition behind lazy VE is that you can partially expand the model and compute lower and upper bounds to the answer to your query by running VE on the partially expanded model. For example, imagine a program that generates a graph of some size and estimates a property of the graph. The size of the graph might not have an upper bound, so it would be impossible to apply vanilla VE to this problem. But lazy VE might be able to partially expand the model and generate graphs up to a certain upper bound and estimate the probability distribution over the property being estimated using that partial expansion.

The Figaro development team is also working on a new general framework for factored inference called *structured factored inference*. This framework includes a structured VE algorithm. This algorithm is in the experimental package and will soon be moving to the main package. (By the time you read this, it may already be there.) The idea of structured VE is to use the structure of the probabilistic program to guide the solution process. Any time a chain is expanded, a subproblem is created to represent all elements created by the chain function. All variables inside this subproblem can be eliminated by a separate VE process that operates on this subproblem. One of the major benefits of this approach is that if the same subproblem appears more than once in your problem, the work involved in solving it the first time can be reused for the other times.

10.3.2 *Designing your model to support efficient VE*

Now that you have an understanding of VE and its complexity, how do you use this knowledge when designing your models? This section provides some tips.

AVOID TOO MANY CLOSED LOOPS

The first and most obvious point is to avoid loops that don't have cross-cutting edges in your models, as far as possible. If you have a loop with no cross-cutting edge, you'll eventually need to add an edge, which will add to the cost of inference. You've seen that if you have a triangulated network, in which every loop of length 4 or more has cross-cutting edges, it will be possible to perform VE without adding any edges.

If you can't avoid loops completely, it's better to have isolated loops than a lot of loops close together. Figure 10.5 shows an example of a network that's hard for VE. This is the image-recovery Markov network you saw in chapter 5. The figure shows a 4×4 network, but you could have hundreds or thousands of pixels along a side.

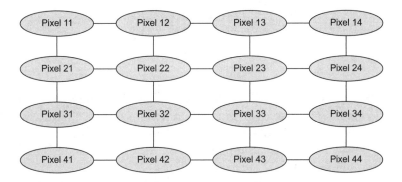

Figure 10.5 Image-recovery network, reproduced from chapter 5. VE on a grid like this is exponential in the number of pixels on a side.

Unfortunately, no matter what elimination order you choose, there's no way to avoid adding edges that create a clique whose size is the number of pixels along the shorter dimension of the image. The cost of VE is exponential in the size of the grid. As a result, although VE works in principle for this kind of network, in practice it takes an extremely long time.

DECOMPOSE CPDS WITH LOTS OF PARENTS

Another contributor to the cost of VE is the size of the factors you start with. Even if you don't add nodes, the algorithm can take a long time if you have large factors. If your original factors come from CPDs, the number of variables mentioned by a CPD is equal to the number of parents plus one for the child. This means that the size of the factor is exponential in the number of parents. Therefore, you should try to minimize the number of parents.

A practical situation where this occurs is with `Apply` elements. Figaro provides `Apply` elements of up to five arguments. If you have a function of five arguments, you have a factor with six variables. And if those arguments have 10 possible values each, then there are 100,000 combinations of values of the arguments. You can see that these factors get big fast.

One trick that often works with `Apply` is to decompose it into multiple functions. For example, suppose you want to add four binomials. You could use the code

```
val x =
  Apply(Binomial(10, 0.1), Binomial(10, 0.2),
        Binomial(10, 0.3), Binomial(10, 0.4),
        (x1: Int, x2: Int, x3: Int, x4: Int) => x1 + x2 + x3 + x4)
```

Each binomial has 11 possible values (0 to 10), so there are 14,641 combinations of values of the arguments, resulting in a large factor. A better representation is to decompose this code into three additions of two arguments each:

```
val x12 = Apply(Binomial(10, 0.1), Binomial(10, 0.2),
                (x1: Int, x2: Int) => x1 + x2)
val x34 = Apply(Binomial(10, 0.3), Binomial(10, 0.4),
                (x3: Int, x4: Int) => x3 + x4)
val x = Apply(x12, x34,(x12: Int, x34: Int) => x12 + x34)
```

This contains three functions of two arguments each. Each of the first two functions has only 121 combinations of its arguments. x12 and x34 could each have a value from 0 to 20 (10 + 10), so the number of combinations of arguments of the third function is $21 \times 21 = 441$. This leads to a total number of 683 rows in the factors, much better than the 14,641 you had before.

In fact, for operations like addition, which you can apply to any number of arguments, there's a natural decomposition into a sequence of `Apply` operations with two arguments each. Fortunately, you don't have to implement this decomposition yourself. Figaro already provides it to you with the `FoldLeft` constructor. `FoldLeft` is similar to Scala's `foldLeft`, which applies an operation iteratively to a sequence of elements. For example, in Scala, you can say

```
val x = List(1, 2, 3, 4)
val y = x.foldLeft(0)((x1: Int, x2: Int) => x1 + x2)
```

which makes y the sum of the x items. Similarly, you can use the following Figaro construct, found in the `com.cra.figaro.library.compound` package:

```
FoldLeft(0, (x1: Int, x2: Int) => x1 + x2)(
  Binomial(10, 0.1), Binomial(10, 0.2),
  Binomial(10, 0.3), Binomial(10, 0.4)
)
```

This automatically decomposes into functions of two arguments each. Figaro also provides `FoldRight` and `Reduce` that are analogous to Scala's `foldRight` and `reduce`, respectively.

EXPLOIT ENCAPSULATION

If you've used object-oriented programming, you'll be familiar with the idea that encapsulation can help manage code by hiding away in the internals of an object all details that are unnecessary for the rest of the program. It turns out that encapsulation also provides a benefit for VE. If an object has an interface that hides away all of the details of the object from the rest of the model, all internal elements representing the details can be eliminated internally to the object without interacting with the rest of the model. The result of eliminating the internal elements is a factor over the interface. This factor captures everything that needs to be known about the object, as far as the rest of the model is concerned.

The key to exploiting encapsulation effectively is to make the interfaces small. This is standard OO design guidance, so good OO design and efficient inference go hand in hand. An example of this is the computer system diagnosis model from chapter 7. In this model, you created separate objects for the Printer, Network, Software, and User. Each of these objects interacts with the rest of the model by using a single variable. For example, the Printer object interacts with the rest of the model through a single State variable. This means that all internals of the Printer object, no matter how complex, can be summarized in a factor over a single variable.

To make the most of this concept, you can use a hierarchical decomposition of the model. For example, the Printer object might contain nested objects for the Paper Feed and the Toner. These nested objects would communicate with the Printer via a small interface, which will in turn communicate with the rest of the model using its own small interface. The following code shows how this might be done. One thing to make sure of is that if you want to be able to query or post evidence about an element, it can't be private. In the following example, you want to post evidence about the toner-low indicator, so the `tonerLowIndicatorOn` element has been brought out of the nested `Toner` class, which is private, and made public in the `Printer` class:

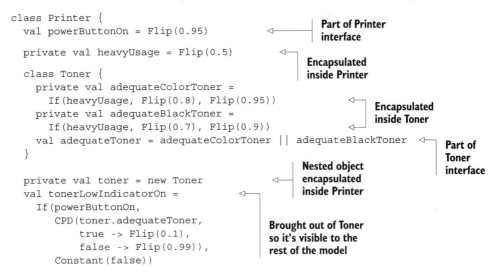

```
class Printer {
  val powerButtonOn = Flip(0.95)                              Part of Printer
                                                              interface

  private val heavyUsage = Flip(0.5)                          Encapsulated
                                                              inside Printer
  class Toner {
    private val adequateColorToner =
      If(heavyUsage, Flip(0.8), Flip(0.95))                   Encapsulated
    private val adequateBlackToner =                          inside Toner
      If(heavyUsage, Flip(0.7), Flip(0.9))
    val adequateToner = adequateColorToner || adequateBlackToner    Part of
  }                                                                 Toner
                                                                    interface
  private val toner = new Toner                     Nested object
  val tonerLowIndicatorOn =                         encapsulated
    If(powerButtonOn,                               inside Printer
      CPD(toner.adequateToner,
          true -> Flip(0.1),              Brought out of Toner
          false -> Flip(0.99)),           so it's visible to the
      Constant(false))                    rest of the model
```

```
val state =
    Apply(powerButtonOn, toner.adequateToner,
        (power: Boolean, toner: Boolean) => {
            if (!power) out
            else if (toner) 'good
            else 'poor
        })
}
```
◁──┐ **Part of Printer**
      interface

You can also get the benefits of encapsulation without explicitly using OO design. The chain construct also provides encapsulation. A chain involves a parent and a child, and, for each value of the parent, a set of elements that are created when applying the chain function to the parent value. As long as these elements don't use elements from outside the chain, they're encapsulated inside the chain by the chain's parent and child. If they do use elements from outside the chain, those used elements become part of the interface. So as long as you keep the number of such elements small, you still benefit from encapsulation. Indeed, structured VE, mentioned briefly in the previous subsection, uses this encapsulation explicitly.

SIMPLIFY THE NETWORK
If you have a network that's too complex for VE, and you want to use VE because it's an exact algorithm, you have to simplify the network. This can be done either by deleting edges or deleting nodes. You'll have to use your judgment about which edges and nodes are least relevant to the model and can also provide the most savings by deletion. An alternative to simplifying the model is to use an approximate inference algorithm, but using VE with a simplified model has the advantage that you know you're getting the right answer with respect to your model and you have control over exactly what's included in the model.

10.3.3 Applications of VE

Because VE is an exact algorithm that perfectly computes the probabilities you're interested in, you might think that it's not suitable for real-world applications with complex models. This isn't the case. VE is widely used; the key question isn't the size of the model but whether it has the right structure—in particular, whether you can eliminate variables without adding too many edges to the VE graph, leaving the size of the largest clique in the VE graph small and the complexity low. This section describes two application domains where VE is widely used.

SPEECH RECOGNITION
One kind of model that's amenable to VE is the hidden Markov model (HMM), which you saw in chapter 8. Figure 10.6 shows an example of an HMM, reproduced from that chapter. An HMM is a dynamic probabilistic model with a state variable that changes over time and an observation that depends on the state variable at each point in time.

HMMs are used in many applications. One popular application is speech recognition. In speech recognition, you typically have an observation sequence that consists of a changing audio signal over time and want to infer what word is being spoken.

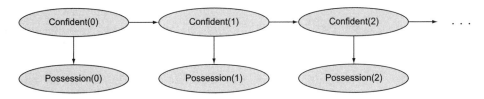

Figure 10.6   A hidden Markov model, reproduced from chapter 8

Each word is modeled as an HMM that goes through a sequence of states corresponding to the types of sounds that the speaker is making during the course of saying the word. For example, if the speaker is saying "car," he might begin by making a *k* sound, then an *ah* sound, and then possibly an *r* sound. The amount of time spent making these sounds is uncertain. The presence of certain sounds might also be uncertain; for example, some people don't pronounce the *r* in *car*. This uncertain pronunciation process is encoded in the transition model of the HMM. Meanwhile, the observation model encodes how features of the audio signal depend probabilistically on the sounds the speaker is making. Thus, the utterance of a word is well modeled as an HMM.

When reasoning about an HMM, you typically have a particular observation sequence (such as an audio signal of a certain length) and want to reason about the hidden states. For example, you might have a sequence of length 4. You can "unroll" the HMM over four time steps to obtain the Bayesian network shown in figure 10.7.

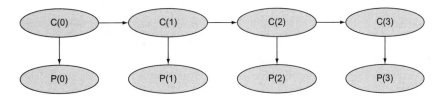

Figure 10.7   Bayesian network for an HMM unrolled over four time steps

One thing to notice about this network is that no node has more than one parent. This implies that when you construct the moral graph for this network, you don't have to connect any nodes. This results in the graph shown in figure 10.8.

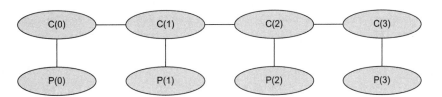

Figure 10.8   Moral graph for the HMM of figure 10.7

The next thing to notice is that the graph in figure 10.8 has no loops. As you've seen, this implies that there's an elimination order that doesn't require adding any edges to the graph. For example, suppose you're interested in the posterior probability of $C(2)$. You can eliminate variables in the following order: $P(0)$, $C(0)$, $P(1)$, $C(1)$, $P(2)$, $P(3)$, $C(3)$. In this order, whenever you eliminate a variable, it's on the edge of the graph and connected to only one other variable, so no edges are added. So the graph in figure 10.8 is also the induced graph of VE under this elimination order.

If you look more closely at figure 10.8, you'll see that pairs of adjacent hidden states are connected, as is each hidden state with its corresponding observation. All of these connections form cliques of size 2. No groups of three variables are all connected to each other, so the largest clique size is 2. This remains true no matter how long the observation sequence is and how many time steps you unroll the HMM. As a result, the cost of VE in an HMM is *linear* in the length of the observation sequence. This is why VE is such an effective algorithm for HMMs.

A variation on HMM inference is used in speech recognition. For one thing, you're generally not interested in a particular hidden state. Rather, you want to know the probability of the observation sequence for the given HMM. For example, suppose you're not sure if the speaker said "car" or "jar," and you want to determine which is more likely. You could use Bayesian reasoning to achieve this. Recall from chapter 9 that in Bayesian reasoning, the posterior probability of something is proportional to its prior times its likelihood.

- The prior might express the fact that *car* is a more common word than *jar*, so in the absence of evidence, you'd believe *car* to be more likely. The prior is often learned from data (how often people use the word *car* versus *jar*). But by the time it comes to classify a word, the prior is given.
- The likelihood of *car*, meanwhile, is the probability of the observed audio sequence given that the word is car, and similarly for *jar*. This probability is defined by the HMM for *car* or *jar*, respectively. In other words, to compute the likelihood, you want to compute the probability of the observation sequence in the HMM.

One easy way to accomplish this is to eliminate *all* of the variables and see what the normalizing factor is at the end. This normalizing factor is equal to the probability of the evidence. Unfortunately, Figaro doesn't currently have a convenient interface for accessing this normalizing factor, although I'm hopeful it'll be added soon. It does, however, provide other algorithms for computing the probability of evidence, which are discussed in detail in chapter 12. In particular, there's a probability-of-evidence algorithm based on belief propagation, which behaves essentially the same way as VE on an HMM.

To use HMMs for an application such as speech recognition, it's also necessary to learn the parameters of the model from data. The data typically consists of examples of audio sequences along with labels of the words being spoken. Learning the parameters of an HMM is also usually accomplished using VE in conjunction with an algorithm called *expectation maximization* (EM). You'll learn how to use the EM algorithm to learn model parameters in chapter 12.

NATURAL LANGUAGE UNDERSTANDING

HMMs aren't the only common structure amenable to inference by VE. In natural language processing, parse trees are often used to express how a sentence is made up of components. The way a sentence is constructed is known as a *parse.*

An example of a parse tree for the sentence "The cat drank milk" is shown in figure 10.9. The top level of the parse is the symbol Sentence, which corresponds to the entire sentence. The parse shows how this top-level symbol is broken into noun-phrase and verb-phrase symbols. The noun phrase covers the words "The cat," and the verb phrase covers the words "drank milk." In this way, the parse describes the hierarchical construction of the sentence.

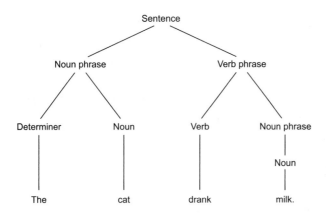

Figure 10.9   A parse of the sentence "The cat drank milk." The sentence as a whole is made up of a noun phrase and a verb phrase. In turn, the verb phrase is made up of a verb (the word "drank") and a noun phrase, and so on.

In natural language understanding, a common task is to determine the correct parse of a given sentence, which helps to understand the sentence. A *grammar* encodes the rules by which a sentence can be constructed. These rules often involve choices. For example, given a verb phrase, it might be composed simply of a Verb (as in the sentence "The cat sat.") or of a verb followed by a noun phrase ("The cat drank milk."). *Probabilistic grammars*, which represent these choices using probabilities, have been found to be effective at generating accurate parses. For example, the probability of a verb phrase being composed of just a verb might be 40%, whereas the probability it's made up of a verb phrase followed by a noun phrase is 60%.

A particularly simple kind of probabilistic grammar that's popular because of its simplicity and ease of inference is a *probabilistic context-free grammar (PCFG)*. I won't go into the details of the definition of a PCFG, but the main characteristic of a PCFG is that the decisions at different points in a parse are independent of each other. This is the essential property that enables VE to work effectively on PCFGs.

The idea is that you have a variable for every nonempty substring of the sentence representing the symbol associated with that substring. In our example, the substrings are *The, cat, drank, milk, The cat, cat drank, drank milk, The cat drank, cat drank milk,* and *The cat drank milk.* By the rules of a PCFG, because "The cat drank milk" can be made up of *The cat* and *drank milk,* the symbol for "The cat drank milk" can influence the symbols for *The cat* and *drank milk.* This general process defines a Bayesian network over all these variables.

In this network, you can determine a parse for a sentence by eliminating variables from the bottom up. For example, you can start with the variables corresponding to individual words. After you've eliminated all of those, you can eliminate the variables corresponding to length 2 substrings. By the independence assumptions of a PCFG, these can all be eliminated separately from each other. You can continue upward in this way; at any point, after you've eliminated variables for all substrings of length less than n, you can eliminate the variables for the length n substrings independently.

It turns out that the cost of VE on a PCFG is cubic in the length of the sentence. For the typical sentences encountered in most applications, this is quite feasible, so this is a widely used algorithm. One variation is that often, you're not interested in a probability distribution over the symbols but rather want to infer the *most likely parse.* This falls into the category of a most likely explanation query. In chapter 12, you'll learn about those queries, including a VE algorithm for computing the most likely explanation, which is what is used for PCFGs.

10.4 Belief propagation

VE produces an exact result when you're able to run it to completion. Unfortunately, sometimes you might not be willing to simplify a model enough to allow you to run VE. You've seen that the complexity of VE is exponential in the size of the largest clique in the induced graph for the elimination order used. What if too many edges have to be added so the induced graph is too dense? Fortunately, an approximate algorithm, called *belief propagation* (BP), can handle cases like this well. I won't explain BP in full detail, but I'll cover the basic principles enough to give you an understanding of how it works and when it works well.

10.4.1 Basic principles of BP

BP operates using the moral graph (the initial VE graph), without adding edges. As long as the largest clique in the moral graph isn't too large, BP is efficient. By not adding edges, BP can avoid creating large cliques, which can potentially result in exponentially faster inference than VE. This comes at a cost. Adding these edges is necessary for correct inference, so not adding the edges will result in errors. Nevertheless, inference can be approximately correct even when these edges aren't added.

You learned in section 10.2.1 that if the moral graph is triangulated, there's some elimination order such that no edges need to be added to produce the induced graph. As it turns out, if you run BP on a triangulated graph, it produces exactly the correct answer. In fact, the complexity of BP and VE is the same in triangulated graphs. But if you run BP on a nontriangulated graph, it's an approximation algorithm that has the potential to be much more efficient than VE. On a nontriangulated graph, BP goes by the name of *loopy BP.*

BP is a *message-passing algorithm.* It can be best understood by considering its operation on triangulated graphs, where it's exact. In this case, it solves a sum-of-product expression, just like VE. But rather than solving the expression by manipulating it using the rules of algebra, it solves it by passing messages between the nodes of the network. These messages are based on factor operations. I'm not going to get into how the messages are computed here, but these messages simulate the same products and sums of factors that VE performs.

There's a significant difference between BP and VE, however. *BP performs these calculations for queries on all variables in the network simultaneously.* After you run BP, you can get the posterior probability of any variable, given the evidence. In a triangulated network, BP can achieve this in two passes over the network, as long as you organize the message passing in the right way. (Unfortunately, as you'll see, Figaro can't organize the messages to achieve this, so you'll need more than two passes, but this property holds in principle for the BP algorithm.) This is a significant advantage of BP over VE, even in triangulated graphs, if you're interested in querying more than one variable.

In a nontriangulated network, loopy BP works in exactly the same way as VE, except that instead of terminating after two passes (if the messages are organized right), it runs repeatedly for as long as you like. Messages are passed around the network, and if the moral graph is loopy, the messages also go around in loops. You can run BP for however many iterations you like, and get the best answer found after the given number of iterations. Ideally, the more iterations you run, the closer you'll get to the true answer.

10.4.2 *Properties of loopy BP*

It's somewhat surprising that loopy BP works at all. It turns out that the reason has to do with statistical physics. In short, loopy BP is computing something called the Bethe free energy of the network; I won't go into exactly what that is. The Bethe free energy can be used to approximate the posterior distribution over the variables in the network, but isn't exactly the same.

As you run more and more iterations of loopy BP, it should, in many cases, converge to the Bethe free energy. Unfortunately, there are no guarantees on how good an approximation the Bethe free energy is to the posterior. The sidebar "Understanding the accuracy of loopy BP" shows two example programs that are almost exactly the same. In one of them, loopy BP gets exactly the right answer. In the other one, loopy BP is far off.

Understanding the accuracy of loopy BP

Consider the following two programs.

Good loopy BP example

```
val e1 = Flip(0.5)
val e21: Element[Boolean] = Apply(e1, (b: Boolean) => b)
val e31: Element[Boolean] = Apply(e21, (b: Boolean) => b)
val e22: Element[Boolean] = Apply(e1, (b: Boolean) => b)
val e32: Element[Boolean] = Apply(e31, (b: Boolean) => b)
val e4: Element[Boolean] = Dist(0.5 -> e31, 0.5 -> e32)
println(BeliefPropagation.probability(e4, true))
println(VariableElimination.probability(e4, true))
```

This chooses randomly between e31 and e32.

Bad loopy BP example

```
val e1 = Flip(0.5)
val e21: Element[Boolean] = Apply(e1, (b: Boolean) => b)
val e31: Element[Boolean] = Apply(e21, (b: Boolean) => b)
val e22: Element[Boolean] = Apply(e1, (b: Boolean) => b)
val e32: Element[Boolean] = Apply(e31, (b: Boolean) => b)
val e4: Element[Boolean] = e31 === e32
println(BeliefPropagation.probability(e4, true))
println(VariableElimination.probability(e4, true))
```

e4 is true if and only if the values of e31 and e32 are equal.

Each of these programs first prints the estimate of the probability that e4 is true produced by BP and then prints the exact answer produced by VE. The better the approximation, the closer the answers will be. If you run the first program, both algorithms will produce the answer 0.5, meaning that the approximation is perfect. For the second program, BP produces 0.5, and VE produces 1.0, meaning that the approximation is terrible.

What's going on? Both programs have exactly the same structure. The moral graph for these programs is shown in the following figure. In fact, the two programs differ only in the definition of e4.

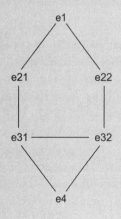

Moral graph for loopy BP example. There's an edge between e31 and e32 because both are parents of e4. The network contains a loop e1-e21-e31-e32-e22 without a cross-cutting edge, so it's not triangulated.

(continued)

If you look closely at these definitions, you see that the secret is in the degree of interaction between e31 and e32 in determining e4. In the first program, e4 chooses randomly between e31 and e32. There's no interaction between e31 and e32 in determining e4; if e31 has an effect on e4 because it's chosen, e32 has no effect, and vice versa. In the second program, e4 is true if and only if the values of e31 and e32 are equal. Here there's extreme interaction between e31 and e32 in determining e4; just looking at the definition of e4, knowing the value of e31 tells us nothing about the value of e4 unless we also know the value of e32. But in fact, we know that e31 and e32 have to be equal, because they're both equal (indirectly) to e1. So e4 has to have the value true, which is why VE produces the answer 1.0.

This brings us to the key point. Getting the right answer in program 2 requires nonlocal reasoning: tracing back the common dependence of e31 and e32 on e1. BP can't do nonlocal reasoning. BP works well when long-distance effects are small. This is true in many problems; effects of variables tend to be attenuated over long paths. This is why BP often works well on typical models. In fact, program 2 is a contrived example. I had to make e21 exactly the same as e1, and e31 exactly the same as e21, to make the point. A typical model probably wouldn't be defined this way.

One more comment on the performance of loopy BP: unfortunately, it's not even guaranteed to converge. Sometimes, as the messages go around in loops, they keep oscillating from one iteration to the next. Fortunately, these cases aren't that common. More significant is the problem that the approximation to which loopy BP converges is sometimes far away from the correct posterior distribution.

The bottom line: loopy BP is a practical algorithm that works quickly and produces reasonably accurate approximations in many cases. But it comes with no guarantees in general, neither as to whether it converges at all nor as to the accuracy of the approximation to which it converges. Therefore, a common strategy is as follows:

1 Try VE. If it terminates in a reasonable amount of time, you've got an exact answer, so it's best.

2 If VE doesn't terminate sufficiently quickly, try BP. Check whether the answer it gives you is reasonable. Hopefully, you'll have some intuition of what the answer should look like, or you have trial data that you can use to check the answer.

3 If BP is also too slow, or you're not satisfied with the answer it produces, try one of the sampling algorithms discussed in the next chapter.

10.5 Using BP

As for VE, I'll first talk about the choices for using BP in Figaro, then provide some general principles for making effective use of BP, and finish with some practical applications.

10.5.1 *Figaro-specific considerations for BP*

The key question when running BP is how many iterations to use. When you run BP, you have three choices:

- Specify how many iterations to use. You do this by passing the number of iterations as an argument to the algorithm creation, for example:

```
val algorithm = BeliefPropagation(100, element)
algorithm.start()
println(algorithm.probability(element, true))
```

- Use an anytime algorithm. In this case, you don't specify the number of iterations, but instead run it as long as you like. To refresh your memory, with an anytime algorithm, you can do something like this:

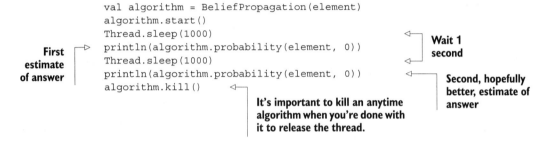

First estimate of answer

```
val algorithm = BeliefPropagation(element)
algorithm.start()
Thread.sleep(1000)
println(algorithm.probability(element, 0))
Thread.sleep(1000)
println(algorithm.probability(element, 0))
algorithm.kill()
```

Wait 1 second

Second, hopefully better, estimate of answer

It's important to kill an anytime algorithm when you're done with it to release the thread.

- Use a one-line shortcut such as BeliefPropagation.probability(element, 0). This shortcut uses a default number of iterations; if you want to specify the number of iterations, you have to use the long form.

How many iterations should you use? Figaro uses an asynchronous form of BP in which the order that messages are passed around the network isn't controlled. In general, if you want to guarantee that information from one node reaches another node, the number of iterations should be at least the distance between the nodes. In section 10.4.1, I said that in a nonloopy network, BP can get the right answer in two passes over the network. For Figaro, that means the number of iterations should be at least twice the diameter of the network, plus one. (The diameter of the network is the maximum distance between two nodes.) This implies that Figaro's BP is more efficient on networks that have a small diameter.

For loopy BP, the story is similar. If you use a number of iterations equal to the diameter of the network, that's equivalent to one loop around the network. So if you're choosing the number of iterations yourself, you multiply the diameter by the number of loops you want. You don't have to get it exact; just choose the number of iterations that ensures you go around the network several times. A common rule of thumb is to run 10 loops around the network. If you don't want to worry about this, use the anytime version of the algorithm.

10.5.2 *Designing your model to support effective BP*

The complexity of BP depends on the size of the largest clique in the moral graph, as opposed to the induced graph for VE. Also, you know that BP is exact when the moral graph is triangulated. Many of the considerations that hold for VE also hold for BP, but some BP-specific considerations exist as well.

AVOID TOO MANY LOOPS

Although loops don't affect the complexity of BP in the way they do for VE, they do introduce error into BP, which, as you've seen, can be hard to estimate. The more loops you have, the more the potential for error. Therefore, avoiding too many loops is still a good idea, although it's not as significant a consideration as for VE.

MERGE ELEMENTS TOGETHER

One way to avoid a loop is to manually eliminate the loop by merging nodes together. Let's look again at the bad program from the sidebar, reproduced here:

```
val e1 = Flip(0.5)
val e21: Element[Boolean] = Apply(e1, (b: Boolean) => b)
val e31: Element[Boolean] = Apply(e21, (b: Boolean) => b)
val e22: Element[Boolean] = Apply(e1, (b: Boolean) => b)
val e32: Element[Boolean] = Apply(e31, (b: Boolean) => b)
val e4: Element[Boolean] = e31 === e32
```

You can eliminate the loop by merging the elements e21 and e22 into an element e2 and by merging e31 and e32 into an element e3, as shown in figure 10.10. Because e21 and e22 are Boolean elements, e2 is an Element[(Boolean, Boolean)] whose value is a pair of the values of e21 and e22. Therefore, the number of possible values of e2 is $2 \times 2 = 4$; similarly for e3.

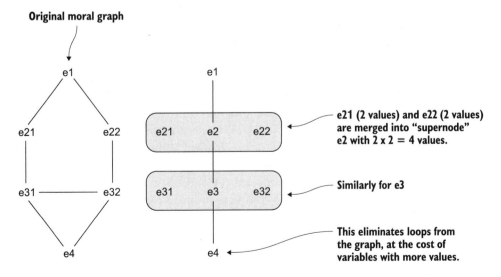

Figure 10.10 Merging nodes to avoid loops. The left shows the original moral graph, which produced inaccurate results with BP. The right shows a graph with merged nodes that has no loops.

You can write the following program:

> Creates an element over pairs, where each
> component is equal to the value of e1, just like
> e21 and e22 were in the original program

```
val e1 = Flip(0.5)
val e2: Element[(Boolean, Boolean)] = Apply(e1, (b: Boolean) => (b, b))
val e3: Element[(Boolean, Boolean)] =
  Apply(e2, (bb: (Boolean, Boolean)) => (bb._1, bb._2))
val e4: Element[Boolean] =
  Apply(e2, (bb: (Boolean, Boolean)) => bb._1 == bb._2)
```

> Creates an element over pairs, where the first
> component equals the value of the first component
> of e2, and similarly for the second component

Clearly, this isn't as natural or easy to read as the original program. But it has the major advantage that BP gets the right answer.

DECOMPOSE CPDS WITH LOTS OF PARENTS

Because BP works on the moral graph, and the moral graph has a clique for every CPD, having CPDs with lots of parents is as much of an issue for BP as it is for VE. In particular, the complexity of BP is exponential in the maximum number of parents of a node. Therefore, you should attempt to decompose these CPDs by using techniques described in section 10.3.2.

USE ATTENUATING CPDS

Loopy BP's error tends to be worse if there are long-distance effects, where the value of a node strongly influences the value of another node far away in the network via a loop. These long-distance effects are strongest when the relationships between variables along the path are deterministic. You saw an example in the sidebar in section 10.4.2, where the intermediate variables were exactly equal to the first variable. The effects are attenuated by relaxing this determinism with CPDs that have some randomness in them.

  Attenuating CPDs not only lead to better BP, but also can be more accurate models. Consider the printer model from chapter 5, for example. In this model, we said that if the printer power button is on, the toner level is high, and the paper flow is smooth, then the printer is in a good state. This is a deterministic relationship. But is it always true? In fact, no; other electrical or mechanical failures could lead to the printer not working. We often use deterministic relationships to simplify models, but adding noise can be more accurate. And, because it leads to better BP, it's generally a good idea. In the next chapter, you'll find that adding a little noise can improve the accuracy of sampling algorithms as well.

SIMPLIFY THE NETWORK

When none of the other options work, simplifying the network can be a good idea, just as for VE. When you simplify the network, you should have two goals. Most important, reduce the number of parents of CPDs to make the inference fast. Secondarily, eliminate long-distance effects as much as possible—for example, by removing loops with no cross-cutting edges.

10.5.3 *Applications of BP*

With VE, models must have a specific structure for the algorithm to be applicable. You saw two examples of such a structure in HMMs and PCFGs. BP has no such limitations. As a result, applications of BP are widespread. Anywhere you have a model with discrete variables, BP is a good candidate technique to use. Even if you have continuous variables, BP can be used if you're willing to limit them to a set of specific possible values. Here are some common applications of BP:

- *Image analysis*—In chapter 5, you saw that a two-dimensional array of pixels can be modeled using a Markov network. Figure 10.5 shows an example of a Markov network for a 4×4 image. In that section, I said that this kind of network is hard for VE, because the cost of inference is exponential in the size the image. In contrast, BP is a fine algorithm to use on this kind of model. The cost of inference is only linear in the size of the image.

- *Medical diagnosis*—In a typical medical diagnosis problem, the patient reports a set of symptoms, and the doctor needs to figure out the cause of those symptoms. An example of a Bayesian network for medical diagnosis is shown in figure 10.11. There's a set of possible diseases the patient might have and a set of symptoms the patient could report. Each symptom could be caused by one of several diseases. These Bayesian networks are usually quite loopy. In general, as the number of diseases and symptoms grow, the cliques can become large, making VE unsuitable. BP has been used successfully on these kinds of networks.

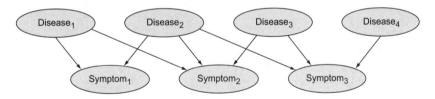

Figure 10.11   A Bayesian network for medical diagnosis

- *Building, vehicle, or equipment health monitoring*—Monitoring the health of a complex system is an important application of probabilistic reasoning. For example, suppose you have a data center and you want to monitor the temperature and power usage of the components of your data center. You might have variables representing the temperature and power usage of each component. The temperature of nearby components is dependent, as heat can transfer between those components. The power usage variables of components that are connected to each other are also dependent. In addition, the power usage of a component influences its temperature. All these factors create a large, loopy probabilistic model. In this example, temperature and power usage are continuous variables that need to be discretized into a set of values. Nevertheless, BP is used effectively for this type of application.

10.6 Summary

- Factors are data structures that organize the calculations performed during probabilistic inference.
- A factor has a set of variables, a row for every combination of values of the variables, and a number for each row.
- Factors support product and sum operations that are defined by multiplying and adding appropriate entries.
- The answer to a query on a probabilistic model can be defined as a sum-of-products expression over factors.
- Variable elimination is an exact algorithm that intelligently manipulates this sum-of-products expression without creating the full joint distribution.
- The complexity of variable elimination depends on the elimination order; for a given elimination order, the complexity is exponential in the size of the largest clique in the induced graph.
- Belief propagation is an algorithm that passes messages around by using factor operations. On a triangulated network, it's exact. On a network with loops, it's a practical approximation algorithm, although it doesn't provide any guarantees.
- Loopy belief propagation is more accurate if there are fewer long-distance effects around loops in the network.

10.7 Exercises

The first five exercises in this chapter are based on the Bayesian network shown in figure 10.12, which describes part of a baby's lifecycle. The figure also shows the CPDs for each of the four variables. Solutions to selected exercises are available online at www.manning.com/books/practical-probabilistic-programming.

1 Write each of the CPDs as a factor.
2 Write the expression for the joint probability distribution over all of the variables, using the chain rule. Compute this joint distribution by multiplying all of the factors together.
3 Write the expression for P(Cry), using the total probability rule. Compute the factor for P(Cry) by summing out Hungry, Eat, and Tired from the joint distribution.
4 Write the expression for the query P(Eat | Cry = True). Starting with the joint distribution, compute the answer to this query as follows:
   a Set the rows where Cry is not True to 0.
   b Sum out the variables Hungry and Tired.
   c Normalize the result.

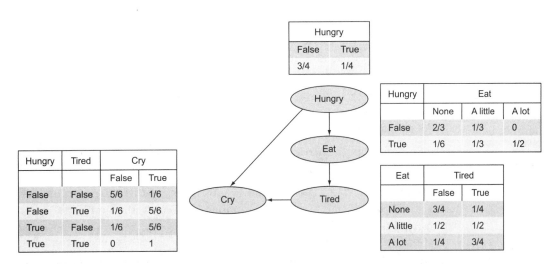

Figure 10.12 Baby lifecycle Bayesian network

5 Consider the process of computing P(Cry) by using variable elimination.

   a Draw the moral graph of the Bayesian network.

   b Draw the induced graph for the elimination order Eat, Hungry, Tired. What is the size of the largest clique?

   c Draw the induced graph for the elimination order Hungry, Tired, Eat. What is the size of the largest clique?

6 For the 4×4-pixel network of figure 10.5, try various elimination orders for variable elimination. Convince yourself that you can't avoid having a clique size of at least 4.

7 Represent an HMM, such as the one in figure 10.6, in Figaro. Write a function that takes an observation sequence as an argument, unrolls the HMM over the length of the observation sequence, and uses variable elimination to compute the probability distribution over the final hidden state. Measure the computation time for observation sequences of different lengths. What trend do the computation times follow, as a function of the length of the observation sequence?

8 Create a generic representation of the pixel network of figure 10.5, with a variable number of pixels on each side, in Figaro. For different numbers of pixels, perform the following experiments:

   a Randomly observe 1/3 of the pixels, not including the top-left corner.

   b Measure the amount of time it takes for variable elimination to compute the probability that the top-left corner is on. You'll find that above a relatively small number of pixels, variable elimination will take a long time, so stop the process. What trend does the computation time of variable elimination follow?

c Measure the amount of time it takes for belief propagation to compute the probability that the top-left corner is on. What trend does the computation time of belief propagation follow?

d If both variable elimination and belief propagation terminate, measure the difference between the answers produced by the two algorithms. Because variable elimination produces the exact answer, this quantity is the error of belief propagation.

9 Consider a medical diagnosis network like that in figure 10.11, with diseases in one row and symptoms in another row.

a Write a function that generates random networks of this sort. The function should take three parameters: the number of diseases, the number of symptoms, and the probability that there's an edge between any given disease and symptom.

b As in exercise 8, experiment with the behavior of variable elimination and belief propagation as the values of these parameters change. What's the trend of the computation time of variable elimination? What's the trend of the computation time of belief propagation? When both algorithms terminate, what's the error of belief propagation?

Sampling algorithms

This chapter covers

- The basic principles of sampling algorithms
- The importance sampling algorithm
- Markov chain Monte Carlo (MCMC) algorithm
- The Metropolis-Hastings variant of MCMC

This chapter continues the theme of the previous chapter, presenting some of the main algorithms used in probabilistic programming inference. Whereas chapter 10 focused on factored algorithms such as variable elimination and belief propagation, this chapter looks at sampling algorithms that answer queries by generating possible states of variables drawn from the probability distribution defined by the program. In particular, the chapter presents two useful algorithms: importance sampling and Markov chain Monte Carlo (MCMC).

After you've finished this chapter, you'll have a solid understanding of inference algorithms used in probabilistic programming systems such as Figaro. This understanding will help you design your models and control inference to make it work well. MCMC, in particular, requires extra effort to make it work well, and the chapter presents a couple of techniques to do that. Chapter 12 then builds on this knowledge to show you how to use similar algorithms to answer other kinds of queries on probabilistic programs.

This chapter is largely self-contained with regard to the previous chapter on factored algorithms. Although I make some comparisons to factored algorithms, you don't need to understand how the factored algorithms work to understand the sampling algorithms. Also, the sampling algorithms make less use of the rules of inference presented in chapter 9. You should, of course, have some understanding of how to write Figaro programs. Finally, the MCMC algorithm builds on the concept of Markov chains, introduced at the beginning of chapter 8, so you should review that material if you want to understand MCMC.

11.1 *The sampling principle*

Sampling algorithms are an alternative to factored algorithms for probabilistic inference. The basic principle behind sampling is straightforward: rather than representing the probability distribution over possible worlds as a set of numbers, you use a set of examples of possible worlds, called *samples.*

The essential idea of sampling is illustrated in figure 11.1. In this example, a single variable has the possible values small, medium, and large. The possible worlds consist of the possible values of this variable. There's some true probability distribution over possible worlds, shown in the top row. This true distribution might be the answer to a query, and is in general unknown. Rather than computing the distribution directly, you generate a set of samples. Each sample is a possible world, and the probability of generating a particular possible world should be equal to the probability of that possible world. In the figure, we've generated the following:

- Two samples in which the variable is set to small
- Five samples where it's set to medium
- Three samples where it's set to large

You can then estimate the probability of a possible world by the fraction of samples equal to that world. To summarize:

- There's a true distribution that you want to compute.
- You generate samples drawn from this true distribution.
- You estimate the distribution by using these samples.

	small	medium	large
True probabilities	0.23	0.46	0.31
Samples	· ·	· · · · ·	· · ·
Estimated probabilities	0.2	0.5	0.3
Values	small	medium	large

Figure 11.1 The sampling principle. There's an unknown true probability distribution that you want to compute. To estimate this distribution, you generate a set of samples. The probability of generating a particular value should equal the true probability of that value. After you have a set of samples, you can estimate the probability of a value by seeing how many samples have that value.

The preceding example has a discrete variable with just three values. Sampling also works for variables with infinitely many values, such as continuous variables. In fact, sampling is perhaps most useful for such variables. Recall that continuous variables use a probability density function. Figure 11.2 shows two continuous variables between 0 and 1; each possible world consists of a value for each variable. The space of possible worlds is divided into regions with different probability densities. The darker the shade of the region, the higher the density. This region is covered with a set of samples. The density of samples in a region roughly reflects the probability density in the region. The number of samples in a region is an estimate of the probability of the region.

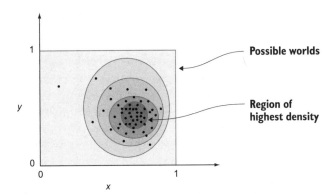

Possible worlds

Region of highest density

Figure 11.2 Covering the space of possible worlds using a set of samples. The darker shaded regions are regions of higher probability density. The density of samples is higher in high-density regions than in low-density regions.

There are two main kinds of sampling algorithms. In the first kind, which is more straightforward, you directly generate a sample from the desired distribution by running the probabilistic program. This kind of sampling is known as *forward sampling*, which I describe next. A practical forward sampling algorithm that's implemented in a number of probabilistic programming systems, including Figaro, is importance sampling, which is presented in section 11.2.

The second kind of sampling algorithm is known as *Markov chain Monte Carlo* (MCMC). The main idea of MCMC is that rather than sampling from a distribution directly, you define a sampling process that eventually converges to the true distribution. All of this is explained in detail in section 11.3.

11.1.1 Forward sampling

In forward sampling, you generate values for the variables in a probabilistic program one at a time. After you've generated a value for all of the variables, you have a possible world, which constitutes a single sample. Each time you generate a value for a variable, you use the definition of the variable: how it depends on its parents using its functional form and numerical parameters. Therefore, the variable's definition defines a probability distribution over this variable. You choose a value for the variable according to this distribution. Forward sampling proceeds in topological order: you always generate values for the parents of a variable before generating a value for the variable, so you always know exactly which distribution to use.

Here's pseudocode for forward sampling. This code generates a single sample consisting of values for all of the variables:

1 Let O be a topological order over the variables.
2 For each variable V in order O:

   a Let Par be the parents of V.
   b Let x_{Par} be the previously generated values for Par.
   c Draw x_V from $P(V \mid Par = x_{par})$.

3 Return **x** (a vector representing the value of x_V for every variable V).

The forward sampling process is illustrated in figure 11.3. The probabilistic program being sampled is shown on the left. The middle presents a tree that shows all possible ways of generating values for the variables in this program. The thick arrows show one particular sampling run. First, a value is generated for the variable `rembrandt1`, indicating whether the first of two paintings is by Rembrandt. Because this variable's definition is `Flip(0.4)`, the value `true` will be generated with probability 0.4, and `false` with probability 0.6. In the shown sampling path, the value `true` is generated. Next, a value is generated for `rembrandt2`. This variable doesn't depend on any other variables and is also defined by a `Flip`, so the process is similar. In the given run, the value `false` is generated for `rembrandt2`. Finally, `samePainter`, which represents whether the two paintings are by the same painter, is generated. (Only two possible painters are considered, so if neither painting is by Rembrandt, they're both by the other painter.) The variable `samePainter` depends on both `rembrandt1` and `rembrandt2`,

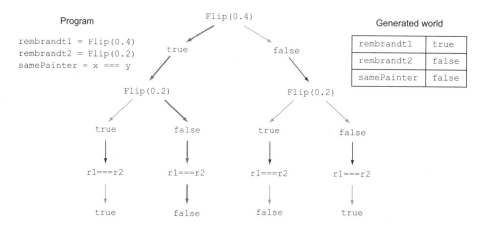

Figure 11.3 The forward sampling process. The tree shows all possible ways of generating values for the given program, along with a particular run through the tree. On the right is the possible world resulting from that run. (The abbreviations r1 and r2 are used for `rembrandt1` and `rembrandt2` in the tree.)

which have already been generated by this time. Because `rembrandt1` is `true` and `rembrandt2` is `false`, `samePainter` is automatically `false`.

In forward sampling, you run this process many times, each time generating a different possible world, or sample. Table 11.1 shows four samples for this program. Notice that the same sample can be generated multiple times; in this example, the second and fourth samples are the same. The probability of a possible world is estimated to be the fraction of samples equal to that world. For example, the probability of the world in which `rembrandt1` is `false`, `rembrandt2` is `false`, and `samePainter` is `true` is estimated to be $1/2$, because two out of four of the samples are equal to this world.

Table 11.1 Four samples generated for the program of figure 11.3

Element	First sample	Second sample	Third sample	Fourth sample
`rembrandt1`	`true`	`false`	`true`	`false`
`rembrandt2`	`false`	`false`	`true`	`false`
`samePainter`	`false`	`true`	`true`	`true`

The estimated sample distribution can also be used to answer queries. For example, what if you want to know the probability that the two paintings are by the same painter? You can see that three out of the four samples have the value `true` for `same-Painter`. So your estimated answer to this query is $3/4$.

WHY USE SAMPLING?

It's important to emphasize that the set of samples is only one possible representation of a probability distribution over the possible worlds. Forward sampling is a randomized process, so it can generate a different result every time. The estimated distribution you get from different runs of forward sampling will usually be different. Furthermore, they'll usually not be exactly the same distribution as the one defined by the probabilistic program. In fact, looking at the example, `Flip(0.4)` is `false` with probability 0.6, and `Flip(0.2)` is `false` with probability 0.8. The probability that they're both `false` is $0.6 \times 0.8 = 0.48$. And in this case, `Flip(0.4) === Flip(0.2)` will always be `true`. So the correct probability of the possible world equal to the second and fourth samples in table 11.1 is 0.48, not 0.5. In this particular example, the value is close, but in general there's no guarantee that the answer will be close, particularly if you don't generate a lot of samples.

Why, then, is sampling a good idea? This example has only three variables, and you can do all necessary calculations directly by using simple multiplication and addition. Many programs, however, have many variables, and these variables can have rich data types with a large number of or infinitely many values. In those programs, it may be impossible even to create all necessary factors to run a factored inference algorithm, let alone to perform all necessary multiplications and additions. With sampling, on the other hand, you need to consider only a relatively small number of possibilities and you get an estimate of the probability distribution you're seeking.

Here's an example program to bring the point home:

```
val x = Apply(Normal(0.4, 0.3), (d: Double) => d.max(0).min(1))
val y = Flip(x)
```

Here, x represents a normally distributed variable that's constrained to lie between 0 and 1. The variable y is defined to be a compound Flip, which is equivalent to Chain(x, (d: Double) => Flip(d)). Figure 11.3 showed the entire tree of possible sampling runs. In practice, however, this full tree is never created—only the subtree corresponding to values that are generated. In this example, the full tree is infinite, so you could never compute the exact probability distribution. Sampling computes only a finite fraction of the tree and uses it to estimate the distribution.

Figure 11.4 shows the tree generated by sampling this program. In each run, a real numbered value is generated for Apply. This is passed as an argument to Chain, resulting in a different Flip element each time. If four samples are generated, only the elements for the four specific Flips will be created; all of the infinitely many rest of the elements will never even exist.

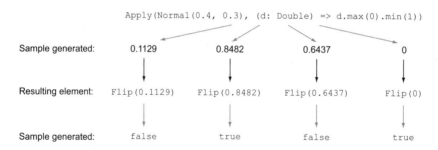

Figure 11.4   Partial tree generated by sampling

If the sampled distribution is only an estimate of the true distribution, what can be said about the result of sampling? Here are two important points, which you probably sense intuitively:

- *On average, the sample distribution will be equal to the true distribution.* Any particular sample distribution will be different from the true distribution, but if you average out all distributions you could take, the average distribution will be equal to the true distribution. Intuitively, this holds because each sample is drawn from the true distribution. The technical term for this property is that the sampling process is *unbiased.*

- *The more samples you use, the closer you expect the sample distribution to be to the true distribution.* Another way of saying this is that if you use the samples to answer a query, the expected error in the answer decreases as you use more samples. This is only the expected error; there are no guarantees. You might be unlucky and find your error increasing with more samples, but on average, your error will decrease. The technical phrase for this property is that *the variance of the sampling process decreases with more samples.*

Figure 11.5 illustrates the typical behavior of a sampling algorithm. The graph shows the probability of a query estimated by sampling as the number of samples is increased over time. You see that at first, the estimate tends to move rapidly toward the true probability and converges to the true probability in the long run, but at times the estimate diverges, and the convergence might be slow.

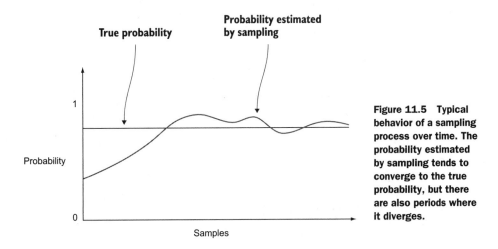

Figure 11.5 Typical behavior of a sampling process over time. The probability estimated by sampling tends to converge to the true probability, but there are also periods where it diverges.

These two properties are the key to why sampling is a useful approximate inference algorithm for probabilistic reasoning. According to these properties, *if you use a sampling process, you'll get an approximate distribution that's centered around the true distribution on average, and you expect it to get closer to the true distribution the more samples you use. If you use enough samples, you can expect to get as close as you want to the true distribution.*

> **WARNING** There's no silver bullet. Inference is a difficult problem, and sampling isn't always a great solution. Sometimes you have to use a really large number of samples to get close enough to the true distribution.

After you've generated a set of samples, it's easy to use them to answer queries. For example, to estimate the probability that a variable takes on a specific value, you compute the fraction of samples in which the variable has that value. To estimate the most likely value of the variable, you see which value is most common in the samples. So to summarize why sampling algorithms are so appealing: *you can get as close as you want to the true distribution if you use enough samples, and it's easy to answer queries by using the samples.*

11.1.2 *Rejection sampling*

So far, you've seen a forward sampling process that generates values for the elements in a model based on the definitions of those elements. The process defined so far hasn't considered evidence in the form of conditions or constraints. Without any evidence, the program defines the *prior distribution* over possible worlds. So the forward sampling procedure generates samples from the prior probability distribution.

Although this can be useful to understand the process, we're normally interested in answering queries about the *posterior distribution*, which is obtained after conditioning on the evidence. You need a way of generating samples from the posterior distribution.

A simple procedure to do this is called *rejection sampling*. Rejection sampling uses a simple principle, which is to use forward sampling as before, but reject any samples that disagree with the evidence. Only the samples that are consistent with the evidence are maintained.

> **NOTE** The algorithm presented here is a special case of a general mathematical concept. The rejection sampling algorithm presented here applies only to probabilistic programs that have conditions but not soft constraints.

Rejection sampling results from the fundamental approach to conditioning on evidence you've seen in chapter 4. Figure 11.6 should remind you how this works. You start with a prior probability distribution over possible worlds. When you observe evidence, you "cross out" the worlds that disagree with the evidence and assign them zero probability. You then normalize the resulting probabilities to get the posterior distribution.

Rejection sampling uses the same principle of crossing out worlds that disagree with the evidence. This is accomplished by deleting all samples that disagree with the evidence. The remaining samples represent the posterior distribution after conditioning on the evidence. You can then use these remaining samples to answer any queries.

Let's consider the same program as used in the example of table 11.1, but now let's add some evidence. Here's the modified program:

```
val rembrandt1 = Flip(0.4)
val rembrandt2 = Flip(0.2)
val samePainter = rembrandt1 === rembrandt2
rembrandt2.observe(false)
```

Table 11.2 shows the same table as table 11.1 except that samples disagreeing with the observation are deleted. The remaining samples represent the posterior probability distribution.

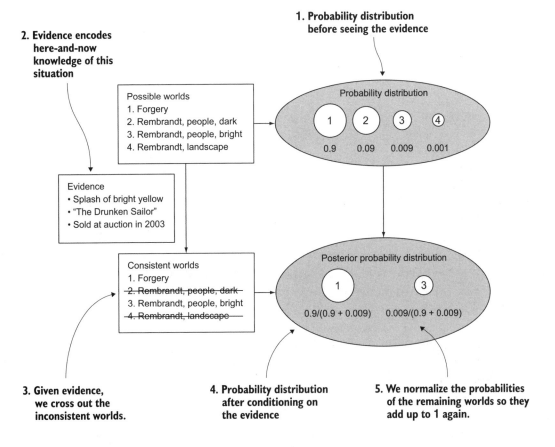

Figure 11.6 Figure 4.4 reproduced: the process of conditioning on evidence

Table 11.2 Rejection sampling with the observation that the `Flip(0.2)` element has the value `true`. Any samples that disagree with this observation are rejected.

Element	First sample	Second sample	Third sample	Fourth sample
rembrandt1	true	false	true	false
rembrandt2	false	false	true	false
samePainter	false	true	true	true

Table 11.2 shows the basic rejection sampling concept, but the actual rejection sampling algorithm has two optimizations. First, it's not an efficient use of memory to store samples that are eventually going to be rejected. Especially if the majority of samples are rejected, this can lead to you running out of memory before you get a decent

set of samples from the posterior distribution. Therefore, samples that disagree with the evidence are discarded as soon as they're created and aren't stored.

Second, it's not necessary to generate an entire sample before checking whether it's consistent with the evidence. It's possible to discard a sample as soon as a value for an element is generated that disagrees with the evidence on that element. In the third sample of table 11.2, as soon as the value `true` is generated for `rembrandt2`, you know that the sample will be rejected, so you don't have to generate `samePainter`. This can lead to significant time savings compared to waiting to reject until after the full sample has been generated.

The following is pseudocode for rejection sampling. This code runs multiple sampling attempts until it generates a single sample that's consistent with the evidence:

1 Let O be a topological order over the variables.
2 For each variable V in order O:

   a Let Par be the parents of V.
   b Let x_{Par} be the previously generated values for Par.
   c Draw x_V from $P(V \mid Par = x_{par})$.
   d If x_v is inconsistent with the evidence about V, start step 2 over again. (The sample is rejected immediately.)

3 Return **x**.

Here are the main things you need to know about rejection sampling:

- The good thing about rejection sampling is that samples that aren't rejected are drawn from the posterior probability distribution, conditioned on the evidence. And, the more samples you use, the closer you expect the sample distribution to be to the true distribution. This is just like forward sampling, with the addition being that you can now take the evidence into account.
- The not-so-good thing about rejection sampling is that the vast majority of samples could be rejected. Then, most of your work is wasted and it will take a long time to generate a decent set of samples. In general, the probability that a sample will be accepted is equal to the probability of the evidence. So if the evidence has low probability, the vast majority of samples will be rejected.

Can you estimate what the probability of evidence is? Suppose you have 10 tosses of a fair coin. The number of possible outcomes is 2^{10}. So any particular observation of 10n tosses has the probability $1/(2^{10})$. If you have 20 tosses, the probability is $1/(2^{20})$. This implies that if you use rejection sampling in this case, only $1/(2^{20})$ of your samples will be accepted—a small number. In general, the probability of the evidence decreases exponentially with the number of variables you have evidence about. This implies that the amount of work you have to do to generate a good sample set when using rejection sampling grows exponentially with the number of evidence variables. You might think that the ability of rejection sampling to reject samples quickly would mitigate this problem. Unfortunately, the savings from that are only linear in the number of evidence variables, which doesn't make up for the exponential cost.

As a result of this problem, although it's useful to illustrate the general principles, rejection sampling is generally not considered to be a practical algorithm. In addition, rejection sampling can handle only Figaro conditions, not more-general constraints. In the next two sections, you'll see two practical algorithms: importance sampling and Markov chain Monte Carlo. Importance sampling is similar to rejection sampling but uses a smarter approach to taking into account the evidence. Markov chain Monte Carlo, on the other hand, uses a completely different approach to sampling.

11.2　*Importance sampling*

Importance sampling is similar to rejection sampling. In fact, when importance sampling encounters a condition that isn't satisfied, it rejects the sample, just like rejection sampling. But two major differences exist. First, recall that in addition to conditions, Figaro provides constraints that aren't just true or false but instead assign a real number to each state. Rejection sampling is unable to handle constraints like this because a sample won't be completely inconsistent with the evidence, but will just have lower probability. Importance sampling is able to handle constraints, which don't result in rejection. Second, in the right circumstances, importance sampling can avoid rejecting with conditions by turning the conditions into constraints on other variables.

> **NOTE** Importance sampling is a more general algorithmic framework than I describe here. I'm focusing on the variation of importance sampling used by Figaro.

Before describing importance sampling, let me go into more detail about the meaning of Figaro conditions and constraints:

- A *hard condition* is a function from the value of an element to a Boolean. It specifies a property that a value must satisfy to have positive probability. To be precise, any possible world in which the element has a value that doesn't satisfy the condition will have probability 0. Therefore, a condition can be seen as multiplying the probability of a possible world by 0 if the value of the element doesn't satisfy the condition, and by 1 if it does satisfy the condition.
- A *soft constraint* is a function from the value of an element to a real number. I've said that a constraint can be interpreted as an "all else being equal" statement. For example, suppose you have an element with a constraint that returns 1.0 if the value of the element is `true`, and 0.5 if the value is `false`. Given two possible worlds that differ only in the value of this element, and whose probabilities would otherwise be equal, the probability of the world in which this element is `true` is twice as high as the world where this element is `false`.

　　Here's a more precise definition. Consider an element E with a constraint C. Ignoring the constraint, any given possible world will have some probability, p_0.

Let the value of the element in that possible world be e. Then the unnormalized probability of the element, taking into account the constraint, is $p_0 \times C(e)$. I say *unnormalized*, because when you interpret constraints in this way, the numbers won't generally add up to 1, so they have to be normalized to make them probabilities.

With that introduction, you're ready to look at how importance sampling works.

11.2.1 *How importance sampling works*

The main principle of importance sampling that makes it different from previous algorithms is that it uses *weighted samples*: instead of counting for a full sample, each sample stands for only a partial sample according to its weight. The probability distribution over possible worlds is then defined by the weights of the samples. I'll explain how this works in the upcoming subsection, and then show how importance sampling can avoid rejections.

WEIGHTED SAMPLES

In importance sampling, each sample is associated with a *weight*. This weight is based on the values of the conditions and constraints for the sample. When you encounter a constraint, you need to multiply the probability of the possible world by the value of the constraint. This is achieved by multiplying the weight of the sample by the value of the constraint. In the end, the value of the weight will be the product of the values of all the constraints.

To see how this works, let's modify the program used in table 11.2 as follows:

```
val rembrandt1 = Flip(0.4)
val rembrandt2 = Flip(0.2)
val samePainter = rembrandt1 === rembrandt2
rembrandt2.addConstraint((b: Boolean) => if (b) 0.1 else 1.0)
```

You've replaced the hard condition with a soft constraint. If `rembrandt2` is `false`, the constraint has the value 1.0; otherwise, the value is 0.1. When you generate the same samples as in table 11.1 and table 11.2, you associate each sample with a weight that is equal to the value of the constraint. The resulting set of weighted samples is shown in table 11.3.

Table 11.3 Weighted samples. Each sample is weighted by the value of the constraint on `Flip(0.2)`.

Element	First sample	Second sample	Third sample	Fourth sample
rembrandt1	true	false	true	false
rembrandt2	false	false	true	false
samePainter	false	true	true	true
Weight	1.0	1.0	0.1	1.0

A set of weighted samples defines a probability distribution over possible worlds. Imagine a process of choosing a sample at random, where the probability of choosing a sample is proportional to its weight. To get the probability of choosing a sample, you simply divide its weight by the sum of all of the weights, which is 3.1 for the four samples shown in table 11.4. For example, the probability of choosing the first sample is 1.0/3.1, whereas the probability of choosing the third sample is 0.1/3.1. Then, the probability of a possible world is the sum of the probabilities of choosing samples that agree with that possible world. So the probability of the world that corresponds to the second and fourth samples is 2.0/3.1. Putting all of this together, the weighted samples in table 11.3 define the posterior probability distribution in table 11.4.

Table 11.4 Posterior probability distribution defined by a set of weighted samples produced by importance sampling. The probability of a possible world is proportional to the sum of weights of samples that agree with that world.

`Flip(0.4)`	`Flip(0.2)`	`Flip(0.4)` `===` `Flip(0.2)`	Probability
true	false	false	1.0 / 3.1 = 0.3226
false	false	true	2.0 / 3.1 = 0.6452
true	true	true	0.1 / 3.1 = 0.0322

Because they define a probability distribution, the weighted samples can be used to answer queries. This can be done simply. For example, suppose you want to know the probability that x (the `Flip(0.4)` element) is true. The samples in which x is true are the first and third samples. Their total weight is 1.1. You divide this total weight by the total weight of all samples (3.1) to get the estimate P(x = true) = 1.1 / 3.1 = 0.3548.

In importance sampling, when you have multiple elements with evidence, you multiply the values of the constraints for each of the evidence elements. For example, suppose you add a second constraint on x to our program:

```
val rembrandt1 = Flip(0.4)
val rembrandt2 = Flip(0.2)
val samePainter = rembrandt1 === rembrandt2
rembrandt2.addConstraint((b: Boolean) => if (b) 0.1 else 0.9)
rembrandt1.addConstraint((b: Boolean) => if (b) 0.8 else 0.3)
```

The weight of a world in which `rembrant1` is true and `rembrandt2` is true is equal to $0.8 \times 0.1 = 0.08$.

Just as with forward sampling, it needs to be emphasized that this isn't the exact posterior probability; it's only an estimate based on the samples that were generated. The same properties hold as for forward sampling:

- On average, the sample distribution will be equal to the true distribution.
- The more samples you use, the closer you expect the sample distribution to be to the true distribution.

Therefore, importance sampling is potentially a good approximate inference method for probabilistic programming.

AVOIDING REJECTIONS

In the previous example, the evidence was specified as a soft constraint. This is a good thing, because one of the goals of importance sampling is to handle constraints. But what happens if you have a condition?

A condition is equivalent to a constraint in which the constraint values are 0 and 1. So, for example, you assert that the evidence

```
y.observe(false)
```

is equivalent to

```
y.addConstraint((b: Boolean) => if (b) 0.0 else 1.0)
```

Because you know how to handle constraints in importance sampling, you can also handle conditions. But there's a catch. If a sample disagrees with a hard condition, its weight will be 0, so it'll contribute nothing to the posterior distribution. This is equivalent to the sample being rejected. Because you know the sample will eventually have weight 0, you might as well reject it right away to save yourself some work.

At this point, it's time to see pseudocode for the basic importance sampling algorithm. The code returns a sample along with its weight:

1 Let O be a topological order over the variables.
2 $w \leftarrow 1$ (The weight is initialized to 1; if there are no constraints, the final weight will also be 1.)
3 For each variable V in order O:
   a Let Par be the parents of V.
   b Let x_{Par} be the previously generated values for Par.
   c Draw x_V from $P(V \mid Par = x_{par})$.
   d If x_v is inconsistent with the conditions on V, go to 2.
   e $w \leftarrow w *$ (product of constraints on V applied to X_V).
4 Return $(\mathbf{x}, w)$.

The preceding algorithm is no better than rejection sampling on hard constraints, which I said tends to be an impractical algorithm, taking too long to generate even a single sample. Rejecting samples that are inconsistent with the conditions is something you want to avoid if at all possible. The solution to this problem is to try to "push the evidence backward" through the program so that hard conditions on later elements turn into soft constraints on earlier elements. The general procedure for doing this is complicated, but I can illustrate with an example:

```
val x = Beta(1, 1)
val y = Flip(x)
y.observe(false)
```

Let's analyze this example. First, you generate a value for x. Let's say you generate 0.9. Next, you generate a value for y by using Flip(0.9). This comes out true with probability 0.9, and false with probability 0.1. So the probability that the observation will be satisfied is 0.1. You don't need to sample y to know this; it follows immediately from the definition of Flip. As soon as you sample 0.9 for x, you can give the sample a weight of 0.1, and you don't need to sample y. Similarly, if you sample 0.3 for x, the probability that the observation will be satisfied is 0.3, so you can immediately give the sample a weight of 0.7.

In general, if you sample the value p for x, the probability of the observation is $1 - p$. You can simulate giving the sample a weight of $1 - p$ by introducing a constraint on x. This constraint is equal to 1 minus the value of x. You can then force y to be false; you know it has to be false because of the observation, and you've already taken into account the effect of this observation in the constraint on x. To summarize, your program is equivalent to the following program:

```
val x = Beta(1, 1)
x.addConstraint((d: Double) => 1 - d)
val y = Constant(false)
```

See how you've turned a hard condition into a soft constraint? As a result, you won't reject any samples in this program but rather give them a weight based on the value of x.

NOTE Figaro doesn't contain a general procedure to do this for all conditions. Rather, it uses a set of simple heuristics that handle common situations. Using program transformation to move conditions and constraints earlier in a program is an active area of research, and we anticipate improving Figaro's capabilities in this regard in the future.

11.2.2 Using importance sampling in Figaro

Using importance sampling in Figaro is straightforward. Figaro provides both a one-time version of importance sampling that you run with a given number of samples and an anytime version that you can run as long as you like and get answers to queries while it's running. To use them, import com.cra.figaro.algorithm.sampling.Importance. The following code runs the one-time importance sampling algorithm with 10,000 samples on the query targets rembrandt1 and rembrandt2 and then issues queries on the result:

```
val algorithm = Importance(10000, rembrandt1, rembrandt2)
algorithm.start()
println(algorithm.probability(rembrandt1, true))
println(algorithm.distribution(rembrandt2).toList)
algorithm.kill()
```

The anytime version of importance sampling collects more and more samples the longer it runs, leading to better and better answers to queries. To specify that you want to use the anytime version, you don't pass it an integer argument for the number of samples, just the query targets. You would typically do something else while the algorithm is running. A simple way to wait for a period of time is to call `Thread.sleep`, which waits for the given number of milliseconds before continuing.

The following code runs anytime importance sampling for 1 second, prints the answer to a query, and then runs it for another second and prints the answer again:

```
val algorithm = Importance(x, y)
algorithm.start()
Thread.sleep(1000)
println(algorithm.probability(x, true))
println(algorithm.distribution(y).toList)
Thread.sleep(1000)
println(algorithm.probability(x, true))
println(algorithm.distribution(y).toList)
algorithm.kill()
```

An anytime algorithm runs in a separate thread. It's important to kill an anytime algorithm at the end to release the thread; otherwise, it will go on using system resources.

If you want to stop the algorithm from working for a while and resume it later, you can use the `algorithm.stop()` and `algorithm.resume()` methods, which do exactly what you expect. For example, you might do the following:

```
val algorithm = Importance(x, y)
algorithm.start()
Thread.sleep(1000)
algorithm.stop()
// Show an interactive visualization and wait for the user to be done
algorithm.resume()
Thread.sleep(1000)
algorithm.stop()
// Show an updated visualization, etc.
```

11.2.3 *Making importance sampling work for you*

When should you use importance sampling? There are usually two main reasons to use importance sampling:

- Your model has continuous variables. As you saw in chapter 10, although factored algorithms can work with continuous variables, they usually have to enumerate a small number of values of those variables, and therefore aren't as effective as with discrete variables with reasonably small ranges. If you want to consider the full range of values of these continuous variables, you should use a sampling algorithm such as importance sampling.

  An example of a model with continuous variables is a model for predicting the sales of various product lines. Sales, which are measured in dollars, are most naturally modeled as continuous variables. If you were to use a factored algorithm, you would have to reduce the sales numbers to a relatively small number of values, which might not give you the resolution you need.

- Your model has variable structure. If some parts of your model exist for only particular values of other variables, importance sampling will generate only the relevant variables for each sample. An example of this is the variable structure dynamic model of a restaurant you saw in chapter 8. The number of people who are seated at the restaurant at any time step is variable. In section 8.2.4, importance sampling was used for reasoning about this model.

It's important to emphasize that importance sampling isn't a magic bullet, even for the types of models where it's appropriate. The problem is that collecting a given number of weighted samples isn't the same as collecting that number of ordinary, unweighted samples. If you collect 1,000,000 weighted samples by using importance sampling, that might be only as good as 100 samples collected by rejection sampling. A concept called *effective sample size* characterizes the number of ordinary samples that a set of weighted samples is equivalent to.

The effective sample size is hard to characterize precisely, but intuitively, the lower the total weight of the samples, the lower the effective sample size. In general, the average weight of a sample is equal to the probability of the evidence as expressed in conditions and constraints. Therefore, the lower the probability of the evidence, the lower you would expect the effective sample size to be. This problem is similar to rejection sampling, where the lower the probability of the evidence, the fewer accepted samples you would expect to get.

With this consideration in mind, the best way to make importance sampling work well for you is to avoid extremely unlikely evidence. For example, instead of a hard condition that's unlikely to be satisfied, which will lead to a lot of rejections, use a constraint that has a low but nonzero value when the condition isn't satisfied. If you have a lot of such conditions and you replace them with constraints like this, you'll find that samples that agree with most of the conditions will have higher weight than samples that agree with fewer of the conditions. This should, in many cases, lead to reasonably good query answers. Unfortunately, although I can explain the intuition, it's hard in practice to get a handle on when exactly this will work well. The key condition for this to work is that samples that agree with more conditions are closer to the truth than samples that agree with fewer conditions. For an example, see the accompanying sidebar.

Example: solving a cryptogram with importance sampling

Let's imagine trying to solve a cryptogram by using probabilistic reasoning. A *cryptogram* is a sentence, written in code, that substitutes each letter of the alphabet with a different letter. You might have a probabilistic model that randomly chooses a specific letter to substitute for each letter. You might have two sets of conditions: that no two letters can be substituted by the same letter and that each word in the sentence has to be a valid English word.

> **(continued)**
>
> For rejection sampling, you'd randomly sample a set of substitutions and then check whether they satisfy the conditions. The probability that you generate a set of substitutions that satisfies all conditions is extremely small, so it'll take a long time before you generate even a single sample. But if you change these conditions to soft constraints, you might generate sets of substitutions that satisfy most but not all of the constraints. And these samples might give you an estimate of the posterior distribution that's useful. Although you're unlikely to generate the completely correct answer, you might find that in most of the highly weighted samples, the letter *E* is replaced by the letter *N*. This can help you make a guess that lets you move forward and solve the puzzle. This is a little bit like how humans solve cryptograms.

The bottom line about importance sampling is this:

- It's a general algorithm that can be applied to just about any model.
- It tends to break down when the evidence is unlikely because of the low effective sample size, but you can help a little by relaxing the evidence.

11.2.4 Applications of importance sampling

You've seen that importance sampling works better when you don't have extremely unlikely evidence. Accordingly, most of the practical applications of importance sampling are where you have little or no evidence.

PREDICTION VIA SIMULATION

When you have no evidence at all (no conditions or constraints in the program), importance sampling is the same as the simplest forward sampling algorithm introduced in section 11.1.1. Forward sampling involves predicting future developments by generating a large number of possible future runs. When used in this way, Figaro is effectively functioning as a simulation system. You can use Figaro's importance sampling algorithm for this purpose. You could use Figaro in this way in many relevant applications, such as elections, military campaign planning, economic systems, and sports predictions.

For example, suppose you want to simulate a soccer season to predict the final position of your team in the league table. You could create a model of an individual match that depends on the strengths of the two teams playing that match, and embed it within a model of the entire season that consists of all of the matches. Your model might allow for things such as injuries to players. When you run forward sampling, you'll simulate playing each of the games across the entire season to come up with a final league table. Using these simulations, you can count the fraction of times your team wins the championship. Taken over the course of a season, this is a complex model, and sampling is a natural approach to reasoning about it.

When you use importance sampling in this way, you'll typically have initial conditions, such as the initial strength of all of the teams in the league. There are three ways to model these:

- *As fixed Scala values*—This enables you to reason with them efficiently, but doesn't allow you to model random changes to the strength over the course of the season. If you're not planning to model changes, this might be the best approach to use.

- *As Figaro* Constant *elements*—For example, if your team has an initial strength of 0.96, you would use Constant(0.96) as the element representing its initial strength. You could then have a different element at each point during the season representing the strength at that point. The advantage of doing it this way is that it allows the strength to vary over the course of the season, but there's no need to introduce evidence about the strength at the beginning of the season. The Constant element can have only one value, so your team's initial strength will always be 0.96. This enables forward sampling to be used and to work efficiently.

- *As Figaro elements with nonconstant distributions*—You'd do this if you have uncertainty about the initial conditions. For example, for each team, you might believe that its distribution is within a certain range—your team might have a strength between 0.94 and 0.98, and you might use a Uniform(0.94, 0.98) element. The advantage of doing this is that you don't have to pick a particular value. But if you do have a particular value in mind (such as 0.96), you're better off using a Constant element, rather than using this element and setting evidence that the value is 0.96.

PREDICTION WITH EVIDENCE ABOUT THE INITIAL STATE

If you don't know the exact initial state, you might have some evidence about it. For example, you might believe that the strength of your team is related to its final position in last year's league table, along with an adjustment for players gained and lost in the off-season. To incorporate this evidence, you could sample the previous season, taking the final league table as evidence, to infer likely strengths of all of the teams last season. Then you could adjust these strengths for players gained and lost. Finally, you could simulate the new season by using these strengths as initial conditions. Here's a Figaro code skeleton to achieve this:

```
val lastYearsStrengths = Array.fill(Uniform(0, 1))
val lastYearsTable = playSoccerSeason(lastYearsStrengths)
lastYearsTable.observe(actualTable)
val thisYearsStrengths =
  lastYearsStrengths.map((strength: Element[Double]) => adjust(strength))
val thisYearsTable = playSoccerSeason(thisYearsStrengths)
println(Importance.probability(thisYearsTable, (t: Table) => myTeamTop(t)))
```

As long as the evidence about the initial state isn't too unlikely, importance sampling is an excellent candidate for this application. If you were to observe an entire season's worth of match results, that would be too much evidence for importance sampling to handle, and you're better off using MCMC.

You could imagine expanding this reasoning over multiple seasons. Maybe you use three past seasons to determine the initial conditions. In each previous season, you'd start with that season's strengths, play the season, observe the league table, and adjust for additions and deletions to get the next season's strengths. All of this reasoning would be done by importance sampling.

What I'm describing here is the basis of the particle-filtering algorithm for reasoning about dynamic models. In particle filtering, you begin with a set of samples representing the current state of the system at a point in time. You then use importance sampling to take into account the evidence at that time point. Particle filtering adds a step, called *resampling*. You can then carry out this process over however many time steps you want. You'll learn all about particle filtering in chapter 12, but I do want to point out that one of the main applications of importance sampling is particle filtering.

INFERENCE ABOUT A COMPLEX PROCESS WITH SMALL EVIDENCE

Importance sampling isn't used only to predict the future. It can also be effective for inference tasks, where the goal is to infer the value of a query variable based on the effects of that variable. Typically, you would use importance sampling in this way when the process by which the effect is generated is complex and there aren't many evidence variables. Here's an example.

Social network analysis uses various types of network-generating models, such as the Erdos-Renyi model and the Barabasi-Albert preferential attachment model. Social scientists might want to know which model is good for a certain observed network. Different models tend to produce different statistics, such as the maximum number of neighbors of a node, or the average distance between two nodes. Using these statistics, it's possible to infer which network-generating process was likely to have been used. In Figaro, the different network-generating models would return `Element[Network]`. The statistics would operate on these and return `Element[Double]`. Here's a code skeleton for this application:

```
class Network { … }
def erdosRenyi: Element[Network] = …
def barabasiAlbert: Element[Network] = …
def maxNeighbors(n: Network) = …
def averageDistance(n: Network) = …
val er = erdosRenyi()
val ba = barabasiAlbert()
val myNetwork = discrete.Uniform(er, ba)
val mn = myNetwork.map(maxNeighbors)           ◁——┐  Shorthand for
val ad = myNetwork.map(averageDistance)            │  Apply(myNetwork,
mn.observe(7)                                      │  (n: Network) =>
ad.addCondition((d: Double) => d > 0.31 && d < 0.35)  ◁——┘  maxNeighbors(n))
println(Importance.probability(myNetwork, er))
```

> Shorthand for Apply(myNetwork, (n: Network) => maxNeighbors(n))

> Uses a range for the condition to avoid it being too unlikely

Importance sampling works here because the evidence is only in the summary statistics of the network. Although a particular single network is unlikely to be generated, many networks have similar statistics, so the summary statistics aren't too unlikely. If, on the other hand, you had observed the exact network produced, it would have been unlikely for either network generation method to have produced the exact network observed, so importance sampling wouldn't have been effective.

From this discussion, you can see that importance sampling is an algorithm that's practical only when there aren't too many evidence variables and the evidence isn't too unlikely. Many real-world situations don't satisfy these conditions, so a different algorithm is needed. Typically, that algorithm is MCMC, discussed in the next section.

11.3 *Markov chain Monte Carlo sampling*

The Markov chain Monte Carlo (MCMC) algorithm addresses a fundamental limitation of importance sampling. In importance sampling, it can take a long time to generate a "good" sample that has high weight. After you generate one, you have to start all over again with the next sample. The main principle of MCMC is to *not* start over on each sample, but instead to start each step of the algorithm where the previous sample left off. This has two major benefits:

- MCMC can more quickly get to samples that have high probability.
- After finding a high-probability sample, MCMC tends to stay in the region of high-probability samples.

MCMC is a flexible and powerful algorithm. Let's take a look at how it works before considering practical issues.

11.3.1 *How MCMC works*

To illustrate the workings of MCMC, let's use the following example program:

```
val x = Normal(0.75, 0.2)
val y = Normal(0.4, 0.2)
x.setCondition((d: Double) => d > 0 && d < 1)
y.setCondition((d: Double) => d > 0 && d < 1)
val pair = ^^(x, y)
println(MetropolisHastings.probability(pair,
        (xy: (Double, Double)) => xy._1 > 0.5 && xy._2 > 0.5))
```

This program defines two normally distributed random numbers and specifies conditions to make sure their values are between 0 and 1. It then creates the pair consisting of the values of the two numbers. Finally, it uses the Metropolis-Hastings algorithm, which is the name of Figaro's MCMC algorithm, to compute the probability that both numbers are greater than 0.5.

Figure 11.7 shows how MCMC works. The figure shows a set of possible worlds (the square in which x and y take on values between 0 and 1). There's some probability distribution over the possible worlds; the circle region shows those worlds that have high probability. The MCMC algorithm goes through a sequence of states. At each time step, it randomly transitions to a new state. Each step is random, but it tends to move

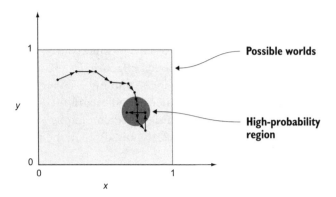

Figure 11.7   The MCMC process: the algorithm moves randomly through a sequence of states, gradually approaching the high-probability states

toward increased probability states. In the end, the algorithm usually reaches the states that have high probability.

WHY MCMC WORKS

Let's try to understand why MCMC works. There are three key points to understand; if you understand the logic of these three points, you'll know the essence of the algorithm.

MCMC, as its name suggests, relies on the theory of Markov chains, which you first encountered in chapter 8. To remind you, a Markov chain is a probabilistic model of a dynamic system that goes through a sequence of states. At each time step, it transitions from the current state to the next state according to some conditional probability distribution. It's easy to see why the MCMC algorithm defines a Markov chain: it goes through a sequence of states of the system, at each point transitioning from one state to the next according to a defined process. Figure 11.8 illustrates this Markov chain, using the same kind of diagram as in chapter 8.

Figure 11.8   A Markov chain showing the states that the MCMC algorithm goes through

Now, let's make a mental leap and move from a *sequence of states* to a *sequence of distributions*. Here's the logic. In any run of the Markov chain, the system goes through a sequence of states. At any time point, the system can be in any one of a number of states. There's always a probability distribution over the current state of the system; at any point in time, there's a probability distribution for that time point. In other words, the Markov chain defines a sequence of distributions, one for each time point.

Let's define this sequence of distributions. Given the current distribution at any time point, the Markov chain's transition model defines the next distribution. In Figaro, this would be accomplished using Chain, as follows:

```
val nextDistribution = Chain(currentDistribution, (s: State) =>
transition(s))
```

The next distribution is defined by the following generative process: start with a state drawn from the current distribution, and then apply the transition function to get the next state. As a result, you get the following property:

- *Point 1*—Starting from a given initial distribution, a Markov chain defines a sequence of probability distributions over states of the system.

Now, here's the subtle and beautiful thing about MCMC, and the reason that it works:

- *Point 2*—For any Markov chain satisfying certain mathematical conditions, the distribution at successive states converges to a single distribution.

This single distribution is called the *stationary distribution* of the Markov chain. The process is illustrated in figure 11.9. The most important thing to understand about this figure is that the shaded region doesn't show the possible states of x and y; rather, it shows the space of probability distributions over x and y. Each point in this space is an entire distribution, not just a single value of x and y.

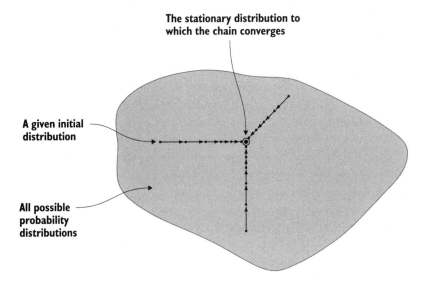

Figure 11.9 Convergence of the distribution over states defined by a Markov chain over time. The shaded area shows all of possible probability distributions over states. Each path shows the sequence of distributions, starting from a different initial distribution each time. No matter what initial distribution you start from, the process converges to the same stationary distribution.

The Markov chain starts with a particular initial distribution. In MCMC, this initial distribution is determined by the process that chooses the initial state of the system for the algorithm. In our example program, it's the process that chooses the initial values of x and y. For example, this process might set x and y to be equal to 0.5; this defines the probability distribution that gives this state a probability of 1.

The arrows in the figure show the process of moving from the distribution at one time point to the distribution at the next; again, this isn't transitioning between states but moving between distributions over states. As the figure shows, no matter what initial distribution you start with, the sequence of distributions converges to a limit, which is the stationary distribution. It may never reach the stationary distribution, but it can get as close as you want by taking enough steps. Furthermore, after the algorithm has converged close to the stationary distribution, it'll stay close.

The final point to MCMC is as follows:

- *Point 3*—If you design the Markov chain in such a way that the stationary distribution is the posterior distribution from which you want to sample, then by sampling from this stationary distribution, you're close to sampling from the posterior distribution.

THE MCMC ALGORITHM DEFINED

The essence of the algorithm is that starting from an initial state, you use the Markov chain to repeatedly move to a new state. After a long time, you know that the distribution over the current state is close to the posterior distribution from which you want to sample. At that point, you record a sample. The number of steps of the Markov chain you take before you record a sample is known as the *burn-in time*. The longer the burn-in time, the closer you get to the true posterior distribution. On the other hand, the longer the burn-in time, the more time MCMC takes to record a sample.

As I mentioned at the beginning of section 11.3, one of the main advantages of MCMC is that after it's found a high-probability state, it continues from that state rather than starting all over again. In MCMC, you never go back to the initial state, but continue using the Markov chain to transition between states. In principle, after you've collected one sample, you know you're near the true posterior distribution, so you should be able to collect a sample at every step.

There's a subtlety, however: the states at successive steps of MCMC aren't independent of each other. Consider our example program. Let's say the value of x at one time step is 0.9. If the Markov chain moves x by small amounts, the value of x at the next time step will be close to 0.9. It will be strongly dependent on the previous value. This can cause the answers to queries to be skewed. For this reason, you can specify an *interval* between samples that you collect in order to ensure that the samples are less dependent on each other. In practice, however, people find that using an interval doesn't necessarily improve the performance of MCMC, as it results in taking far fewer samples.

Figure 11.10 shows the progression of an MCMC sampler using a burn-in and interval. As you can see, the use of the burn-in has ensured that the first sample collected is already in the high-probability region. There's no way to guarantee this. You just have to guess how long it'll take and hope that your burn-in is large enough. Also in the figure, you see that the use of an interval of 2 has ensured that successive samples are far apart, meaning they're reasonably independent.

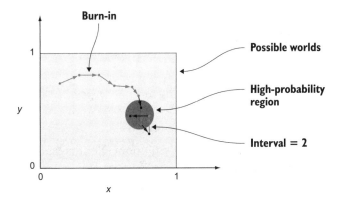

Figure 11.10 Progression of an MCMC sampler using a burn-in and interval. The burn-in samples are skipped; then, every second sample is taken due to the interval of 2.

More formally, here's a specification of the MCMC algorithm. The algorithm takes three parameters: a number of samples, a burn-in time, and an interval time.

1 Draw an initial state from the initial distribution of the Markov chain.
2 *Burn-in phase*—repeat for the burn-in time:
   a Transition to a new state using the transition model.
3 Record the current state as the first sample.
4 *Sampling phase*—repeat until the number of samples has been collected:
   a Repeat for the interval time:
      i Transition to a new state using the transition model.
   b Record the current state as a sample.

11.3.2 Figaro's MCMC algorithm: Metropolis-Hastings

Point 3 indicates that if the Markov chain is designed so that the stationary distribution is the posterior distribution from which you want to sample, you get the basis of an algorithm to sample from the posterior distribution. There are many ways to design a Markov chain with this property. Figaro's MCMC algorithm uses one approach, based on an algorithm known as *Metropolis-Hastings* (MH). MH is a widely used algorithm because of its general applicability, which also makes it suitable for probabilistic programming, with its ability to express many kinds of models.

The basic idea of Metropolis-Hastings is to use a Markov chain in which the transition model has two steps:

1 Given the current state (the set of values for variables in the model), propose a new state. This new state is chosen according to a proposal distribution, which is a probability distribution over the next state given the current state. This proposal distribution depends on the current state; for example, it might favor making small steps away from the current state. Much of the art of designing an MH algorithm is in choosing the proposal distribution.

2 Choose whether to accept the new state or keep the current one according to an acceptance probability. The acceptance probability depends on properties of the proposal distribution, as well as the relative probabilities of the new state and the current state.

In Figaro, the proposal distribution is specified by using a *proposal scheme*. There's a default proposal scheme, as well as an API for specifying your own custom proposal schemes. The default proposal scheme works as follows:

1 Choose a single nondeterministic element at random. Nondeterministic means that the value of the element is random even if its arguments are known; for example, `Flip` and `Normal` are nondeterministic, but `Constant` and `If` aren't.
2 Propose a new value for the chosen element.
3 Update the values of elements that depend on this chosen element.

In the default scheme, you have no control over which element gets chosen in step 1; it's chosen uniformly from all nondeterministic elements. In a custom proposal scheme, you can propose multiple elements, and you get control over which elements you propose. In some cases, the default scheme will work well, and it's generally worth trying first. In other cases, you'll need to design your own custom scheme. Custom proposal schemes are discussed in section 11.4.1.

CREATING A METROPOLIS-HASTINGS ALGORITHM IN FIGARO

Figaro provides ways to create an instance of MH with different configurations of arguments. The most common way specifies the number of samples you want to take, the proposal scheme, and the query targets. For example,

```
MetropolisHastings(100000, ProposalScheme.default, x, y)
```

specifies that you want to take 100,000 samples by using the default proposal scheme to obtain approximate posterior distributions for x and y. This is a one-time version of the algorithm that runs until a specified number of samples is completed. There's also an anytime version of the algorithm, where you don't specify the number of samples and can run it for as long as you like; for example,

```
MetropolisHastings(ProposalScheme.default, x, y)
```

In these versions of the algorithm, there's no burn-in, so MH starts collecting samples right away. The interval is 1: every single state gets collected as a sample. You can also provide an optional burn-in and an optional interval. For example, to specify a burn-in of 1,000 with 100,000 total samples taken, you can use

```
MetropolisHastings(100000, ProposalScheme.default, 1000, x, y)
```

In this example, the interval is 1. As you can see, you can specify a burn-in with the default interval of 1. It's common to specify a burn-in, because you want to avoid sampling from the early distributions defined by the Markov chain, which might be far from the true distribution. But in most cases, you don't need to worry about the interval and can leave it at 1. If you do want to specify the interval, you also have to specify the burn-in. The burn-in argument appears first, followed by the interval. For example, to specify a burn-in of 1,000 and an interval of 10, you would use

```
MetropolisHastings(100000, ProposalScheme.default, 1000, 10, x, y)
```

Anytime versions of all of these variants can also be used. Figure 11.11 shows the structure of an MH constructor, including all of the optional arguments.

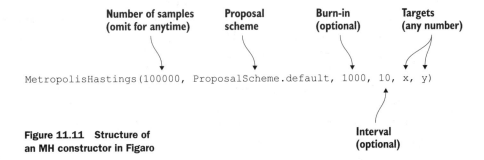

Figure 11.11   Structure of an MH constructor in Figaro

PROPERTIES OF MH

MH is a widely used algorithm because of its general applicability. Its main advantage is that rather than randomly sampling a new state at every iteration, the sampling process guides the algorithm to sampling high-probability states. Once more, after it has found the high-probability region, it tends to stay there. This can make sampling feasible in cases where importance sampling doesn't work well because the probability of the evidence is too low.

To understand why MH can find high-probability states, whereas importance sampling can't, let's take our simple example with the two variables x and y. Suppose you have a constraint on each of x and y that's hard to satisfy. To be concrete, let's say the constraints on x and y have high value within a narrow band that occurs 1 in 10 times when you sample x and y from their prior probability distribution. For the other 9 out of 10 times, the constraints have low value. Using importance sampling, you'll generate a new x and y every time from the prior distribution, so the probability that both constraints have high value is 1 in 100. So it'll effectively take 100 iterations of importance sampling to get a single usable sample.

On the other hand, let's imagine an MH process where you can propose either x or y separately. On average, after 10 total proposals of either x or y, one of them will have a constraint with high value. Let's say this is for variable x. When MH later proposes x again, it will almost always reject a move that makes the constraint have low value. So x will almost always stay in the high-probability region. Meanwhile, after a few more proposals of y, its constraint will also have a high value.

Now imagine the same situation except that you have 100 variables. For importance sampling, the probability of generating a sample that has high value for all constraints is 10^{100}, meaning that it'll effectively never happen. But MH can move each variable to its likely region one at a time, eventually finding a state where all variables have high constraint values.

Although this advantage makes MH attractive for many applications, it has disadvantages. *The main disadvantage is that it can be a slow algorithm.* If you don't specify an interval between samples, you generally have to collect many more samples than for importance sampling because the samples aren't independent. Depending on the problem, the number of samples that you need can be orders of magnitude higher than for importance sampling. If you do decide to use an interval, the interval has to be large to make the samples effectively independent, so it takes a correspondingly long time to generate even a single sample. Furthermore, it can take a long time to burn in and get close to the high-probability region in the first place. Therefore, in situations where the evidence doesn't have extremely low probability, importance sampling is a better choice.

A second disadvantage of MH is that it can be hard to understand, predict, and control its behavior. The effectiveness of MH depends on defining a good proposal distribution. Intuitively, you want the algorithm to move around the state space fairly quickly, so it doesn't take too long to find the high-probability region, but not so quickly that it tries to leave the high-probability region as soon as it finds it. These properties are sensitive to the proposal distribution; designing a good proposal distribution with these properties can be tricky, and it's often hard to predict how a particular proposal distribution will behave. What's more, it's easy to accidentally define a proposal distribution that doesn't fully explore the state space at all. I'll have more to say about this in the next section.

A side effect of the difficulty predicting the behavior of MH is that it's hard to know how long to make the burn-in time and how many samples to take in total. If you don't know how long it'll take to reach the high-probability region, how do you know when to stop the burn-in? And if you don't know how long it takes to move from one state to a nearly independent state that nevertheless stays in the high-probability region, how do you know how many samples to take? Therefore, what you generally have to do is run MH for a long time and see whether your answers look reasonable. One option is to use multiple runs to see whether the answers you get in different runs are similar; if they're not, you're probably not taking enough samples.

As a result, despite its power and generality, I often consider MH an algorithm of last resort. Try it if none of the other algorithms works, but recognize that it might take more effort to get it to work well. The next section covers techniques that can help make MH work better.

11.4 Getting MH to work well

This section presents techniques for getting MH to work well. I'll use a challenge problem that's hard to make work without these techniques.

Imagine that you're trying to predict the winner of the best actor award at the Oscars. There's a set of candidates. Each candidate is an appearance of a specific actor in a specific movie. According to your model, whether or not an appearance wins the award depends on the fame of the actor and the quality of the movie.

Our first attempt to model this situation in Figaro is as follows:

```
class Actor {
  val famous = Flip(0.1)
}

class Movie {
  val quality = Select(0.3 -> 'low, 0.5 -> 'medium, 0.2 -> 'high)
}

class Appearance(val actor: Actor, val movie: Movie) {
  val award: Element[Boolean] =
    CPD(movie.quality, actor.famous,
        ('low, false) -> Flip(0.001),
        ('low, true) -> Flip(0.01),
        ('medium, false) -> Flip(0.01),
        ('medium, true) -> Flip(0.05),
        ('high, false) -> Flip(0.05),
        ('high, true) -> Flip(0.2))
}
```

This code uses object-oriented modeling patterns from chapter 7 and should be self-explanatory. But the code has a problem. There's nothing to stop the award attribute of different appearances from having the value true. So in any given possible world, any number of appearances can have an award. You know this can't be the case, so you add a condition to enforce that exactly one appearance is awarded. This is achieved as follows:

```
def uniqueAwardCondition(awards: List[Boolean]) = {
  awards.count(b => b) == 1
}
val allAwards: Element[List[Boolean]] =
  Inject(appearances.map(_.award): _*)
allAwards.setCondition(uniqueAwardCondition)
```

> **Check whether the number of true awards is 1**

> **Create an element whose value is the list of award Booleans, collected from an array of appearances**

> **Set the condition of this element to enforce the unique award condition**

To complete the description of a situation, you need to create some instances of actors and movies and connect them together in appearances. In practice, the actors, movies, and appearances might be created from a database. In the book code repository, I create the appearances at random as follows:

```
val numActors = 200
val numMovies = 100
val numAppearances = 300

val actors = Array.fill(numActors)(new Actor)
val movies = Array.fill(numMovies)(new Movie)
val appearances =
    Array.fill(numAppearances)(new Appearance(
        actors(random.nextInt(numActors)),
        movies(random.nextInt(numMovies))))
```

Unfortunately, if you naively apply MH to this problem, it won't work at all. The problem is this: In a possible world with positive probability, exactly one appearance has an award. You want MH to explore the space of possible worlds with high probability. If you start in one possible world in which one appearance has an award, you want to move to another state in which this appearance doesn't have an award and exactly one other appearance has an award. Figure 11.12 shows why this won't happen. The figure shows the Bayesian network for a case with two actors, movies, and appearances, but the same problem holds with any number. Under the default proposal scheme, a proposal could change the fame of a single actor, the quality of a single movie, or the award of a single appearance. Changing the fame of an actor or quality of a movie is fine. But if the current state satisfies the unique award condition, changing the award

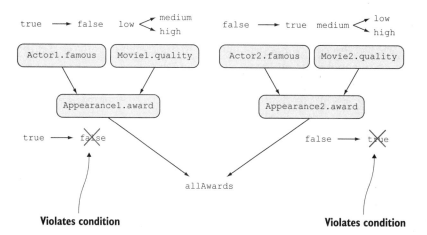

Figure 11.12 Possible single-step proposals for the naïve application of MH to the actors and movies example. Variables are shown in rounded rectangles. For each variable, the current value is to the left of the arrow, and possible alternative values are to the right. Under the default proposal scheme, in a single step, MH can change any one of the variables from the current value to a different value. Two values can't be changed simultaneously. Therefore, any proposal that changes the value of an award variable will violate the unique awards condition, so it won't be accepted.

of a single appearance will necessarily violate that condition. If you change the award of the appearance that currently has an award, you'll move to a state where zero appearances have an award; if instead you change the award of an appearance that currently doesn't have an award, you'll move to a state where two appearances have an award. In either case, the new state violates the condition and will be rejected. There's no way to switch the award from one appearance to the other in a single MH step.

How do you get MH to work on this problem? There are two main ideas. The first is to use proposal schemes that are different from the default scheme. These custom schemes can, for example, propose to change two elements at once. The second idea is to avoid hard conditions that can never be violated. One of the problems in our example is that the unique award condition absolutely has to be satisfied for a proposal to be accepted. If you could relax this and sometimes accept proposals with zero or two awarded appearances, the MH algorithm would occasionally be able to change an award. The next two subsections elaborate on these two ideas.

11.4.1 *Customized proposals*

The first problem is that you're using the default proposal scheme. Figaro provides a language for describing custom schemes. Recall that the default proposal scheme chooses a single nondeterministic element at random, but a custom proposal scheme lets you propose multiple elements and gives you control over which elements they are. In particular, a custom proposal scheme lets you do the following:

- Propose multiple elements in sequence
- Choose between multiple alternatives
- Start with one element, and then decide how to continue based on the value of that element

The accompanying sidebar provides details as to how each of these is achieved. I'll now show you how to create a custom proposal scheme for the actors and movies example. In this example, you want to be able to propose two appearances at the same time. Figaro lets you propose multiple elements in sequence by using the following construct:

```
ProposalScheme(element1, element2, …)
```

So if appearances is an array of instances of the Appearance class whose length is numAppearances, you can create a proposal scheme that proposes the award elements of two random appearances by using this:

```
ProposalScheme(
  appearances(random.nextInt(numAppearances)).award,
  appearances(random.nextInt(numAppearances)).award)
```

You also want to propose the fame of an actor or the quality of a movie sometimes. To get the effect you want, you can use a DisjointScheme, which lets the algorithm choose between several proposal schemes, each with a given probability. In our example, you create a Scala value called `scheme` that contains the `DisjointScheme` you want:

```
val scheme: ProposalScheme = {
  DisjointScheme(
    (0.5, () =>
      ProposalScheme(appearances(random.nextInt(numAppearances)).award,
                     appearances(random.nextInt(numAppearances)).award)),
    (0.25, () =>
      ProposalScheme(actors(random.nextInt(numActors)).famous)),  .
    (0.25, () =>
      ProposalScheme(movies(random.nextInt(numMovies)).quality)))
}
```

Now you have the proposal scheme you want. You either propose the awards of two random appearances, possibly leading to a switch, or the fame of a random actor, or the quality of a random movie.

Proposal schemes in general

Figaro provides a little language for defining proposal schemes. Besides the default proposal scheme, here are some things you can do:

- *Choose between multiple alternatives*—Suppose you want to randomly choose between a number of proposal schemes, each with a given probability. `Disjoint-Scheme(probability`$_1$` -> schemeFunction`$_1$`, …, probability`$_n$` -> scheme-Function`$_n$`)` achieves this. Each scheme function is a function that takes zero arguments and returns a proposal scheme. In the actors and movies example, `() => ProposalScheme(actors(random.nextInt(numActors)).famous)` is an example of a scheme function. The `DisjointScheme` chooses one of the scheme functions with the appropriate probability, and then applies the scheme function to get the proposal scheme to use.
- *Propose multiple elements in sequence*—`ProposalScheme(element`$_1$`, …, element`$_n$`)` will propose `element`$_1$` to `element`$_n$` in turn. Because you ordinarily don't want to propose exactly the same elements in every iteration of MH, this proposal scheme is typically used as the result of a scheme function, such as one used in a `DisjointScheme`. This is how it's used in our example.
- *Start with one element, and then decide how to continue based on the value of that element*—Sometimes, you want to propose one element and then decide how to continue proposing based on the chosen value for that first element. An example is proposing an actor's fame and a movie's quality when they become awarded. `TypedScheme` is used in this kind of situation. It takes two arguments. The first argument is a function that returns the first element to propose. Its type is `() => Element[T]`, where `T` is the value type of the first element. The second argument to `TypedScheme` has type `T => Option[Proposal-Scheme]`. That is, it takes the generated value for the first element, which has type `T`, and based on that value, it either returns `None`, indicating that proposing should stop, or it returns `Some[proposalScheme]`, indicating that proposing

(continued)

should continue with the given `proposalScheme`. For example, consider the following code:

```
val appearance = appearances(random.nextInt(numAppearances))
TypedScheme(
  () => appearance.award,
  (b: Boolean) =>
    if (b) Some(ProposalScheme(appearance.actor.fame,
                               appearance.movie.quality))
    else None)
```

This proposal scheme chooses a random appearance and first proposes the award of that appearance. If the new value of `appearance.award` is `true`, it goes on to propose `appearance.actor.fame` and `appearance.movie.quality` in sequence. Otherwise, it stops proposing.

There's also an `UntypedScheme`, where the decision of how to continue doesn't depend on the value chosen for the first element proposed.

Unfortunately, there's still a technical snag in our actors and movies example, which results from the way Figaro's MH algorithm works. Let's take another look at the definition of the `award` attribute:

```
class Appearance(val actor: Actor, val movie: Movie) {
  val award: Element[Boolean] =
    CPD(movie.quality, actor.famous,
        ('low, false) -> Flip(0.001),
        ('low, true) -> Flip(0.01),
        ('medium, false) -> Flip(0.01),
        ('medium, true) -> Flip(0.05),
        ('high, false) -> Flip(0.05),
        ('high, true) -> Flip(0.2))
}
```

The problem is that in the program, the `award` attribute of `Appearance` is defined as a CPD. A CPD is a deterministic element; although there are `Flips` inside the CPD, if the values of those `Flips` are fixed, the value of the CPD is fully determined. The `Flips` inside the CPD are arguments to the CPD element. When an element is proposed, the arguments are kept fixed and the value of the element is sampled. Because the CPD is deterministic, the same value will always be sampled, given the values of the `Flips`. As a result, you won't ever propose a switch in the value of `award`.

Although the preceding explanation is a bit technical, the bottom line is this: *always try to make elements you propose nondeterministic elements.* Atomic elements are generally nondeterministic, except for `Constant`. Compound elements, meanwhile, are usually deterministic. CPD is a compound element, and it's deterministic. A few exceptional compound elements are nondeterministic: compound `Flip`, compound `Select`, and compound `Dist`. Other compound elements, however, such as compound `Normal`, are defined using `Chain` and are deterministic.

How do you make `award` a nondeterministic element? The trick is to transform the program into an equivalent program in which `award` is nondeterministic. This can be achieved through the following definition:

```
class Appearance(val actor: Actor, val movie: Movie) {
  def getProb(quality: Symbol, famous: Boolean): Double =
    (quality, famous) match {
      case ('low, false) => 0.001
      case ('low, true) => 0.01
      case ('medium, false) => 0.01
      case ('medium, true) => 0.05
      case ('high, false) => 0.05
      case ('high, true) => 0.2
    }
  val probability: Element[Double] =
    Apply(movie.quality, actor.famous,
          (q: Symbol, f: Boolean) => getProb(q, f))
  val award: Element[Boolean] =
    Flip(probability)
}
```

Function that determines the probability to use, based on the quality of the movie and the fame of the actor

Element representing the probability to use

Chooses the value of award by flipping a coin with the appropriate probability

You can see why this definition is equivalent to the original definition of `award`. In the original definition, every clause of the CPD resulted in a `Flip` with some probability. In this new definition, you also use a `Flip`, and the probability is equal to exactly the same probability in every case. This `Flip` is a compound `Flip`, which, as I've just said, is nondeterministic. So proposing this `Flip` can result in a switch of values. This enables MH to work well on this example.

11.4.2 Avoiding hard conditions

Even with the custom proposal scheme and program transformation from the previous section, our example still might not work properly. Here's the problem. Suppose you start in a state where four movies are awarded. In any one step, with our custom proposal, the most awards you can change are two. You'll have at least two movies awarded at the end of the step, so the proposal won't satisfy the unique awards condition and will be automatically rejected. As a result, you'll never be able to move to states that satisfy the condition.

The crux of the problem is that you have a hard condition that absolutely has to be satisfied for a proposal to be accepted. You saw in section 11.2.3 that hard conditions can be a problem for importance sampling. The same is true for MCMC. With hard conditions, it can be difficult to find any state that satisfies the conditions in the first place. And then, after the algorithm has found one, it can be hard to move to any other.

The solution is to replace the hard condition with a soft constraint. Ideally, the constraint will guide the algorithm toward the best states. In our example, you can use the following constraint:

```
def uniqueAwardConstraint(awards: List[Boolean]) = {
  val n = awards.count(b => b)
  if (n == 0) 0.0 else 1.0 / (n * n)
}
```

This constraint counts the number of award values that are true and assigns this number to a variable, n. It then returns a score based on the value of n. If n is nonzero, the score is $1/n^2$. This means that if n is 1, the score is 1, and the score decreases rapidly as n increases. Meanwhile, if n is 0, the score is 0, making this state impossible according to the constraint.

What is the effect of this constraint? Let's consider what state you start in:

- If you start in a state for which the number of awards is zero, any new state with at least one award will automatically be accepted.
- If you start in a state with one award, the algorithm usually will accept only new states with one award, but occasionally (1/4 of the time) will accept new states with two awards, and even less often (1/9) will accept new states with three awards.
- If you start in a state with more than one award, the algorithm will always accept states with fewer awards, because the constraint value is higher. It'll also occasionally accept states with a higher number of awards, but in general the tendency will be to move toward the good state of one award.

You can think of this constraint as a "lubricant" that facilitates flow of the Markov chain between states, tending toward the states with one award. Without this lubricant, the chain is too stiff and can't move around properly. This technique of using a constraint as a lubricant is commonly used. It can help not only to reach the high-probability states in the first place but also to move freely among the high-probability states after it has found them.

You can find the full code for this example in the book's code repository. As this example illustrates, you sometimes need to go to considerable lengths, including custom proposals, program transformations, and tailoring the constraints, to get MCMC to work. If you're lucky, the default proposal scheme will work, but if not, the degree of difficulty in getting the algorithm to work is significantly greater than for other algorithms. This is a major reason that I consider MCMC to be an algorithm of last resort. Nevertheless, if you're willing to invest the effort, the rewards can be significant, as you can get results on problems where no other algorithm works.

11.4.3 Applications of MH

MH has been applied to a wide variety of problems, but, as discussed, applying it to a given problem can take some work. Each application is unique, and unfortunately I don't know of any magical formulas that will make your particular application work well. I can say that the applications where MH tends to work best are those where the observations are the result of lots of small interactions between variables, without depending on combinations of many variables. In the previous section, you saw that the unique awards condition depended on combinations of the awards variables, and that significant work was required to make sure the correct combinations were always used. When this isn't required, MH will work much more easily.

Let's revisit the soccer prediction model discussed in section 11.2.4. In that section, I said that importance sampling might work well when the only observation is the league table, but if the results of all of the matches are observed, it wouldn't work well and MH might be better. In fact, this is the kind of application that MH can work well on out of the box. What are the random variables in the model? There are the strengths of the players and other aspects of the team, as well as the results of all of the matches. No single variable governs all of the other variables, and the match outcomes depend on the other variables in a cumulative way. For example, if a team's center forward is good, that will tend to lead them to winning more matches, no matter what the values of the other variables. The default proposal scheme is likely to work reasonably well on this problem.

A practical application domain where MH is used is image and video analysis. If you're just trying to recognize a single object in an image, you might be best off using a nonprobabilistic approach such as a deep neural network. But if you want to interpret an image or video more deeply (for example, to recognize relationships between objects or activities), a probabilistic model can be beneficial. The probabilistic model can provide a frame of knowledge with which to interpret the image. For example, consider the action sequence of a soccer player kicking a ball toward the goal and the goalie attempting to make a save. A dynamic probabilistic model can encode a probability over such event sequences. Each particular event in the sequence will produce an image or video properties as evidence. A probabilistic inference algorithm can be used to infer likely action sequences, given the evidence.

MCMC algorithms are generally used for this task, for several reasons. First, the structure of the action sequences is flexible and variable, making them difficult to capture with a small number of random variables, and therefore less amenable to factored inference. Second, the images or videos have variables with many possible values for brightness and color, again making factored algorithms less practical. Finally, importance sampling isn't applicable because the images or videos constitute unlikely evidence.

A practical application of MH to this problem might treat the variables representing the action sequence as a single unit for the purpose of proposals. For example, suppose the current action sequence has the center forward kicking the ball to the left side of the goal and the goalie diving to her right (the center forward's left) to make the save. If you then propose the center forward kicking the ball to the right, it doesn't make sense for the goalie to continue diving to her right. Therefore, you need a proposal scheme that also sends the goalie to her left. By carefully crafting the proposal schemes, MH can be made to work effectively.

> **SCIENTIFIC APPLICATIONS OF MH** The MH algorithm is particularly popular in sciences such as biology and physics. In biology, for example, a probabilistic model can be used to capture the relationship between the genotype of an organism, which represents its genetic material, and its phenotype, which represents how these genes are manifested in the organism to produce traits. One query of interest is to find out which gene causes a given trait of interest. Complicating matters is that we don't always know which version of a gene a particular organism has, but the versions of nearby genes on the same chromosome are correlated. The different versions of genes, as well as the traits, can be represented by random variables, and a joint probabilistic model can be expressed over the genotype and phenotype. With this model, MH can be used both to learn general relationships between genes and traits and to infer specifically which versions of genes a given individual has.

In the preceding two chapters, you've learned a lot about the algorithms used for inference in probabilistic programming. I've focused on the problem of computing the posterior probability distribution over query variables given evidence, but other queries are also useful, such as finding the most likely values of variables or computing the probability of evidence. These tasks require their own algorithms, which are variants of the algorithms you've seen in these two chapters. It's also important to be able to learn the parameters of probabilistic programs from data. The next chapter shows you how to do all of these things.

11.5 *Summary*

- Sampling algorithms generate states drawn from the probability distribution over possible worlds and answer queries by looking at the frequency of values in the samples.
- On average, the distribution represented by the samples will be equal to the true distribution, but any given sample distribution will vary from the true distribution by some amount.
- The more samples you generate, the closer you expect the sampling distribution to get to the true distribution, and the more accurate your query answers. Unfortunately, getting as close as you want may require many samples.
- Rejection sampling is a simple sampling algorithm that generates samples from the prior probability distribution defined by the program and rejects any samples that don't satisfy the conditions. It doesn't handle constraints and works poorly with many conditions.
- Importance sampling uses weighted samples to factor in constraints and avoids rejections where possible, leading to better performance than rejection sampling. But importance sampling can require many samples with hard-to-satisfy conditions or constraints with small values due to the low effective sample size.

- Markov chain Monte Carlo (MCMC) is a type of algorithm that reuses its work as it goes along. It randomly searches for the high-probability region of the state space, and after it has found that region, tends to move about it. This can lead to better performance than importance sampling with hard-to-satisfy constraints or low-value conditions.

- MCMC can require a large number of samples and can be hard to understand and control. Making MCMC work on real problems often requires extra effort, using techniques such as custom proposals and tailored constraints.

11.6 *Exercises*

Solutions to selected exercises are available online at www.manning.com/books/practical-probabilistic-programming.

1 For the following program:

```
val x = Flip(0.8)
val y = Flip(0.6)
val z = If(x === y, Flip(0.9), Flip(0.1))
z.observe(false)
```

a Run variable elimination to compute the exact posterior probability that y is true, given the observation about z.

b Run importance sampling using 1,000 samples, 2,000 samples, and so on up to 10,000 samples. For each number of samples, run the experiment 100 times. Compute the *root-mean-square error* of importance sampling with the given number of samples, defined as follows:

  i For each experiment, measure the difference between the probability estimated by importance sampling and the exact probability computed by variable elimination. This is the error.

  ii Compute the square of this error for each experiment.

  iii Compute the mean of all these squared errors together.

  iv Take the square root of the mean. This is the root mean squared error, which is a common way to measure the error of an inference algorithm.

c Plot the root-mean-square error on a chart. What kind of trend do you notice?

2 Repeat exercise 1 for Metropolis-Hastings using the default proposal scheme. This time, use 10,000 samples, 20,000 samples, 30,000 samples, and so on up to 100,000 samples.

3 Now let's change the program slightly by making the numerical parameters more extreme:

```
val x = Flip(0.999)
val y = Flip(0.99)
val z = If(x === y, Flip(0.9999), Flip(0.0001))
z.observe(false)
```

    a Run variable elimination to get the exact posterior probability of y.

    b Run importance sampling with 1,000,000 samples.

    c In this program, the evidence is unlikely. But you should see that importance sampling is accurate on this program. Why do you think that is?

4 Run Metropolis-Hastings on the same program using the default proposal scheme with 10,000,000 samples. You should see a poor result. (This may not happen every time, but over multiple runs the results will tend to be poor.) Why do you think this problem is hard for Metropolis-Hastings?

5 Try writing a custom proposal scheme for Metropolis-Hastings:

    a Because we'll be proposing the `Flip`s inside the definition of z, we have to make them separate variables that we'll refer to. Make the `Flip(0.9999)` a variable named z1, and the `Flip(0.0001)` a variable named z2, and use the new variables in the definition of z.

    b Create a custom proposal scheme that behaves as follows:

        i With probability 0.1, propose z1.

        ii With probability 0.1, propose z2.

        iii With probability 0.8, propose both x and y.

    c Run Metropolis-Hastings using this proposal scheme. This should produce better results. Why do you think this is the case?

6 Chapter 6 included an exercise to write a probabilistic program to represent the game Minesweeper. Try using this program to compute the probability that a square contains a mine. Experiment with different algorithms.

12

Solving other inference tasks

This chapter covers

- How to query the joint probability of multiple variables
- How to compute the most likely values of all variables in your model
- How to compute the probability of your observed evidence

So far, you've looked at ways of answering questions such as "What's the probability that the printer power switch is off, given that it's not printing correctly?" or "What's the probability that I'll win the Oscar, given my skill and the movie's quality?" All of these questions can be summarized as answering the query of computing the posterior probability distribution over a single variable, given the evidence. A variety of other inference tasks can be performed using probabilistic programming. These include the following:

- Computing the joint probability distribution over multiple variables
- Computing the most likely values of the variables, given the evidence
- Computing the probability of the evidence (the probability that a possible world generated by the model will satisfy the evidence)

- Monitoring the state of a dynamic system over time
- Learning the parameters of a model so they can be used for reasoning later

This chapter shows how the first three of these tasks are performed. The remaining two tasks are covered in the next chapter. For each task, I describe what it is and why it's useful, and then present examples before showing you how the algorithms work and how you perform them in Figaro. Fortunately, the algorithmic principles you learned in the previous chapters carry over to these tasks, so the material should be mostly familiar to you, with some interesting new ideas.

To follow this chapter, you should have a basic understanding of Figaro modeling, although advanced techniques will generally not be used. Because the algorithms in this chapter build on those of chapters 10 and 11, you should have a good understanding of those chapters.

12.1 Computing joint distributions

Until now, you've seen a variety of algorithms for computing a probability distribution over a single variable. This distribution is known as the *marginal distribution* over that variable. When you call the various algorithms, such as variable elimination or importance sampling, you supply them with a list of query targets. For example, suppose you have a probabilistic program that predicts the amount of sales for different product lines. You would supply each product line's sales element as a query target. You can then query the probability that sales of a given product line will exceed a certain level or meet the expected level of sales of the product line.

But what if you wanted to query the joint distribution over multiple variables? Why would you want to do that? Because the joint distribution contains information that the individual marginal distributions don't. For example, you might be interested to know the probability that the sales of two product lines would simultaneously be low, because that would be particularly bad for your business. Here are some possibilities for the joint distribution:

- The sales of the two product lines are independent; one line's sales being high or low has no bearing on whether the other line's sales are high or low.
- The sales of the two product lines are correlated, so that when one is low, the other is also more likely to be low. This indicates a risky situation.
- The sales of the two product lines are anti-correlated, so that when one is low, the other is more likely to be high. This is a less risky situation, because it's unlikely that both will be low at the same time.

Given only the individual marginal distributions, you have no way of knowing which of these possibilities holds. So how can you query joint distributions?

Figaro doesn't have a specialized algorithm for computing joint distributions. Instead, you have to create a special element to capture the joint behavior of the elements whose joint distribution you want to query. You can then use any of the inference algorithms from the previous chapters. To create the special element, you use Figaro's tuple constructor, which is the `^^` operator.

For example, suppose you have an array of sales elements. The following creates a pair of the first two sales elements:

```
val salesPair = ^^(sales(0), sales(1))
```

In contrast, this creates a four-tuple of sales elements:

```
val sales4Tuple = ^^(sales(0), sales(1), sales(2), sales(3))
```

> **NOTE** The tuple constructor `^^` is defined for up to five arguments. If you need more than five, you can use nested tuples, as in `^^(^^(sales(0), sales(1), sales(2)), ^^(sales(3), sales(4), sales(5)))`.

You can then query these tuples as single elements whose values are tuples. For example:

```
VariableElimination.probability(salesPair,
  (pair: (Double, Double)) => pair._1 < 100 && pair._2 < 100)
```

Creating tuples and reasoning about them isn't without cost for factored algorithms. Creating a tuple is equivalent to creating a factor over all components of the tuple. So for `sales4Tuple`, you have a factor over `sales(0)`, `sales(1)`, `sales(2)`, and `sales(3)`. You may have had such a factor already, in which case there's no problem. But maybe you didn't have such a factor, and creating this factor significantly increases the cost of the algorithm.

For sampling algorithms, this isn't an issue. You'll create only select values of each of the tuple components, and each combination of the components translates into one value of the tuple. So if you find that your factored algorithms are getting too expensive when computing joint probabilities, try a sampling algorithm.

In general, as you increase the number of elements being joined, the number of possible values of the tuple grows exponentially. Not only is it harder to compute, but it can also be difficult to interpret joint distributions over many variables. If you find yourself wanting to query joint distributions over many variables, try using a summary statistic instead. For example, instead of the joint distribution over the sales of many product lines, why not compute a distribution over the total sales? This can be accomplished easily by using Figaro collections. For example:

```
val allSales = Container(sales:_*)
val totalSales =
  allSales.foldLeft((x: Int, y: Int) => x + y)
println(Importance.probability(totalSales,
          (i: Int) => i > 1000))
```

The notation `:_*` turns the sales array into a variable argument list for the Container constructor.

The foldLeft method folds the addition function through all sales elements to get the total sales element.

NOTE You'll find a full code example illustrating the concepts in this section in the book's code repository. The same goes for all sections in this chapter.

12.2   *Computing the most probable explanation*

Sometimes, rather than knowing a probability distribution over outcomes, you want to know which outcomes are the most likely. Let's consider the printer diagnosis problem. You observe symptoms of the printer; for example, it's printing slowly. The goal of probabilistic inference in this case is to find out the most likely state of the system (the printer, the software, the network, and the user, that led to the observed symptoms). Identifying the most likely state tells you the most likely cause of the problems you're seeing, which you can then fix.

The query that tells you the most likely state of variables in the model is known as the *most probable explanation*, or MPE. When you're performing diagnosis, you want the overall best hypothesis so you know how to fix it. You'll typically operate using the following process, illustrated in figure 12.1:

1 Observe initial symptoms as evidence in the model. For example, a printer user might complain that there's no print result, so the evidence "none" is observed in the printer network for the Print Result Summary variable.

2 Compute the MPE to determine the most likely state of the system. The figure shows that in the most likely explanation, the printer power button is off, but all of the other possible causes of poor printing aren't present. So the most likely reason for no print result is that the printer power is off.

3 Check whether the fault or faults identified in step 2 are actual faults, and if so, attempt to fix them. In our example, the user might check the power button and see that it's on.

4 Check to see if the fix solved the problem. If it did, you're finished. In our example, the power button being off wasn't the issue, so the printer problem isn't yet solved.

5 If the fix didn't solve the problem, add additional evidence, and return to step 2. The bottom half of the figure shows the added evidence that Printer Power Button On is true and the resulting MPE. In this MPE, the most likely fault is that the network is down. The user can then check this fault and attempt to correct it. In our example, the user found that the network cable was unplugged, and the problem was solved by plugging it back in.

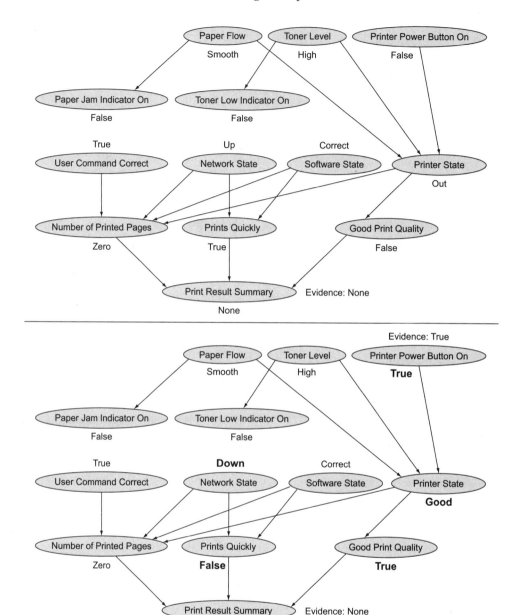

Figure 12.1   Using MPE for diagnosis. The top image shows the first inference on the printer network of chapter 5. The user is complaining that there was no print result, so the evidence "none" is asserted for the Print Result Summary variable. An MPE query is run, and the figure shows the most likely value of each variable. According to the MPE, the most likely fault is that the printer power button is off. A test is performed to see whether the button is on or off, and it's found to be on. So the evidence "true" is asserted for the Printer Power Button On variable. The bottom image shows the MPE query with this added evidence. Most likely values that have changed since the first query are shown in bold. Now the most likely fault is that the network state is down.

Let's take another example. Say you have a degraded image that you want to complete. You can use probabilistic inference to recover the true image, given the pixels that you observe. You have some choices:

- Compute the marginal probability distribution of each individual pixel. Although this is computationally feasible, it's not ideal for recovering the full image, because it gives you only a separate distribution for every pixel. It doesn't tell you which pixel values are likely to go together. It may be that the choice that you make for some pixels should affect your choice about other pixels, which isn't captured in the marginal distributions.
- Compute a joint probability distribution over all pixels in the image. Unfortunately, this isn't computationally feasible. The number of possible values of all pixels is exponential in the number of pixels, which can be quite large.
- Compute the most likely *joint* value of all pixels in the image. This value, the MPE, is the most likely value of all pixels taken together, not a composite of the most likely values of individual pixels. This has the advantage of being computationally feasible, because you're computing only one value. In addition, the MPE captures the interactions between the pixels, unlike the individual marginal distributions.

The MPE is illustrated in table 12.1. Here you have two pixels that are either On or Off. The table shows four possible worlds for these two pixels, along with their associated probabilities. If you consider just pixel 1, the sum of probabilities of possible worlds in which pixel 1 is Off is 0.65, whereas it's 0.35 for On. So the most likely value for pixel 1 is Off. Similarly, the most likely value for pixel 2 is Off. But the possible world where pixel 1 is Off and pixel 2 is On has probability 0.45. This is the highest probability of any possible world, so it's the MPE. You see clearly that the MPE isn't the composite of the most likely values of individual variables.

Table 12.1 The most probable explanation isn't necessarily a combination of the most likely values of individual variables. Here, the most likely value of each pixel is Off, but the most probable explanation has pixel 1 = Off and pixel 2 = On.

Pixel 1	Pixel 2	Probability
Off	Off	0.2
Off	**On**	**0.45**
On	Off	0.35
On	On	0

To summarize, MPE is a useful kind of query for many applications. Let's see how you compute the MPE in Figaro.

12.2.1 Computing and querying the MPE in Figaro

The interface for computing and querying the MPE in Figaro is simple. Figaro contains three algorithms for computing MPE: two factored algorithms, `MPEVariable-Elimination` and `MPEBeliefPropagation`, and a sampling algorithm, called `MetropolisHastingsAnnealer`. I'll describe how these algorithms work in the next section, but first, I'll show you how to use them.

Each of these algorithms is an instance of `MPEAlgorithm`. Like other algorithms, `MPEAlgorithm` has one-time and anytime variants. `MPEBeliefPropagation` and `MetropolisHastingsAnnealer` have both one-time and anytime variants, but `MPE-VariableElimination` is only one-time. This example illustrates the use of the one-time algorithms, but you can use the anytime variants in the same way as usual.

Let's recall the image-recovery scenario from chapter 5. In this scenario, you were trying to predict the color of a pixel in an image. The image is defined by a Markov network. Each pixel has a unary constraint specifying that its individual probability of being On is 0.4. Each pair of adjacent pixels also has a binary constraint, specifying that, all else being equal, they're twice as likely to be the same as different. The Markov network for this example is shown in figure 12.2, where the arrays start from Pixel 11 as they do in the image-recovery scenario in chapter 5.

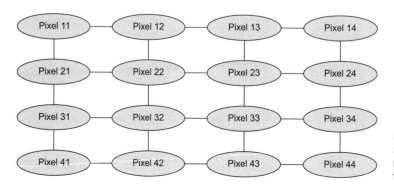

Figure 12.2 Image-recovery Markov network, reproduced from chapter 5

The following listing shows some code that illustrates how to use each of these algorithms to compute MPE for the image-recovery example. In the following listing, the pixel indices start from 00.

Listing 12.1 Recovering an image using MPE

```
val pixels = Array.fill(4, 4)(Flip(0.4))         ◁───┐  Create the pixel
                                                      │  elements and add unary
def makeConstraint(pixel1: Element[Boolean],          │  constraints on them
                   pixel2: Element[Boolean]) {
  val pairElem = ^^(pixel1, pixel2)
  pairElem.setConstraint(pair                        Add binary constraints
      => if (pair._1 == pair._2) 1.0 else 0.5)       on pairs of pixels
}
```

```
for {
  i <- 0 until 4
  j <- 0 until 4
} {
  if (i > 0) makeConstraint(pixels(i-1)(j), pixels(i)(j))
  if (j > 0) makeConstraint(pixels(i)(j-1), pixels(i)(j))
}
```
Apply the binary constraints to neighboring pixels

```
pixels(0)(0).observe(true)
pixels(0)(2).observe(false)
pixels(1)(1).observe(true)
pixels(2)(0).observe(true)
pixels(2)(3).observe(false)
pixels(3)(1).observe(true)
```
Observe the values of some of the pixels as evidence

This method applies the given algorithm to the model defined in the preceding lines. The pixels are the elements in the model, and the algorithm will be applied to them.

```
def run(algorithm: OneTimeMPE) {
  algorithm.start()
  for { i <- 0 until 4 } {
    for { j <- 0 until 4 } {
      print(algorithm.mostLikelyValue(pixels(i)(j)))
      print("\t")
    }
    println()
  }
  println()
  algorithm.kill()
}
```
Query the most likely value of the given pixel and print the result

Create and start a one-time MPE algorithm to compute the MPE. After this call completes, the most likely value of every pixel will have been computed.

```
def main(args: Array[String]) {
  println("MPE variable elimination")
  run(MPEVariableElimination())
  println("MPE belief propagation")
  run(MPEBeliefPropagation(10))
  println("Simulated annealing")
  run(MetropolisHastingsAnnealer(100000, ProposalScheme.default,
                Schedule.default(1.0)))
}
```
MPEVariableElimination takes no arguments.

MPEBeliefPropagation takes the number of BP iterations as argument.

The three arguments to MetropolisHastingsAnnealer are described in the next section.

As you can see in listing 12.1, the pattern for computing and querying MPE is similar to ordinary probability queries:

1. Create all of the elements.
2. Add any conditions and constraints that are part of the definition of the model.
3. Observe evidence.
4. Create an instance of the appropriate algorithm.
5. Start the algorithm.
6. Query for the most likely values of individual elements. Although you query one element at a time, these are the values of these elements in the most likely joint state.

When run, this program produces the following output:

```
MPE variable elimination
true    true    false    false
true    true    false    false
true    true    false    false
true    true    false    false

MPE belief propagation
true    true    false    false
true    true    false    false
true    true    false    false
true    true    false    false

Simulated annealing
true    true    false    false
true    true    false    false
true    true    false    false
true    true    false    false
```

This example is particularly easy, and all of the algorithms quickly produce the right answer. But on more challenging problems, each algorithm has its own advantages and disadvantages. Let's take a closer look at these algorithms and when and how they work well.

12.2.2 *Using algorithms for solving MPE queries*

Algorithms for solving MPE queries are typically variants of algorithms for solving ordinary probability queries. As with ordinary queries, you can use a factored algorithm or a sampling algorithm. I'll first describe the two factored algorithms together and then describe the sampling algorithm. Because you already understand the basic principles of these algorithms, I won't go into as much detail as in chapters 10 and 11, but just point out the main ideas.

FACTORED MPE ALGORITHMS

The goal of MPE is to compute the possible world that has the highest probability. For example, suppose a possible world consists of pixel value p_{00} for Pixel 00, value p_{01} for Pixel 01, and so on through value p_{33}. The probability of this world is P(Pixel 00 = p_{00}, ..., Pixel 01 = p_{01}, ..., Pixel 33 = p_{33}). You want to maximize this probability. This means that you want to know this:

$$\max_{p00} \max_{p01} ...\max_{p33} P(\text{Pixel } 00 = p_{00}, ..., \text{Pixel } 01 = p_{01}, ..., \text{Pixel } 33 = p_{33})$$

Recall from chapter 10 that the probability of a possible world is a product of factors. In this case, it's a product of the unary factors over individual pixels, and the binary factors over adjacent pixels. The maximum probability of any possible world is the max of the product of factors. This is known as a *max-product* expression. If the unary factors are U and the binary factors are B, you can write the following max-product expression:

$$U(\text{Pixel } 00 = p_{00})\, U(\text{Pixel } 01 = p_{01})\, ... U(\text{Pixel } 33 = p_{33}) \times$$

$$\max_{p00} \max_{p01} ... \max_{p33} B(\text{Pixel } 00 = p_{00}, \text{Pixel } 01 = p_{01})\, ... B(\text{Pixel } 32 = p_{32}, \text{Pixel } 33 = p_{33}) \times$$

$$B(\text{Pixel } 00 = p_{00}, \text{Pixel } 10 = p_{10})\, ... B(\text{Pixel } 23 = p_{23}, \text{Pixel } 33 = p_{33})$$

In this expression, the first row contains unary factors, the second row contains binary factors over pairs of pixels that are adjacent horizontally, and the third row contains the binary factors for pixels that are adjacent vertically. Altogether, you take the maximum, over all variables, of the product of these factors.

Just like ordinary variable elimination (VE) operated by manipulating a sum-product expression, so MPE VE operates by manipulating a max-product expression. It eliminates one variable at a time. The process of eliminating a variable is illustrated in figure 12.3. It begins in a way similar to ordinary variable elimination. As with ordinary variable elimination, you first multiply all factors that mention that variable. Instead of summing out the variable being eliminated, you *max out* that variable. This produces a factor over all variables that were mentioned in a factor with the variable being eliminated. In this example, it creates a factor over pixel 21 and pixel 12.

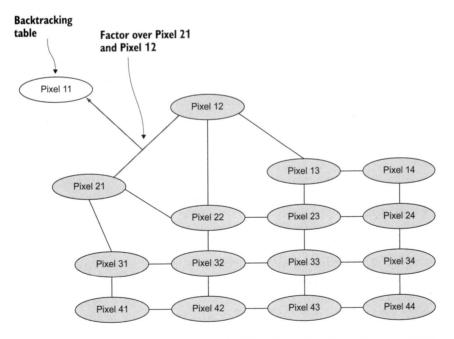

Figure 12.3 Result of eliminating pixel 11 in the MPE VE algorithm. A new factor is created over pixel 11 and pixel 12. In addition, a backtracking table is created that enables recovering the most likely value of pixel 11 after the values of pixel 21 and pixel 22 are known.

The operation of maxing out a variable is analogous to summing out a variable. In both cases, you remove the given variable from the factor. In the case of summation, for each combination of values of the other variables, the factor contains the sum of numbers associated with those values. Similarly, in the case of maximization, the factor contains the maximum of the numbers associated with each of the values of the remaining variables.

The process is illustrated by the example in table 12.2, which shows two variables, pixel 1 and pixel 2, connected by the factor shown in the table. Table 12.3 shows the factor resulting from maxing out pixel 2. The variables in this factor are taken from all factors mentioning the variable being eliminated, except for the eliminated variable itself. In this example, the only variable in this factor is pixel 1. For any given value of pixel 1 (say, Off), the entry in this factor is the maximum entry of any row in the input factor consistent with this value. The two rows consistent with pixel 1 being Off have entries 0.2 and 0.45, so the maximum is 0.45.

Table 12.2 Input factor for eliminating pixel 2

Pixel 1	Pixel 2	Entry
Off	Off	0.2
Off	On	0.45
On	Off	0.35
On	On	0

Table 12.3 Factor resulting from maxing out pixel 2 from the factor in table 12.2

Pixel 1	Entry
Off	0.45
On	0.35

In addition to the factor produced from maxing out a variable, a second table is created when eliminating a variable. This is a *backtracking table* that enables the algorithm to recover the most likely value of the variable being eliminated, after the most likely values of the other variables have already been determined. When solving an MPE problem, you're not interested only in finding the possible world with highest probability. You're also interested in finding the values of variables in this possible world. The backtracking table produced is intended to achieve this. This table lists, for every possible value of the non-eliminated variables, the value of the eliminated variable that leads to the highest entry in the input factor.

In our example, the backtracking table is shown in table 12.4. The non-eliminated variable is pixel 1, and the eliminated variable is pixel 2. The table shows, for each value of pixel 1, the value of pixel 2 that leads to a maximum entry in the factor in table 12.2. Suppose pixel 1 is Off. In the input factor, a value of Off for pixel 2 leads to an entry of 0.2, whereas a value of On leads to 0.45. So when pixel 1 is Off, the maximizing value of pixel 2 is On. You record this value in the table.

Table 12.4 Backtracking table produced when eliminating pixel 2 from the factor in table 12.2

Pixel 1	Pixel 2
Off	On
On	Off

At the end of the process, all of the variables have been eliminated. You can then trace backward through the tables to find the MPE. Let's start with the last variable to be eliminated; let's say it's pixel 1. Because no other variables are eliminated after that variable, you have a table with only a single value for pixel 1; let's say that value is Off. You can read that value as the most likely value of pixel 1. Then, you move back to the one before the last variable eliminated; let's say this is pixel 2. You go to the backtracking table produced when eliminating pixel 2, shown at the bottom right of table 12.2. You look for the row with pixel 1 = Off and read off pixel 2 = On as its most likely value. You continue in this way through all of the variables in reverse order of elimination and end up with the full MPE.

MPE belief propagation (BP), meanwhile, is extremely similar to ordinary BP. Just like BP, it works by passing messages between the nodes and performing factor operations on these messages. The only difference is that instead of performing a summation operation at every node, you perform a maximization. The maximization operation is the same as the one shown at the bottom-left of table 12.2. MPE BP is often called the *max-product algorithm.*

The main thing to remember about MPE VE and MPE BP is that their properties are similar to the ordinary algorithms. MPE VE is an exact algorithm, so if it's feasible, it's the best choice. Its complexity is the same as for ordinary VE: exponential in the size of the largest clique in the graph induced by the elimination order. So it will work well on precisely the same set of problems as ordinary VE. For image recovery, the size of the largest clique is equal to the number of pixels on a side of the image. In the preceding example, with only four pixels, MPE VE was feasible, but as the number of pixels is increased, the cost will be exponential in the number of pixels per side.

MPE BP is an approximation algorithm, with properties similar to BP. It often works well and quickly, but there are no guarantees that it will produce the optimal result. The same ideas that work well for ordinary BP can help make MPE work well: avoiding too many loops, merging elements together, decomposing CPDs with lots of parents, and using attenuating CPDs. Simplifying the network can help both MPE VE and MPE BP.

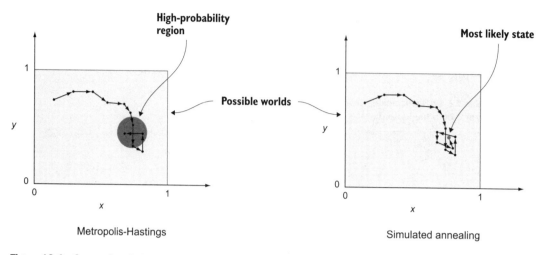

Figure 12.4   Comparison between Metropolis-Hastings and simulated annealing

SIMULATED ANNEALING

The most common sampling MPE algorithm is known as *simulated annealing* (SA). SA is closely related to Metropolis-Hastings. In MH, the sampler wanders around the state space, eventually reaching a state with probability equal to the probability of that state. It doesn't necessarily find the most likely state; rather, it tends to move around the various high-probability states. SA, in contrast, seeks out the most likely state. It moves around the state space, generally moving toward states with higher probability, although occasionally it takes "backward" steps toward lower-probability states. Figure 12.4 illustrates the difference between MH and simulated annealing trajectories.

The reason SA sometimes moves toward lower-probability states is to help it explore the state space better. If it were to move toward only higher-probability states, it might get stuck in a local maximum, where it's in a state that has higher probability than its neighboring states, but other states further away have much higher probability. Exploring the state space lets SA avoid being stuck in a local maximum and find an overall better part of the state space. SA tries to find a balance between exploring the state space and moving toward high-probability states. At the beginning, it tends to favor wandering around, and at the end it focuses on finding the nearby states with high probabilities.

SA achieves this balance by using the concept of temperature. Intuitively, the temperature controls how SA explores the state space. If the temperature is high, SA tends to randomly explore the state space. If the temperature is low, it aggressively moves toward more likely states. The SA strategy is to start with a high temperature and cool it down over time, so it starts out with more exploration and ends by honing in on the likely states.

Different implementations of SA use the temperature in slightly different ways. Figaro's implementation essentially works as follows. Let the state you start in have probability p_0 and the proposed new state have probability p_1. If the temperature is t, the probability of accepting the new state is given by

$$\left(\frac{p_1}{p_0}\right)^{1/t}$$

What effect does the temperature have? Let's examine how likely it is for the new state to be accepted, as a function of the temperature. If p_1 s greater than p_0, this number will be greater than 1 and the new state will always be accepted. Otherwise, the probability of acceptance depends on the temperature. If the temperature t is infinity, the probability of acceptance is always 1, so the new state will always be accepted. This corresponds to pure exploration. If t is 0, the new state will never be accepted unless it's at least as likely as the previous state, so this corresponds to purely moving toward the high-probability states. In between, values of t will lead to different balances of exploration and probability maximization. In general, the smaller the value of t, the less the algorithm will explore.

> **NOTE** In the technical definition of the algorithm, the probability of acceptance also depends on properties of the proposal distribution being used to propose the new state. In Figaro, the terms that depend on properties of the proposal distribution usually cancel out, so as far as you're concerned, it depends on the ratio between the probabilities of the states.

The rate at which the temperature changes over time is controlled by the *cooling schedule*. The cooling schedule determines when and how fast the temperature gets colder. In other words, the cooling schedule controls how much the algorithm explores before it starts maximizing the probability. Figaro provides a default cooling schedule that's standard; it should be good enough for you in most cases.

The default cooling schedule has one parameter that controls the cooling speed. Higher values for this parameter make the cooling slower. In general, the higher this parameter, the longer annealing will take to find the most likely value, but the less likely you'll be to end up with a local maximum. One approach is to start with a value of 1.0 and increase it if you suspect you're getting to a local maximum.

> **CONTEXT** In physics, annealing is a technique to find low-energy states of a material by gradually cooling it down. Low-energy states correspond to states of high probability. At hot temperatures, the material moves around different energy states, whereas at cooler temperatures, it tries to reduce the energy directly. The cooling schedule controls how much different energy states are explored and how rapidly a minimum energy state is found.

You can create an instance of SA as follows:

```
MetropolisHastingsAnnealer(100000, ProposalScheme.default,
                Schedule.default(1.0))
```

The standard `MetropolisHastingsAnnealer` constructor takes three arguments: the number of samples to take, the proposal scheme (here we're using the default scheme), and the cooling schedule (here we're using the default schedule with a parameter of 1.0).

SA has many of the same properties as MH. It's a general algorithm that works on a wide variety of models. But it can be slow, and getting it to work well can be tricky. You have to not only provide the proposal scheme, but also specify the cooling schedule. Even if you have a good proposal scheme, a subtle interaction occurs between the cooling schedule and the number of iterations. The best way to manage this interaction is through trial and error.

One technique is to compare the results of different iterations. If you're consistently getting the same result, it's probably the right answer. If you're getting different results, you're probably hitting local maxima and should slow down the cooling schedule by increasing the parameter. If you're getting similar but not quite the same results, SA probably hasn't converged to a maximum yet. You should either speed up the cooling schedule or run for more iterations.

12.2.3 *Exploring applications of MPE algorithms*

In practice, computing the MPE is almost as widely used as computing the probability of query variables given evidence. Examples of applications include the following:

- *Recognizing likely action sequences*—Given a sequence of images or a video, you might want to know what activity is being performed. For example, if you have a video of a soccer match, you might want to detect which actions are being performed (the corner kick is taken, the center forward leaps up and heads the ball toward the goal, the goalie dives and saves the ball). The possible action sequences and resulting images in a soccer game can be represented as an HMM.

  In an HMM, the MPE task is to compute the most likely sequence of hidden states, given the observations. In chapter 10, you saw that VE is a good algorithm for HMMs because of their linear structure. Likewise, MPE VE is good for solving the MPE task in HMMs. For HMMs, MPE VE is known as the *Viterbi algorithm*.

- *Producing the most likely parse of a natural language sentence*—In chapter 10, you learned that PCFGs are simple and popular frameworks for representing probabilistic models over sentences. Given a PCFG, you can ask for the most likely parse of the sentence according to that model. Again, MPE VE works well here.

- *Image analysis*—You've seen the example of image completion in the text, and it's a typical application of MPE reasoning. Given a partial image, you want to work out likely completions of the image. For example, given a picture of part of a person's face (in the photograph, only part of the person's face is showing), you want to produce a full image of the person. This might be useful to help identify the person. Both MPE BP and SA are used here.

- *Diagnosis*—The printer diagnosis model seen at the beginning of this section is an example of a diagnosis problem. Another example is medical diagnosis, where the goal is to diagnose the diseases of a patient, given the reported symptoms and tests. In diagnosis, you often want to know the most likely states of all of the variables—for example, the most likely joint state of the printer, network, software, and user. This would help indicate which tests to perform first and which likely faults to tackle.

  Any MPE algorithm can be used for diagnosis, depending on the structure of the model. For example, chapter 10 showed you a two-layer network for medical diagnosis with diseases in the first layer and symptoms in the second layer. As in chapter 10, MPE BP is a good algorithm for this structure.

- *Scientific applications*—Chapter 11 discussed an application of MH to biology, where the goal is to determine the probability that a person has certain genes given their phenotype, which is the manifestation of their genes as traits. You can turn this query into an MPE query, where the goal is to find the most likely genotype of the individual. Just as MH is a good algorithm for the marginal probability computation in chapter 11, SA is a good algorithm for the MAP query here.

Marginal MAP

Another kind of query is a combination of computing marginal probabilities of query variables given evidence and MAP, called *marginal MAP*. In marginal MAP, you want to compute the most likely values of certain variables, while summing out or marginalizing over other variables. For example, in the printer diagnosis application, you might want to know the most likely state of the printer while marginalizing over the network, the software, and the user.

Marginal MAP is a generally useful kind of query, but it can be much harder to answer marginal MAP queries than either ordinary marginal probability queries or MAP queries. Marginal MAP defines a max-sum-of-products expression involving both maximizations and summations. In factored algorithms such as VE and BP, it's important to be able to move variables around arbitrarily. In marginal MAP, the problem is that you can't legally move a maximization inside a summation, which severely restricts the operations that the algorithm can perform. Algorithms for marginal MAP are at the forefront of research in probabilistic reasoning. Figaro doesn't include any marginal MAP algorithms, but we're planning to add them in the future.

12.3 Computing the probability of evidence

In addition to computing the probability distribution over query variables or the most likely explanation, sometimes you want to compute the *probability of observed evidence*. Suppose, for example, you're trying to monitor your network and detect intrusive attacks. You'd like to use a probabilistic approach to determine whether an activity is normal or intrusive, but unfortunately, you don't have a lot of examples of intrusive attacks to learn a model of them. Furthermore, you're worried about new kinds of intrusive attacks that are different from anything seen before.

In this situation, you could try to create a joint probability distribution with variables for (a) whether the activity is normal or intrusive, and (b) the activity, which depends on the kind of activity. But this won't work, because you don't know the conditional probability of the attack, given that it's intrusive. An alternative approach is to create a model of normal activity and flag anything that's especially unusual under this model. In this approach, known as *anomaly detection*, you'd create a probabilistic model of normal activity. Given a specific activity, you'd assert the characteristics of the activity as evidence in the model and ask for the probability of evidence. If the probability is sufficiently small, you'd flag the activity as anomalous. This doesn't mean for sure that it's an intrusion, but it does flag it as something worth investigating.

Another application of probability of evidence calculation is *classification*. Let's think about the speech recognition application discussed in chapter 10 in the context of HMMs. In speech recognition, each word is modeled as an HMM, in which the hidden states correspond to stages in uttering the word and the observations correspond to the audio signal produced. To determine the probability of a word by using Bayesian inference, you need to consider (a) the prior probability of the word, and (b) the likelihood of the word, which is the probability of the observation sequence, given the word. This likelihood is equal to the probability of the observations in the HMM corresponding to the word. Therefore, to compute the posterior probability distribution over words, you'd compute the probability of evidence in the HMM for every word.

Because computing probability of evidence is a rather different way of using probabilistic reasoning than before, let me illustrate it by using figure 12.5, which is similar to diagrams found in chapter 1.

The first two steps are just like those in ordinary probabilistic reasoning: encode general knowledge in the probabilistic model, and specific knowledge about the situation in the evidence. In this case, the general knowledge is about normal network activity. Then, the query is to compute the probability of evidence, and the system uses the inference algorithm to answer the query and return the probability of evidence. This use of probabilistic reasoning includes a final step: a decision module that decides what to do with this answer. This decision module would encode a policy. For example, a simple policy is to raise an alert whenever the probability of evidence is less than some predetermined threshold.

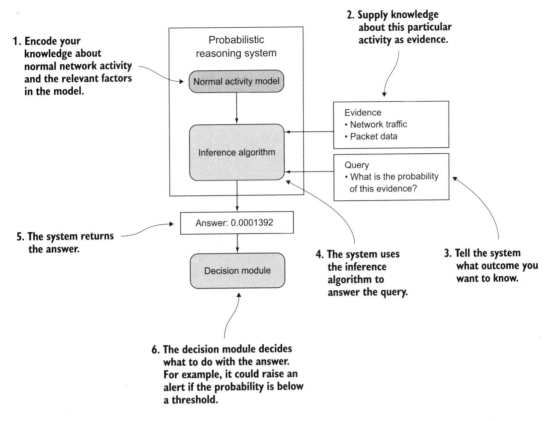

1. Encode your knowledge about normal network activity and the relevant factors in the model.

2. Supply knowledge about this particular activity as evidence.

5. The system returns the answer.

4. The system uses the inference algorithm to answer the query.

3. Tell the system what outcome you want to know.

6. The decision module decides what to do with the answer. For example, it could raise an alert if the probability is below a threshold.

Figure 12.5 Steps for using probabilistic reasoning to compute the probability of evidence in a network intrusion–detection application

12.3.1 Observing evidence for probability-of-evidence computation

This section continues with the image example in the previous section, except that now you're going to compute the probability of the observed pixels. The model is the same as before. Next, I'll show you how to observe the evidence.

You might be saying that you already know how to observe evidence; you use conditions or constraints. But conditions and constraints may be part of the model rather than evidence. For example, in the image model, the constraint that adjacent pixels are likely to be the same is part of the model, not evidence. When you're computing the probability of evidence, you don't want to compute the probability of these constraints; you want to compute the probability of the evidence under the model that includes these constraints.

NOTE The reason for this problem is that conditions and constraints serve two purposes in Figaro: to modify the model, and to assert evidence. Until now, this hasn't been an issue, because both purposes of conditions and constraints affect queries in the same way. But when computing probability of evidence, you need to know explicitly what the evidence is.

For this reason, Figaro provides an additional mechanism for explicitly specifying evidence. To use this mechanism, you take the following steps:

1　Associate the element on which you're asserting evidence with a name and an element collection. In our image example, you'll apply evidence to individual pixels, so you use the following line:

```
val pixels =
  Array.tabulate(4, 4)((i: Int, j: Int) =>
    Flip(0.4)("pixel(" + i + "," + j + ")", Universe.universe))
```

This creates a 4×4 array of pixels. Each pixel is a `Flip(0.4)` associated with a name that depends on the indices of the pixel. For example, the pixel at (0, 0) will be named `pixel(0,0)`. Each pixel is also associated with the element collection `Universe.universe`, which is the default universe. (Remember that a universe is an element collection.)

2　Turn each item of evidence into an instance of the `Evidence` class. Examples of the `Evidence` class include the following:

  – `Observation(true)`, which asserts that a `Boolean` element has value `true`
  – `Condition((i: Int) => i > 0)`, which asserts that an `Integer` element has a positive value
  – `Constraint((d: Double) => 1 / (d + 1) * (d + 1))`, which applies the constraint to a `Double` element

3　Associate each item of evidence with a specific element by using an instance of the `NamedEvidence` class. `NamedEvidence` takes two arguments: a reference to the element on which evidence is being applied, and an instance of `Evidence` representing the evidence. For example, the following code specifies evidence that the pixel at index (0,0) has value (true):

```
NamedEvidence("pixel(0,0)", Observation(true))
```

4　Put all instances of `NamedEvidence` you want to assert in a list. The following code creates all of the evidence in our image program:

```
def makeNamedEvidence(i: Int, j: Int, obs: Boolean) =
  NamedEvidence("pixel(" + i + "," + j + ")", Observation(obs))
val evidence =
  List(makeNamedEvidence(0, 0, true),
       makeNamedEvidence(0, 2, false),
       makeNamedEvidence(1, 1, true),
       makeNamedEvidence(2, 0, true),
       makeNamedEvidence(2, 3, false),
       makeNamedEvidence(3, 1, true))
```

Using named evidence in this way functions in the same way as specifying evidence using conditions and constraints. All elements (the pixels, in this case) are generated as usual according to the generative model. Then, any element that has named evidence has a condition or constraint applied to it. The effect of adding the named evidence is the same as the effect of adding the condition or constraint. The named evidence lets you access the elements on which to apply the condition or constraint.

Now that you know how to express your knowledge about the particular situation in the form of named evidence, let's see how to ask the probability-of-evidence query and receive the answer.

12.3.2 *Running probability-of-evidence algorithms*

Now you're ready to compute the probability of evidence. The basic interface to achieve this is simple. Figaro provides two algorithms for computing probability of evidence: a sampling algorithm, similar to importance sampling, named `ProbEvidence-Sampler`; and a factored algorithm called `ProbEvidenceBeliefPropagation`. For example, to run the `ProbEvidenceSampler` for 10,000 samples on given evidence, and print the resulting probability, call

```
println(ProbEvidenceSampler.computeProbEvidence(10000, evidence))
```

To run a `ProbEvidenceSampler`, for a fixed amount of time (say, 1 second), use

```
println(ProbEvidenceSampler.computeProbEvidence(1000L, evidence))
```

Make sure to include the `L` in `1000L`. This tells Scala that the value is a long integer, which indicates that it represents a time in milliseconds, rather than a number of samples. To run a fixed number of samples, use an ordinary integer; to run for a fixed amount of time, use a long integer.

`ProbEvidenceBeliefPropagation` is similar. You simply provide the number of iterations and the evidence, as in

```
println(ProbEvidenceBeliefPropagation.computeProbEvidence(20, evidence))
```

The BP probability-of-evidence algorithm has the same benefits and drawbacks as ordinary BP. It can be fast, but it's an approximation algorithm, and the answer it converges to can be significantly different from the correct answer, particularly in a loopy network. This is the case for the image network; if you run the program in the book's code repository, you'll see that BP gives a different answer from sampling, even when you run sampling many times with many samples. So for this example, BP isn't a good algorithm.

How good is the sampling probability-of-evidence algorithm? It depends on what you mean by *good*. Let's define absolute error and relative error:

- *Absolute error* is the magnitude of the difference between the estimated value and the true value. For example, if the true probability of evidence is 0.0001 and your computed answer is 0.001, the absolute error is 0.0009, which might be quite good.
- *Relative error* is equal to the absolute error divided by the true value. In this example, the computed answer (0.001) is 10 times as large as the true probability (0.0001), so in relative terms, it's not so good. Indeed, the relative error is 0.0009/0.0001 = 9.

Sampling the probability of evidence tends to produce good absolute error, but struggles with relative error. Another way of saying this is that it can tell you that the probability is close to zero, but has a hard time deciding how many zeros are in the decimal expansion before the first positive number. Whether this is good enough depends on your application. For detecting anomalies, it depends on whether the normal cases also have probability of evidence that's close to zero. If the normal cases tend to have probability that's separated from zero by some amount, the sampling algorithm will work well because it will quickly detect when a case doesn't fall into this category. But if normal cases also have probability close to zero, but the anomalous cases are even closer, the sampling algorithm will have trouble. Although this is a property of sampling algorithms in general, it's especially an issue for a probability-of-evidence calculation, where you're often concerned with small probabilities.

The same techniques that helped sampling for ordinary probability queries can help here. Most important, *avoid hard conditions*. If your model has a lot of hard conditions such that few states satisfy all conditions, it'll be hard for the sampler to find any of them. The estimated probability will usually be 0, instead of a small positive number. In absolute terms, this is correct, but in relative terms, it's terribly wrong.

12.4 *Summary*

- You can compute the joint probability distribution over multiple variables by creating a tuple of the variables and using ordinary inference. But if you want to query the joint distribution over many variables, you might be better off creating a variable that summarizes them in a single statistic instead.
- You can use MPE queries to compute the most likely joint value of all of the variables. Figaro provides factored and sampling (simulated annealing) algorithms for this task. MPE queries can be used as an alternative to marginal probability queries in many applications.
- Computing probability of evidence can be useful for applications such as anomaly detection and classification. Figaro also provides factored and sampling algorithms for this task.

12.5 *Exercises*

Solutions to selected exercises are available online at www.manning.com/books/practical-probabilistic-programming.

1. Using the printer diagnosis program from chapter 5, compute the joint probability of the printer state and network state given a poor print result. Are these variables correlated, anti-correlated, or independent?

2. Using the same program, go through diagnosis steps as described at the beginning of section 12.2.

3. Using the same program, compute the probability of the evidence that the print result is poor.

4. Following from exercise 10.7 (in chapter 10), create a representation of an HMM in Figaro. Given a particular sequence of observations, compute the most likely sequence of hidden states that generate those observations.

5. This question concerns the image-recovery network in chapter 5. For both of the following tasks, experiment with different algorithms for computing probability of evidence.

   a. Compute the probability of the evidence that the top-left pixel is on.

   b. Compute the probability of the evidence represented in the data field in the code.

13

Dynamic reasoning and parameter learning

This chapter covers

- How to monitor the state of a dynamic system
- How to learn the parameters of a probabilistic program

The preceding chapter described several alternative kinds of queries you could ask of a probabilistic model. This chapter continues the theme by presenting two more reasoning tasks, both of which are important and widely used. The first task, discussed in section 13.1, is monitoring the state of a dynamic system over time as you receive information from sensors. The second task, presented in section 13.2, is learning the parameters of a probabilistic model from data. Although the techniques used for these two kinds of reasoning are different, both fall in the category of advanced methods that are necessary in many applications. It's well worth your while to understand these methods and how to use them. The chapter concludes with a brief section on taking what you've learned in this book and moving beyond it in your use of Figaro.

Section 13.1 on monitoring dynamic systems relies heavily on chapter 8, which covered dynamic probabilistic models. The particle-filtering algorithm described in that section is based on importance sampling, which was discussed in chapter 11. Section 13.2 on learning model parameters uses material from chapter 9. In particular, you should understand the different approaches to learning, such as the maximum a posteriori (MAP) and Bayesian approaches.

13.1 *Monitoring the state of a dynamic system*

Chapter 8 discusses how to represent dynamic probabilistic models. There are two ways to reason about the dynamic model, illustrated in figure 13.1:

- As shown in the top half of the figure, you can unroll the dynamic model over a fixed number of time steps. For example, starting from an initial state describing the start of a soccer match, you could unroll it forward over 90 time steps, where each step represents 1 minute. This produces an ordinary probabilistic model, which you can then reason about in the usual way described in the previous chapters. The main advantage of this approach is that it enables you to reason both forward and backward in time. For example, you could use conditions at the beginning of the game to predict the outcome or use the outcome of the game to infer the initial conditions.

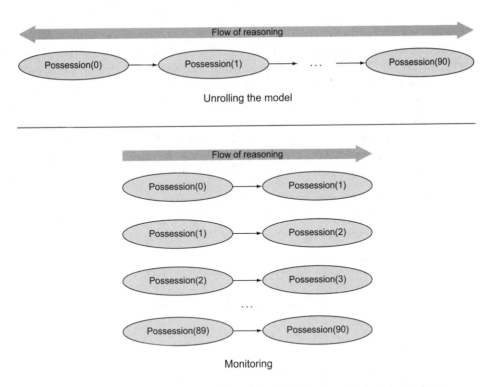

Figure 13.1 Two ways of reasoning about dynamic models. The top part of the figure shows unrolling the model for the full number of time steps to create a single Bayesian network. The gray arrows show the flow of reasoning, which in this case can go both forward and backward through time. The bottom part of the figure shows monitoring, where the reasoner moves forward recursively from one time step to the next. Here the flow of reasoning is only forward.

- As shown in the bottom half of the figure, you can recursively keep track of the state of the system over time. In this approach, you don't unroll the model over a number of time steps. Instead, at each point in time, you maintain the current and previous time steps. When you advance forward in time, you generate a new time step to become the current time step. What was formerly the *current* time step becomes the *previous* time step, and what was formerly the previous time step is discarded. The major advantages of this approach are that you maintain only two time steps in memory at any time and can continue going as long as you like. The disadvantage is that you can reason only going forward.

This section covers how to use the second approach. This kind of reasoning goes by several names: *monitoring the state of the system, state estimation,* or the more technical *filtering.*

13.1.1 *Mechanics of monitoring*

Chapter 8 showed how to perform this kind of reasoning mechanically, which I'll review here. Monitoring in Figaro uses the concept of a universe. There's a different universe for every time step. When advancing forward in time, a new universe is generated to represent the current time step. The penultimate (second to last) universe is discarded and garbage collected. To set this up, you create an initial universe to represent the initial state and a transition function that takes the previous universe and returns the next universe. Elements that are carried over from one universe to the next must be given a name. Elements that are observed or queried must also be given a name.

Here are the steps in more detail, together with excerpts from the program for monitoring a restaurant's capacity in chapter 8. Recall that this model includes two state variables, each given a name:

- seated—A list of integers representing the amount of time that each of the groups sitting at tables has been seated
- waiting—An integer representing the number of people waiting for a table

Here are the steps:

1 Create a universe to represent the initial state of the system. Give each of the relevant elements a name and put it in the initial universe.

Create the universe representing the initial state

```
val initial = Universe.createNew()

Constant(List(0, 5, 15, 15, 25, 30, 40, 60, 65, 75))("seated", initial)
Constant(1)("waiting", initial)
```

Create two elements and place them in the initial universe with the names "seated" and "waiting"

2 Create a transition function. Any elements from the previous universe that have an effect on the current universe are gotten by name. Corresponding elements with the same name must be created in the next universe.

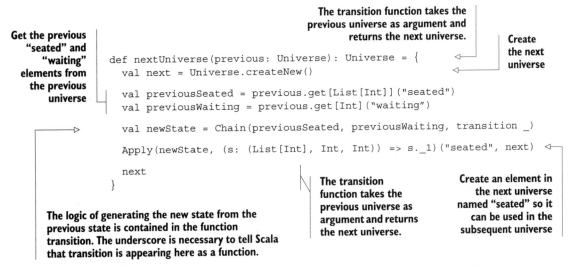

The transition function takes the previous universe as argument and returns the next universe.

Create the next universe

Get the previous "seated" and "waiting" elements from the previous universe

```
def nextUniverse(previous: Universe): Universe = {
  val next = Universe.createNew()

  val previousSeated = previous.get[List[Int]]("seated")
  val previousWaiting = previous.get[Int]("waiting")

  val newState = Chain(previousSeated, previousWaiting, transition _)

  Apply(newState, (s: (List[Int], Int, Int)) => s._1)("seated", next)

  next
}
```

The logic of generating the new state from the previous state is contained in the function transition. The underscore is necessary to tell Scala that transition is appearing here as a function.

The transition function takes the previous universe as argument and returns the next universe.

Create an element in the next universe named "seated" so it can be used in the subsequent universe

3 Create an instance of a monitoring algorithm. Figaro provides two monitoring algorithms: particle filtering and factored frontier. Particle filtering is a sampling algorithm, whereas factored frontier (as its name implies) is factored. Particle filtering is the most commonly used algorithm, and I describe it later.

```
val alg = ParticleFilter(initial, nextUniverse, 10000)
```

4 Start the algorithm. This generates a probability distribution over the initial time step.

```
alg.start()
```

5 Repeatedly advance the algorithm one time step at a time by using the advance-Time method. This method enables you to assert evidence at each time step. Evidence is asserted by using the NamedEvidence interface. This is why elements that are observed as evidence have to be named.

```
alg.advanceTime(List(NamedEvidence("waiting", Observation(1))))
```

6 At each time point, you can query the distribution over elements at the current time point. The query elements must be named. For example, to get the expected length of the list of people who are seated at the restaurant, you can use

```
alg.currentExpectation("seated", (l: List[Int]) => l.length)
```

Now that the mechanics of using filtering algorithms is understood, let's take a look at particle filtering, which is the most widely used filtering algorithm.

13.1.2 *The particle-filtering algorithm*

Particle filtering is an algorithm based on importance sampling. The word *particle* is a synonym for *sample*, and *filtering* is another word for *monitoring*, so this is an algorithm for monitoring by using samples.

OPERATION OF THE ALGORITHM

The operation of particle filtering is shown in figure 13.2. The main concept in this algorithm is that the state distribution at any time point is represented by a set of samples. On the left side of the figure is the set of particles representing the previous state distribution, and on the right is the set of samples representing the current state distribution. Two intermediate stages are shown in between.

The first step of the algorithm is to take each sample of the previous state and propagate it through the dynamics of the system, as represented in the transition function. This creates a new distribution over the current state of the system, but it doesn't take into account evidence that has been provided about the current state. The next step, then, is to condition on the evidence. This is achieved in the same way as importance sampling, but giving each sample a weight corresponding to the probability of the evidence for that sample. (Specifically, the weight is 0 if the sample violates any conditions; otherwise, it's the product of the values of the constraints defined on the elements.)

At this point, you have a set of weighted samples, as shown at number 3 in figure 13.2. In the figure, the size of the black circle intuitively shows the weight of the sample. To

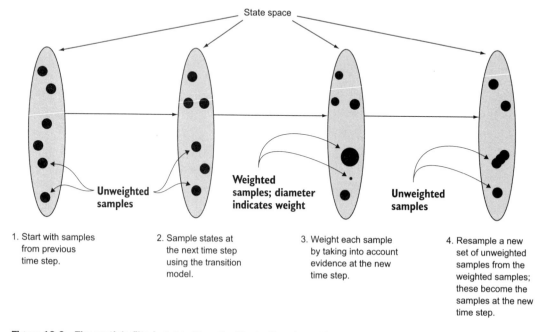

Figure 13.2   The particle-filtering algorithm: the illustration shows the process of moving from the estimate of the state distribution at the previous time point to the one at the current time point.

finish the algorithm, however, you need to get back to a set of unweighted samples to represent the distribution at the current time step.

This is achieved by a *resampling* process. In resampling, you create a new set of unweighted samples that approximates the same probability distribution as the weighted samples. The algorithm chooses each new unweighted sample from the set of weighted samples. The probability of a given weighted sample being chosen is proportional to its weight. For example, suppose one weighted sample has weight 1/3 and another one weight 2/3. The one weighted 2/3 will appear roughly twice as often in the new set of unweighted samples as the other one. So the probability of that state will be about twice as much in the unweighted particles, just as in the weighted particles.

PROPERTIES OF PARTICLE FILTERING

Resampling is a critical component of the particle-filtering algorithm. You might be wondering why you need it at all. Why don't you just use weighted particles the whole way through? Can't you propagate the weighted particles through the dynamics and then condition on the evidence by computing new weights? The problem with doing that is that you would end up with a set of samples with extremely small weights. At every time step, the algorithm would multiply the current weight of the sample with the value of the constraints, resulting in an even smaller weight. Over time, if a trajectory is long enough, it's unlikely that any sample will represent a high-probability trajectory. So the set of samples won't be representative of the true state distribution.

Resampling resolves this problem by getting rid of the lowest-probability particles at every iteration, and keeping only the ones that are more representative of the true state. This isn't guaranteed to give you the high-probability samples; there's a small probability that samples with low weight will be chosen. But on average, the resampling process will tend to keep the high-weight samples the most. So the samples that are maintained will generally represent more likely trajectories.

Although resampling helps in this way, it also has the detrimental effect of reducing the diversity of the samples at each iteration. If one weighted sample has much higher weight than all of the others, it's likely that nearly all unweighted samples at the next time step will correspond to this sample. This is all well and good if this sample is the true state of the system, but what if it's not? It can be hard for particle filtering to recover from "mistakes" made early on.

This phenomenon is known as *particle starvation*. Here's an example. Suppose you're using particle filtering to monitor the state of a soccer match between team A and team B. Let's say there's a variable indicating the relative strength of the teams. If team A scores first, it's possible all of the samples will say that team A is stronger than team B. At that point, the algorithm can't recover if this is wrong, even if team B scores the next 10 goals! There aren't any samples left where team B is stronger than team A. Figure 13.3 shows how particle starvation can happen even in a single time step.

As this example illustrates, particle starvation is particularly a problem with variables that don't change over time. Team strength, in the model just described, is fixed,

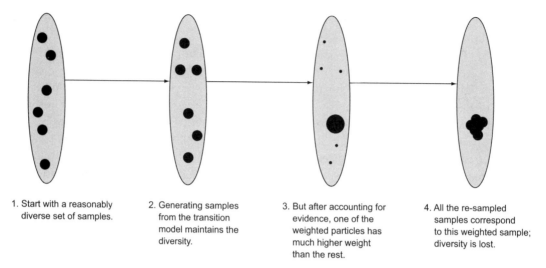

1. Start with a reasonably diverse set of samples.

2. Generating samples from the transition model maintains the diversity.

3. But after accounting for evidence, one of the weighted particles has much higher weight than the rest.

4. All the re-sampled samples correspond to this weighted sample; diversity is lost.

Figure 13.3   Particle starvation happens when the diversity in the sample set is lost due to resampling. This can happen in a single time step.

so after the particle filter has made a determination about team strength, it can't change it. This also suggests a potential mitigation of the problem: introduce some probability of change in these variables over time. For example, if you have a 1% probability that the relative team strength switches every minute, then even if the algorithm has decided that all samples show team A being the better team after they score, some of them will change their mind at the next time step. Then, when team B scores, those particular particles will have higher weight and will be resampled more times. Eventually, if team B scores repeatedly, the samples where team B is stronger will dominate.

Besides this issue with particle starvation, the usual considerations of importance sampling apply to particle filtering. If the evidence within a single time step is unlikely, the set of samples won't be a good representation of the posterior distribution. The standard mitigations apply:

- Avoid hard conditions and use soft constraints wherever possible. For example, observing that exactly five people are waiting for a seat at the restaurant may be hard to satisfy and can lead to many samples with weight 0, which are useless. Instead, add a constraint whose value is highest when exactly five people are waiting and whose value tapers off the further away the number is from five.
- Weaken soft constraints by avoiding extremely small constraint values.

Both these mitigations operate using the same principle. You replace your probabilistic model with an approximation of the model that's more "smooth." Although it's an incorrect model, it's easier to reason about by using a sampling algorithm, and the results can be better. Of course, if you do this too much, the model ends up being far from the true model, so the results aren't useful. It's a balancing act that can be best managed by trial and error.

13.1.3 Applications of filtering

Dynamic models are ubiquitous in probabilistic reasoning, and filtering is perhaps the most widely used way of reasoning about dynamic probabilistic models. As a result, many possible applications of filtering exist. Here are some examples:

- *Monitoring the health status of a person or a system*—For example, you might have a patient in a trauma ward connected to various sensors such as temperature and heart rate. You want to monitor the medical condition of the person so you can intervene quickly if problems arise. The patient has hidden variables such as amount of blood loss. The goal is to infer these variables over time, based on the sensor readings.

- *Robot localization*—If a robot is navigating an environment, it needs to keep track of its location based on its sensors, which may include, for example, radar. The hidden variables in this application pertain to the robot's location and speed. The goal is to maintain these hidden variables over time based on the sensors. A variant of this application is known as *simultaneous localization and mapping* (*SLAM*). In SLAM, the robot is placed in an unknown environment and must make a map of the environment at the same time that it's working out where it is in the environment.

- *Surveillance and tracking*—In a surveillance application, a certain number of sensors cover a region and receive signals when an object is present in the region. For example, the sensors might be video cameras, and the signals might be sequences of images of people or vehicles. The hidden variables in this application are the objects present in the region. Based on the sensors, you want to calculate which objects are in the region. In the related tracking application, the goal is to take individual observations of objects and turn them into tracks of objects as they move through the region over time.

- *Modeling complex ongoing processes*—Filtering is useful in modeling long-running complex processes. One example is elections. In a model of an election, the hidden state includes variables pertaining to the candidates, such as the popularity of the candidate with different segments of the population. This hidden state changes dynamically over time. You might model this system by using a dynamic model in which each time step corresponds to one day. The sensors are polls. Over the course of the election season, poll results come in that shed light on the hidden state. If you want to predict the election results based on the polls, you can keep track of the state of the hidden variables from day to day. Let's say it's 30 days before the election. Using filtering, you have a probability distribution over the state of the candidates at this time point. Now you can unroll the dynamic model over 30 steps, beginning with your current estimate of the initial state, to predict the ultimate outcome of the election.

13.2 Learning model parameters

Part 3 of this book has focused on *inference*: computing the answers to queries, given evidence. Another important task a probabilistic programming system needs to do is *learning*: improving the model based on data. In learning applications, you don't know exactly what numerical parameters to use in the model, so you use past data to help estimate those parameters. In the Bayesian learning paradigm, you use the past data to create a posterior probability distribution over parameter values, whereas in the maximum likelihood (ML) and maximum a posteriori (MAP) paradigms, you use a learning algorithm to estimate a single set of parameter values, which you then use in your model.

I've focused on inference rather than learning for two reasons:

- In the Bayesian learning paradigm, learning is performed by an inference algorithm.
- In the ML and MAP learning paradigms, inference algorithms are used as the inner loop of learning, and the learning algorithm is a relatively simple wrapper around them.

This section elaborates on these points and shows you how learning is performed in the Bayesian and MAP paradigms. I describe both the algorithms used and how you accomplish these tasks in Figaro. I focus on the problem of learning model parameters, leaving structure learning to a brief sidebar.

13.2.1 Bayesian learning

In the Bayesian approach to learning, which was first described in chapter 9, the probabilistic program consists of two main parts:

- A prior distribution over model parameters. Let's call this $P_0(\text{Parameters})$. The 0 indicates that these are the parameter values before seeing any data.
- A conditional probability distribution, for each data instance, over the values of the data variables in that data instance. Let's call this $P(\text{Data} \mid \text{Parameters})$. Note that because this is a probabilistic program, the data could have variable structure in different data instances. For example, the data in a given instance could be a sentence in English, which will have a different length in different instances.

Given these two parts, you can define a joint distribution over the parameters and the data by using the chain rule:

$$P(\text{Parameters, Data}) = P_0(\text{Parameters})\ P(\text{Data} \mid \text{Parameters})$$

You can then use the total probability rule to get a probability distribution over the data by summing out the parameters. You get the formula in figure 13.4.

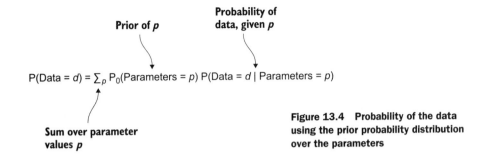

Figure 13.4 Probability of the data
using the prior probability distribution
over the parameters

NOTE Because the parameters are usually continuous variables with infinitely many parameters, you use integration rather than summation. Integration is the continuous analog of summation.

The data consists of a set of data instances, and each instance consists of a set of values for the data variables. The *likelihood* of a given set of parameter values given the data is the probability of the data given those parameter values. This is equal to the product, over all data instances, of the probability of the data in each instance, given the parameter values.

The key concept in Bayesian learning is Bayes' rule. Bayes' rule says that the posterior probability of the parameter values p given the data is proportional to the prior of p times the likelihood of p. Let's call the posterior distribution P_1(Parameters) and the data that was observed d. Then the posterior distribution can be computed by using the formula in figure 13.5.

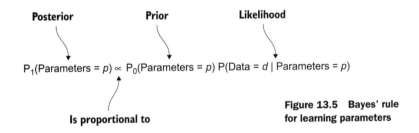

Figure 13.5 Bayes' rule
for learning parameters

USING BAYESIAN LEARNING TO PREDICT FUTURE OBSERVATIONS

In the Bayesian approach, you compute this posterior distribution and use it to predict future data instances that you didn't learn from. Another way of saying this is that for a future data instance, the posterior becomes your prior distribution. Let's call the posterior distribution P_1(Parameters), and let's use $Data_1$ to represent the future data instance. Using the same reasoning as in figure 13.4, you get the formula in figure 13.6.

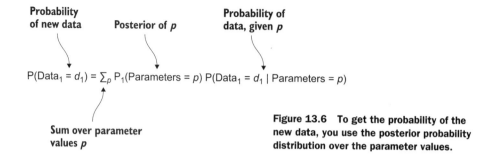

Probability of new data   Posterior of *p*   Probability of data, given *p*

$$P(\text{Data}_1 = d_1) = \sum_p P_1(\text{Parameters} = p)\, P(\text{Data}_1 = d_1 \mid \text{Parameters} = p)$$

Sum over parameter values *p*

Figure 13.6 To get the probability of the new data, you use the posterior probability distribution over the parameter values.

Now, taking this formula and plugging in the formula in figure 13.5 for P_1, you get the final formula for the prediction of the new data (Data_1), having learned from the original data (Data_0), in figure 13.7.

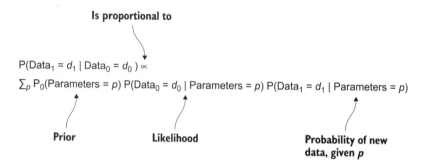

Is proportional to

$$P(\text{Data}_1 = d_1 \mid \text{Data}_0 = d_0) \propto$$

$$\sum_p P_0(\text{Parameters} = p)\, P(\text{Data}_0 = d_0 \mid \text{Parameters} = p)\, P(\text{Data}_1 = d_1 \mid \text{Parameters} = p)$$

Prior   Likelihood   Probability of new data, given *p*

Figure 13.7 Final formula for the probability of the new data given the observed data

This quantity, $P(\text{Data}_1 = d_1 \mid \text{Data} = d_0)$, is known as the *posterior predictive*, because it's the prediction of the new data based on the posterior distribution over parameter values. Now, here's an important point: *The formula for the posterior predictive is a sum-of-products expression. You can use any inference algorithm to compute it. Bayesian learning is performed by inference and doesn't need a special algorithm.*

USING BAYESIAN LEARNING IN FIGARO

Now that you know you don't need a special algorithm to do Bayesian learning, you already have all of the tools you need. To illustrate how it works, I'll use an abbreviated version of the spam filter model from chapter 3. You proceed in several steps:

1 Define the parameters and their prior distributions.

Parameter representing the probability a given email is spam

```
val spamProbability = Beta(2,3)

val wordGivenSpamProbabilities =
  featureWords.map(word => (word, Beta(2,2))).toMap
val wordGivenNormalProbabilities =
  featureWords.map(word => (word, Beta(2,2))).toMap
```

Parameters representing the probability of individual words appearing in the email given that it is or isn't spam. featureWords represents the words being used as features derived from training emails.

2 Create a class that defines individual data instances (that is, an email) and the probability distribution over the instance, given the parameters.

An element representing whether the email is spam. This uses the spam probability parameter.

```scala
class EmailModel {
  val isSpam = Flip(spamProbability)

  val hasWordElements = {
    for { word <- featureWords } yield {
      val givenSpamProbability =
        wordGivenSpamProbabilities(word)
      val givenNormalProbability =
        wordGivenNormalProbabilities(word)
      val hasWord =
        If(isSpam,
          Flip(givenSpamProbability),
          Flip(givenNormalProbability))
      (word, hasWord)
    }
  }

  val hasWord = hasWordElements.toMap
}
```

Class representing an individual email

Elements representing the presence of individual words, depending on whether the email is spam. This uses the appropriate parameters for the presence of words, given spam or normal.

Create a map from words to their associated elements

3 Create instances of the class, one for each data instance (each individual email in the training set). Observe the evidence about each email in the model of that email. Notice how all of the emails in the training set use the same email model with the same parameters.

Go through all emails in the training set

```scala
for { email <- trainingEmails } {
  val model = new EmailModel
  for { word <- featureWords } {
    model.hasWord(word).observe(email.text.contains(word))
  }
  model.isSpam.observe(email.label == "spam")
}
```

Create a new email model for each email

Observe the evidence about email's file in the model

4 Create an instance of the class for all future data instances you want to predict (future email). In this example, a single future email is being predicted, but you could have any number. Again, this future email uses the same email model with the same parameters as the training emails.

```scala
val futureModel = new EmailModel(dictionary)
```

5 Now you can answer queries about the future instance in the usual way. For example, you might want to observe the words in the future email and query whether it's spam.

```
for { word <- featureWords } {
  futureModel.hasWord(word).observe(futureEmail.text.contains(word))
}
println(MetropolisHastings.probability(futureModel.isSpam, true))
```

**Infer whether the future email is
spam based on its words, using
the learned parameters**

**Observe the words of the future
email, but don't observe its
label because it's unknown**

What algorithm should you use? In this example, I've used Metropolis-Hastings, and it's usually a good candidate for Bayesian learning. Although factored algorithms can be used, they'll sample a set of parameter values from the prior and use those as the only possible parameter values. This runs the risk of failing to identify good parameter values that have high posterior probability. Importance sampling, meanwhile, can be troublesome because with many data instances, the probability of the evidence is extremely low. This leaves Metropolis-Hastings as the best candidate.

As discussed in the previous chapter, Metropolis-Hastings can require effort to make it effective. The dataset in the code repository for this chapter is simple, unlike chapter 3. For this simple dataset, the default settings of Metropolis-Hastings work reasonably well. For a realistic dataset, you'll need to use many more samples or let it run for a long time. Unfortunately, it's hard to know in advance how long you should let it run, so you should try to see how many samples give you reasonably consistent results. You might also want to use a custom proposal.

13.2.2 *Maximum likelihood and MAP learning*

This section shows you how to perform MAP learning, which was first covered in chapter 9. I first describe the mechanics of doing this in Figaro and then explain the algorithms used. Remember, in MAP learning, you choose the values of the parameters that maximize the prior times the likelihood. You then use these parameter values for future data instances.

> **NOTE** Maximum likelihood (ML) learning is just MAP learning using a uniform prior that assigns the same probability to every value. So what I explain here for MAP learning applies to ML learning too.

MECHANICS OF MAP LEARNING IN FIGARO

Figaro provides a common pattern for MAP learning. The main challenge in coding MAP learning, illustrated in the top half of figure 13.8, is that you want to use the same model for learning the parameters and for subsequent inference about test cases, but these two models use different parameters. During learning, the parameters are learnable. For example, you might use a beta distribution to represent the spam probability. During subsequent inference, however, the parameters are fixed to a specific value. For example, you might have learned that the spam probability is 0.4 and will want to use this value subsequently. Because the parameters are different elements,

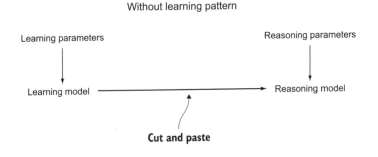

Without learning pattern

Using learning pattern

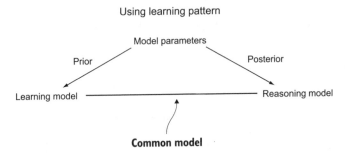

Figure 13.8 Creating models for learning and reasoning. The top part shows what you would need to do without the learning pattern. Because the learning and reasoning use different parameter elements, you'd need to create two models and share code by cut-and-paste. Using the learning pattern (bottom), the parameters are encapsulated in the `ModelParameters` class, and a common model is used, which is specialized to the learning or reasoning model depending on whether the prior or posterior parameters are chosen.

you have to create two different models and share code between them by cut-and-paste, which is error prone.

Figaro's learning pattern, shown in the bottom half of figure 13.8, enables you to use the same model for learning and inference. It uses the `ParameterCollection` data structure, which is an element collection that's specifically designed to hold model parameters. To use the pattern, you create an instance of the `ModelParameters` data structure. From the `ModelParameters`, you can get either the `priorParameters` for learning or the `posteriorParameters` for subsequent inference; each of those is a `ParameterCollection`. The parameters in the `ParameterCollection` are given a name, and you refer to them in your model by name.

Here are the steps you'd use. You can follow the full program in `MapLearning` `.scala` in the book code repository.

1 Create an instance of `ModelParameters`.

```
val params = ModelParameters()
```

2 Give each of the parameters a name and associate them with your Model-
Parameters.

```
val spamProbability = Beta(2,3)("spam probability", params)
val wordGivenSpamProbabilities =
  featureWords.map(word =>
    (word, Beta(2,2)(word + " given spam", params))).toMap
val wordGivenNormalProbabilities =
  featureWords.map(word =>
    (word, Beta(2,2)(word + " given normal", params))).toMap
```

For each feature word, make two elements with the appropriate name for normal and spam emails. Put these elements in two maps.

3 Make your model take a ParameterCollection as an argument.

```
class EmailModel(paramCollection: ParameterCollection) {
```

4 Within the model, get the parameters by name.

```
val isSpam = Flip(paramCollection.get("spam probability"))
```

5 For the training instances, make them use the ModelParameters' priorParame-
ters to create the model.

```
for { email <- trainingEmails } {
  val model = new EmailModel(params.priorParameters)
```

6 To learn the MAP parameter values, use an instance of the expectation maximization (EM) algorithm. As I describe next, EM is a "meta"-algorithm that wraps
itself around any one of a number of inference algorithms. Figaro contains variants of EM with VE, BP, importance sampling, and MH.

EM is an iterative algorithm that loops through a certain number of iterations. The first argument to any of the EM variants is the number of iterations.
The rest of the arguments are as usual for the algorithm variant. For example,
for EM with BP, you'd specify the number of BP iterations, whereas for EM with
importance sampling, you'd supply the number of samples. The final argument
to the EM variants is ModelParameters, containing the parameters whose values
you want to learn. In this example, I use EM with VE. Here's how you create and
run the algorithm:

```
val learningAlg = EMWithVE(10, params)
learningAlg.start()
```

7 At this point, the MAP parameter values have been learned. You can now use the
posterior parameter values in a model for a future data instance.

```
val futureModel = new EmailModel(params.posteriorParameters)
```

8 Now you can reason about the future instance in the usual way, observing evidence and running a standard inference algorithm.

```
val result = VariableElimination.probability(futureModel.isSpam, true)
println("Probability new email is spam = " + result)
```

THE EXPECTATION MAXIMIZATION ALGORITHM

The goal of the expectation maximization (EM) algorithm is to learn a specific set of parameter values from data. The algorithm relies on the notion of *sufficient statistics*. To explain sufficient statistics, I'll revisit the beta-binomial model, which you saw in chapters 4 and 9. As a reminder, figure 13.9 reproduces the model from chapter 4.

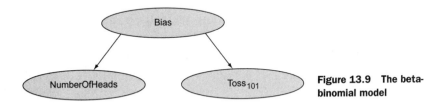

Figure 13.9 The beta-binomial model

Let's review the model:

- There's a variable representing a continuous parameter, modeled by a beta distribution. This variable represents, for example, the bias of a coin. The beta distribution has two parameters, known as α and β. Because they're parameters of a parameter, they're sometimes called *hyper-parameters.*
- There's a variable representing the number of successes in a given number of trials using the parameter, modeled by a binomial distribution. This variable represents, for example, the number of coin tosses that come out heads, when the bias of the coin is represented by the beta parameter.

Remember in the prior distribution over the beta parameter, α represents the imagined number of successes seen before observing any data, plus 1. Meanwhile, β represents the imagined number of failures, plus 1. And if you observed N_S successes and N_F failures, the posterior distribution over the parameter is Beta$(\alpha + N_S, \beta + N_F)$. And the mode of this distribution, which represents the MAP value of the parameters, is

$$\frac{\alpha + N_S - 1}{\alpha + N_S + \beta + N_F}$$

It's not important to remember the precise formula. What's important is to recognize that after you know the number of successes N_S and the number of failures N_F, you have all of the information you need to compute the posterior parameter distribution and the MAP parameter values. It doesn't matter what order the successes and failures happened in. For this reason, N_S and N_F are called *sufficient statistics* for the beta distribution, because they're summary statistics of the data that are sufficient for computing the posterior. And because N_S and N_F are typically observed for a binomial distribution, observing the outcome of the binomial distribution provides sufficient statistics for the beta parameter.

There are many examples of parameter distributions and sufficient statistics for them. Figaro includes only a small number of examples, but is easily extensible. The most common examples are as follows:

- Beta and Binomial, as you've seen.
- Beta and Flip; each Flip provides one success or failure for the beta parameter, and if you have many Flips depending on a beta parameter, you add together all successes and failures, just as for a binomial.
- Whereas Flip lets you choose between two outcomes (true and false), Select lets you choose between multiple outcomes—for example, Select(0.2 -> 1, 0.3 -> 2, 0.5 -> 3). Just as Flip can be parameterized by a beta parameter, Select can be parameterized by a *Dirichlet* parameter. A Dirichlet parameter is just like a beta parameter except that it allows for multiple outcomes and has a hyper-parameter for every possible outcome. As for a beta, a parameter of a Dirichlet represents the number of times you've seen a certain choice, plus one. For example, Dirichlet(2, 4, 3) might be a prior distribution for selecting one of three choices. It corresponds to imagining having seen the first outcome once, the second outcome three times, and the third outcome twice. Given a Dirichlet parameter d, you can use Select(d, List(1, 2, 3)) to create a Select parameterized by d in which the possible outcomes are 1, 2, or 3.
- A normal distribution representing the mean of other normal distributions. For example, suppose you have a variable m defined by Normal(2, 1) representing the mean of other normal distributions. Each of these other distributions is defined by Normal(m, 0.5). Let's say you have observations of each of these other distributions. Then the average value of those observations is sufficient for determining the MAP value of m, which is equal to that average. So in this case, the average value of the observations is a sufficient statistic for m.

The basic principle is simple. If you know the sufficient statistics, you can compute the MAP parameter values. Unfortunately, however, in most cases you don't get to observe the data instances directly, so you don't know the sufficient statistics.

On the other hand, if you have a well-defined probabilistic model, you could use probabilistic inference to compute the expected values of the variables you'd ordinarily have to observe. In the beta-binomial case, you could compute the expected number of successes and failures. In the normal-normal case, you could compute the expected value of the average of the normals. These expected values are called the *expected sufficient statistics*. And, given the expected sufficient statistics, you could compute the MAP parameter values. Unfortunately, this still isn't good enough, because you don't have the parameter values, so it's hard to compute the expected sufficient statistics.

To summarize the situation:

- If you know only the expected sufficient statistics, you could compute the MAP parameter values by formula.
- If you know only the MAP parameter values, you could compute the expected sufficient statistics by inference.

It seems like you're in a bind, but these two facts suggest a solution, embodied in the EM algorithm. A flowchart of the algorithm is shown in figure 13.10. You start with a random guess of the parameter values to start the process. You then iterate between two steps that give the algorithm its name: an Expectation, or E, step, where you use the current parameter values to compute expected sufficient statistics by probabilistic inference; and a Maximization, or M, step, where you use the computed expected sufficient statistics to compute the MAP parameter values. You repeat these two steps until the prespecified maximum number of iterations has been exhausted or the parameters have converged. Convergence means that the parameters on two successive iterations are almost exactly the same; if that happens, you know the algorithm isn't going to make much more progress, so you might as well stop.

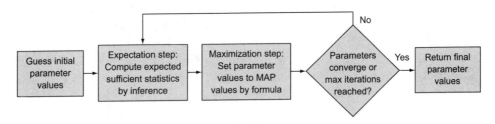

Figure 13.10   **Flowchart of the expectation maximization algorithm**

CONSIDERATIONS WHEN USING EM

It's not hard to show the running EM until convergence leads to a maximum in the space of parameter values. But it might be a *local maximum*; the parameter values returned will have higher posterior probability than any other nearby parameters, but other parameter values elsewhere in the space might have higher probability. EM can return different results on different iterations because of different initial guesses. In practice, this means that you might want to run EM several times with different random initial guesses and see which produces best results. This technique is known as *random restarts*.

I call EM a *meta-algorithm* because it relies on another algorithm for inference in the E step. This is why EM can wrap around any inference algorithm, and Figaro provides several options. EM spends almost all of its time in the E step, so it's important to choose the right inference algorithm. The considerations for choosing the inference algorithm are the same for ordinary inference on each of the individual data instances. An algorithm that's good on a particular model for ordinary inference will also be good for learning using EM. In the email model, you can use exact inference by VE for each individual data instance, so you can also use EM with VE.

But EM is generally a lot slower than inference on a single data instance. First of all, in every EM iteration, you have to run inference on all data instances, which can be a large number. Second, you have to run it for a number of iterations. Third, you might want to use random restarts to run EM multiple times.

How many iterations should you run? This is highly problem dependent, and it's impossible to give a good general answer. But as a rule of thumb, I sometimes find that after 10 iterations, you reach a point of diminishing returns and might be better off restarting the algorithm with a different initial guess.

One issue that can arise in EM with a large dataset is memory requirements. Running EM on all of the data instances simultaneously requires storing all of the instances in memory, including the data structures used for inference. This is especially an issue for factored algorithms because factors can be large data structures, but it's also an issue for sampling algorithms. So with large datasets, you may find yourself running out of memory.

ONLINE EM

To avoid the memory problems, Figaro provides an alternative online expectation maximization algorithm. Instead of operating on all data instances simultaneously and performing the E step on all of them in every iteration, this algorithm goes through each of the data instances one at a time. It performs the E step on the single data instance, and then performs the M step by adding the expected sufficient statistics from that instance to the previously accumulated statistics from all previously seen instances.

Typically, you'll go through all of your data instances and apply EM once to each instance. But you might also have a situation where you have an ongoing stream of data, and you want to continually learn from data as it comes in. At any time point, you can use the parameters learned so far to reason about new instances and continue learning afterward. Here's some code showing how you can use online EM in Figaro.

Listing 13.1 Online EM

The Model class takes the parameter collection and the universe as arguments for maximum flexibility.

```
val parameters = ModelParameters()
val d = Dirichlet(2.0,2.0,2.0)("d",parameters)
```

Use the ModelParameters pattern to make it easy to use the prior and posterior parameters in the same model.

```
class Model(parameters: ParameterCollection, modelUniverse: Universe) { //
  val s = Select(parameters.get("d"), 1, 2, 3)("s", modelUniverse) //
}

def f = () => {
  val modelUniverse = new Universe
  new Model(parameters.priorParameters, modelUniverse)
  modelUniverse
}
```

Every data instance lives in its own universe. The function f takes zero arguments and produces this universe.

```
val em = EMWithVE.online(f, parameters)
em.start()
```

The first argument to online EM is the function that produces the universe. The second argument is the ModelParameters.

For every data instance, you create a list of Named-Evidence containing the evidence for that instance (perhaps by reading a file).

```
for (i <- 1 to 100) {
  val evidence = List(NamedEvidence("s", Observation(1)))      //
  em.update(evidence)
}
```

Call the update method of online EM using that evidence.

```
val futureUniverse1 = Universe.createNew()                     //
val futureModel1 = new Model(parameters.posteriorParameters, futureUniverse1) //
println(VariableElimination.probability(futureModel1.s, 1))
```

```
for (i <- 101 to 200) {
  val evidence:  List(NamedEvidence("s", Observation(2)))      //
  em.update(evidence)
}
```

Call the update method of online EM using that evidence.

```
val futureUniverse2 = Universe.createNew()                     //
val futureModel2 = new Model(parameters.posteriorParameters, futureUniverse2) //
println(VariableElimination.probability(futureModel2.s, 1))
```

After reasoning, you might encounter more training data. You can interleave training and reasoning as often as you like.

When you're done learning, you can create a model using the posterior parameters and reason about it in the usual way.

When you run this code, it prints something like

```
0.9805825242718447
0.4975369458128079
```

The first time you reason, the training data has consisted of 100 1s, so the learned probability of generating a 1 is close to 1. Then you add 100 2s to the training data, so now the learned probability of generating a 1 is close to 1/2.

Learning model structure

This section has focused on the problem of learning model parameters from data. I've assumed you know the structure of the model (the variables, the functional forms, and the dependencies) but are uncertain about the numerical parameters. But what if you don't know the structure?

Ideally, you'd learn both the structure and parameters of a model from data. Unfortunately, structure learning is hard, because the space of possible program structures is enormous. Imagine that you're given examples of the inputs and outputs of a program and want to learn the program that transforms those inputs into outputs. This problem is known as *program induction*, and despite years of research, there aren't yet reliable general-purpose methods.

(continued)

So if you don't know the structure of your model, what can you do? The best approach is to encode uncertainty about the structure explicitly in the model. For example, if you don't know whether a certain variable should be in the model, create two versions of the model with and without the variable. If you don't know whether a dependency goes in one direction or the other, again encode both possibilities in your model. If you don't know whether a variable is normal or uniform, again encode both dependencies. In all cases, add a variable representing which model is the correct model. This is called a *structural variable*.

You could end up with an awful lot of models if you try to encode every combination of possibilities in a separate model. Fortunately, many of the structural decisions are independent. For example, whether or not the model contains one variable might be independent of whether another variable is normal or uniform. The trick is to encode as much flexibility about the structure in as compact a model as you can.

After you've represented multiple alternative structures in the model, deciding between them is done by probabilistic inference. Using inference, you can determine the posterior probabilities of the structural variables. Alternatively, you could use MPE inference to determine the most likely values of all the structural variables. You could then use these most likely values to reduce the model to a single model used for future instances.

13.3   Going further with Figaro

Congratulations! If you've made it all the way through the book, you've learned an awful lot about probabilistic modeling and probabilistic programming, including the basics of modeling and inference, a variety of modeling paradigms, and several inference algorithms and how to use them. You're at the end of this book, but if you'd like to deepen your knowledge of probabilistic programming and your use of Figaro, here are some tasks you could try:

- Create your own library of atomic element classes. There may be probability distributions you want to use that aren't provided in the current Figaro library. It's not hard to add your own. You can look at the element class definitions in `com.cra.figaro.library.atomic`, whether continuous or discrete, to get ideas and see how this is done.

- Create custom compound elements. This is even easier than creating atomic element classes. If you find yourself writing and reusing a function that takes some elements and returns another element, consider turning it into a compound element class. This will make it easy for you to use it in any model you like. Again, you can look at the element class definitions in `com.cra.figaro .library.compound` for ideas.

- Explore the debug versions of algorithms. Most Figaro algorithms provide a flag named `debug`, which is ordinarily set to `false`. If you set it to `true`, it will generally provide verbose output that can help you figure out why an algorithm isn't performing as you expected. Of course, understanding the debug messages requires that you have some understanding of what the algorithms are doing, but the basic information provided in this book should be enough. For example, the debugging output for variable elimination shows all the factors that are created at any point during the solution process. When you're debugging your models, you'll find that giving unique names to all of your elements will be helpful.

- Also, if you're using Metropolis-Hastings, you might find the `Metropolis-Hastings.test` method useful. In this method, you set up the system in a particular state by setting the values of any variables you want using the `Element.set` method. You can then test to see the possibilities that can result from running MH for one step from this state. You specify a number of predicates that the resulting state could satisfy and find the fraction of times each predicate is satisfied.

- Use the universe concept to help with difficult inference tasks. For example, you might break up a model into one universe over which you perform simulated annealing to search for the most likely values of a set of variables, and another universe in which you compute the probability of evidence resulting from values of these variables. In fact, variable elimination already has built in this concept of using a different algorithm to compute probability of evidence in a dependent universe, but the idea of using multiple universes is a general one. The Figaro team is upgrading the universe framework to provide a uniform algorithm interface that enables the same algorithm to operate on multiple universes and to combine algorithms seamlessly across different universes, so the potential to use this technique will only grow with coming releases.

If you have ideas on how to make Figaro more useful, please consider sharing them on our GitHub site (https://github.com/p2t2/figaro). We welcome contributions and we're always happy to answer any questions you might have. Thanks for reading, and I hope you make good use of probabilistic programming.

13.4 Summary

- You can reason with a dynamic probabilistic model either by unrolling it over a fixed number of time steps or by using a filtering algorithm to monitor it over time. Unrolling lets you reason both forward and backward through time, but filtering lets you go as long as you want and saves memory.

- You can use any standard inference algorithm to perform Bayesian learning, in which you learn a posterior probability distribution over parameter values and use this posterior distribution to predict new cases.

- Figaro's `ModelParameters` construct helps MAP learning, which is performed by the expectation maximization (EM) algorithm, which wraps around a standard inference algorithm.

- Online EM is useful when you have many data instances and memory could be an issue or when you want to learn from an ongoing stream of data.

13.5   *Exercises*

Solutions to selected exercises are available online at www.manning.com/books/
practical-probabilistic-programming.

1 One in a thousand cars produced by the factory that made your car is faulty. On
   any given day, the fuel efficiency of a car is either high or low, and follows the
   following distribution: If the previous day had low fuel efficiency, then the current day's fuel efficiency is low with probability 90%. If the previous day had
   high fuel efficiency, then the current day's fuel efficiency is low with probability
   90% for faulty cars and 5% for normal cars. Your car also has a fuel-economy
   gauge that shows whether your car has high or low fuel efficiency that day. The
   gauge shows the correct value with probability 0.95 and the incorrect value with
   probability 0.05.

   a Draw a dynamic Bayesian network to represent this system.
   b Write a Figaro program to represent this system.
   c Create two observation sequences of length 100 from this program, one for a
      normal car and one for a faulty car.
   d Use particle filtering to monitor the state of this system. Run the particle fil-
      ter on your two observation sequences. Use 100 samples. You'll probably find
      that most of the time, you cannot detect a faulty car. Why do you think this is?
   e Now repeat part (d) with 10,000 samples. You should usually get a different
      result. Can you explain why? (Make sure to run the experiment multiple
      times—particle filtering will not always produce the same answer.)

2 Now let's change the model of the previous exercise slightly, in an attempt to
   make particle filtering run more smoothly. A faulty car doesn't always stay
   faulty; it has some probability to correct itself at each time step. Likewise, a normal car could become faulty. Specifically, a car maintains the same faulty state
   from one time step to the next with probability 0.99, and flips state with probability 0.01.

   Run particle filtering using this model with 100 samples.
   What are the differences between your new results and the
   previous ones? Repeat the experiment with 10,000 samples.
   Evaluate the trade-off.

3 This exercise points out a pitfall with the EM algorithm. Consider the simple Bayesian network shown in figure 13.11.
   You're going to learn the parameters of this network.

   a Create a Figaro program to represent this network using
      the model parameters learning pattern. Use a Beta(1, 1)
      prior for all parameters.
   b Create a training set of about 10 instances in which only
      the variables X and Z are observed. Make sure that in

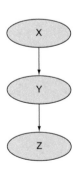

**Figure 13.11
Bayesian network
for exercise 3**

every training instance, X and Z take on the same value. Sometimes they're both true and sometimes they're both false.

   c Use the EM algorithm to learn the parameters of the model. Experiment with different variants of EM.

   d Now create a test case using the posterior parameters. Observe that X is true and compute the probability that Z is true. You'll probably find that this probability is not close to 1, even though X is true and X and Z were always equal in the training set. Try to explain why this might be.

   e Now let's fix the problem. Change the prior for Y given that X is true to Beta(2, 1), and the prior for X given that Y is true to Beta(1, 2). Again, use EM to learn the parameters and run your test. This time, the probability that Z is true should be close to 1. Why do you think learning worked in this case? What moral can you derive for your own use of EM?

4 Now repeat question 3, using Bayesian learning instead of EM.

   a Try different inference algorithms on this problem. Which algorithm works best? Why do you think that is?

   b Compare and contrast the results of Bayesian learning with the EM results. Do the results of Bayesian learning differ significantly whether you use Beta(1, 1) priors for all variables or you use Beta(2, 1) and Beta(1, 2) priors for Y? Are the results with the Beta(2, 1) and Beta(1, 2) priors significantly different from EM? If so, why do you think that is?

5 Now that you've seen how parameter learning works, it's time to revisit the spam filter example from chapter 3.

   a Rewrite the example to use the model parameters learning pattern.

   b Change the learning method from the basic EM method used in chapter 3, which trains on all emails simultaneously, to an offline learning method.

appendix A
Obtaining and installing
Scala and Figaro

This appendix contains instructions for getting Figaro installed and running on your computer. The easiest way by far is to use the Scala Build Tool (sbt). Instructions for running Figaro using sbt are described in section A.1. If for some reason you can't or don't want to use sbt, instructions for a manual installation are presented in section A.2.

The official version of Figaro for the code in this book is 3.3. Earlier versions of Figaro don't support all features described in the book. We'll try to make future versions backward compatible if at all possible, so you should be able to use later versions of Figaro as well.

Figaro 3.3 uses Scala 2.11.*x*. Unfortunately, the Scala developers don't maintain backward compatibility between versions, and it takes time to migrate Figaro to the latest version of Scala, so Figaro doesn't always work with the most recent Scala version. sbt takes care of the dependencies for you and makes sure the appropriate version of Scala is used.

A.1   *Using sbt*

The simplest way to run the code in this book is to use the sbt. If you download the code for the book, it comes prepackaged in an sbt project. All you need to do is download and install sbt from www.scala-sbt.org. Then, when you run sbt in this project, it will automatically pull in the relevant versions of Scala and Figaro, so there's nothing else for you to install. sbt also makes sure the classpath is configured correctly for your project, saving you some hassle.

The main sbt commands you need to know to use the book are as follows:

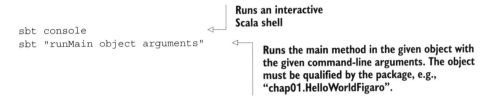

```
sbt console
sbt "runMain object arguments"
```

Runs an interactive Scala shell

Runs the main method in the given object with the given command-line arguments. The object must be qualified by the package, e.g., "chap01.HelloWorldFigaro".

To run these commands, you need to navigate to the PracticalProbProg/examples directory, which is the top-level directory of the project.

> **NOTE** If you're already in the sbt console, you don't need to type sbt again and can just type runMain object arguments.

sbt has a lot of features and would also be a good way to build and run your own code. You can use the Build.scala in our project as a starting point. sbt can also be used with Eclipse.

A.2 *Installing and running Figaro without sbt*

Although sbt is a useful tool, you may want to manage your own workspace differently. The rest of this installation guide describes how to install and run Figaro without using sbt.

To run Figaro, you first need Scala. The Scala compiler can be run either from the command line or within an integrated development environment (IDE). Available IDEs that support Scala development include Eclipse and IntelliJ IDEA. NetBeans also has a Scala plugin, but it doesn't appear to support recent versions of Scala. In the following guide, I show you how to obtain Scala and Figaro and run Scala programs that use Figaro from the command line. I don't provide instructions for specific IDEs. Please see the documentation of your IDEs and Scala plugins for details of how to include the Figaro library.

1 To get started with Scala, download the appropriate version of Scala for your Figaro version from http://scala-lang.org/download/. Follow the Scala installation instructions at http://scala-lang.org/download/install.html and make sure you can run, compile, and execute the Hello World program provided in the documentation.

2 The next step is to obtain Figaro. The Figaro binary distribution is hosted at the Charles River Analytics Inc. website. Go to www.cra.com/figaro. Make sure the Figaro version you use matches the Scala version. Each available download link is a compressed archive containing the Figaro JAR (JAR is the Java/Scala format for compiled byte code), examples, documentation, Scaladoc, and source code files. In the distribution, the Figaro JAR name ends with "fat," indicating that this is a fat JAR containing all the necessary libraries to run Figaro. Click the appropriate link and then uncompress the downloaded archive to access the file.

3 [Optional] Add the fully qualified path name of the Figaro JAR to your class-path. This can be done by adding the Figaro JAR to the CLASSPATH environment variable in your operating system. The process for editing the CLASSPATH varies from operating system to operating system. You can see details about using the PATH and CLASSPATH environment variables at http://docs.oracle.com/javase/tutorial/essential/environment/paths.html.

a If the CLASSPATH doesn't exist yet, create it. I always like the CLASSPATH to include the current working directory, so set the CLASSPATH to ".".

b Now you add the Figaro JAR to the CLASSPATH. For example, on Windows 7, if figaro_2.11-3.3.0.0-fat.jar is in the C:\Users\apfeffer folder and the CLASSPATH is currently equal to ".", change the CLASSPATH to C:\Users\apfef-fer\figaro_2.11-3.3.0.0-fat;. Replace 2.11 with the appropriate Scala version number, and 3.3.0.0 with the appropriate Figaro version number.

4 Now you can compile and run Figaro programs just like any Scala program. Put the test program that follows in a file named Test.scala. First, let's assume you followed step 3 and updated the CLASSPATH.

a If you run scala Test.scala from the directory containing Test.scala, the Scala compiler will first compile the program and then execute it. It should produce the output 1.0.

b If you run scalac Test.scala (note the c at the end of scalac), the Scala compiler runs and produces .class files. You can then execute the program by running scala Test from the same directory.

c If you didn't follow step 3, you can set the CLASSPATH from the command line by using the -cp option. For example, to compile and execute Test.scala, assuming figaro_2.11-3.3.0.0-fat.jar is in the C:\Users\apfeffer folder, you can run scala -cp C:\Users\apfeffer\ figaro_2.11-3.3.0.0-fat Test.scala.

Here's the test program:

```scala
import com.cra.figaro.language._
import com.cra.figaro.algorithm.sampling._

object Test {
  def main(args: Array[String]) {
    val test = Constant("Test")
    val algorithm = Importance(1000, test)
    algorithm.start()
    println(algorithm.probability(test, "Test"))
  }
}
```

This program should output 1.0.

A.3 Compiling from source

Figaro is maintained as open source on GitHub. The GitHub project is Probabilistic Programming Tools and Techniques (P2T2), located at https://github.com/p2t2. P2T2 currently contains the Figaro sources, but we plan to update it with more tools. If you want to see the source code and build Figaro yourself, please visit our GitHub site.

Figaro uses the sbt to manage builds. To build Figaro from GitHub source, make a fork of the repository to your GitHub account, and then use Git's clone feature to get the source code from your GitHub account to your machine:

```
git clone https://github.com/[your-github-username]/figaro.git
```

Several branches are available; check out "master" for the latest stable release or the latest "DEV" branch for more cutting-edge work and features (this is a work in progress and therefore less stable). Download and install sbt, start the program to get its command prompt, and enter these commands in order:

```
> clean
> compile
> package
> assembly
> exit
```

This creates a version of Figaro for the relevant Scala release; you can find the artifacts in the "target" directory.

appendix B
A brief survey of probabilistic programming systems

A growing number of probabilistic programming systems (PPSs) are under development. In this survey, I briefly describe some of the more widely used systems and mention their key features. Where possible, I also provide you with URLs to download the systems. I don't attempt to cover all of the systems out there; I apologize to any developers whose system I don't cover. I also apologize in advance for any errors or key omissions in the description of the systems.

PPSs can be characterized along various dimensions:

- How expressive is the language? For example, does it support user-defined functions, undirected models, discrete and continuous variables, open-universe models, and variables with arbitrary data types?
- What is the deployment strategy of the system? Does it provide a standalone language, a library in an existing language, or a new implementation of an existing language with probabilistic extensions? And if it's a standalone language, does it provide an interface from an existing language?
- What kind of programming style does it use, such as functional, logical, imperative, or object-oriented?
- What kinds of inference algorithms, such as factored and sampling algorithms, does it provide? Does it support dynamic reasoning?
- What kinds of queries does it support?

Following are some examples of PPSs.

BUGS (WWW.MRC-BSU.CAM.AC.UK/SOFTWARE/BUGS/)

BUGS stands for *Bayesian Inference Using Gibbs Sampling*, and, as its name suggests, is built around a Markov chain Monte Carlo (MCMC) algorithm called Gibbs sampling. BUGS was one of the first PPSs and has become popular in disciplines such as social sciences. Representationally, BUGS doesn't allow user-defined functions and focuses mainly on continuous variables, but it provides a wide range of distributions for the variables. BUGS is implemented as a standalone language.

STAN (HTTP://MC-STAN.ORG/)

Stan is a popular probabilistic programming system, especially in statistics circles, and is able to perform many kinds of statistical inference. Stan's main inference algorithm is an efficient form of MCMC. Like BUGS, Stan focuses on continuous variables and provides a wide range of distributions. Also like BUGS, Stan is a standalone language, but it provides interfaces to popular languages, such as R, Python, and MATLAB.

FACTORIE (HTTP://FACTORIE.CS.UMASS.EDU/)

FACTORIE is a probabilistic programming system that has had a lot of success in natural language processing applications. Unlike most other PPSs, FACTORIE uses an imperative style to explicitly create factor graphs, on which it can perform algorithms such as MCMC. Similarly to Figaro, FACTORIE is a library in Scala.

PROBLOG (HTTPS://DTAI.CS.KULEUVEN.BE/PROBLOG/)

ProbLog is different from the other PPSs in this survey, because it's based on logic programming. If you like using a logic programming language like Prolog, ProbLog might be a good choice for you. ProbLog can be thought of as an extension of Prolog with probabilities. The basic idea in probabilistic logic programming is that there's a set of uncertain basic facts and a set of logical rules from which other derived facts follow. The probability of any derived fact is then the probability that a set of basic facts holds, such that the derived fact follows from them. ProbLog is restricted to discrete variables. For inference, ProbLog uses logic programming techniques such as proof derivations.

BLOG (HTTPS://SITES.GOOGLE.COM/SITE/BLOGINFERENCE/)

BLOG (Bayesian Logic) is a kind of hybrid between a logical and a functional PPS. Statements in BLOG are like statements in logic, except that there's a generative flow to BLOG models that represents how possible worlds are generated, similar to a functional PPS like Figaro. BLOG makes open-universe modeling, in which you don't know the number and identity of objects, front and center, and is a good choice if you have that kind of model. BLOG uses MCMC for inference. It's a standalone language, but you can write custom proposal schemes in Java.

CHURCH (HTTPS://PROBMODS.ORG/PLAY-SPACE.HTML)

Church is a functional PPS based on Scheme, a LISP-like language. Representationally, it's similar to Figaro in that it supports complex control flow and recursion as well as rich data structures, although it's not object-oriented. Church has several implementations. The preceding URL is to WebChurch, which is a web app with a nice interactive probabilistic programming tutorial.

ANGLICAN (WWW.ROBOTS.OX.AC.UK/~FWOOD/ANGLICAN/)

Anglican is a relatively new language similar to Church in its representation. The main feature of Anglican is efficient and accurate sampling algorithms.

VENTURE (HTTP://PROBCOMP.CSAIL.MIT.EDU/VENTURE/)

Venture is a new language from some of the developers of Church. Venture's major innovation is *inference programming*, which gives the user expressive, fine-grained, and interactive control over inference, mainly using sampling algorithms.

DIMPLE (HTTP://DIMPLE.PROBPROG.ORG/)

Dimple is a PPS produced by Gamalon. Although it can represent both discrete and continuous variables and directed and undirected models, it's limited to finite, fixed-structure models. For these models, Dimple offers some highly efficient factored inference algorithms.

index

RELATED MANNING TITLES

R in Action, Second Edition
Data analysis and graphics with R
by Robert I. Kabacoff

 ISBN: 9781617291388
 608 pages, $59.99
 May 2015

Practical Data Science with R
by Nina Zumel and John Mount

 ISBN: 9781617291562
 416 pages, $49.99
 March 2014

Functional Programming in Scala
by Paul Chiusano and Rúnar Bjarnason

 ISBN: 9781617290657
 320 pages, $44.99
 September 2014

Grokking Algorithms
An illustrated guide for programmers and other curious people
by Aditya Y. Bhargava

 ISBN: 9781617292231
 300 pages, $44.99
 April 2016

For ordering information go to www.manning.com